ISLAM, GENDER, & SOCIAL CHANGE

ISLAM, GENDER, & SOCIAL CHANGE

Edited by
Yvonne Yazbeck Haddad
& John L. Esposito

New York   Oxford
OXFORD UNIVERSITY PRESS
1998

Oxford University Press

Oxford   New York
Athens   Auckland   Bangkok   Bogota   Bombay   Buenos Aires
Calcutta   Cape Town   Dar es Salaam   Delhi   Florence   Hong Kong
Istanbul   Karachi   Kuala Lumpur   Madras   Madrid   Melbourne
Mexico City   Nairobi   Paris   Singapore   Taipei   Tokyo   Toronto   Warsaw

and associated companies in
Berlin   Ibadan

Copyright © 1998 by Oxford University Press, Inc.

To Sana Sabbagh

Published by Oxford University Press, Inc.
198 Madison Avenue, New York, New York 10016

Oxford is a registered trademark of Oxford University Press

Library of Congress Cataloging-in-Publication Data
  Islam, gender, and social change / edited by Yvonne Yazbeck Haddad, and John L. Esposito.
    p.   cm.
  Includes bibliographical references
  ISBN 0-19-511356-X; 0-19-511357-8 (pbk.)
  1. Women in Islam.   2. Muslim women—Social conditions.   3. Sex role—Religious
aspects—Islam.   I. Haddad, Yvonne Yazbeck, 1935– .   II. Esposito, John L.
BP173.4.I73 1998
297'.082—dc21   97-2845

9 8 7 6 5 4 3 2 1
Printed in the United States of America
on acid-free paper

Contents

Contributors

Vivienne SM. Angeles teaches World Religions, Islam, and Dynamics of Religion at La Salle University in Philadelphia. She received her Ph.D. in religion (major in Islamic Studies) from Temple University. The contribution to this volume is part of her ongoing research on Muslim women in the Philippines and Southeast Asia.

Margot Badran has written extensively on women's history and feminism in the Arab world. Her books include: *Feminists, Islam, and Nation: Gender and the Making of Modern Egypt*; and a co-edited volume, *Opening the Gates: A Century of Arab Feminist Writing*. She is Professor of Women's Studies and History at Oberlin College.

Laurie A. Brand is Associate Professor of International Relations and Director of the Center for International Studies at the University of Southern California. She is the author of *Jordan's Inter-Arab Relations: The Political Economy of Alliance Making*. She has recently completed *Women, the State and Political Liberalization in Jordan, Tunisia and Morocco*.

John L. Esposito is Professor of Religion and International Affairs, Georgetown University, and Director of the Center for Muslim-Christian Understanding: History and International Affairs at Georgetown University's Edmund A. Walsh School of Foreign Service. Esposito is Editor-in-Chief of *The Oxford Encyclopedia of the Modern Islamic World*. Among his publications are: *The Islamic Threat: Myth or Reality?*; *Islam and Democracy* (with John O. Voll); *Islam: The Straight Path*; *Islam and Politics*; *The Contemporary Islamic Revival* (with Yvonne Haddad and John O. Voll); *Voices of Resurgent Islam*; *Islam in Asia: Religion, Politics, and Society*; and *Women in Muslim Family Law*.

Yvonne Y. Haddad is Professor of the History of Islam and Christian-Muslim Relations at the Center for Muslim-Christian Understanding, Georgetown University. She is past President of the Middle East Studies Association and a former Editor of the *Muslim World* quarterly. Her published works include: *Contemporary Islam and the Challenge of History*; *Women, Religion and Social Change*; *Islamic Values in the United States*; *The Contemporary Islamic Revival* (with John O. Voll and John L. Esposito); *The Islamic Understanding of Death and Resurrection* (with Jane Idleman Smith); *The Muslims of America*; *Islamic Values in the United States* (with Adair T. Lummis); *Mission to America* (with Jane

Idleman Smith); *Muslim Communities in North America* (with Jane Idleman Smith) and *Christian Muslim Encounters* (with Wadi Z. Haddad). She is an associate editor of *The Oxford Encyclopedia of the Modern Islamic World*.

Mervat F. Hatem is Associate Professor of Political Science at Howard University in Washington, D.C. Her latest article, "Political Liberalization, Gender and the State," appeared in *Political Liberalization and Democratization in the Arab World*. She is presently working on a manuscript on *Ethnicity and Gender* as modern forms of governmentalities.

Nadia Hijab has been Senior Human Development Officer at the United Nations Development Programme since 1989. A writer and journalist based in London, she was Editor-in-Chief of *Middle East Magazine* (1981-84) and commented frequently on political, economic and social developments in the Arab region on the BBC and in other media. She is the author of *Womanpower: the Arab Debate on Women at Work*.

Afsaneh Najmabadi is Associate Professor of Women's Studies at Barnard College. Her publications include *Daughters of Quchan: Remembering the Forgotten Gender of Iranian Constitutional Revolution* (forthcoming); *Ma'ayib al-Rijal. [Vices of Men]* (editor); *Women's Autobiographies in Contemporary Iran* (editor); *Land Reform and Social Change in Rural Iran*; and *In the Shadow of Islam: The Women's Movement in Iran* (with Nahid Yeganeh).

Carol Riphenburg is Associate Professor of Political Science at the College of DuPage in Glen Ellyn, Illinois. She is the author of several articles on gender relations in the Middle East and Africa. Her current research interest is state formation and development in Oman.

May Seikaly is Associate Professor of Middle East History at Wayne State University, Department of Near East and Asian Studies. She is the author of *Haifa: Transformation of an Arab Society 1918-1939*, and a number of articles on Middle East history and gender issues in the Arabian Gulf. She is currently conducting research on oral history of Arab society.

Barbara F. Stowasser is Professor of Arabic in the Department of Arabic, College of Arts and Sciences, Georgetown University, and Director of the Center for Contemporary Arab Studies at Georgetown University's Edmund A. Walsh School of Foreign Service. She is the author of *Women in the Qur'an, Traditions and Interpretation*, and the editor of *The Islamic Impulse*. In addition, she has published articles on religion and gender, early Islamic *hadith* literature, and Ibn Khaldun.

Anita M. Weiss is Associate Professor of International Studies at the University of Oregon. She has published extensively on socioeconomic development and women's issues in Pakistan and is the author of *Walls Within Walls: Life Histories of Working Women in the Old City of Lahore*; *Culture, Class and Development in Pakistan: The Emergence of an Industrial Bourgeoisie in Punjab*; editor of *Islamic Reassertion in Pakistan: the Application of Islamic Laws in a Modern State*; and co-editor of *Power and Civil Society in Pakistan*.

Women in Islam and Muslim Societies

In the early post–WWII independence period, many emerging Muslim nations pursued paths of modernization and development that were Western inspired or informed, ranging from "modern" Western dress to the institutions of state and society. Implicit were pre-suppositions that modernization would entail increased secularization—separation of religion from public life. Western models of development (political, economic, educational, and social) were adopted or adapted—nationalism and/or socialism, parliaments, legal codes, and modern educational curricula.

National liberation and emerging forms of nationalism provided the context and idiom for political and social development in many arenas, from politics to gender relations. Gender relations, however, proved more complex and enigmatic. In no area was the force of tradition felt more strongly and the clash of civilizations more apparent than that of the status and roles of women. Secular modernists were seen by religious leaders and more Islamically oriented Muslims as Westernizers whose reforms threatened religion and culture, family and society. The modernization paradigm, with its purported Western values of freedom, equality, and self-determination, seemed to be an indictment of Islam that threatened to undermine the Muslim community and Muslim family. It affected everything from dress, education, and employment to personal status or family laws (marriage, divorce, and inheritance). Women replaced the veil with Western dress, and the sex-segregated ideals and realities of Muslim societies were bridged by the greater visibility and participation of women in public life—that is, outside the more traditional confines of the home. Implicit in educational and employment reforms were new or additional roles for women beyond those of wife and mother. These new roles were seen by some as countering traditional Islamic belief, namely, that men have the primary religious duty to support the family and women have the duty to nurture the family at home. No place was the conflict more visible than in Muslim family law reform.

While Muslim governments had borrowed heavily from the institutions of the West in political, economic, and legal development, Muslim family law was generally not replaced by Western civil codes but reformed through legislation that affected laws of marriage, divorce, and inheritance. Like most of the modern reforms, reform came from the state, not from the people. They were initiated not from below but from above; they did not come from the desire or demand of religious leaders and the people but from rulers and a minority of modernizing elites. They were imposed or "legislated" from above, often rationalized by the belief that it was the "modern" educated, enlightened few who were charting the future for the more "traditional," less privileged or enlightened conservative sector of society.

Change did occur. Educational reforms improved literacy and opened up new opportunities for women, who became more visible in public life, in government, and in the professions. However, many questions remained. How deep and representative were these changes? To what extent were the primary beneficiaries of modern reforms a very small minority of urban elite women of the upper classes and upper middle classes? To what extent had reforms substantively changed gender relations—that is, the definition of gender roles and the status of women—in society in terms of authority and decision making? In other words, to what extent had modern reforms trickled down and across society, rather than remaining a testimony to the social and economic cleavages or gaps (which, ironically, often seemed to be the product of modernization programs in which a minority benefited from advances of the new order to a disproportionate extent).

In more recent years, the "project of modernity" has seemed under assault—some would say discredited—as the nationalist and secular idioms have been challenged by the reassertion of Islamic alternatives. Muslim rulers, states, and elites have been threatened by those who speak of the failures of the state and cast their grievances and solutions in an Islamic idiom, often summarized in the slogan, "Islam is the solution." Integral and perhaps most visible has been the gender issue. For if, for some, Islamic revivalism or "fundamentalism" is symbolized by *mullahs* with *kalashnikovs*, it has equally been symbolized by the veil and calls for reimplementation of Islamic law. Under the impact of Islamic revivalism, many women from North Africa to Southeast Asia have donned Islamic dress and sought to redefine their identity in a manner that they perceive as a more authentic accommodation of modernity to their religion and culture. Like many of their male counterparts in the Islamist movement, they constitute a newly emerging alternative elite, modern educated but more formally Islamically oriented than their mothers and grandmothers. The implications of this movement raise new questions about gender relations and the roles of women in Muslim societies.

For several decades, much of the Muslim world has experienced a contemporary religious resurgence or revival. The reassertion of Islam in personal and public life has taken many forms, from greater attention to religious practice (prayer, fasting, dress, and family values) to the emergence of Islamic organizations, movements, and institutions. Islam has become a significant social and political force. Governments have appealed to Islam to enhance their legitimacy and mobilize popular support; Islamic organizations and parties have challenged the failures of the status quo, maintaining that "Islam is the solution" and calling for social and political reforms.

If some have welcomed the promise of a new Islamic order, many others have feared the creation of new Islamic states or the implementation of *shariah* (Islamic law). In response to those who see Islam as a source of liberation, others charge that Islamists will turn back the clock, retreat from the gains of modernization in recent decades, and put Muslim societies back on a medieval path that will retard rather than sustain progress, as well as promote extremism and intolerance. The stereotypical images of a resurgent Islam are often those of bearded mullahs with AK-47s and women in black *chadors*, all with the words "Death to America" or "Death to the West" on their lips. Many have charged that calls for a return to Islam or "Back to the Quran" is a cover for those who would return modern Muslim societies to a medieval past, which, among other things, would reverse the gains made by Muslim women and return them to a life of segregation behind the walls of their homes.

The challenge of contemporary Islamic activism (what some also call political Islam or Islamic fundamentalism) spanned the 1980s with its fear of Iran's export of Islamic revolution, or the growth of clandestine violent radical groups such as those that assassinated Egypt's Anwar al-Sadat, bombed the Marine barracks in Beirut, or engaged in hijacking and hostage taking from North Africa to South Asia.

In the 1990s, political liberalization and calls for greater democratization have witnessed the emergence of Islamic activism in a new role as a potent political force. Islamists or Islamic parties have proved to be the leading alternative or opposition to regimes in Tunisia, Egypt, Jordan, Algeria, Kuwait, Yemen, and Turkey, among others. The extent to which Islamic revivalism has become institutionalized as a social and political force, through its schools, social service agencies, banks, dominance of professional associations, and track record at the ballot box, has again caused many to fear an Islamic threat and to charge that Islamists were out to "hijack democracy," with the net result proving detrimental to women and minorities in particular.

Feminist organizations from Algeria to Malaysia have warned that Islamist power sharing would in fact reverse the educational and social gains of the postindependence period, remove women from public life, and again restrict their roles solely to that of wife and mother. The issue of women and Islam has thus become an emotionally charged one in Muslim societies and is reflected in recent international conferences like the United Nations Population and Development Conference in Cairo (September 1994) and the United Nations' Fourth World Conference on Women (Beijing, September 1995). Thus, it remains important to view the religious, historical, and political reconstruction of Islam in Muslim societies and its impact on gender. *Islam, Gender, and Social Change* provides these perspectives through historical reviews and case studies of Muslim societies from North Africa to Southeast Asia.

Women in Islam—Women in Muslim Societies

Few issues in Islam and Muslim culture have attracted more interest—and yet proven so susceptible to stereotyping—as issues involving women. Women in Muslim societies have been the subject of images and generalizations, romantic orientalist tales and feminist exposé, Muslim reformers and apologetic tracts. For many non-Muslims, the subject of women in Islam is characterized by the images of deserts and harems, chadors and *hijabs*, segregation and subordination. Subjugation and second-class citizenship probably best describes the perception of Muslim women in the West. Some Muslims counter that Islam has liberated women, but, at the same time, they often present an ideal not accompanied by the problems and issues encountered in the diversity of the Muslim experience. In an ironic way both non-Muslim observers as well as Muslims often fall into the same pitfall in cross-cultural affairs, comparing one's ideal to someone else's reality.

The study of women in Islam and Muslim society is complex, reflecting the diverse and varied realities of Muslim women and Muslim societies throughout the ages. Alongside ideals embodied in the Quran and the traditions (*hadith*) of the Prophet Muham-mad, one must look at the actual condition of Muslim women in diverse time periods and sociohistorical contexts. The status of women in Islam was profoundly affected not only by the fact that Islamic belief interacted with and was informed by diverse cultures, but also, and of equal importance, that the primary interpreters of Islamic law and tradition were men (religious scholars or *ulama*) from those cultures.

The subject of gender relations in Islam is highly charged not only at the popular level, but among scholars as well. If some blame Islam for the accumulated ills of Muslim women, others see it as a beacon of light and reform. Still others insist that the status and role of women in Muslim societies should be attributed more to socioeconomic forces than to religious belief. The explanations often seem as numerous as the subjects.[1] Yet, one cannot overlook the formative influence of Islam on the roles of women and men in Muslim societies both in the past and in the present.

It is often said that women and the family are the foundation of the Islamic commu-nity, the heart of Muslim society. That centrality is reflected in Islamic law, the ideal blue-print for Muslim society, within which family law has often seemed sacrosanct. The Quran, Islam's book of revelation, and the *Sunnah* (example) of the Prophet Muhammad provided textual sources for the development of law. The Word of God, however, was in-terpreted and applied in sociohistorical contexts by human beings. Using reason and in-fluenced by diverse geographic locations and customs, early jurists developed a body of laws which, while somewhat uniform in its essentials, reflected the differences of juristic reasoning and social customs of a patriarchal society. Islamic law is thus the product of di-vine law (shariah) as understood (*fiqh*), interpreted, and applied by male religious schol-ars in the past and preserved in legal texts and manuals.

The Quran is not a law book; it does, however, provide principles and guidelines that were incorporated into Islamic law through selection and interpretation. The Quran re-formed, but did not replace, Arabian patriarchal tribal society and customary laws. Quranic reforms enhanced or reinforced the status of women. Throughout much of Ara-bia, women had often been treated as chattel, as property with no rights in a totally male-dominated society. The tribal societies of pre-Islamic Arabia were in every sense of the term patriarchal societies, in which women's only identity and rights came from their sta-tus as wives, mothers, or daughters. There were exceptions in some areas that seem to have been polyandrous and in which women were able to select and divorce their hus-bands. The Quran outlawed female infanticide, emphasized a woman's right to contract marriage, granted her inheritance rights and control over her dower and property, and (in innumerable passages) sought to protect the rights of widows and orphans.

In a society in which men had unfettered rights to marry and divorce, some restric-tions were introduced. Though polygamy (polygyny) continued to be permitted, the number of wives was restricted to a maximum of four and guidelines were provided for the just and equal treatment of co-wives. While only males possessed the right to initiate di-vorce, the Quran counseled equity and responsibility and stipulated maintenance, child support, and a period for reconciliation. In the contexts of the family and in society, the Quran was quite explicit in maintaining women's religious and moral equality with men before God. Reflecting the realities and values of patriarchal society, however, women re-mained subordinate to the men of their family. They received less inheritance and a woman's testimony was counted as half that of a man, for example, in societies where males were seen as more experienced in public life and were primarily responsible for the livelihood and conduct of the family.

Historically, women's role in society was determined as much by social and economic factors as by religious prescriptions. Social custom, poverty, and illiteracy often eroded or subverted Quranic intent. While Islamic law did provide the parameters for behavior regarding marriage, divorce, and inheritance, the actual rules in practice—whether or not men took more than one wife, or whether divorce was common, or how modesty expressed itself in terms of women's dress or participation in the work force—were the result of local conditions and social class, which often differed from urban to rural settings and from one country or region to another. Women in Africa and Southeast Asia were never as secluded nor covered (chador or *burqa*) as their sisters in Saudi Arabia or some women in Pakistan. Islamic laws that protected women's right to inherit were often circumvented by families who sought to protect the property of the patriarchal family.

The role of women in religious observances and education was similarly restricted. During the Prophet's time, examples of strong public figures are to be found, such as Khadija, Muhammad's wife of twenty-five years, who owned her own business and played a prominent role in the birth of the Islamic community. After her death, other wives, notably Aisha and Umm Salama, were particularly prominent as advisers. Aisha was regarded as a major source of religious knowledge; she was a transmitter of Prophetic traditions and also took to the battlefield. Another woman, Umm Waraqa, was a prominent scholar of the Quran and was among a small group of female *imams* (prayer leaders). Other women earned reputations for their knowledge of the religious sciences (Quran, hadith, and law). However, these were regarded as "exceptional" personalities.

Similarly, while women in the Quran have the same religious duties and are promised the same rewards (and during the time of the Prophet, were said to have prayed in the mosque), historically, their religious role and practice, particularly their access to the mosque, became restricted. In the centuries after the death of Muhammad, religious scholars increasingly cited a variety of reasons, from moral degeneration in society to woman's tendency to be a source of temptation and social discord, to restrict both her presence in public life and in the mosque.[2] In the mid-twentieth century Muhammad al-Ghazzali could go so far as to observe, "Ninety percent of our veiled women do not pray at all; nor do they know of the other duties of Islam more than their names."[3]

Sufism, or Islamic mysticism, was something of an exception, providing greater religious space for Muslim women. The ranks of the mystics included Rabia al-Adawiyah (d. 801), one of the great early formative influences in the development of Sufi doctrine. In popular Sufism, women and men have been recognized as saints (*walis*, "friends" of God) who perform miracles and intercede with God. After death, their tombs have become shrines for pilgrimage or visitation, places of prayer and devotion. However, even within Sufism, due to the prevailing cultural attitudes toward women and women's sexuality in particular, such examples remained a minority in a world in which women were often seen as seductresses and potential sources of moral and social disorder. As in all the world's major religious traditions in premodern societies and cultures, in Islam both the reassertion of tribal custom and historical interpretations and practice often undermined Quranic reforms and reaffirmed a male dominance that perpetuated the inequality of women. In the twentieth century, the tension between ideal and real would become compounded by conflicts between tradition and modernity.

Women in the Modern Muslim World

During the late nineteenth and early twentieth centuries, governments, intellectuals, and religious leaders responded to the challenge of European colonialism and the impact of the modern West. The object was to resurrect a seemingly impotent, if not moribund, community, to restore its strength and vitality through a new renaissance. For many the hope was that, in time, an Arab or Muslim rebirth would lead to national liberation from the yoke of European (Christian) colonial dominance. The challenge existed on all fronts: political, economic, religious, educational, and sociocultural. Approaches varied widely, ranging from those of the more conservative ulama, to that of rulers and Western-oriented elites, as well as Islamic modernists.

For many of the ulama the options for the community were clear: armed struggle (*jihad*) in defense of Islam or emigration (*hijra*)—both patterned on Muhammad's response to his enemies—or withdrawal and noncooperation. In contrast, Muslim rulers wished to learn from the West, that is, to master the techniques that had given Europe its military and technological advantage. New schools with Western curricula were established, students were sent to the West to be educated, consultants, and advisers were hired. Rulers were more interested in military, scientific, and economic modernization rather than significant political change, and a new crop of Western-oriented elites wished to emulate the West, advocating widespread reforms.

At the same time, a third alternative emerged: Islamic modernism. In the Middle East, reformers like Jamal al-Din al-Afghani and Muhammad Abduh in Egypt, and in South Asia Sayyid Ahmad Khan and later Muhammad Iqbal, attempted to bridge the gap between the more isolationist position of many religious leaders (ulama) and more Western secular Muslim modernists. They argued that Islam was a dynamic, progressive religion capable of change and that Islam was compatible with the pillars of modernity (reason, science, technology). All criticized the ulama's tendency to cling to tradition (*taqlid*) and called for a fresh reinterpretation (*ijtihad*) of Islam to respond to the new challenges faced by the Muslim community. Their programs included religious, educational, and social reforms based on a distinction between those aspects that were immutable in Islam and those that were subject to change. Thus, reformers distinguished between religious observances (*ibadat*) in Islamic law and social relations or regulations (*muamalat*), which were historically and socially conditioned and thus capable of reinterpretation or reformulation. Reformers espoused a process of reinterpretation that adapted traditional concepts and institutions to modern realities, resulting in a transformation of their meaning to accommodate and legitimate change.

While primarily concerned with revitalizing Muslim societies and achieving national liberation, the process of reform inevitably raised questions of social and educational reforms that affected the status and role(s) of Muslim women and the family. This inaugurated a period of debate and reform that encompassed the areas of dress, family relations, education, and employment. The disciples of Abduh and Ahmad Khan, Qasim Amin and Chiragh Ali, advocated greater educational opportunities for women, arguing that educated wives and mothers would strengthen the Muslim family and thus Muslim society. At the same time, they provided rationales for reforms in Muslim family law, arguing that the Quranic ideal was monogamy, in order to restrict polygamy as well as to restrict a male's unfettered right to divorce or repudiate his wife. If, initially, males were the advocates for the "emancipation" of women, it was not long before Muslim women—as individuals and through newly established women's organizations—pressed for religious, educational, and social reforms.

During the twentieth century, significant changes occurred in the lives of many Muslim women. Influenced by the West and by Islamic modernism, legal reforms, voting rights, and educational and employment opportunities altered and broadened women's role in society. In addition to being wives and mothers, women have entered many areas of public life, ranging from politics to the professions. Admittedly, this is true for a relatively small percentage of women and it varies greatly from one region of the Muslim world to another (and often from urban to rural settings).

Perhaps no area is more indicative of the process of modernization in the Muslim world and, more specifically, the struggle to redefine gender relations, than Islamic legal reform. At one end of the spectrum, for example, Turkey's modernization program included a wholesale adoption of Western-based reforms including the adoption of a European legal code. On the other hand, Saudi Arabia proclaimed itself an Islamic state governed by shariah law. In general, however, the vast majority of Muslim states pursued a more modified process. However much countries adopted Western political, economic, social, and legal institutions and codes, family law remained untouched at first, and then it was reformed rather than replaced. Failure to replace family law with Western codes was a tacit, if not explicit, recognition of the importance and sensitivity of issues of women and the family in Islamic history and tradition. For, while other areas of Islamic law might remain an ideal often not implemented, the Islamic law of marriage, divorce, and inheritance had remained historically intact.

Modern Muslim family law reforms were initiated then by governments, implemented from the top down, and often rationalized and legitimated in the name of Islam by using (or, as some would charge, manipulating) Islamic principles and legal techniques. While the ulama were generally resistant, at best they were only able to restrict the scope of reform. The power of authoritarian states and modernizing elites prevailed. The power and sacrosanct nature of classical family law was reflected in the fact that even where modern legislation reformed it, failure to comply rendered an act illegal but not invalid.

Nationalists and Islamists have responded to the impact of social change on gender in Islam and thus have been engaged in formulating a reconstituted tradition. In Chapter 1, "Islam and Gender: Dilemmas in the Changing Arab World," Yvonne Haddad draws on Arab history and scholarship to demonstrate the central (and yet conflicting) role that women have experienced in modern Arab history at the hands of Arab nationalists and Islamists alike. "For both the nationalist and the Islamist ideologies, women are a crucial component for the preservation of the nation. Both, however, have placed increasing contradictory demands on women" (p. 21).

The Arab world and the broader Muslim world have struggled to redefine women's role in society and, in the process, to identify continuities as they seek to reconcile tradition and modernity. On the one hand, as Arab nations and leaders struggled to modernize, often drawing inspiration from the West, they had to overcome the force of tradition, which was regarded as an obstacle to change. Arab reformers of every stripe and shade have recognized the need for modernization and change. Indeed, for many elites, Western values were uncritically embraced and seen as superior to Islamic norms. On the other hand, Arabs of many different orientations have remained cognizant of, and have had to contend with, the role of religion as a source of transnational Arab identity and unity, a source of legitimacy and popular mobilization.

This has been seen time and time again in twentieth-century Arab politics: the emergence of Arab nationalism in the early twentieth century, the spread of Nasser and the Baath Party's Arab nationalism/socialism in the 1950s and 1960s, the Arab–Israeli conflicts, and more recently Saddam Hussein's call for an Arab and Muslim *jihad* in the Gulf war of 1991. No place was the tension and conflict between tradition and modernity more evident than in the ambivalent and contradictory paths pursued with regard to women's role and emancipation. Thus, universal education, open government employment, and family reforms were introduced by Arab governments in Egypt, Syria, and Iraq. Yet they continued to exist alongside traditional values of shame and honor based on a "hymen mystique" (p. 12) and fear of loss of virginity. At the same time, Saudi Arabia and many of the Gulf countries maintained strict laws of segregation of the sexes, restricting education, employment, and political participation. These differences are as much the product of political economy as of religion and culture. For men and women in the non–oil-producing states, employment in the Gulf brought wide-ranging changes: women were left at home as the primary parent while their husbands labored in the Gulf. Other women found employment opportunities that altered their role and family relationships. Those families in countries with both weak economies and rising expectations often find a two-paycheck family an attractive option, if not a financial necessity. At the same time, women in the Gulf have lived in societies where oil wealth and cheap foreign labor reinforced more traditional norms and values regarding a woman's place in society and in the family.

Since the 1970s and the Islamic resurgence, Islamists have insisted that in contrast to the tendency to modernize (equated with westernizing and secularizing) society and Islam, the real task at hand is, or should be, the Islamization or reIslamization of society. For Islamists, the primary threat of the West is cultural rather than political or economic. Cultural dependency robs one of faith and identity and thus destroys Islam and the Islamic community (*umma*) far more effectively than political rule. Women and the family have been identified as pivotal in this contest. Women, therefore, are regarded as the primary culture bearers, "as the maintainers of the tradition, relegated to the task of being the last bastion against foreign penetration" (p. 21). The hijab has become not only a sign of modesty but also the symbol for the defense of Islam, for the preservation of the family, and thus the Islamic identity of Muslim societies.

Yet, as Haddad notes, there are diverse Islamist perspectives. Many continue to reassert traditional values and perspectives that promote the "macho myth" of the strong, aggressive, dominant male, the unquestioned head of the household and leader in society, and the weak, fragile, subservient female. Others have increasingly come to accept the fact that education and employment are an inherent right of women as of men. However, like many nationalists, Islamists remain caught in contradictions, unable to reconcile recognition of the right of women to determine their futures with the need to redefine the role of men as well as women in society.

Given the centrality of the Quran in Islam and the development of Islamic law, would-be reformers, whatever their orientation, have had to contend with the text of the Quran. Barbara Stowasser, in "Gender Issues and Contemporary Quran Interpretation" (Chapter 2), discusses how reformers have engaged in the reinterpretation of sacred scripture to buttress and legitimate new Islamic paradigms. Today, as in the past, the word of God has sustained multiple levels of discourse. Stowasser focuses on a pivotal Quranic verse, Sura 4:34, which has long been regarded as a key text to support the authority of men over women and the obligation of women to be obedient to man. She demonstrates how this verse has been interpreted and applied in classical and contemporary Islamic discourse by diverse authors (the more traditional religious establishment, Islamists, and modernists, respectively), often yielding diverse paradigms but, at the same time, sometimes revealing surprisingly similar ideological linkages. Muhammad Abduh, the Islamic modernist and Egyptian religious leader, in his writings and legal opinions (*fatwas*) condemned the abuses of polygamy and divorce and advocated reforms to protect women's rights in marriage, divorce, and education. However, for Abduh as well as other Islamic modernists, women's education was less an inherent right than a necessary means to strengthen the family and reislamize society. Man's leadership in the family and in society continued to be regarded as part of the natural order, a combination of innate and acquired qualities.

In a similar manner, while Islamists are often critical of the ulama and claim the right to reinterpret Islam, "In letter and spirit, hermeneutic approaches and political stances, Islamism differentiates itself from mainstream conservatism" (p. 37). Yet, as Stowasser notes, when it comes to its vision of women, Islamism often remains quite similar to establishment Islam, as when Sayyid Qutb, an ideologue of the Egyptian Muslim Brotherhood, reaffirmed that the "guardianship" or "superiority" of men is part of nature (*fitra*); and thus (Western) gender equality would bring societal and cultural destruction (p. 38).

In recent years, many Muslim modernists and some Islamists have more boldly struggled with the relationship of the Quran's eternal nature and historical and cultural specificity. For some like Fazlur Rahman and Ismail al-Faruqi, a distinction is drawn between extrahistorical universal values and their application to specific sociohistorical contexts. This enables reformers to distinguish between past theological and legal doctrines (interpretations and applications) and the need for fresh formulations or reformulations of Islam. Stowasser shows the reader the dynamism and diversity of contemporary Muslim paradigms.

How, then, is theory being translated into social reality? In Chapter 3, "Islam, Social Change, and the Reality of Arab Women's Lives," Nadia Hijab takes us beyond the world of texts—which are interpreted to buttress conservative and reformist positions—to an analysis of the social conditions that have reigned in the Arab world. Hijab notes perceptively that Arab women today are in the unenviable position of having to choose between rights and the respect that has been accorded to them by their traditional roles within the family. The situation is intensified in the midst of rapid social and economic change when traditional security and support systems are increasingly eroded and replaced by the state. Hijab maintains that the state has failed to provide equal rights for men and women because the debate has been conducted within the Islamic framework, which "provides women with equivalent rather than equal rights within the family" (p. 50). While constitutions in countries may provide for political and labor rights, family law, which continues to be based on Islamic law in most Arab countries, does not provide for equality. Thus, there is often a contradiction between a woman's constitutional right to work and a family law that enables her husband to require that she obtain his permission to work outside the home.

Hijab notes that Islam has remained central to the issue of women's roles in society, not only because of the family but also because of its linkage to the debate over the role of Islam in the state and its close ties to the Arab quest for authentic identity and self-reliance. Hijab, however, sees some signs of change, particularly in Arab regional meetings in preparation for the United Nation's Fourth World Conference on Women in Beijing (September 1995). In contrast to the United Nation's Economic and Social Commission for Western Asia (ESCWA) 1985 meeting in Nairobi, where women felt a need to place their discussions within the framework of "the heritage of Arab–Islamic civilization," by 1995 the framework had shifted from "the ethos of the Arab–Islamic heritage to the international arena, and from prescriptions of an Islamic perspective to that of a secular one" (p. 50). Hijab discusses the debate that ensued between those who voiced religious objections and others who denounced the use of Islam as a weapon against women. In many ways, the discussions and debates mirrored the Islamic politics of the Arab world today and the spectrum of positions, from secular to Islamist. Explanations for this apparently significant shift are many: fear of fundamentalism is driving many governments away from their formerly close relations with and sensitivity to religious conservatives; the presence and input of more progressive North Africans; the significant presence of nongovernmental organizations (NGOs); and the increased presence of women in the labor force and at international women's meetings. Finally, Hijab underscores the extent to which resources, rather than culture, determine the educational and employment roles of women today; women in Qatar and Jordan, for example, have far higher enrollment of females in school than Sudan and Egypt. Similarly, in countries where a need for extra manpower emerged, women have been able to take advantage of job opportunities—only to discover that when circumstances change, they are expected to go back to their homes.

No study of gender in Islam and in Muslim societies can be credible without moving beyond the textual and beyond broad comparative overviews to specific sociopolitical case studies. Part Two of this volume brings together examples that take us beyond, but also include, the Arab world. The examples reflect the broad sweep of the Muslim world from Africa to Southeast Asia, from Egypt to the Philippines.

Few images better capture the stereotype of gender relations in Islam, and the threat of a resurgent Islam to women's status and roles in society, than that of Iranian women covered by black chadors during and after the revolution. For many in the Western world, and for some in the Muslim world as well, the reality and threat of political Islam, or "Islamic fundamentalism," has been epitomized by the Islamic Republic of Iran. Iran in the 1960s and 1970s was regarded by many as the model of a modernizing state. The Shah's White Revolution had as its goal to bring Iranian development, within decades, into the twentieth century. With its rich oil reserves, powerful Western-armed and trained military, strong ties with America and Europe, and a seemingly enlightened social policy toward women, many saw Iran as an island of stability in a turbulent Middle East. Then, in 1979–1980 the unthinkable occurred, as a mighty Shah was overthrown by an "Islamic revolution" led by its leader and primary ideologue, the Ayatollah Ruhollah Khomeini.

If Islam and the Muslim world were often seen through the prism of Khomeini/Iran, for many, its medieval character was symbolized by veiled women, seemingly snatched from their liberated roles during the days of the Shah and forced to return to the oppressive days of an ancient past. Afsaneh Najmabadi's "Feminism in the Islamic Republic: 'Years of Hardship, Years of Growth'" (Chapter 4) offers an unusual, finely nuanced picture of the complexities and contradictions of women's status in postrevolutionary Iran. For if legislation and regulations have circumscribed and restricted women's rights and public space, "the past decade has also witnessed incredible flourishing of women's intellectual and cultural productions in Iran" (p. 59). Najmabadi provocatively notes that the deepest fear of many, that women would disappear from public life, has in fact not come to pass. Indeed, women are visible and active "in practically every field of artistic creation, professional achievement, educational and industrial institutions, and even in sports activities" (p. 59). The real challenge is to understand why and how this has happened. Is it a tribute to secular feminists who have somehow resisted or escaped the oppressive Islamic framework of the mullahs? Is Iran's brand of revolutionary Islam to be credited?

The logic of revolutionary Iran's worldview, like that of many other Islamists, is to regard the real threat of Western imperialism as less one of political, military, or economic hegemony than of a direct attempt to undermine religion and culture. As a Tehran journal noted:

> Colonialism was fully aware of the sensitive and vital role of woman in the formation of the individual and of human society. They considered her the best tool for subjugation of the nations. . . . women serve as the unconscious accomplices of the powers-to-be in the destruction of indigenous culture. . . . woman is the best means of destroying the indigenous culture to the benefit of imperialists (p. 60).

This logic, which can often lead to the oppression of women, has also meant that women's issues have been center stage in defining the new order. With women's role no longer scripted by the opposition, as in the days of the Shah, Najmabadi sees an explosion of new possibilities and feminisms: "New configurations of Islam, revolution, and feminisms are now emerging" (p. 60).

Najmabadi characterizes the changing roles of women from early post-revolutionary purification campaigns and attempts to enforce veiling and to dismiss and bar women from certain positions as "incontestably misogynous interpretations of Islamic notions of gender [that] set the political agenda of the new government" (p. 61). It was not long, however, before women countered with a variety of responses. "Years of Hardship, Years of Growth" uses the women's press to demonstrate how secular as well as Islamically oriented women redefined the roles of women. The early years of Islamic women's activism generated the drive to rethink gender in Islam in new and sometimes radical ways. Iran offers a good case study of reinterpretation (ijtihad) not simply of traditional Islamic theological and legal sources, but rather an effort that went directly to interpreting sacred texts. Both the "what" and the "who" are important, for they also reflect a process that is beginning to occur in other Muslim contexts. Women, not simply men, are claiming their right to interpret Islamic sources and to leave behind or go beyond classical formulations to develop new paradigms and to reformulate Islamic concepts and laws. The result is a lively debate over competing visions of male–female relations and the status and roles of women in Islam and in Muslim societies, yielding new understandings of spiritual, professional, and social equality. The new directions evident in Iran today reflect a new awareness of the need for greater inclusiveness as secular and Islamic feminists think, struggle, and in some cases, contribute to the same journals. While future results are not predictable, Iran's example may point to current realities and future possibilities within the Islamic world and beyond.

Like Iran, Egypt had long been seen as among the leading modernizing states in the Muslim world. In many ways, Egypt was the leader in the Arab world in educational and employment legislation as well as family law reforms. Like Iran, Egypt has also experienced the impact of the Islamist movement. Egypt was the birthplace of the Muslim Brotherhood in the 1930s and a launching pad for the spread of Islamic activism to other parts of the world in the 1970s, as both the government of President Anwar al-Sadat and its opposition turned to Islam. By the late 1970s, the regime was challenged by radical Islamic organizations, one of which assassinated Sadat in 1981. Since that time, the Mubarak government has contended with a diverse and dynamic Islamic opposition, ranging from the Muslim Brotherhood, which has become a major political and social force within society, and radical extremists like the Gamaa Islamiyya (Islamic Group) that has sought to destabilize and overthrow the regime and impose an Islamic state.

Mervat Hatem, in Chapter 5, "Secularist and Islamist Discourses on Modernity in Egypt and the Evolution of the Postcolonial Nation-State," maintains that women play a critical role in the current debate between competing secularist and Islamist discourses and visions of the state and civil society. Secularists argue that Islamists threaten the universal political and economic projects of modernity and will reintroduce religious and gender divisions. Islamists maintain that in their envisioned new state, women "will simultaneously represent cultural differences (through the Islamic mode of dress and an Islamist definition of femininity) and the exercise of full and universal political rights to vote and run for office" (p. 85). Hatem believes that the differences between Islamists and secularists are often exaggerated to reduce the argument to one of tradition versus modernity, and to demonstrate that both share a common national history in which cultural nationalism can be reconciled with "the universal project of modernity and the role that gender plays in it" (pp. 85–86).

The postcolonial state under Gamal Abdul Nasser and then Anwar al-Sadat reveal the complexity of gender relations. Nasser introduced reforms that reflected universal rather than religious or cultural-specific gender norms through legislation in education, employment, and political participation. These resulted in an increase in the numbers of women in the professions. However, these universal rights were also associated with new forms of social control in a state that often used reforms to divide and control women of different classes (p. 87). Reforms benefited the middle class, a minority of women. Women were often channeled into feminine professions (teaching, nursing, medicine) with only a few token women ever obtaining prominent positions. More important, "despite the multiplication of the number of professional women in the public arena, their professional consciousness did not routinize or internalize relations of equality or empowerment. These modern professional identities associated authority and leadership with maleness" (p. 88). Not only were these reforms irrelevant to the majority of rural women, but the regime's land and agricultural reforms often reinforced their economic dependence on men: "rural labor laws carried old disparities into the present and also contradicted the modern constitutional commitment to equality irrespective of religion and gender" (p. 89).

Perhaps nowhere was the perpetuation of disparities more evident than in the refusal of Nasser to respond effectively to requests by some middle-class and upper-class women to introduce family law reforms to restrict polygyny and divorce.

Anwar al-Sadat's rule ushered in a reassertion of Islamist discourses, as Sadat initially developed a strategic alliance with the Muslim Brotherhood and used Islam to enhance his legitimacy, discredit Nasserites and leftists, and mobilize popular support. Hatem maintains that, while Sadat did not alter the basic relationship of religion to the state, his use of Islam in public life—and his granting greater public space to the Brotherhood and other Islamists—enabled Islamists to challenge Nasserites in the institutions of civil society and created an atmosphere from which Islamist organizations and discourses were able to reemerge and prosper, and, in some cases, challenge the government. Contrary to the characterizations of some, Islamists like the Brotherhood did not seek to retreat to the past, but, in fact, developed a "competing Islamist–modernist discourse" aimed at the new educated middle-class audience of professionals, a discourse that "succeeded in persuading a majority of middle-class college women and working women to adopt the Islamic mode of dress as a visible sign of this attempted synthesis of Islam and modernity" (p. 92). Hatem skillfully shows how Islamists redefined the private and public roles of men and women to respond to the realities of the modern middle-class nuclear family.

Hatem points out that both secularists and Islamists have provided conservative and modern interpretations of gender and that there is more than one interpretation of modernity. Egypt today is not simply witnessing a struggle between tradition and modernity, between rural and urban environments, or between uneducated peasants and educated elites, but rather between competing definitions of modernity—secularist and Islamist—often aimed at the new middle class.

Jordan provides a case study distinctive from the Arab world. King Hussein is the longest ruling monarch (and one of the last) in the Arab world. Jordan has been a state characterized by religious moderation and tolerance. Its Christian minority (10%) has often held government positions disproportionate to its size. The monarchy has generally had good relations with the Muslim Brotherhood and, in contrast to many other states, the Brotherhood has long functioned as a political party and held positions in the Jordanian cabinet. In 1989 the Brotherhood and other Islamist candidates won thirty-two of eighty seats in Parliament and at one point held five cabinet positions.

The status of women in Jordan reveals similarities and differences with that of their sisters in other states. In Chapter 6, "Women and the State in Jordan: Inclusion or Exclusion?," Laurie Brand maintains that, while religion is important, it is only one determinant of women's status and role in society. Traditional religious attitudes prevail regarding women's nature, primary role as wife and mother, and appropriate function in society. In recent years, as Islamists have become more visible in public office, attempts have been made to introduce legislation regarding women's education and role in society. However, Brand believes that political and socioeconomic conditions are equally important, if not more so. She acknowledges the advancements but emphasizes the contradictions and setbacks experienced by Jordanian women. Analyzing women's education, employment, legislation, and the activities of political and religious leaders as well as women's organizations, Brand concludes that meaningful participation as opposed to mere appearance in the public sphere remains the exception.

Progress in women's rights has been affected by many factors. Politically, long years of repression and a primary focus on the struggle with Israel limited the development of civil society for all citizens and detracted from attention to social issues. While women often enjoy a good deal of power within the family, cultural traditions, social forces, and limited resources have combined to produce a situation in which women, both in the family and in the state and its policies, continue to be second-class citizens. Like many other Muslim societies, middle-class urban women in particular have enjoyed improved levels of education and social mobility. This, however, has not translated into significant power in civil society where women have been excluded from, or marginal to, the decision-making process. Although in 1982 women received the right to vote and be candidates in municipal elections, Brand notes that no women candidates were successful until the municipal elections of July 1995 and that national legislation both implicitly and explicitly relegates women to a citizenship status inferior to that of men. Only males can be recognized as heads of households; only men can automatically pass on citizenship to their children; women cannot obtain a passport without permission. While the king has intervened in recent years to prevent Islamist-inspired legislation, such as calling for sex segregation in education, Brand notes that the government has shied away from meaningful legislation in areas affecting women, such as the Personal Status Law that limits polygamy and arbitrary divorce by men, and male enforcement of the honor code. At the same time, it has tended to repress or control the development and activities of women's organizations.

In contrast to Brand's conclusions about Jordan, Anita Weiss characterizes the experience of women in Pakistan as "The Slow Yet Steady Path to Women's Empowerment in Pakistan" (Chapter 7). Yet, a fundamental irony exists. In the Indian subcontinent both secularists and Islamic reformers were united in pressing for the empowerment of Muslim women. Islamic modernist movements (like that of Sayyid Ahmad Khan) and the Muslim League's struggle for independence from Britain supported this goal. The Muslim Family Law of 1937, which enabled Muslim women to reclaim rights under Islamic law that had been taken away by British law, was hailed as a victory by the Muslims of British India. As Weiss documents, the situation in Pakistan from independence to today, though informed by this legacy, has been far more divisive and complex. South Asian religious and cultural norms and a distinctive set of political developments have produced the anomaly of a government led by a Western-educated modern secular-oriented Muslim woman prime minister from 1988 to 1990 and from 1993 to 1996 in a state in which the vast majority of women continue to live in an environment in which *purdah* (segregation) and "purdah psychology or ethos" has produced "the practical as well as figurative curtain separating the everyday worlds of women and men" (p. 125). Thus, while changes are occurring in homes and the workplace, pressures for a return to sexual segregation in public life remain strong.

Elite women have generally enjoyed greater access to education and employment; thus their status has changed less dramatically than those of the non-elite majority. Weiss skillfully utilizes the lives of women within the Walled City of Lahore to provide a window on the central role of the male-dominated family in determining women's lives. Technology, the mass media, and education have introduced changes in education, mobility, and employment that provide new opportunities for women but that also create new sources of conflict within the family as men seek to maintain their status, authority, and social control.

The advent of the martial law rule of General Zia ul-Haq (1977–1988) and his program of Islamization attempted institutional transformation within an Islamic framework "which constructed an image of women as not having identical civil liberties as men and which justified such laws in the name of Islam" (p. 133). Weiss shows that while the government promoted an ideal of the faithful veiled Muslim woman, women's lives were increasingly becoming more visible in the public realm. She analyzes how subsequent governments (especially that of Benazir Bhutto) and women in particular have had to contend with the implications of this legacy and its impact on issues of parliamentary representation, women's employment, family planning, and increased violence against women.

In contrast to many other areas of the Arab and Muslim world, the Gulf states tend to be among the most conservative, and yet they have experienced an intense drive toward modernization within a relatively compressed period of time. In nations with substantial oil revenues and small populations, many of the Gulf rulers have undertaken ambitious modernization programs while having to remain sensitive to their Islamic and cultural traditions. Oman is among the latest; it was only when the present ruler, Sultan Qaboos, took power in 1970 that the process began. Carol Riphenburg's "Changing Gender Relations and the Development Process in Oman" (Chapter 8) demonstrates the extent to which political economy can be both a catalyst and an obstacle to change.

Oman has an oil-based economy (95% of its income) with limited additional resources. Although Sultan Qaboos has recognized the importance of increasing women's presence in the labor force, the economy has not been able to absorb them. The country's oil income is affected by its limited oil reserves as well as the extent to which, like other oil-producing states, it has been affected by the sharp drop in oil prices since the mid-1980s. In addition, the oil industry is capital rather than labor intensive.

Nevertheless, a significant minority of women is employed in the public sector (government, 13%; oil, 10%), and to a lesser extent in the private sector (8%) due to the influence of traditional social mores. As in other parts of the Gulf and the Arab world, there is a correlation between work participation and class, education, and income. Working women tend to be elite and middle class and many have been educated overseas, especially since Oman lacks the developed educational systems of some other Arab countries. Riphenburg believes that Omani women are hampered, as in many other countries, by a state that officially recognizes their need and their right to work, but that also perpetuates a gender ideology that stresses family roles, gender differences, and the need for distance between men and women. Their job opportunities are therefore more limited and they are often restricted to those professions that are seen as more appropriate for females: teaching, nursing, accounting, pharmacy, medicine. Riphenburg notes that the significant advances (in health, education, and employment) made by women are in large part due to Sultan Qaboos, who has gained public support by casting reforms within the context of Islam's support for women's rights. Nevertheless, she maintains that "such policies, however, serve to fulfill women's practical gender needs rather than advance their strategic gender needs, preserving existing gender relations rather than transforming them" (p. 160). Traditional Islam has been used to support change; little emphasis has been given to an Islamic reform that would support substantive change in gender relations: "Although Islam itself improved women's status in the seventh century, women in Oman today have few legal rights regarding land tenure, marital relations, income and social security" (p. 161). Oman, like other Gulf states and many Arab states, remains dominated by patriarchal family practices and family law that perpetuates male privilege and control, sexual difference and complementarity, and thus stratification based on gender.

Bahrain, like other Gulf states, has gone through a period of intense political and socioeconomic change in the past two decades. Its political stability was challenged in the early 1990s by the Ayatollah Khomeini's call for the spread of Islamic revolution and the overthrow of Gulf rulers. A Shii majority population ruled by a Sunni ruler seemed an explosive mix. Political disturbances erupted and were crushed by the government. Some Shii leaders were deported. In 1994 a new antigovernment uprising (*intifada*) broke out. This time the protest movement was backed by both Shii and Sunni elements. It took the form of petitions to the ruler, calling for greater political participation (a return to constitutional democracy), an end to corruption, and socioeconomic reforms. A variety of interest groups participated, including religious leaders, merchants, professionals, and women, many of whom were members of religious organizations or movements.

May Seikaly's "Women and Religion in Bahrain: An Emerging Identity" (Chapter 9) studies the rapidly changing identities and roles of Bahraini women from their educational advances in the 1960s and greater visibility in the 1970s, to their increasing participation in contemporary protest politics. In particular, Seikaly asks the question, "Are Bahraini women consciously protesting against the patriarchy and subordination of the state or are they part of the male-led political activism. . . . How much does this protest reflect the emerging identity of women especially within the religious currents that have assumed political struggle as a platform?" (p. 171).

As we have seen in other parts of the Gulf and the Arab world, while women have made some educational and employment gains, the primary beneficiaries have been urban elite women who have obtained greater access to higher education and to certain professions but with little or no access to decision-making positions. Through a study of political and socioeconomic developments in recent decades, Seikaly documents the extent to which Bahrain's oil boom created rising expectations and then increased the gap between those who benefited significantly and others who did not. Thus, with a reversal of fortunes in the 1980s, Bahrain has increasingly witnessed the growth of Islamic revivalism. In particular, Seikaly's study enables us to understand the broad-based appeal of Islamism, why "followers of this current are not only from among the economically depressed and youthfully impressed women, but it has also cultivated women of the liberal eras who had considered themselves politically radical and socially liberal. This is a wave that has swept most of the middle class and practically all of the lower, economically depressed strata" (p. 180).

Seikaly explores the reasons for the rapid spread and attractiveness of the Islamist message among women. "While in the 1960s and 1970s the idiom was one of national liberation, constitutional democratization, Western dress, and political radicalization, in the 1980s and 1990s the idiom of Islam is used" (p. 185). Bahrain's crisis of state legitimacy, socioeconomic inequities, and the breakdown of traditional structures generated a growing political opposition with a strong religious leadership that warned that Islam, tradition and culture were endangered. Islamists in Bahrain, as in other examples encountered in our case studies, have proclaimed Islam as the source for a reconstruction of authentic identity and have politicized gender by giving women "the roles of upholders of authenticity, propagators of generations, and transmitters of morality and social values" (p. 180). Bahrain reveals the extent to which the failures (or perceived failures) of the government and its brand of nationalism, and of "the West" itself, have made the Islamic alternative attractive.

Seikaly analyzes the positions of Sunni and Shii women and their religiosocial perceptions of the veil, education, employment, and social services and highlights their commonalities and differences. A fascinating picture emerges of the impact of demographics and education upon a younger generation, raised in the 1970s and 1980s, and the extent to which education has been the primary vehicle for bringing women from the rural middle and lower classes to the Islamist movement, to an embracing of the veil as a symbol of emancipation and liberation, and to an involvement in political protest. At the same time, it has raised questions about women in the workplace. The political and socioeconomic realities of Sunni and Shii communities have not only produced commonalities in women Islamists responses, but have also led Sunni women to identify with more conservative definitions of women's role while Shii women have adopted more "radical feminist" perspectives.

In the post-Gulf War (1991) period, the Amir of Kuwait restored Parliament and held elections in 1992 as Kuwait moved hesitantly toward greater political participation and democratization. Yet, Kuwait is a country in which only a fraction of the population (and all male) can exercise full political rights. Despite the fact that Kuwaiti women are highly educated, hold positions in most professions from government and education to the private sector, they cannot vote or be elected to Parliament. Indeed, even Kuwaiti women with first-class citizenship lack political rights, like second-class citizens (naturalized citizens) and stateless residents (bidun).

In Chapter 10, "Gender, Islam, and the State: Kuwaiti Women in Struggle, Pre-Invasion to Postliberation," Margot Badran discusses the status and role of Kuwaiti women, particularly their decades-long struggle to exercise their full political rights. Kuwaiti women have played an integral role in society in two major instances: (1) in a premodern political economy in which women often ran the community while their men were off at sea; and (2) during the resistance to Iraq. Historically, however, politics, class, and religion have conspired to undermine women's suffrage.

Kuwait's first parliamentary election in 1963 was an important stage in women's struggle for equal political rights, the beginning of Kuwait's suffrage movement. It was a time marked by the burning of abayas, symbols of their exclusion from society, in a public demonstration for the creation of the first women's associations. Women's associations, however, such as the Arab Women's Development Society and the Women's Cultural and Social Society, neither attracted a broader social base nor proved capable of transcending their class differences to achieve gender solidarity and cooperative action.

The politics of women's suffrage have been used or manipulated by the Kuwaiti government in the 1980s. The state dissolved Kuwaiti women's organizations when it deemed necessary, and then initially encouraged the formation of Islamic women's organizations that emphasized women's domestic role and were against political rights for women (to counter Arab nationalist forces). Islamist groups like the Muslim Brotherhood, however, began their own organizations that advocated the right to vote, though not to stand for election.

The solidarity that had previously eluded Kuwaiti women occurred in their resistance to Iraq's invasion and the occupation of Kuwait in 1990–1991. As Badran notes, women of all classes and ages came together in public demonstrations, using mosques (normally designated as male space) as centers for organization and sanctuary. In contrast to the early 1960s, women donned abayas, not as symbols of a retreat to the home, but as a symbol of Kuwaiti identity and solidarity, "a weapon in the defense of women and the nation," whose anonymity provided protection and enhanced their ability to carry information and arms. Class and sectarian (Sunni and Shii) differences were left behind. They were active both in non-cooperation and armed resistance, risking capture, torture, rape, and death. Badran contends that, during the resistance, gender roles and space were reversed as women became the protectors and men the protected, and women were more visible and men more invisible, either fleeing the country or going underground. Kuwait became "a city-state of women" in which women were able to function more freely than men in public.

Despite the enormous contribution of women during the resistance, Kuwaiti women, like their sisters in other countries who had fought in wars of independence, have found that the postwar reconstruction has not meant recognition of their entitlement to full political rights. Badran analyzes the politics of political rights, demonstrating how women's new gender consciousness, sense of empowerment, and solidarity experienced during the war, have been undermined by continued male domination of the Parliament and *diwaniya*. She notes, moreover, that while some women became more vocal and visible in renewing the call for full political rights, "it was not long before class, kin, ethnic, and sectarian divisions resurfaced, dissipating the cohesion they had achieved under occupation" (p. 200). The situation is further complicated by regional politics, Saudi Arabia's opposition, the fear that Islamist women will use the vote to increase significantly the number of Islamists in power, and an opposite concern that more secular-oriented and independently minded women might use the vote to disrupt the status quo.

Muslim women represent 60% of the six million Muslim population of the Philippines. However, in Chapter 11, "Philippine Muslim Women: Tradition and Change," Vivienne SM. Angeles contends that Muslim women remain a minority within a minority in decision making. Living as a minority (8.6% of the population of 63 million) in a Christian majority country, the experience of Muslims in general and Muslim women in the Philippines in particular is quite different from that of other countries represented in this volume. Like most, however, gender relations have been affected and influenced as much by the distinctive sociopolitical realities of the Philippines as by Islamic traditions, the implementation of Muslim family laws, and Muslim institutions. Although there are numerous examples of aristocratic women who exercised power as wives of sultans, the majority of Muslim women followed traditional patterns that were centered on their role in the home, a role that gave them little control over their education or marriage. While American colonial rulers tended to avoid interference in Muslim life, the Marcos government pursued a policy of national integration and had to contend with the Moro National Liberation Front (MNLF) secessionist movement for self-determination and autonomy.

Like many areas of the Muslim world, since the 1970s the Philippines has experienced its own version of an Islamic revival, reflected in the rapid growth of Muslim schools (*madrasas*), the increased number of women studying the Quran and wearing the headscarf (*kombong* or hijab) and Islamic dress, as well as of men wearing a turban (*kopia*). Once regarded as a sign of backwardness, the scarf is now seen as a source of identity. The impact of the global Islamic resurgence, the experience of those who have studied in the Middle East (Egypt and Saudi Arabia in particular), and the influence of foreign Muslim teachers also contributed to a new sense of identity, pride, and religiocultural assertiveness. The struggle (jihad) for some went beyond consciousness raising, education, and the building of Islamic institutions, and included the armed struggle by the MNLF for self-determination and autonomy. Focusing on the participation of women in

Muslim Women's organizations and in the MNLF revolution, Angeles discusses how conscientization and politicization have given some Muslim women the opportunities to rediscover and empower themselves (p. 228).

As with Muslim women elsewhere, women in the Philippines represent diverse religious orientations, classes, and interests. These have been remarkably visible in the multiplicity of Muslim women's organizations and in the involvement of women in politics, in particular MNLF. Angeles analyzes the agendas and activities of women's organizations, revealing three major orientations. The Philippines Muslim Women's Association (PHILMUSLIMA) and the Muslim Professional and Businesswomen's Association (MBPWAP) are primarily concerned with political and economic advancement, seeking to open up new positions for women in government and the professions and tend to be supported by and of, government programs and policies. Those that mix professional concerns with an Islamic orientation, such as the Muslim Women Fellowship of the Philippines and the Sarang Bangun Foundation, seek to educate women regarding their rights under Islam and to promote preaching Islam to non-Muslims. And finally, there are the MNLF Women's Committee and the Bangsamoro Women's Professional and Employees Association, in which women have been integral to the MNLF struggle for self-determination and autonomy. MNLF women have represented a cross section of society, old urban aristocracy and rural women, well educated and illiterate, and those educated in public and Catholic schools as well as graduates of the Islamic schools. At one level, the revolution broke down traditional barriers as women left their homes and traditional roles. However, despite activities during the period of armed struggle, which included smuggling supplies, making explosives, and engaging in battle, few women were involved in key leadership or decision-making positions. In the postwar period, the struggle for national liberation, which somewhat bridged gender barriers, has been replaced by the struggle for women's rights and empowerment. The question, Angeles observes, remains "whether the men they work with will continue to see them as equal partners in the struggle" (p. 227).

At the dawn of the twenty-first century, Muslim societies continue to define and redefine their identities and place within the international community. Through the ages, from the beginning of the first Muslim community at Medina to the present, Islam, gender, and culture have been intertwined in defining the nature of the Muslim family and of the broader community. The twentieth century has witnessed a major period of transformation and transition, yielding a new map of the Muslim world, politically, economically, socially and religioculturally. Critical to the process is the question of the relationship of tradition to change. The contemporary Islamic resurgence has raised many of these issues quite vividly. Gender relations, particularly the status and roles of women in society, have been part and parcel of the debate over the role of religion in politics and society. As this volume demonstrates, today, as in the past, despite some advances, the struggle for equality—indeed to define the meaning of equality and gender roles and relations—remains contentious and unresolved. It is a battle that is about gender, class, and political and economic power as often it is about religious faith and identity.

Notes

1. See Nikki Keddie's comments in "Introduction: Deciphering Middle Eastern Women's History," *Women in Middle Eastern History*, ed. Nikki R. Keddie and Beth Baron (New Haven Conn.: Yale University Press, 1991), pp. 1–2.

2. Valerie J. Hoffman Ladd, "Women's Religious Observances,"in *The Oxford Encyclopedia of the Modern Islamic World*, vol. 4, ed. John L. Esposito (New York: Oxford University Press, 1995), p. 327.

3. Muhammad al-Ghazali, *Our Beginnings in Wisdom*, trans. Isma'il R. al-Faruqi (Washington D.C.: American Council of Learned Societies, 1953), p. 111.

PART ONE

ISLAM, GENDER, AND SOCIAL CHANGE

A Reconstituted Tradition

Islam and Gender: Dilemmas in the Changing Arab World

Over the last two centuries, the role of women and the family in Islamic society has been a central component of the debates over modernization and progress. While the socio-economic and political changes that have taken place as a consequence of modernization and programs for development, along with the legislation introduced by Arab governments, have left their mark on society, the debates have been instrumental in keeping a check on indiscrimate change—and in some cases reversing what was conceived as gains for women.

The discussions during this century regarding women and the family are constantly being shaped, reshaped, and changed by reference to internal as well as external factors. Internal factors include: (1) the consequences of economic, political, and cultural policies implemented by various nation states; (2) legislation adopted by governments regarding personal status law that affects women's lives; (3) the availability of opportunities for women in education and employment; and (4) the dominant belief that national liberation should take precedence over liberation of women, since the latter would lead both to subservience to the West through consumerism and to the degradation of women. External factors include: (1) the awareness of Western distaste for and criticism of Islamic family institutions; (2) international pressure, through agencies such as the United Nations, the Agency for International Development, and the International Monetary Fund; (3) the reality transforming the lives of Western women; and (4) a backlash against radical feminism in the West, identified as the wearing of miniskirts, bra burning, and free sex.

Regardless of the gender or ideological orientation of the author, one of the main features of the literature about women is its apologetic nature, betraying a belief that there are Western values against which it must justify itself. Increasingly the apologetic tone identifies the West with Christian and at times both Jewish and Christian values; hence recent promulgation of Islamic doctrine is placed in a comparative context to show the superiority of Islam over other religions.

In the nineteenth century, Arabs who had visited the West, such as Rifa'at al-Tahtawi, al-Tahir al-Haddad, and Qasim Amin, focused on the need to bring about change in the role of women and the family in order to usher in an Arab renaissance. Modernists such as Muhammad Abduh opened the way to reinterpretation (*ijtihad*) by distinguishing between *ibadat* (doctrines, beliefs and rituals), which they defined as eternal and not open to reinterpretation, and *muamalat* (human relations),[1] the political, economic, cultural, social, and educational issues that should be reinterpreted for each age. They wrote that it is legitimate to borrow from other cultures what is deemed useful for raising the standard of society. For those who participated in the endeavor, change in the role of women was from the beginning among the most important concerns, especially in areas of education, seclusion, polygyny, and divorce. The survival of the nation was seen as contingent on these changes, not so much out of belief in the innate equality of male and female as for the utilitarian goal of achieving parity with Europe.

Westernizers at the turn of the century debated whether women were required to adhere to tradition or needed to be educated to operate outside its parameters. Advocacy of Western values and norms became so pervasive that it fostered an atmosphere among elites in various Arab countries in which whatever pertained in the West was perceived as superior to its Islamic counterpart. The "sorry state" of Muslim countries and particularly the "unfortunate" circumstances for women have been portrayed as due directly to the religion of Islam itself. For Europeans who sought to Westernize the Arab world, the expectation was that Muslims should abandon their tradition and religious teachings about women in order to become modern.[2]

Upon achieving independence, the various Arab governments instituted universal education and opened government employment to educated females. With the coming to power of socialist regimes in several Arab countries, the debates began to include Marxist authors who looked to the Soviet Union as the model to be emulated. Efforts to thwart capitalist influence in the Arab world produced several studies that attempted to delineate the influence of colonialism, and of Western efforts to incorporate Muslim countries into the capitalist system, on the family and the role of women in society.[3] The socialists stressed the importance of labor and of economic development. The model of woman as worker was idealized within the overall ethos of participation in development. Children were to be cared for in nursery schools rather than at home. This model fostered a reaction in traditional Islamic circles and generated virulent Islamic rhetoric reaffirming traditional values.

Faulting Islam for prevalent backwardness are such authors as Amira al-Durra, Director of Family Planning in Damascus, who is reported to have said publicly:

> I see religion as a potent and very dangerous weapon, a double-edged sword. It is true that the backwardness of the Arab person whether male or female has many roots, but the fundamental root is religion. From it come the conventions, customs, and practices that dominate the Arab person. It has strong chains that pull backward, especially the Arab woman. . . . She finds herself at times considered to possess half a brain and [half the] religion. At other times she is a rib from the ribs of man. In whatever she does she is evil, obsessed with that which is forbidden. . . . Unless we find a new modern interpretation for religion, and a way to distance religion from forming the Arab person, we will not be successful in changing the social structures.[4]

The Islamic response to such statements was to denounce those who have been duped into the Western scheme of undermining Islam. They affirmed that Arab national experiments in Western liberalism and socialism had not only failed to deliver parity with the West, but that they had also failed in the societies that fostered them—in France, the

United States, and the Soviet Union. They point to such phenomena as the Western feminist movements of the late 1960s, the sentiment against the Vietnam War, the illegal drug trade, the hippie movement, the student rebellion in France, etc., to prove that Westerners themselves have found these social values wanting. Islamists wonder, if these systems do not work in their own contexts, why should they be imported? Islamic values concerning the role of women, the family, and the social order are increasingly being portrayed not only as divine prescription for humanity, but also as the last vestiges of resistance to total anarchy in the world.

Islamists who seek the reestablishment of Islamic *sharia* as the constitution of the state ascribe more sinister intent to Western penetration of Islamic lands. They see a conspiracy aimed at separating Islam from the Muslims in order to disempower them:

> The colonizers of the Islamic East are fully knowledgeable of this truth. They fear nothing as much as the rise of an Islamic movement that reconnects us with our history and joins us directly with our nature and inclinations and launches us to fulfil our duty in a manner that revives [the glory days of] Islamic civilization, the day we spat on Tartar ascendancy and turned off their lights and confronted the Crusader invasion and dismantled it and washed away its filth.[5]

Muslim experience of European colonialization has left a residue of resentment over attempts of the colonial bureaucrats and Christian missionaries to alter political, economic, and criminal law through both pressure and direct legislation. The only area that seemed immune to their interference, but not to their derision and sanction, was that dealing with personal status law. Colonial occupiers are still depicted as obsessed with weakening Muslim societies by various means. Consequently, the Western call for unveiling and for restriction on divorce and polygyny is understood as proceeding from this context, that is, the desire to sap the strength of the Muslim people.[6]

Authors committed to the preservation of a distinctive Islamic society have glutted the market with works that at first appear to vary very little in content, perspective, or ideas. This literature tends to project woman as endowed with a special mystique of domesticity interpreted as an essential part of God's plan for humanity, a religious duty. It depicts the home as the center of peace, civility, tranquility, and love, a safe haven and protection from the brutality of the outside world. The home is the domain of the woman; the man is her protector. A closer look at this literature reveals a variety of emphases identifying works as conservative or Islamist. The conservative writing is produced by al-Azhar professors and reactionaries; while the Islamist work is by those who are engaged in the Islamic revivalist movement.

The 1967 Arab defeat in the Six Day War inaugurated a period of intense debate concerning the direction that Arab countries should take. It raised questions about the values that had been adopted and the fact that they failed to create a vibrant and strong society able to withstand Western attacks.

The oil boycott that followed the war brought in a transformation of Arab economic power. The northern tier states became labor-exporting countries, poor and dependent on remittances from the southern-tier oil-producing Gulf states. Labor migration created new conditions for which the debates had not prepared Arab society. Among them were what one author called the "feminization of Arab families"; women of all classes of society whose husbands were working in the Gulf assumed the responsibility for management of the family, while the husbands played the role of periodic guest in the home. In some cases, women were employed in the Gulf and their husbands, who could not find employment, became economically dependent on them. (In 1979, for example, there were 7,817 Egyptian women working in the Gulf.) While some welcomed this as a way to force the liberation of women on a reluctant society, it nevertheless served to undermine the social structure in which the tradition of a male head of household continues to be revered.[7] With a growing economy in Arab countries during the 1970s and early 1980s, and a rise in the standard of living, it became clear that two salaries were often necessary to provide for better schooling of the children and for the enjoyment of modern comforts.

The women of the Gulf countries, however, do not generally participate in the labor force. With governments providing sufficient wealth to a husband and with cheap foreign labor easily available as domestic help, it has become unnecessary for wives to be economically productive. This wealth has created a disjuncture in the socioeconomic and cultural forces in society and has enhanced the drive toward retraditionalization. While the wealth has provided the latest technology and the most modern infrastructure, women's lives have become more, rather than less, restricted. Their status is by virtue of belonging to a wealthy state, rather than achieved. Even parenting has been relegated to Filipino or Sri Lankan maids; this has some officials concerned, because some studies have shown that Kuwaiti students in kindergarten classes have better knowledge of Sri Lankan than Arabic.

It is clear to many observers that the goals proposed by various national leaders as to what society should achieve vis à vis women have been subverted by the traditions enshrined in the various national constitutions. While affirming equality for both genders under the law, all constitutions have a clause insisting that the sharia is the operative norm, a reference (understood by all concerned) accepting the Islamic principle that men are in charge of women. A survey by Naseef Nassar of national constitutions showed a marked difference in the political definition of the state in the various countries and its source of legislation. Nassar identified three types of constitutional parameters. The traditional (*al-taqlidiyya*) group included Kuwait, the Arab Emirates, Bahrain, Qatar, and Northern Yemen, as well as the Sudan. (Nassar believes that if Oman and Saudi Arabia had constitutions, they would have similar definitions.) In the constitutions of these countries the woman is wife and mother and her identity is bound by her relationship in the family.[8] The second group is identified as those countries that have a progressive (*al-taqaddumiyya*) view of women. Aside from her role as mother and wife, the woman is treated as educated and cultured, as a working woman, and as one engaged in the political proccess. This is reflected in the constitutions of Syria, Southern Yemen, Algeria,[9] and Iraq.[10] The third group of nations Nassar calls the accommodationists (*al-tawfiqiyya*), best illustrated by the Moroccan and Egyptian constitutions. The Egyptian constitution, issued under Sadat as a corrective to Nasserists in 1971, affirms the traditional roles of mother and wife, while guaranteeing women opportunities in political, social, cultural, and economic spheres, contingent on not subverting the principles of the Islamic sharia.[11] This has had serious ramifications for the role of women throughout the Middle East given the dominance of Egypt on the Arab scene. Furthermore, all the constitutions, including those of the progressive countries, affirm the importance of the religion of Islam as a source of the constitution. Nassar concludes that there is real conflict among the views of women in these constitutions, and that the Egyptian attempt at accommodation has failed to come up with a depiction of the progressive view as being of the essence of Arabic Islamic thought.[12]

The changes that have taken place in the Arab world regarding women have not been radical according to some observers, but were mostly formalities because the sharia remained operative and affirmed the authority of the father, brother, and husband over the woman. Traditional values of shame and honor have been maintained as the operating principle of relationships, rather than the conclusions of the human conscience.[13]

The intellectual debates between advocates of tradition and modernizers begun in the middle of the last century intensified in the 1970s as new arguments and interpretations were incorporated. The situation has become more complex with the rise of Islamism. Whereas the modernists focused their efforts on a reinterpretation of Islam in order to modernize its teachings and traditions, the Islamist movement at present is engaged in the process of Islamizing modernity. Both groups have used the religious traditions in order to buttress their arguments, and both focus on women as one of the key elements in their respective platforms. As Nadia Hijab notes, by the 1970s, "the status of women seemed to have become the major indicator of a country's modernity."[14]

All participants in the discussion agree that the Quran and the Sunna of the Prophet liberated women from unacceptable conditions that prevailed in pre-Islamic Arabia, and that Islam has given women a position superior to that accorded them by other religious traditions. Women in non-Muslim religious systems have to expend a great effort to achieve the high level and status assured to them by the Quran fourteen centuries ago.[15] This is expressed both as an appreciation for the equity promised by the Quran and an indictment of other religions.[16] Among the rights guaranteed for women by Islam are the right to life, to education, to conduct business, to inherit, to maintain property, and to keep their names. Discussants note that these rights long preceded the recognition on the part of the West that they were appropriate for women (a result of the extension of the Renaissance concept of the rights of man, which was challenged to include women).

While such rights for Muslim women have been affirmed, however, social customs continue to dominate, still making them unavailable. Such customs include arranged marriages in which the consent of the woman (and sometimes of the man) involved is not sought; the appropriation of the dowry by the father as a compensation for the loss of his daughter, even though Islamic law guarantees it to the bride alone; the lack of equal treatment of wives in polygamous marriages; and the abuse of the privilege of divorce (especially in the Gulf region) in which the husband simply states "you are divorced" three times, without recourse to arbitration or attempt at reconciliation.

For many Muslim authors, therefore, issues relating to women have become a kind of final frontier, a place to take a stand against what is perceived as the pervasive cultural intrusion of Westernization that is raging in Muslim countries and wreaking havoc in their family institutions.

Regardless of the debates that have kept radical change under relative control, modernization in fact has had a serious impact on women's lives and their relation in the family. Since the 1970s, several new factors intensified the process of change. These include the dramatic economic fluctuations of the 1970s and 1980s; the increase in labor migration (especially of young males); women's participation in salaried work, state ideology, and politics; the growth of the popularity of the Islamist movement; and international input such as United Nations studies and recommendations and Western feminist demands. Those eager to incorporate women in development projects and to insure them an ability to earn a living, for example, tend to agree with the assessment of the United Nations and the World Bank that the domination of women is primarily conditioned by economic factors. "We believe that all social relations of dependence and oppression, of which the subordination of one sex to the other is only one example, take their origin exclusively in economic domination."[17]

It is clear that modernization in the Arab world has served to sharpen the conflict between traditional expectations of women and their role and the real demands of daily life in a developing society. Yet there is little information about how changes have actually affected family life, the decision-making processes, and the real contributions of women to the economy. Certainly the emphasis on universal education has made a great difference for many women. At the turn of the century, debates concerning women's education centered on whether women should be educated at all. Today the tendency is to look at a woman's education as a fulfillment of her Islamic duty. Although questions persist concerning what kind of education is appropriate for a woman and for what purpose, it is nonetheless possible for females to seek advanced training at most of the eighty-four Arab institutions of higher learning. Modernization has produced an educated professional corps of women who are employed in various sectors of society.

Women's education has increasingly become a sign of status in some circles. One illustration of this is that educated women are receiving higher dowries. A study in Syria shows that:

> The dowry of [women] engineers is the highest in Syria. In the city, the second highest is for government employees and teachers. In rural areas, the highest dowry is for students, followed by those engaged in secretarial tasks and then teachers. The lowest dowry goes to factory workers, home makers, and agricultural workers.[18]

There is a flip side to this, however, as a growing number of men who cannot meet the exorbitant and prohibitive demands of such high dowries tend to marry Western women. This has led to the growth in the number of unmarried women, a situation that became acute in Kuwait where one estimate put the number at two-thirds of the eligible female population.

While a large number of urban women have received university training, the trend is for them to drop out of the job market when they get married. This has led to what some authors consider a squandering of resources. Others insist that their education, although not used in economic development, does help in creating a better-educated society with long range benefits, because they influence the lives of their children and prepare them for the future. As for tribal, rural, and working-class women, modernization appears to have had a negative effect by reducing or eliminating their traditional means of making a living. Their economic contribution is not generally appreciated; government figures tend to ignore or underestimate their contribution in the agricultural sector unless they are salaried or in domestic production.[19]

Even insofar as women are part of the labor force they continue to have little significant public role outside the home.[20] Most authors appear to agree that women can work, although some wish to restrict them to housework, others to "feminine" jobs such as teaching children, nursing, and medical care of other women, and some are loathe to allow even that.[21] Shaykh bin Baz of Saudi Arabia, for example, says that women should not be teachers since teaching young boys might induce eroticism in the children, which is unacceptable. He also insists that having women work in any environment where there is the opportunity for men to see or work with them is a grave sin. Having women work with men as a response to the call for modernity is a serious danger and is contrary to the sharia, which demands that women stay at home and confine themselves to housework:

> He who wants to know the countless evils that mixing has wrought need only look at the plagues that have afflicted the nations that have made such choices. . . . He will find concern on the personal and collective level over the escape of women from the home and the disintegration of the family.[22]

Conservative Muslim authors consider woman's work outside the home to be contrary to her basic nature and against the role for which she is biologically determined:

> There is no argument that the woman's work is inside providing for the comfort and happiness of the family and managing the house and keeping it in order. . . . If the woman competes and participates with the man in his work while she is exhausted by menstruation, pregnancy, childbirth, and raising the children, given the fact of her natural incapacity, she would have transgressed her condition and deviated from her nature. Then the family system would be undermined and its bond would disintegrate and there would be no love and mercy between them. . . . Woman was created crooked, lacking in intelligence and religion.[23]

Not all writers are so categorical in their determination of the role of women. Tunisian scholar Rashid al-Ghannushi insists that in choosing workers, qualifications and not gender should be the deciding factor in making the choice for hiring. He goes on to say, however, that if the qualifications of a male and female applicants are equal, then preference should be given to the man. "Islam does not allow women to work while a battalion of men are unemployed, especially since the woman can take care of the home."[24] This sentiment is shared by others. It was expressed to the author in Jordan when an official in the government asked, "If you wanted me to hire your son and daughter and I had only one job, who do you think I should hire, given the fact that our society expects the man to be the provider?" And the President of Algeria, in a statement on March 8, 1966, said, "There is the problem of unemployment; when a job is available, should it be given to a man or a woman? Should men stay at home while women go out to work? That is the problem."[25]

Furthermore, even though women may have high-status professional jobs and make important decisions in the course of the day, and even though Islamic sharia insists that women have the right to keep their income, it appears that husbands continue to control the decisions concerning expenditures.[26] The husband is pivotal in allowing his wife to work in the interest of the welfare of the family; he is also the final arbiter in defining what constitutes that welfare. In many instances, while accepting that she may work outside the home, he will not allow her to participate in public events. As already noted, given the power of the constitutions of various countries affirming the determination of the sharia that men are in charge of women, there is little chance for change in the foreseeable future.[27]

Modernization and urbanization, however, have brought about certain changes in family life. One is a preference for nuclear families. This has altered the traditional power of the mother-in-law which has been undermined by the new system. Instead of being a guest in her mother-in-law's home, the bride gets to be in charge of her own household. But, if she also has to go out to work in order to maintain private residence, her workload is doubled. In addition, the change in housing design from the traditional open courtyard with a garden and opening to the sky to the small apartment has confined the woman and restricted her contact with other members of the family as well as with nature. If her husband restricts her going out, she feels imprisoned and lacks contact with friends and intimate relations.[28]

The contradictions in roles and expectations in many cases appear to be taking a toll on women's lives, sometimes leading to psychological dysfunction at all levels of society. Recent studies have shown that the conflict between opposing values has resulted in a rise in the number of clinically depressed women. This is especially true among young urban working women, who find persistent traditional values incompatible with their new status.[29] Modernity and the stress it has placed on the social fabric has also had an impact on the psychological well-being of rural and working-class urban women.

It is clear that both the secular nationalist and the religious models propagated for women have contradictions at their core. According to Mouinne Chelhi, the nationalist expectations subject women to two contradictory ideologies. One ideology is modern, stating that both officially and legally women are equal to men and should have equal access to power. The other ideology is the traditional perspective which, while usually unspoken, continues its centuries-old message that it is age and gender that give men authority. "What is worse," says Chelni, "[is] that it is an individual's sex, even more than their age, that now permits or forbids this access—which may even be a retrograde step compared to previous centuries."[30]

Fouad Zakaria notes a similar contradiction in the Islamic perspective when he says that the view of women among contemporary Muslim fundamentalists suggests a duality of overt praise and flattery on the one hand and covert humiliation and degradation on the other. This duality occurs in order to perpetuate the "degraded and marginalized state of women" at the same time that they are made to look free and honorable.[31] He continues:

> Wearing the veil, therefore, falls at the junction between the repudiation and denunciation of the body. . . . and excessive concern for the body and the danger it could pose to the woman herself as well as to others. . . . She is supposed to have an ascetic appearance, to be suspicious and aggressive toward others and their possible motives, and to minimize mixing with men. At the same time, however, she is supposed to behave towards her husband as a wholly sexual female. . . . A woman is expected to encompass both extreme chastity and lustful sexuality. She must constantly reverse her modest, even drab, appearance and prove to her husband that she is a desirable woman.[32]

It is taken for granted by various sectors of society that woman must play the dual role of housewife and worker. Modernizers admit that there is inequity in the burden of work. Some Islamist authors advocate that the husband help his wife with household chores, following the example of the Prophet. One author insists that there is a need to provide help for the working woman, not only by providing ready-made foods, or labor-saving devices for the home, but also in encouraging the man to change his attitude and participate in the housework. This is presented in the context of national development; since society has asked the women to take on an additional burden of working in order to develop the economy, the man must do his share by helping at home.[33]

It is clear that there is no consensus in the Arab world as to the role and status of woman in the family in the modern world. The various models have their male and female defenders. Following are three representative models, illustrating the disparities in understanding.

A Social Psychological Profile

One of the themes that emerges from contemporary writing about Muslim women is that of woman as victim of the experience of oppression in developing countries. The oppression is not unique to the Arab context but is a consequence of disempowerment and feelings of impotence. The condition of the woman serves to demonstrate the extremes of disempowerment. She is used to compensate for the socially oppressed man. She has become the projection of the inadequacy of the society, shackled with the burden of failure and weakness. Her inherent worth is devalued in relation to her physique, intellect, gender, productivity, and status. At the same time, her role as mother is symbolically elevated. She is the "Goddess, the source of love and compassion, symbol of sacrifice."[34] Her role thus fluctuates from being the center of honor, of human purity as mother, to the lowest degradation "as the woman of imperfection, *aura*, the symbol of shame and weakness, the immature, ignorant woman, symbol of castration, the tool used by man to service his needs."[35]

Mustafa Hijazi identifies what he sees as the roles for women, determined by the tripartite class structure of Arab society: the working class, the middle class, and the upper class. In the working class, he says, a sharp distinction is made between feminine and masculine characteristics. There is a clear exaggeration of the man's status, his strength, his masculinity, his capacity to persevere, his ability as a provider and manager of the household, his aggressiveness, and his anger. He is ascribed powers he rarely has. "It is necessary to deny any evidence of his weakness, fear, and inability to cope. It is by this denial alone that the family is able to find comfort in the presence of such powerful support."[36]

In order for the man to be transformed into the embodiment of the "macho myth," it becomes necessary for the woman to be weak and oppressed. She becomes the articulation of suffering who is in dire need of a supporter. She takes on the role of the emotional being, while the man is rational; she is in the home, he challenges the world; she surrenders, he is empowered and capable; she becomes the symbol of shame and need, he the symbol of pride, self-fulfillment and power; she is the dependent follower, the obliging servant of the master, he the master whose word is obeyed.[37] "She is transformed into a utensil for his self-pleasure with no regard for her wishes and desires. She dies in her psyche that he may gain the illusion of life; she is crushed that he may gain the mirage of self-fulfillment."[38]

In the middle-class family, says Hijazi, the relationship is more flexible and open to change. The woman is able to break out of her traditional prison to acquire knowledge and live a productive life and share responsibilities with her husband inside as well as outside the home. The man understands that the woman's development is a necessary condition of his own progress. Yet both are depicted as trapped by the dilemma of being pulled in the direction of modernity and progress on the one hand and traditional conditioning and defined roles on the other. Members of this class suffer from the claims of the past. While the woman longs to be free and to realize her rights, and the man wants her to be free, both are bound by internal chains:

> The woman is prisoner of chronic conditioning that pushes her to play a subservient role, one of an instrument. She is comfortable in that role because she is psychologically prepared for it. However, consciously she is dissatisfied with it and is aware of her rights. The man talks about equality and the liberation of woman but is incapable of giving up his privileges."[39]

The middle-class woman is unable to achieve her independence because she is fearful of assuming responsibility for her destiny. She is controlled by ingrained fears that maintain her in a state of dependency, fears that make her bound to protect her reputation. In dependency she finds order, a sense of protection against the hostile outside world depicted as "evil or a raging bull about to devour her."[40] As for the middle-class man, while intellectually and consciously ascribing to the ideals of liberation and equality, he persists in being a hostage of traditional roles. He expects the woman to achieve without his participation. In many cases he fears that he will lose control of the woman. His masculinity is contingent on his ability to control rather than his capacity to achieve.[41]

Hijazi sees the upper-class woman as a tool. Her role is to preserve family status and privilege. She is totally absorbed in her role and has no independent identity. She demonstrates the wealth and status of the family,[42] and thus is the consummate consumer.

For Hijazi, women's oppression has three aspects: economic, sexual, and ideological. Because she is a victim, the economic productivity of woman has been devalued. She is assigned a secondary role and not afforded equal opportunity. As an instrument of sexual pleasure, she is controlled by the "hymen mystique" and the fear of losing her virginity. Her body is considered a shameful entity that needs to be protected. Her husband possesses her body by law, rather than by emotional bond. Finally, the woman has appropriated the social and cultural myths that bind her and maintain her in a subservient role. She appears to accept the definition that she is incompetent, ignorant, gossipy, and emotional and cannot confront any problem with seriousness.[43]

A Conservative Islamic Profile

In another model that has been proposed by conservative Muslims, the role of the woman is confined to that of mother and wife and defined by the parameters of the Quran. There are about a hundred verses in the Quran that have been used by the *ulema* in defining the role of women and the family in Islam. The modernists have used the reinterpretation of these same verses as well as traditions (*hadith*) of the Prophet in order to create a more modern interpretation. While the teachings and example of the Prophet have been contextualized in some cases, the serious debate has centered on the Quranic verses.

According to the Quran, man and woman are created of one spirit. They are to be each other's protectors, supporters, and comforters. Their relationship is one of equality, mutuality, and cordiality. "God created from a single life-cell and from it created its mate and from them twain spread abroad a multitude of men and women" (S. 4:1).[44] The Prophet taught that "Whosoever has a daughter and does not favor his sons over her, God will cause him to enter into paradise."[45] Male and female are accountable in the sight of God.[46] Marriage is a source of joy and blessing to both partners.[47] The Quran encourages marriage of chaste men and women (S. 4:32).[48] It recommends marrying a slave girl if one can't afford a free woman (S. 4:25). The Quran also teaches that men are in charge of women[49] and are a degree above them.[50]

The Quran and the hadith advocate reverence for parents, especially mothers.[51] Muslims point out that the Quran guaranteed women the right to live by condemning female infanticide.[52] In cases of adultery and fornication, man and woman are to receive identical punishment.[53] The Quran warns against slandering a chaste woman (S. 24:4–5). The witness of one man is equal to that of two women (S. 2:282). Other verses have been interpreted to sanction segregation and seclusion (S. 33:33),[54] as well as define proper clothing and public behavior (S. 33:59; 24:31). While the verse understood to sanction veiling appears to address only the wives of the Prophet, some Muslims see in it a prescription for all Muslims.[55]

While there is not a single statement in the Quran that contains a condemnation of divorce (which in Arabic literally means "to be free"), men have the right of unilateral divorce. Islam regards marriage as a contract and like other contracts it is subject to dissolution. Social disapproval of divorce is attributed to the hadith of the Prophet. "Of all things permissible, the most displeasing to God is divorce."[56]

From the outset, restricting polygyny has been linked to the issue of women's liberation. Modernists have insisted that while it is sanctioned in the Quran it is contingent on men's capacity to be just in their treatment of women.[57] Some have argued that polygyny is an impediment to progress insofar as it fosters a turbulent home life, with discord among wives competing for the attention of the man and tensions among other members of the family.

Others have advocated polygyny, arguing that in fact it is a means of liberating woman. It lifts her from her condition of humiliation, grief, and squalor to a noble state of matrimony in which she experiences purity, dignity, and honor. One author even argues, "Polygyny is one of the manifestations of the liberation of woman, empowering her will, since the man does not marry other wives without her permission."[58] 'Ali 'Abd al-Wahid insists that polygyny appears only in distinctly advanced societies. He claims many sociologists believe that the practice will increase and will be adopted by other societies as they become modern and progressive. "It is an error to link the multiplicity of wives to primitive society while considering the multiplicity of mistresses as signs of a progressive society," he says.[59]

Defenders of Islamic traditionalism believe that in a genuine Islamic society current inequities will disappear. Islamic laws, they argue, guarantee the woman's control of her household. She is to have independent dwelling, with no single wife superior to another.[60] They point out that the enemies of polygyny see the custom as primitive and insist that liberation of women as well as the progress of the nation is contingent on the elimination of such practice. This, they affirm, is false. The Quran has sanctioned marrying four wives and there is no connection between this divine approval and the degree of civilization of a nation. In fact, insists one author, such practices have existed in all countries, in all ages, whether manifested as multiple wives, or multiple mistresses.[61] Bin al-Sharif affirms that polygyny is the law of nature and shall persist until the end of the world; in forbidding polygyny, Christianity has "led to three dangerous plagues: prostitution, old maids, and illegitimate children." In Europe and America, there are tens of thousands of mistresses.[62]

One issue of contention that has received a great deal of commentary is that of equality of the sexes and the ramifications of such an understanding on the family unit. Is the equality in worth or function? Is it in value as a human being or is it setting up women as contenders with men over all issues of life? For some authors, an acknowledgment of the true nature of the two genders involves the realization that men are in fact superior to women. Reference is made to the tradition (non-Quranic) that while Adam was created from the mud of the earth woman was created from man, with all creation proceeding from the two of them.[63] Some Muslims assert that man's superiority did not occur because some partiality has been shown for males over females, but rather out of a necessity predicated on the nature of the two sexes. Women of all places and ages have sought man's strength, superiority, steadfastness, and constancy.[64]

Therefore, there are disparities between the genders because God has endowed men and women with different qualities to perform their different tasks. A woman must bear children, for which God has given her the quality of compassion. Because she needs to breastfeed infants and talk "baby talk" to them she has been given a specific nature to find pleasure in that task.[65] Referring to Sura 4:34, Shaban says God has endowed man with more than women (twice the inheritance, *imama* and *qada'*), making him responsible for her. This is not an honor but a burden involving responsibilities and duties:

> [Man] is superior over woman by nature and physical constitution. This is not a special privilege for man as much as his grave responsibility to carry heavy burdens of spending [on his wife]. . . . It also places the burden of jihad on him to protect his homeland and his home.[66]

A person who bears such responsibilities in the home inevitably also is responsible for the religious and political leadership of the community.[67]

Shaban insists that not only is male superiority inherently the case, but women actually prefer it that way.[68] He cites a study of German women in which men value a woman who stays at home exuding self-confidence, compassion, intelligence, motherhood, attractiveness, obedience, and management skills. For her part the German woman prefers a man who is self-assured, honest, and superior to her. "This study proves without any doubt that woman's nature has a vacuum that needs man's superiority and strength and men's nature requires an obedient woman."[69]

Yaljin concurs that the course of human history demonstrates the superiority of males. As one observes the flow of history and the history of knowledge it is evident that the most famous scholars, including philosophers, doctors, mathematicians, and inventors have been male. "Knowledge progresses on the shoulders of males."[70] Men excel in sciences, sports, and economics.[71] This is true despite the fact that there have been increased educational opportunities for females in all fields over the past hundred years. It is also the case that the greatest political and military leaders are male.[72] Even if one descends to what Yaljin calls the lowest ranks, one finds that the most famous chefs, dressmakers, and artisans are also male. The excellence of women, instead, comes in their gentleness of spirit and the intensity of their emotions, as well as their abilities at homemaking and raising their children to appreciate music and literature and to be merciful and kind.[73] They are especially suited to secretarial work, social work, and teaching on the elementary level.[74]

Yaljin is particularly specific when it comes to the matter of women's inherent intelligence as compared with men's. Before puberty, he says, women excel in intelligence. But then men's intelligence increases during puberty so that they catch up with women, and from then on move far ahead. "Intelligence increases among the males and decreases among the females, therefore the number of geniuses among males increases as does weakness in intelligence among females."[75]

It is clear that the corollary of men's superiority is that they are to be in charge of women. Women are "a bundle of love and emotion,"[76] limiting their ability to be responsible. Thus men are in charge because of their rationality and their ability to exercise authority, do justice, and perform *jihad*.[77] Sha'ban even goes so far as to say that the woman is not allowed to eat the food of a man's house except with his permission, with the exception of that which is damp and thus liable to rot. If she eats with his permission she will be given appropriate recompense, and if she eats without his permission she will be punished.[78]

Marriage, readers of these works are assured, is a perpetual contract which ends only by death or separation. It affects not only the couple involved but all of society.[79] Building a wholesome society begins with building a wholesome home, and a home cannot be built without marriage. Marriage is a social bond that fulfills necessary biological and psychological needs. It is necessary as a way of preventing disease, it provides pleasure, it offers the structure for producing progeny, and it is the fulfillment of a religious duty.[80] It is a holy bond and the means of implementing an Islamic principle.[81]

"Marriage," said the Prophet, "is my way (*sunna*). Whoever seeks other than my sunna seeks an alternative to me."[82] The ulama have defined marriage as a contract between two partners where intercourse is permissible. But, says Shaban, such definitions ignore what is really essential to married life, that is, love, mercy, cooperation, and the mutual rest of souls. He cites Muhammad Abu Zuhra as having said that marriage is a contract that allows intimacy between man and woman, that it is their cooperation that defines their rights and duties toward one another.[83] He supports that by saying:

> Marriage is a contract between man and woman sanctioned by the book of God and the sunna of the Prophet to strengthen the self, to cooperate in life's issues on the basis of companionship, love and mercy, and to form a family and seek progeny.[84]

God created men to live on this earth with natural instincts, tendencies, and desires. He did not create them to be angels walking on earth, but to be humans of two different kinds, each seeking its perfection and continuity in conjunction with the other through legitimate marriages.[85]

The man is in a constant struggle to gain his livelihood and to feed his family. He faces danger and life-threatening situations. Because of this he is strong in body and clear in thought with a sharp intellect, a strong will, and a steadfast intent. He needs these qualities to deal with people outside his home. He does not need overwhelming emotion, but rather relies on his strong brain and wholesome communication skills to fulfill his role.[86] He needs a wife who will support and enhance those necessary male qualities. It is most important that a man not choose his prospective wife for the wrong reasons. If it is to be a choice among the attributes of wealth, status, beauty, or religion, Shaban strongly advises the suitor to choose religion.[87] Most of all, a man should not choose a woman who is not able to bear children. He cites a hadith in which a man says to the Prophet that he has met a woman who is beautiful and of high status, but is not able to bear children. The Prophet advises him not to marry her, saying:

He who marries a woman for her eminence, God will increase him in nothing but humiliation. He who marries her for her wealth, God will increase him in nothing but poverty. He who marries her for her status, God will increase him in nothing but degradation. But he who marries a woman and seeks only to cast down his gaze, secure his private parts, and form kinship, God will bless him in her and bless her in him.[88]

A related gender issue in Islamic traditions deals with the right of the man to examine the woman that he is going to marry, after they are engaged. Despite the prohibition on engaged couples being alone together, it does seem to these writers that a man should at least be able to look at some parts of his prospective bride as long as the couple is in the company of a chaperone. Shaban quotes a hadith that says "If a man gets engaged to a woman, if he can look at her [in such a way that it would] lead to marrying her, let him do so."[89] This is cited as support that the Prophet felt that an engaged man should look for what would lead to marriage. He is not restricted to her physical looks alone, says Sha'ban, but should also consider her personality and character, her behavior, and her mental maturity and capacity to solve life's problems.[90]

There does, however, seem to be some contention among the ulama as to how much of the woman can be viewed physically. The consensus is that it is limited to the face and the hands in order to see how much beauty she has or lacks, although some have said more and some less.[91] Qasim Amin had advocated that they should have a chance to see each other. "I see a common man unwilling to buy a sheep or a donkey before seeing it and checking its characteristics carefully making sure it has no imperfections. . . . This rational man enters marriage quickly and irresponsibly, which makes one wonder."[92]

The majority have felt that the man has the right to look without the women's permission, although Malik (founder of one of the four Islamic schools of law) insisted on that permission. Sha'ban argues that this inspection is not restricted to one time, but can be done several times. He also feels that the woman must look at the man she is to marry since there are things in him that might make her recoil.[93] There is also considerable discussion about how much a man should be able to see of his wife after he is married. 'Alam al-Din concludes that a husband can look at all of his wife except her private parts, which are considered repugnant (*makruh*).[94]

In return the wife must be obedient. That is her primary and most important responsibility. This is so much part of the fabric of Islam that it is said that she will be punished on the day of judgment for the failure of such obedience. That, of course, is contingent on the husband not demanding things that are contrary to religion. She must preserve his honor; forbid anyone from coming into his house without his permission; treat him with respect, kindness, gentleness, and gratitude; not ask him for what is beyond his means: and be faithful over his wealth and home and the raising of his children [95] After obedience, the second right of the husband is for his wife to look nice and to please him so that he can see her at her most beautiful and smell the best of her scents.

It is clear by the attention given to it that obedience of the wife to the husband is the highest priority. It is not fitting for a man to allow his wife to do what she pleases and for him always to follow her wishes. If that were the case he would lose his ability to control the family. The man should supervise the wife and make sure that she fulfills all her religious duties.[96]

A variety of other traditions from the Prophet are cited as proof of the necessity of a woman being obedient to her husband, including: "She whose husband dies and he is pleased with her will enter the Garden"; "If a man calls his wife to his bed and she does not come and he sleeps angry with her the angels will curse her until the morning"; and "If it is possible for one to prostrate oneself for a being other than God, I would order the wife to prostrate herself before her husband."[97]

Shaban goes on to describe the stages of dealing with a recalcitrant wife, one who is rebellious or whom one fears will be rebellious (that is, one who disobeys her husband and refuses to follow his orders). First he should admonish her, gently but with frequent repetition. If she does not recant, the husband can initiate the second stage, which is abandonment of the bed. This is a way to break her and her haughtiness. The last stage is that of beating, gently so as to avoid the face. If the wife obeys then the husband is to be gentle.[98] "God has made men more perfect in intelligence, more insightful, more power-ful, and possessing better judgment," hence they are in charge.[99] Man has the power, the leadership, and the dominance; he punishes her lest she contradict him or embarrass him.[100]

One author who finds physical punishment to be the proper way to deal with a dis-obedient wife, in conjunction with isolation and mediation, notes that if society were to give the woman the same right, she would not be physically capable of beating the man. Furthermore, he maintains, psychology books inform us that women do not enjoy sex until they are beaten up. Although this phenomenon may be rare, it may have deep roots in the essence of womanhood.[101]

Muslims have always believed that female sexuality is potent with a predilection to create havoc and chaos in the male. Thus it is necessary to control the woman in order to preserve order and well-being in society. This conviction is at the heart of contemporary Muslim writing about sexuality in Islam, a subject to which increased attention has been paid. Recent works address the issues raised by the sexual revolution in the West, as well as psychological studies on sex. They stress that a woman's honor is to be guarded at all costs, and they give much attention to the danger of men submitting to sexual urges in in-appropriate ways. One of the authors who gives considerable attention to the subject is 'Alam al-Din. Sexual contact with anyone but one's wife or a slave is strictly forbidden, he says. Sex with anyone else is adultery and is to be punished by a hundred lashes admin-istered in public. Likewise homosexuality is forbidden, which he puts into the context of a critique of British society.[102]

'Alam al-Din observes that the sharia has taken steps to get the sexual instincts re-stricted to *halal* (what is permissible). He recommends keeping one's gaze cast down so as not to get desire going in oneself. Casting down the eyes keeps one from looking at things that arouse, which is like charging wires with electicity. When the eyes are cast down the current is cut off.[103] It helps if the woman's body cannot be seen, so he recommends that everything but the hands and face be covered.[104] He notes that women today have turned things around. They wear long robes with long sleeves at home, and short dresses with short sleeves in the street. They should reverse this to be in accord with Islam.[105] (Shaban adds that Islam preserves women and orders them to veil from men. "Seeing is one of the arrows of Satan," he says. It is unfitting for a woman to be seen by a man unless there is a necessity."[106]) In addition, 'Alam al-Din feels that sexuality is controlled by making other people's homes forbidden. No man should enter a home other than his own until he asks and receives permission.[107]

Within the context of marriage, sex is not only legitimate but an essential ingredient.

It is a gift from God. "Intercourse is blessed by heaven as well as by family and friends."[108]
It keeps people from being led into sin and allows for building up the world through pro-
creation. Many warnings are given, however, about the temptations of premarital and ex-
tramarital sex. Sexual maturity precedes intellectual, emotional, and financial maturity,
which may lead the male to try to respond to sexual desires without love, emotion, or reverence for marriage. One of the ways in which to reduce the temptation that engaged couples may feel to have premarital sex is for a man and a woman not to be alone with each
other. Because of human weakness that leads to desire, Islam forbids a man to be alone
with a strange woman (that is, one who is not his wife) without the presence of a chaperone (*mahram*). Shaban cites the well-known hadith, "Anyone who believes in God or the
last day, let him not be alone with a woman without mahram for their third would be the
devil."[109] This is to protect the sexual honor of women. Even an engaged couple should
not see each other without a chaperone or travel together. Currently some families do
allow those who are engaged to be together. This is a foreign custom, however, and has
brought the Islamic people many problems. "The engaged man, as long as he is not married, can leave [a woman] after getting from her what he wants, which the devil leads him
to. [If that is the case] he will burden her with eternal shame and pain and suffering heavy
to bear."[110]

'Alam al-Din advises young men to refrain from indulgence in temptation by avoiding movies, plays, magazines, pornographic pictures, and looking at half-naked women on
the beach. If a good girl loses her honor it cannot be restored. Would you, he asks the
young men, want one of your female relations to be an instrument of entertainment for
others? Learn patience and get involved in beneficial things. "It is sinful for a man to look
at a woman as a hunter looks at his prey, the fox at the sheep, and to see her as a body for
enjoyment."[111]

He warns women that they may be viewed as mere sex objects rather than as potential
marriage partners. The dangerous thing is that the woman may fall for the man's smooth
talk. Once he fulfills his desire he will leave her rather than marry her. "Do not be reluctant to refuse his advances even though he may use it as a test of his love," he warns
girls.[112] He notes that men who engage in premarital sex are more likely to divorce, separate, or be unfaithful in marriage.

The teachings regarding sex as articulated by these writers are in no way an attempt
to accommodate the temptations of modern society. Rather they are aimed at combatting
it. Teenagers are urged to fight the temptations of sexual allure that are all around them so
as to avoid falling into sin. Such deeds lead to the degradation of the woman, the birth of
illegitimate children, and consequently to the collapse of society. Thus acts of self-indulgence are not only detrimental to the individual and the partner, but they also have serious
social ramifications because they undermine the righteousness of the whole social fabric.

For some authors the purpose of sexual relations is to increase the *umma* (community). A small umma is seen as powerless and fearful for its existence. "Islam is strong and
seeks to expand; it desires the Islamic kingdom to extend over all the world." Furthermore, increasing the number of Muslims is fulfilling the injunction of the Prophet who
said, "Copulate, procreate, I will be proud of you before the nations on the Day of Resurrection."[113]

In Arab society, women continue to derive status through fertility. Sociopolitical change appears to have had little effect on the reward system associated with being a mother:

> Muslim women are fully cognizant of the need to attain marital position and motherhood for commanding respect and status in their own kin group and community. They are not about to deemphasize willingly the only role that now gives them a bargaining position in the social structure. Children represent much more than a form of social insurance against the threat of divorce or polygamy, for women derive status from motherhood even when divorced or rejected for a second wife. Hence we may expect women to continue childbearing activities throughout their reproductive years.[114]

There is little agreement among Muslim authors on the subjects of birth control and abortion. While medieval scholars did not have a problem with aborting fetuses before the onset of the second term of pregnancy, "when they are quickened in the womb," more recent opinions that life begins at conception have increased the condemnation of abortion. Those who support a complete ban on abortion as well as birth control cite both the Quranic injunction against infanticide,[115] and the hadith of the Prophet sanctioning unrestricted intercourse.[116]

Proponents of birth control often turn to the same traditions of the Prophet as the opponents to buttress their arguments. Some writers find these traditions supportive of "family planning," while others interpret them in such a way as to forbid it. Some authors appear to say that it is acceptable in Islam to have birth control because the Prophet and his companions practiced *coitus interruptus* (*'azl*). Others feel that if the reason for birth control is fear that one will be unable to provide for the children, then birth control is un-Islamic on the grounds that it raises questions about God's providence. However, if birth control is for the purpose of saving a woman's life or because of illness, then it is permissible.

A number of factors, then, seem to contribute to the high rate of birth among Muslims today. Among them are the conviction that abortion is un-Quranic and morally wrong, the belief that dissemination of contraceptives leads to illicit sex, the emphasis on the importance of a woman bearing children, and the desire of both parents to have more male children.

An Islamist Model

Islamist literature puts a new emphasis on the role of woman. Rather than dwelling on her role as temptress, one who plays havoc with men's lives and keeps them from fulfilling their religious duties, these writings depict woman as a partner in a family structure predicated by divine design as the paradigmatic social unit. There is an awareness of the increase in leisure time in the middle classes, especially among nonworking women, as a result of the decline in household production. Therefore, an effort is made to channel some of women's energies into public religious and charitable activity directed towards the common good. Hence the Islamist movement incorporates into its ideology a combination of religious commitment, moral indignation, and political participation.

Among those who are concerned with a new interpretation of the Islamic role of women, the work of Rashid al-Ghannushi is most instructive. While most Islamists are motivated by a kind of evangelical zeal, al-Ghannushi is considered to occupy a moderate position on this subject. He observes that his visits to Sudan showed him that the role of women does not have to be as restrictive as other Islamists have tried to argue. He justifies his more moderate interpretation as necessary for political and strategic purposes. He sees women's participation as necessary for the missionary outreach of the movement, the da'wa, and argues that the role of woman is essential in the effort to convert the world, beginning with the Muslims themselves. Women are crucial not only in implementing a kind of moral rearmament, a moral jihad to create a virtuous society, but also as workers for a political agenda that refuses to participate any longer in subservience to the foreigner.

Islamists fault the Arab woman for appropriating the concept of equality and liberation from the West. In this she has become an importer, they say, an imitator rather than a creative originator. Her body dwells in her country, while her mind is in the West. She suffers from spiritual alienation and has lost her sense of security. She is obsessed lest her decor, her clothing, her etiquette become obsolete.[117] Many women wore the maxiskirt without any concern that it would make them falter while walking. "That was their excuse when their parents or the Islamists asked them to put on a modest long dress. But when the long dress is suggested by the Parisian designers and not the Lord of the World, then they hear and obey."[118] al-Ghannushi continues, "The truth is that we do not like what we like because it is innately good, nor do we reject it because it is evil; rather it is determined by whether the West accepts it or rejects it. It is sufficient that Western opinion change about what we believe is good or bad and we change our opinion."[119]

al-Ghannushi argues that the depiction of women is a relic of the age of decadence that set in after the early glory days of Islam. From this perspective:

> The woman is born hated and despised. . . . she has to be compassionate, pliant, an obedient being to her husband as a means to affirm his power and strength. She is raised in oppression by the father and the brother—regardless of the fact that he may be younger than she is—and then the husband. Despite the fact that Islam banned burying females, the period of decadence prepared a new burial for her personality and dignity. It instilled in her a sense of dependency, a lack of confidence, and an openness to ridicule and abuse.[120]

al-Ghannushi explains that this kind of upbringing created a family structure based on abuse and oppression, where the individual is crushed in the family. It created a woman who is confined to interests in clothing, cosmetics, children, and gossip rather than the urgent cultural and political issues of society. "This was a fruit of the seclusion which kept her from knowledge and made her into an instrument of reproduction and a cheap thrill to be enjoyed by the man who crushes her and casts her aside." This kind of social behavior was then sanctioned by religious leaders who worked for oppressive authoritarian governments.[121]

al-Ghannushi suggests that women must be enlisted in order to build a populist Islamic movement. They cannot be ignored or relegated to a secondary role. "A movement whose aspirations do not go beyond teaching women to cover themselves and perform their religious duties will be elitist and not populist."[122] Women must be encouraged to possess the spirit of daring, not of fear and retreat.[123] Nothing in Islam says that a woman must take care of the house or raise the children. If she chooses to do that, she is to be compensated. If she decides that she does not wish to be paid, then gratitude for her work must be expressed. Furthermore, the husband must help with the housework. This is the way of the Prophet, who used to help his wives.[124]

al-Ghannushi's critics have questioned whether his apparent openness is a public relations effort, or whether it is the only way he can sell Islamism to his followers. He admits that the Islamic movement needs women to participate in the political, cultural, and social (labor) field to counter the model of the secular woman that has been created by Bourguiba, former president of Tunisia.[125] He goes on to say that education is an effective tool to liberate men and women. He also admits that presenting a model of the educated Islamic woman is necessary to confront the infamous woman of the Bourguiba model.[126] This has caused his critics to wonder whether the promises of Islamism are merely tactical in order to appeal to those who benefit from the Bourguiba reforms.

Conclusion

The United Nations definition of modernity and progress, especially where it pertains to women, has tended to emphasize that maintenance of tradition is a central problem of underdevelopment. For Arabs who are aware of their weakness and repeated defeats at the hands of Israel, rejection of tradition would be tantamount to self-destruction. The fragmented entities that constitute the Arab nations are perceived as doomed to perpetual weakness unless they unite. The tradition is crucial for bonding in order to undergird the drive to unity. It is the one thing that the varied people of the Arab world hold in common. For both the nationalist and the Islamist ideologies, women are a crucial component for the preservation of the nation. Both, however, have placed increasingly contradictory demands on women.

For the nationalists, the situation is complicated by the fact that Israel, which is identified as the enemy, sought to destroy the Arabs, claiming that attachment to the heritage is the cause of retardation. At the same time the "chauvinistic ideology of 'God's chosen people' justifies its expansion over Arab land basing it on the myth of the 'Land of Return.'"[127] For the Islamists, women are maintainers of tradition and are relegated to the task of being the last bastion against foreign penetration. Their role is to safeguard the umma from annihilation, by upholding the faith in the face of what is perceived as a long-standing Western design to destroy Islam by converting its people.

For some, the West continues to exploit the region, including the Islam of the neo-conservatives. Western companies know how to market Islamic consumer products in exchange for the wealth of the nation. These companies sell products that counter Islam, the veil, local customs, and traditions. "The covers for the body and the head manufactured in the capitals of the West that invade our markets and our homes are not made to protect our traditions, but to ridicule our religion, heritage and customs."[128]

Because of the defensive nature of most contemporary Islamic writing about women, the debate has assumed a special character in which the central issue is basically a resistance to defamation and dishonor. For the nationalists the integration of women in public life is in line with the projected modern image that seeks to blunt the ridicule of the West. Their participation continues to be tempered, however, by traditional controls whose transgression would bring shame and dishonor. Consequently, there has developed an internal as well as an external dialogue. To agree with the foreign detractors is to participate in self-defamation and succumb to humiliation:

Islam sought to make the woman a veiled queen; she refused so as to be a common market. Islam wanted her to shorten her gaze and confine her to the home; she refused so as to gaze at others than her husband and to go out for unnecessaary matters. Islam wanted to make her the symbol of perfection, out of reach, respected, under strong protection. She refused so as to be the place where gazes meet, surrounded by questions and suspicions. Islam granted her dignity and she considered it degradation. . . . It directed her to strength and she considered it abasement. Noting that men have a degree over them and are in charge of them, she rejected it and became haughty. It called against the adornment of the age of ignorance, and she rebelled. It said, stay at home and she went out. Islam allowed the plurality of wives as mercy and she found it as oppression. She was assigned half the amount of inheritance and she thought it was oppression. It prescribed for the man because of the girth of his body, greatness of his brain, and strength of his forebearance that he should earn a living, strive and struggle, and provide leadership and protection for women. But despite all this she attempted to alter the natural order and did not obey the man's leadership nor did she recognize his superiority."[129]

Given the perception of the collapse of Western society, it is clear that traditional family values in the Arab world will be propagated strongly for fear of loss of social cohesion. While the Western model may continue to be alluring to some, the inability of Arab observers to decipher where to draw the line in order not to fall in the same trap has given impetus to the traditional affirmation of values.

This perception will also enhance the selling of Islamism as a divine antidote to exploitative "manmade" ideologies. Islamism is represented as a divine system designed out of God's mercy and compassion for women, with arguments similar to the following: Whereas women in Western countries are seeking the right to domestic upkeep, under Islam such provision is guaranteed. Whereas Western women are seeking legislation to force men to support their children, under the Islamic system this is assured. Whereas women in the West are cast away when their husbands seek mistresses or divorce them to marry new wives, Muslim women in a polygynous marriage are guaranteed respect, equal treatment in love, as well as material support.

In dialogue with the dominant cultural traditions, where women have no say in the selection of a marriage partner, Islamism promises a right of assent. In Arab culture where women bear the onus of honor for the family, under Islamism both will be responsible, both are punishable, both are to cast down their gaze. In the current Arab culture the tendency is for the men to maintain control of women's wealth. Consequently we see fathers and brothers depriving their women of the right of inheritance or dispossessing them of their wealth, or husbands taking over the management of women's property. Islamism gives women the right to manage their own wealth, as guaranteed by the sharia. Whereas the current rate of mahr has become so exorbitant that Islamists argue it debases women because it treats them as property, Islam would assure that it is kept within reasonable means for the general welfare, decreasing the number of men marrying foreigners and consequently leading to a more cohesive society.

It is no surprise that authors from within the Islamic tradition quote misogynist Western sources with relish. None seem to be interested in quoting approvingly any Western feminist literature. Yet their arguments appear to have taken the feminist movement head on. While Western feminists seek to abolish division of labor based on gender, Islamists see such a division as safeguarding woman's interests and not taxing her abilities. While feminists seek resources for child care outside the home, Islamists warn of the consequences that have led to the deterioration of the family and what is perceived as the general breakdown of society in the West. They affirm that child care is primarily a woman's business and should be her first concern. This is to safeguard the future of the next generation and create a stronger and more viable society.

While Western feminists have focused on physical abuse of women and sought to have it considered to be criminal activity, disciplining one's disobedient wife is depicted by some in Islamic literature as prescribed by God as an alternative to the destruction of the family unit. It guarantees obedience, hence harmony, and some even argue that it fits the nature of women. Furthermore, while Western feminists have called for reproductive freedom and the right to abortion, Islamic literature continues to debate the efficacy of birth control. Some insist that while Islam allows birth control it should be restricted to conditions that threaten women's lives, and pursued not in order to abide by Western perceptions, or out of lack of trust in God to provide. They tend to impute to the West the more sinister motive of reducing the number of Muslims in the world, perceiving programs of family planning as tantamount to genocide.

Examination of recent writings on women, then, reveals an intensification of emphasis on purity and modesty, and on women's chastity before marriage. The traditional role for women is accepted as natural, rational, and scientific. Sex itself is not evil, but natural when pursued in appropriate contexts. Celibacy is neither moral nor natural, and was not the way of the prophets.

Since the 1970s, growing disenchantment with the Western democratic model has led to the model being judged as a particular development in a unique setting and not necessarily applicable to the Arab world. The Western model's foreign roots and goals will continue to accord with an alien society and not coordinate with Arab culture.[130] Arab women who participated in the conference on women in Copenhagen came to realize that their own issues were different from those being raised by Western feminists, and that problems faced by developing countries cannot be understood or measured by Western norms or models, because Western issues and concerns are basically irrelevant to their reality.[131]

Debates over social and cultural values during this century have focused on the legitimate source of universal values. Westernizers have advocated Western values as rooted in rationality and fostering modernity and progress. The current state of Western society, which is perceived by many Muslims as degenerate, has not only encouraged the questioning of these values, but also has provided fodder for the attack against them. Critics see values in the West as grounded in human whims and desires, fads that are here today and gone tomorrow. Advocacy of such issues as human rights, equality under the law, reproductive freedom, freedom for self-fulfillment, work, and sexuality is seen as the underlying cause of the corruption and apparent disintegration of Western society. Muslims increasingly challenge the assumption that the Western experience is the only legitimate analytical framework for assessing the role of women, or that the Western family must serve as the universal model. Many have decided that Western values are to be avoided at any cost. Can the West, they ask, allow for other cultures and traditions to posit universals?

Notes

A longer version of this essay appeared as "Socio-Economic Change and its Influence on Women and the Family in the Arab World," in the proceedings of a conference published in *Journée Roman* (Rome: the Vatican, 1993).

1. Malcolm H. Kerr, *Islamic Reform: The Political and Legal Theories of Muhammad Abduh and Rashid Rita* (Berkeley: University of California Press, 1966), pp. 189ff; cf. John L. Esposito, *Women in Muslim Family Law* (Syracuse, N.Y.: Syracuse University Press, 1982), pp. 129–130.

2. See, for example, Annie van Sommer and Samuel M. Zwemer, *Our Moslem Sisters: A Cry of Need from Lands of Darkness Interpreted by Those Who Heard it* (New York: Fleming H. Revell, 1907); A. E. Zwemer and S. M. Zwemer, *Moslem Women* (West Medford, Mass.: The Central Committee of the United Study of Foreign Missions, 1926); Evelyn Baring Cromer, *Modern Egypt*, 2 vols. (New York: Macmillan, 1908).

3. See for example: Bu'Ali Yasin, "Matabbat fi Masirat al-Mar'ah al-'Arabiyah 'Ala Tariq al-Taharrur wa-al-Musawat," *al-Wahdah*, 1 (9) (June 1985): 41–54. .

4. Amira al-Durra in response to a lecture, as quoted in *al-Mar'ah wa-Dawruha fi Harakat al-Wahdah al-'Arabiyah*, ed. Ali Shalaq et al. (Beirut: Markaz Dirasat al-Wahdah al-'Arabiyah, 1982), p. 82.

5. Muhammad al-Ghazali, *Min Huna Na'lam* (Cairo: Dar al-Kitab al-Haditha, 1370H), p. 11.

6. Muhammad Atiya Khamis, *al-Shari'ah al-Islamiyah wa al-Harakah al-Nisa'iyah*, Cairo: Dar al-I'tisam, 1987, p. 71.

7. Sa'd al-Din Ibrahim, *al-Nizam al-Ijtima'i al-'Arabi al-Jadid* (Beirut: Markaz Dirasat al-Wahdah al-Arabiyah, 1982), p. 145.

8. For example, the constitution of the United Arab Emirates of 1971 notes that "the family is the foundation of society, it is built on religion, morality, love of country. The law guarantees its composition and protects it from deviance." Also, "Society includes in its protection infancy and motherhood." The Bahraini constitution of 1973 notes that "The family is the foundation of society, it is built on religion, morality, and love of country. The law conserves its legal rights and strengthens its bonds and values, and protects under its shade motherhood and infancy." Naseef Nassar, "Wad' al-Mar'ah fi al-Dasatir al-'Arabiyah, *al-Wahdah* 1 (9) (June 1985): 7.

9. The Algerian constitution of 1976 affirmed the need for a cultural, agricultural, and industrial revolution in order to complete national independence according to socialist principles. The woman is given rights as a citizen equal to the man. The constitution talks about equality in economic, social, and cultural spheres. The Syrian constitution of 1970 says that "the government guarantees for the woman all opportunities for effective and complete participation in political, social, cultural, and economic life and acts for the eradication of bonds that might impede her progress and participation in the building of Arab socialist society." Nassar, *Wad'*, p. 9.

10. Polygyny in the Iraqi constitution is contingent on the ability of the man to provide upkeep and maintain equality of treatment; it is also seen as being in the public interest. 'Abd al-Nasir Tawfiq al-'Attar, *Ta'addud al-Zawjat* (Cairo: Silsilat al-Buhuth al-Islamiyah, 1972), p. 272.

11. Nassar, *Wad'*, p. 9.

12. Nassar, *Wad'*, p. 10.

13. Suhayr Lutfi, "Wad' al-Mar'ah fi al-Usrah al-'Arabiyah wa 'Alaqatuh bi-Azmat al-Hurriyah wa al-Dimuqratiyah," in *al-Mar'ah wa Dawruha fi Harakat al-Wahdah al-'Arabiyah*, ed. Ali Shalaq et al. (Beirut: Markaz Dirasat al-Wahdah al-'Arabiyah, 1982), pp. 130–131.

14. Nadia Hijab, *Womanpower: The Arab Debate on Women at Work* (Cambridge: Cambridge University Press, 1988), p. 2.

15. Mahmud 'Abd al-Sami' Sha'ban, *Nizam al-Usrah bayn al-Masihiyah wa al-Islam: Dirasah Muqaranah*, vol. 1 (Cairo: Dar al-'Ulum, 1983), p. 341.

16. One of the ways in which Islam provides for women, for example, is through the *mahr*, which Sha'ban calls "the proof of Islam's respect for women." The enemies of Islam depict this as a kind of bride-price, but they forget the bitter reality of their own customs in which women present themselves openly in competition for a husband. Sha'ban, *Nizam*, vol. 1, p. 128.

17. Alya Baffoun, "Research in the Social Sciences on North African Women: Problems, Trends and Needs," in *Social Science Research and Women in the Arab World* (Paris, Unesco, 1984), p. 41.

18. Abu Ali Yasin, *Azmat al-Mar'ah fi al-Mujtama' al-dhukuri al-Arabi*, Lataqiya, Syria: Dar al-Hiwar, 1992, p. 48.

19. Aicha Belarbi, *Research in the Social Sciences on Women in Morocco*, UNESCO SS-81/CONF. 804/7. Paris: UNESCO, 1981; Alya Baffoun, *Research in Social Sciences on North African Women: Problems, Trends and Needs*. UNESCO SS-81/CONF. 804/4. Paris: UNESCO, 1981; Fatma Oussedick, *The Conditions Required for Women Themselves to Conduct Research on Women in the Arab Region*, UNESCO SS-81/CONF. 804/6. Paris: UNESCO, 1981.

20. Yasin, *Azmat*, p. 43.

21. Khamis, *al-Harakah*, p. 115.

22. Abd al-Aziz ibn Abd Allah ibn Baz, *Majmu' Fatawa Samahat al-Shaykh Abd al-Aziz ibn Abd Allah ibn Baz*, Riyad: Dar al-Watan, 1995, 17.

23. Khamis, *al-Harakah*, p. 56.

24. Rashid al-Ghannushi, *al-Mar'ah bayn al-Qur'an wa-Waqi' al-Muslimin* (Tunis: Matba'at Tunis Qurtaj al-Sharqiyah, n.d.), p. 25.

25. Fatma Oussedik, "The Conditions Required for Women's Studies," p. 115.

26. Nawal El Saadawi, "The Political Challenges Facing Arab Women at the End of the 20th Century," in *Women of the Arab World: The Coming Challenge*, ed. Nahid Toubia (London: Zed, 1988), p. 17.

27. El Saadawi, "The Political Challenges," pp. 8–9.

28. Yasin, *Azmat*, p. 43.

29. Baffoun, "Research in the Social Sciences," p. 56.

30. Mouinne Chelhi, "The Modern Tunisian Woman Between Hysteria and Depression," in *Women of the Arab World: The Coming Challenge*, ed. Nahid Toubia (London: Zed, 1988), p. 116.

31. Fouad Zakaria, "The Standpoint of Contemporary Muslim Fundamentalists," in *Women of the Arab World: The Coming Challenge*, ed. Nahid Toubia (London: Zed, 1988), p. 29.

32. Zakaria, "The Standpoint," p. 32.

33. Henry 'Azzam, "al-Mar'ah al-'Arabiyah wa al-'Amal: Musharakat al-Mar'ah al-'Arabiyah fi al-Quwah al-'Amilah wa Dawruha fi 'Amaliyyat al-Tanmiyah," *al-Mar'ah wa Dawruha fi Harakat al-Wahdah al Arabiyah*, ed. Ali Shalaq et al. (Beirut: Markaz Dirasat al-Wahdah al'Arabiyah, 1982), pp. 276–278.

34. Mustafa Hijazi, *al-Takhalluf al-Ijtima'i: Madkhal ila-Susiyulujiyat al-Insan al-Maqhur* (Beirut: Ma'had al-Inma' al-'Arabi, 1976), p. 307.

35. Ibid., p. 308.

36. Ibid., p. 313.

37. Ibid., p. 314.

38. Ibid., p. 315.

39. Ibid., p. 319.

40. Ibid., p. 320.

41. Ibid.

42. Ibid., p. 321.

43. Ibid., pp. 325–337.

44. "God has made your mates for you out of yourself"(S. 16:72);

45. Despite this teaching, the preference for sons is prevalent in Arab society. The birth of

daughters is seen as a test and a responsibility rather than a gift from God. Girls are not given the privileges given to sons, who are seen as a permanent part of the home, providing economic support for its dependent members. The Prophet also taught: "Act kindly toward women, for woman is created from a rib, and the most crooked part of the rib is the top. If you attempt to straighten it, you will break it, and if you break it, its crookedness will remain there."

46. The following Quranic verses are quoted in support of this teaching: "And their Lord hath accepted of them, and answered them 'never will I suffer to be lost the work of any of you, be he male or female: ye are members one of another'"(S. 3:295); "If any do deeds of righteousness, be they male or female and have faith, they will enter heaven, and not the least injustice will be done to them"(S. 4:124), "The believers, men and women, are protectors, one of another: they enjoin what is just, and forbid what is evil: they observe regular prayer, practice regular charity and obey God and His apostle. On them will God pour His mercy: for God is exalted in power, wise" (S. 9:71–72); "For Muslim men and women, for believing men and women, for devout men and women, for men and women who are patient and constant, for men and women who give in charity, for men and women who fast, for men and women who guard their chastity, and for men and women who engage much in God's praise, for them has God prepared forgiveness and great reward" (S. 33:35).

47. "And among His signs is this, that He created for you mates among yourselves, that ye may dwell in tranquillity with them, and He has put love and mercy between your [hearts] verily in this are signs for those who reflect"(S. 31:21).

48. Hadith supporting the importance of marriage include: "The messenger said, Young man, those of you who can support a wife should marry, for it keeps you from looking at strange women and preserves you from immorality, but those who cannot, should devote themselves to fasting, for it is a means of suppressing sexual desire,"and "When a man marries he has fulfilled half of the religion; so let him fear God regarding the remaining half."

49. "Men are in charge of women because Allah has made the one of them to excel the other, and because they spend of their property [for the support of women]. So good women are the obedient, guarding in secret that which God has guarded. As for those from whom ye fear rebellion, admonish them and banish them to beds apart, and scourge them. Then if they obey you, seek not a way against them. Lo! God is ever high exalted, great" (S. 4:34).

50. "And women shall have rights similar to the rights against them, according to what is equitable; but men have a degree over them" (S. 2:288).

51. "Revere the womb that bore you" (S. 4:1); "Show gratitude to me and to thy parents" (S. 31:14); "Your Lord has decreed that you worship none but Him and that ye be kind to parents. Whether one or both of them attain old age in thy life, say not to them a word of contempt, nor repel them, but address them with honor" (S. 17:23).

52. Verses cited in support of this argument include the following: "It will be asked regarding those hapless girls whom society buried alive and who have no caretaker for what crime, after all, were they slaughtered" (S. 81:3, 9); "They even have this belief that God has daughters, whereas for themselves they desire something else [sons] and when any one of them receives the news that a daughter has been born to him, his countenance grows dark and he is lost in grief. He considers the news of the birth of a daughter to be so shameful that he hides his face from people and reflects whether he ought to keep his daughter alive and subject himself to perpetual humiliation or bury her alive and be rid of the degradation. Ah! how iniquitous is the judgment these people pass on their innocent daughters" (S. 16:57–59).

53. "The man and the woman guilty of adultery and fornication, flog each of them with a hundred stripes: let not compassion move you in their case, in a matter prescribed by God, if ye believe in God and the Last Day: and let a party of the believers witness their punishment" (S. 24:2); "The crime of a slave woman receives half the punishment of that of a free woman" (S. 4:25); "The punishment for the wives of the prophet is double that of a free woman" (S. 33:30).

54. "Say to the believing men that they should lower their gaze and guard their modesty: that will make for greater purity for them. God is well acquainted with what they do. And say to the believing women that they should lower their gaze and guard their modesty, that they should not display their beauty and ornaments except what appears thereof; that they should draw their cover over their bosoms and not display their beauty except to their husbands, their fathers, their husband's fathers, their sons, their husbands sons." (S. 24:30–31); "Such elderly women as are past the prospect of marriage, there is no blame on them if they lay aside their outer garments" (S. 24:60).

55. "Prophet, enjoin your wives, your daughters, and the wives of the true believers to draw their veils close round them.That is more proper, so that they may be recognized and not molested. Allah is forgiving and merciful" (S. 33:59).

56. For Quranic references on divorce, see: S. 2:229; 2:231; 65:1–2; 2:241; 65:6; 4:20; 2:236–237.

57. "If you fear that you will not be able to deal justly with the orphans, marry what you desire of women, two or three or four; but if you fear that you will not be able to deal justly, then only one, or what your right hand possesses to prevent from injustice" (S. 4:3); "You will never be able to be just among women even if it is your ardent desire" (S. 4:129).

58. From Abbas Mahmud al-'Aqqad in *al-Mar'ah fi al-Qur'an* as quoted in 'Abd al-Nasir Tawfiq al-'Attar, *Dirasah fi Qadiyyat Ta'addud al-Zawjat* (Cairo: Dar al-Ittihad al-'Arabi, 1968), p. 8.

59. 'Ali 'Abd al-Wahid in an article published in *Minbar al-Islam*, 30 (9): 55, as quoted in al-'Attar, *Dirasah*, pp. 7–8.

60. al-'Attar, *Dirasah*, p. 9.

61. al-'Attar, *Ta-'addud*, p. 8.

62. Mahmus bin al-Sharif, *al-Islam wa-al-Hayat al-Jinsayah*, (Cairo: Maktabat al-Injlu al-Misriyyah, 1960), p. 93.

63. Sha'ban, *Nizam*, vol. 1, p. 335.

64. Ibid., p. 345.

65. Ibid., p. 341.

66. Ibid.

67. Ibid.

68. Ibid., p. 345.

69. Ibid., p. 346.

70. Miqdad Yaljin, *al-Bayt al-Islami* (Cairo: Kitab al-Hilal, 1972), p. 69.

71. Ibid., p. 66.

72. Ibid.

73. Ibid., p. 69.

74. Ibid., p. 66.

75. Ibid.

76. Sha'ban, *Nizam*, vol. 1, p. 350.

77. Ibid., p. 360.

78. Ibid., p. 381.

79. Ibid., p. 243.

80. Yaljin, *al-Bayt*, p. 13.

81. Ibid., p. 157.

82. Sha'ban, *Nizam*, vol. 1, p. 219.

83. Ibid., p. 156.

84. Ibid., p. 158.

85. Ibid., p. 216; see 'Alam al-Din says that God created the angels without desire, the beasts with desire and without intellect, and man with both desire and intellect. Therefore, if one has his intellect in control of his desires he is, in fact, like the angels. Muhammad 'Alam al-Din, *al-Tarbiyah*

al-Jinsiyah bayn al-Waqi' wa 'Ilm al-Nafs wa-al-Din (Cairo: al-Hay'ah al-Misriyyah al-'Ammah lil-Ta'lif wa al-Nashr, 1970), p. 83.

86. Sha'ban, *Nizam*, vol. 1, p. 342.

87. Ibid., p. 244.

88. Ibid., p. 245.

89. Ibid., p. 123.

90. Ibid., p. 124.

91. Ibid., p. 126. Looking for classical references, Sha'ban cites Uza'i who said that one has the right to see everything except the 'awra, and Ibn Hazm who said one could see everything except the front and back. He then concludes that the hadith implies that viewing is not restricted to face and hands but to other parts of the body such as arms and legs. The engaged person is doing nothing wrong in looking, because if he found the woman unattractive it would lead later on to the destruction of the home. Ibid., p. 24.

92. Qasim Amin in *Tahrir al-Mar'ah*, as quoted in Mukhtar al-Tuhami, *Thalath Ma'arik Fikriyah: Al Sihafah wa-al-Fikr wa-al-Thawrah* (Cairo: the author, 1976), p. 16.

93. Sha'ban, *Nizam*, vol. 1, p. 125.

94. al-Din, *al-Tarbiyah*, p. 79.

95. Yaljin, *al-Bayt*, pp. 85–91.

96. Sha'ban, *Nizam*, vol. 1, p. 354. He quotes the following tradition:

> A woman came to the Prophet and said, "I am deputized by the women to you. God decreed for men on jihad that, if they are hit and killed they are alive with the Lord. And we women have to take care of them—what is in that for us?" The Prophet said, "Tell whomever you meet of the women that obedience to the husband and acknowledgment of his rights balances that and few of you do it." (Ibid., p. 372.)

97. Yaljin, *al-Bayt*, p. 77; cf. Sha'ban, *Nizam*, vol. 1, p. 339.

98. Sha'ban, *Nizam*, vol. 2, p. 535.

99. Khamis, *al-Harakah*, p. 57.

100. Ibid., p. 65.

101. Ali Shalaq in response to a lecture, as quoted in *al-Mar'ah wa-Dawruha fi Harakat al-Wahdah al-'Arabiyah*, ed. Ali Shalaq et al. (Beirut: Markaz Dirasat al-Wahdah al-'Arabiyah, 1982), p. 49.

102. "I prophesy that God will do to the British what he did to Lot's people because their parliament allowed homosexuality for which they deserved punishment." Masturbation is also disallowed if it is done as a result of specifically getting oneself aroused; if, however, if it done on rare occasion out of necessity and does not become a habit it is acceptable. al-Din, *al-Tarbiyah*, p. 75. See also Fathi Yakan, *al-Islam wa-al-Jins* (Alexandria: Mu'assasat al-Risalah, 1972), p. 24.

103. al-Din, *al-Tarbiyah*, p. 80.

104. Ibid., p. 81.

105. Ibid., p. 81, 83.

106. Sha'ban, *Nizam*, vol. 1, p. 378.

107. al-Din, *al-Tarbiyah*, p. 83.

108. Ibid., p. 74.

109. Sha'ban, *Nizam*, vol. 1, p. 128.

110. Ibid., p. 128.

111. al-Din, *al-Tarbiyah*, p. 95.

112. Ibid., p. 98.

113. al-Sharif, pp. 78–79.

114. Nadia Youssef, "The Status and Fertility Patterns of Muslim Women," in *Women in the Muslim World*, ed. L. Beck and N. Keddie (Cambridge, Mass.: Harvard University Press, 1977), p. 86.

115. "Kill not your children for fear of want: We shall provide sustenance for them as well as for you, verily the killing of them is a great sin" (S. 17:31).

116. "Your wives are a tilth unto you, so approach your tilth when and how you will; but do some good beforehand, and fear God, and know that ye are to meet Him- [in the Hereafter], and give these good tidings to those who believe" (S. 2:223). The hadith quoted include: "When a woman spends the night away from the bed of her husband, the angels will curse her until morning"; "Allah's Messenger said: By Him in Whose hand is my life, when a man calls his wife to his bed, and she does not respond, the one who is in heaven is displeased with her until he [her husband] is pleased with her."

117. Yaljin, *al-Bayt*, p. 53; cf. Muhammad Zaki Ibrahim, *Ma'alim al-Mujtana' al-Nisa'i fi al-Islam* (Cairo: Dar al-'Ashirah al-Muhammadiyah, n.d.); al-Bahi al-Khuli, *al-Islam wa-al-Mar'ah al-Mu'asirah* (Kuwait: Dar al-Qalam, n.d.)

118. al-Ghannushi, "al-Mar'ah," p. 46.

119. Ibid., p. 47.

120. Ibid., p. 14.

121. Ibid.

122. Ibid., p. 21.

123. Ibid., p. 24.

124. Ibid.

125. Ibid., p. 25.

126. Ibid., p. 27.

127. Hikmet Abu Zayd, "Imkanat al-Mar'ah al-'Arabiyah fi al-'Amal al-Siyasi." In *al-Mar'ah wa-Dawruha fi Harakat al-Wahdah al-'Arabiyah*, ed. Ali Shalaq et al. (Beirut: Markaz Dirasat al-Wahdah al-'Arabiyah, 1982), pp. 163–164.

128. Muhammad 'Ubayd, "Ta'liq" In *al-Mar'ah wa Dawruha fi Harakat al-Wahdah al-'Arabiyaha*, ed. Ali Shalaq et al. (Beirut: Markaz Dirasat al-Wahdah al-'Arabiyah, 1982), p. 258.

129. Khamis, *al-Harakat*, pp. 19–20.

130. Abu Zayd, "Imkanat," p. 160.

131. 'Ubayd, "Ta'liq," p. 260.

Gender Issues and Contemporary Quran Interpretation

This chapter is about new trends in contemporary Muslim Quran interpretation and their interrelationship with contemporary Islamic paradigms on gender issues. From the beginning, Muslims have interpreted their eternal and inimitable, *mu'jaz* scripture in the light of specific socioeconomic and political situations. The eternal text has thus served as both the foundational basis and as the point of convergence of many different, specific, human interpretations. "Classical Islam" produced a number of methodological approaches to the text (traditionist, rationalist, or a combination of the two), as well as some variations in the paradigms of the status of women. These paradigms had been given shape in Islamic law (*sharia*) well before the lifetime of the first great Quran interpreter whose exegesis (*tafsir*) has survived in its entirety. Thus medieval scholastic divergences in approaches to the Quranic text failed to find an "application" in equally divergent readings on questions of women's status. Change came with the modern age and its modernist and reformist scholars. While the nineteenth century produced new approaches to the Quran that were equally "applied" to social questions, the contemporary age has brought forth a whole new Islamic epistemology where scripture-sanctioned gender paradigms play an important part. In what follows, the interrelationship of Muslim exegetic methodology and its "application" to gender issues is pursued by examining different readings of Sura 4:34, a Quranic verse that puts men "in charge of" or as "protectors of" women.

Approaches to the Quran

When al-Ash'ari (d. 935) declared the Quran "eternal in God," an "attribute of God's essence" (and therefore uncreated) but its "expression in words created in time," he formulated the orthodox scholastic doctrine of the nature of scripture. That the Quran is divine speech (*kalam Allah*) is proclaimed by the Quran itself (for example, in Sura 9:6). Ash'ari's doctrine of the Quran's manifestedness or expressedness in time was the response of mainstream Islam to the challenge of the Mu'tazila, rationalist school of Islamic theology, which in the eighth and ninth centuries had defined the Quran, while being God's speech, as "attribute of act" (not essence) and therefore "created" (not eternal).

Contemporary establishment theology is far removed from the urgency and creativity of medieval debates about the nature of God's word. While scholars within the modern and contemporary religious establishments perpetuate al-Ash'ari's doctrine of the Quran as eternal in nature, they increasingly place the emphasis on its implication, that is, the tenet that the Prophet Muhammad was merely the intermediary in the Quran's transmission, with neither his person nor his environment involved in the process of its formulation.

Classical theology did not distinguish between "principal cause" and "instrumental cause" of revelation; thus it had no room for a concept of God as the first and absolute cause of revelation using the mental resources of his "instruments," the prophets, to cast his revelation into a specific human setting of place and time.[1] This emphasis on the absolute, hence timeless, nature of the Quranic revelations, however, did not impede the medieval legal and theological experts from studying and recording the chronological sequencing of Quranic verses and the precise situations in which they were revealed to the Prophet. This was deemed necessary especially with legal matters, when the doctrine of *naskh* (abrogation of an earlier Quranic verse by one revealed later) demanded attention if not to the precise date then at least to the relative sequencing of the revelations. More generally, the medieval *hadith*, *sira*, and tafsir literature demonstrates a keen interest of pious scholars in recording the precise situation in which a revelation was first received; such information constitutes a category of literature known as *asbab al-nuzul* (occasions of revelation). The interplay between eternal word and early Islamic realities is here then quite simply understood as God's active involvement in the affairs of Muhammad's *umma* (community), without much further thought given to the metaphysical implications.

By contrast, modern and contemporary traditionalist Muslim thinkers tend to dwell much less on chronology and, especially, the "occasions of" specific Quranic revelations. Undoubtedly this comes of fear that such reflection might wrongly suggest that revelations were "determined" by historical necessity, that is, that the asbab al-nuzul be misconstrued as "occasions *for* (not *of*)" revelation. This fear is clearly a reactive stance against the accusations of Western Orientalist tradition. It is also a reaction against some recent "liberal" voices in the inner-Islamic dialogue that are now proposing new approaches to the problematic of sacred text and its cultural formation.[2] Medieval theologians and scripturalist experts showed interest in asbab al-nuzul, while also fully maintaining the Scripture's eternal nature and literal applicability in all areas of the faith; this combined interest illustrates the interplay of the symbols of divine word and sacred past, the inspiring and the inspired.

A related mechanism that transforms the past into paradigm is also present in the formation and function of the hadith in classical Islam. As a corpus of traditions on the life and actions of the Prophet, the actions of his companions and followers, and those of the first few generations of righteous Muslims after his death, the hadith was second in sanctity to the Quran and first in its function as interpreter of scripture. Over time and in a different culture (that is, changed political and socioeconomic situations occasioned by the Arab Muslim conquests of vast areas beyond the birthplace of Islam), the original nucleus of Muhammadan and Arabian traditions was expanded to legitimize foreign customs and facilitate their incorporation into the developing structures of the Islamic order. Even though far-reaching efforts of hadith criticism preceded and underlay the compilation of the six "canonical" collections of the ninth century said to contain only "sound," *sahih* traditions, ultimately the focus of the compilers was not historicist (seventh-century documents only) but based on a larger concept of authenticity as "spiritually and morally beneficial to the community." Included as "genuine" were items approved of by legal–theological consensus, with the result that the authenticated hadith came to contain strands of differing, sometimes even contradictory, traditions but which were at some time past or contemporaneous carried by their supporters' consensus. The consensus principle, in turn, by the tenth century had been recognized as one of the "infallible and inspired" sources of Islamic law. Historically a record as well as a dynamic vehicle of earlier processes of Islamization, the hadith continued to provide the faithful with understanding of scripture as applied and lived in a symbolic sacred past that provides a model of contemporaneous relevance.

Muslims experience the Quran as God's living presence, and they and their scripturalist experts have always interpreted it in this fashion. Tafsir, one of the most important Islamic sciences, has traditionally followed two main methodological approaches, interpretation by traditions (*tafsir bil-ma'thur*) and interpretation by way of philosophical speculation, personal opinion, individual initiative, and expression (*tafsir bil-ra'y*). In the classical sources, the end results—especially on issues of ethics—differed less than this bifurcation might suggest. The reasons for this lie both in the multifaceted nature of the hadith, already outlined, and also in the fact that ra'y (individual opinion) in premodern establishment scholarship often referred more to form and manner of argument than to its substance. The aim of the medieval tafsir as a whole was to disclose the Quran's norms to the faithful, to explicate in detail just in what manner they were called to discern truth and achieve goodness. The relative similarity of medieval Quran-based definitions of social morality and other questions of ethics derived from the fact that in the world of medieval Islam, the religious institutions were solid. The sharia, that venerable superstructure perched on scripture (*sunna*) and scholarly consensus, was not only a defining but largely an unchallenged coordinate of the medieval paradigm. Conquests by non-Muslim forces did occur (the Christian Crusaders, the pagan Mongols), but Islamic law, education, and the status of Arabic as Islam's sacred language formed part of the traditional structures and coherences that firmly underlay the medieval Muslim worldview and provided for its transregional solidarities.

The first complete "traditionist" (tradition-based) tafsir still extant was authored by Tabari (d. 923), on whose work all later exegeses of the same genre have heavily relied. The medieval "rationalist" school was represented by the Mu'tazilite Zamakhshari (d. 1144) and the Ash'arite Razi (d. 1149), whose works remained widely read even though by the end of the thirteenth century the preferred form of tafsir was once again tradition-based. It was during the modern age, especially the nineteenth century, that the rationalist tradition emerged afresh, as is visible, for instance, in the many textual echoes of Razi's interpretation in the tafsir of the Egyptian modernist Muhammad Abduh (d. 1905).

Sura 4:34 and Classical Exegesis

To gain a reading on the stance of the medieval authorities on gender issues, it may be useful to examine Tabari's (d. 923) and Baydawi's (d. 1286?) interpretations of the pivotal Quranic verse on gender relations, Sura 4:34. The verse in question says:

Men are in charge of [are guardians of/are superior to/have authority over] women (*al-rijalu qawwamuna 'ala l-nisa'*) because God has endowed one with more [because God has preferred some of them over others] (*bi-ma faddala Allahu ba'dahum 'ala ba'din*) and because they spend of their means (*wa-bi-ma 'anfaqu min amwalihim*). Therefore the righteous women are obedient, guarding in secret that which God has guarded. As to those from whom you fear rebellion, admonish them and banish them to separate beds, and beat them. Then if they obey you, seek not a way against them. For God is Exalted, Great.

To Tabari, this verse is primarily concerned with the domestic relations between husband and wife. It legislates men's authority over their women, which entails the male's right to discipline his women in order to ensure female obedience both toward God and also himself. This system is deemed equitable in that it sets out men's obligation to pay the dower for women, spend their wealth on them, and provide for them. Female obedience consists of marital fidelity, friendly behavior toward the husband and his family, and good household management, while male authority includes the right of bodily chastisement as long as such is deserved. Rebellion (*nushuz*), on the other hand, is interpreted to mean female appropriation of superiority over the husband, undue freedom of movement, objection to sexual contact when desired by the husband, and other acts of defiance. While Tabari's main point of exegesis of the phrase "because God has endowed the one with more/preferred some of them over others" rests on the men's economic ability to support their wives and the concomitant obligation to do so, several traditions quoted by Tabari also indicate that men in general have precedence or excellence over women.[3]

This point is made much more clearly by Baydawi, whose tafsir is a concise recapitulation of the gist of previous exegetic works, especially those of Zamakhshari and Razi. In this commentary, men's "guardianship of" or "superiority over" women as revealed in Sura 4:34 is likened to that of rulers over their subjects. The reason for this is twofold: one is concerned with innate abilities and the other with acquired qualities. "God has endowed the one with more" refers to the fact that:

> God has favored men over women by endowing them with a perfect mind, good management skills, and superb strength with which to perform practical work and pious deeds. Hence, to men [alone] were allotted the prophethood, the imamate, government, performance of the religious ceremonies, witnessing in all (legal) matters, the duty to fight for the sake of God (*jihad*), attend Friday prayers, to wear the turban, receive the greater inheritance share, and the monopoly in the decision to divorce.[4]

Modern Methodologies and Paradigms

Compared to the classical tradition, modern and contemporary tafsir works generally dwell more on the ethical issues in culture, society, politics, and economics and less on points of theology or aspects of language (grammar and rhetoric) in the Quranic text. Nevertheless, most of these works are still "traditionalist" in nature in that they echo their predecessors' conclusions, especially on gender issues where the latter have been enshrined in sharia law. Especially in works authored by conservative establishment *ulama*, the hallowed, "authentic" (that is, consensus-based) tradition is seen as endangered; emphasis is placed on its defense against the forces of "alienating" innovation.

This traditionalism on gender issues was modified and altered by Islamic modernism whose various strands are more than just a rethinking of tradition, including the medieval rationalist tradition. The prominent trait of the modernist school is its spirit of reformism that seeks to grasp the value system of the Quran as a whole, therefrom to win fresh and new guidance, signposts in a world so unlike that of the past. To derive the living value system as first revealed to, and practiced-by, the righteous early community of Islam, modernists assume the right to *ijtihad* (individual interpretation of scripture), while also propagating legal reform, which they perceive as separation of the true sharia from its medieval juridic formulation (*fiqh*).

Sura 4:34 and Muhammad Abduh

The Egyptian theologian and jurist Muhammad Abduh (d. 1905), Islamic modernism's most important early representative in the Arab world, saw Islam as eminently compatible with modernity. His main goal was to "renew" Muslim morality and reform the traditional social structures of his day—and particularly his region, Egypt—by way of a return to the dynamic faith and pristine morality of Islam's first generations. Although familiar with the classical tafsir literature, to which he frequently referred, Abduh's approach to the Quran in his own exegesis[5] showed a new attention to the literal meaning of the Quranic verses and also their contextualization, both within the particular sura as well as the entire Quran. This he did in tandem with deemphasis of the hadith as a whole and most especially its *isra'iliyyat* (Bible-derived and extrabiblical traditions). A radical breakthrough on "how to read" the Quran's commands and injunctions came with Abduh's new rationale to separate the *ibadat* (laws on religious duties) from the *muamalat* (laws on social transactions) in the Quran and sharia. He argued that while ibadat by nature lie beyond interpretative change, the muamalat by nature require interpretation and adaptation by each generation of Muslims in light of the practical needs of their age.[6] A third "modernist" characteristic recognizable in Abduh's writings, which grew ever more important with later modernists, was his desire to express both his exegesis and also his Qurano-centric blueprint for moral reform in language aimed at a wider reading public.

Abduh's interpretation of the Quran's social laws led him to some daringly innovative Quran interpretations and *fatwas* (legal opinions) on women's issues, most prominent among them the practice of polygamy. He argued that while polygamy was a sound practice among the righteous early believers, it had developed into a corrupt practice of unbridled lust, without justice or equity, in his own time. "A nation that practices polygamy cannot be educated. Religion was revealed for the benefit of its people; if one of its provisions begins to harm rather than benefit the community . . . the application of that provision has to be changed according to the changed needs of the group."[7] "Exceptions will always be possible—as in the case of the barren wife—but must be decided upon by a judge. There is no impediment to this in religion. What prevents [its implementation] is merely custom (*'ada*)."[8] Abduh was equally concerned with the harmful effects of divorce on public morality. He described at great length and in passionate language the inequities of the divorce system for women. A wife should have the right to request divorce with a judge in the case of "harm" from her husband, such as unlawful neglect, unlawful beating, abuse, etc.; in these cases, the burden of proof would rest with the wife. More important, men should mend their ways and live up to their religiously sanctioned obligations toward their wives, former wives, and children.[9]

Abduh's ijtihad was not put forth to benefit women in and of themselves but as a means to bring about the moral rebirth of Islamic society which Abduh perceived possible only through the "re-Islamization" of the family.[10] He proceeded from the premise that women's status is causally linked with the well-being or decay of social life as a whole, as demonstrated in the Quranic revelations. The community, however, "takes of the revelations only that for which it is ready," and so this truth was disregarded as the people reverted to the ignorance of the Jahiliyya (pre-Islamic Arabia) to which they added the licentiousness and animal drives they had learned from the Franks. "See how we have become an argument against our religion."[11]

Among the reform measures Abduh proposed were, first, the education of women in the obligations and rights established for them by their religion. "How can a nation prosper in this life and the next when one half of its members are like beasts of burden, neglecting their duties toward God, themselves, and their relatives?"[12] Second, he called for the education of men "in the true meaning of Islam," which would make them give up all selfishness, material greed, power hunger, and love of tyranny, so they would begin to deal with their wives in the spirit of love, compassion, and equality that the Quran enjoins.[13] "Know that the men who try to be masters in their houses by oppressing women beget but slaves for others."[14] Third, this would lead to the reestablishment of righteous marriage as a solemn covenant that is part of the natural order of being and reconfirmation of the "exact equivalence" of the spouses in the family.[15]

This, then, was Abduh's reading on Sura 4:34, in concert with that of his editor, commentator, and later spokesman Rashid Rida (d. 1935): that in the God-willed natural order of the family, the man is charged with leadership (*qiwama*) to protect domestic life and well-being. He is to the wife as the head is to the body. Men merit this "superiority" because of qualities they alone possess, some innate and some acquired. Among them are a stronger, more perfect, more complete, and more beautiful constitution, as is the case with the males in all species. This physical constitution is linked to a stronger mind and sounder perceptions, the ability to earn money and administer affairs in a creative way. Women, in turn, should be gratified that their dependency, even though it is a matter of natural constitution, is actually rewarded with "remuneration" or "wages" (dower and maintenance). The husband's qiwama over his wife consists not of acts of tyranny but of guidance toward righteous behavior, education, domestic efficiency, houseboundness, and fiscal responsibility to his budgetary guidelines. Then the woman can keep her house in safety, and order and bear and raise the children.

God has not "preferred" men over women. In individual cases, wives can even surpass their husbands in knowledge, work, bodily strength, and earning power. But it is by their biological and social functions in the family that the sexes as a whole are addressed and organized in Sura 4:34. From this system follows the man's leadership in concluding the marriage contract and deciding upon divorce. Man's exclusive obligation to fight holy war also derives from his role as protector of the woman, and his larger inheritance share relates to fact that his expenses are greater. According to Abduh, all other prerogatives mentioned by the classical interpreters (prophethood, government, prayer-leading, religious ritual, call to prayer, sermonizing on Friday), while following from man's more perfect disposition and lack of preoccupation (with other things), have nothing to do with his "guardianship" of women (of Sura 4:34). Because even if the law had endowed women with all these prerogatives, by innate nature men would still be "in charge" of them in the family.[16]

Sura 4:34 and Mid-century Modernism

The Abduh/Rida tafsir was written in the traditional style as an interlinear (verse by verse) Quranic exegesis, although it had cross-references to other Quranic sections dealing with the same topic. Many later Quran interpreters, especially of the modernist kind, have chosen to present their commentary on selected Quranic passages in formats other than tafsir, such as monographs, collections of lectures, sermons, and the like. This tendency was strengthened by the creative impulse of disciplines other than theology; one example can be seen in the work of the Egyptian philologist and literary critic Amin al-Khuli (d. 1967) who, though not the author of a tafsir work himself, propagated the importance of thematic tafsir (*tafsir mawdu'i*).[17] By the 1940s, al-Khuli had introduced some new, Western-inspired courses and projects in literary criticism at Fu'ad (now Cairo) University; he had also decided to work toward a new methodology in Quranic interpretation that, though being mainly literary and philological, also was to use various other disciplines such as history, psychology, and sociology. Thus, textual background studies and what we would now call "close reading" of the Quran as literary text were thought essential to the proper understanding of the Quran.[18] As indicated, al-Khuli was not a theologian but an Arabist, a specialist in language and literature.

Here it is perhaps useful to compare the Arabic linguists of the present age, such as al-Khuli and Nasr Hamid Abu Zayd (to be dealt with later), with the Arabic linguists of the classical age. The latter were among the major constructors of the meaning of the Quranic text. Much of their lexicographic work related to pre-Islamic (that is, pagan) literature, especially poetry, and many of their methodological approaches and grammatical categories may at least partially have been influenced by foreign (Greek, Indian, Persian) traditions. However, Arabic linguistics in the Middle Ages had a secure place within the religious sciences, as had the Arabic linguists within the religious establishment. It is only now, as new (originally Western) theories of literary criticism and new approaches to text, its formation and meaning, have found some creative proponents among Arab Muslims in Arabic linguistics, that theology views this discipline as a new menace.

With al-Khuli, as with Abduh/Rida and increasingly so with later interpreters, theologian and lay alike, emphasis lies with the Quranic text as an organic unity, whence the arrangement of verses in the suras, and the arrangement and progression of suras themselves, are hermeneutically significant.[19] Mahmud Shaltut (d. 1963), the Egyptian modernist Rector of the Azhar from 1958 to 1963, represents this trend on the theological side. Shaltut approached the Quranic text as an organic whole, emphasized interpretation by themes, considered the hadith at best a secondary source of interpretation and legislation (with large parts of it unreliable), and stressed muamalat, sociopolitical issues and the like, with the purpose of moral reform of the community.[20] For Shaltut, the asbab al-nuzul traditions could be useful in clarifying the original intention behind a Quranic law; nevertheless, the Quran itself remains universal, valid for all Muslims and at all times. To understand it properly requires not reliance on old tafsir scholarship but a new inner-Quranic interpretation that includes a consideration of context, of a verse or phrase, instead of the atomistic approach of the classical interpreters.[21] Nevertheless, to Shaltut, all information in the Quran, including the stories on events that occurred long before the Prophet's time, is absolutely true; perhaps these stories are primarily told to teach the believers "lessons," but nevertheless they also impart historical truth.[22]

Surely this traditional stance represented a rejection of more literary-critical approaches to the Quranic text, such as those of al-Khuli and, especially, al-Khuli's student Muhammad Ahmad Khalafallah, whose dissertation on *The Art of Storytelling in the Qur'an* raised a public furor in Egypt because of the underlying premise that the Quran's narratives are to be taken as principles of direction and guidance, not historical fact.[23] Therefore, and even though the reformist tenor is a central aspect of Shaltut's paradigm, its roots lie securely in tradition. Like his ideological predecessor Muhammad Abduh, Shaltut and many others like him of the modernist school maintain the validity of background studies for a better understanding of the Quran's original meaning (in seventh-century Arabia) but insist on the universality and absolute truth of all of the Quran's tenets.

On women's issues, Shaltut's position was both tied to tradition and had a modern apologetic aspect to it; this modern aspect pitted the humaneness and morality of the Quranic family laws and other women-specific laws in general against their narrow literalist readings by the critics of Islam. To Shaltut, marriage is not about demanding one's personal rights, but rather about achieving spousal cooperation and harmony (as addressed elsewhere in the Quran). Therefore, man's "authority" over his wife, while established as such by Sura 4:34, is not a right as much as an obligation that entails the burdens of domestic leadership. In Shaltut's view, this is the nature of authority in general, on all levels of society. The specific formulation of 4:34, "because God has given the one more/because God has made some of them to excel others," does not indicate men's superiority over women in an absolute sense, but rather it indicates their superiority within an organic whole, just as the right hand is superior over the left in the human body.[24]

Islamism (Islamic "fundamentalism") differs from the modernist school established by Abduh by way of its politicization and engagement. In their active struggle to Islamicize (infuse Islamic values into) immoral and corrupt (and often "Western") structures and practices, Islamists translate the sacred text directly into contemporary thought and action. Thus, an individual textual approach to the Quran ijtihad as well as some interpretations, especially on gender, indicate the existence of tight ideological links between Islamism and the Abduh tradition—except that a spirit of revolution sets Islamism apart from the modernists' spirit of reform.

Islamism by nature differs more profoundly from traditionalism. The latter is the mainstream conservative school of thought that views Islam as an inherited, balanced system of faith and action based on and sanctioned by scripture and its interpretation through the verifying authority of past scholarly consensus. In letter and spirit, hermeneutic approaches and political stances, Islamism differentiates itself from mainstream conservatism. Yet its vision of women (and minorities) remains similar to that of establishment Islam, and it also derives from a fairly literal application of the Quran's gender laws. Thus, the Islamist Sayyid Qutb (d. 1966) interprets Sura 4:34 in a mixture of traditionalism and some modernist ingredients, all clad in the language of Islamism's warning that gender equality (in the Western sense) would bring societal and cultural destruction in its wake. Qutb sees the social and psychological import of 4:34 within the institution of the family, that cornerstone of Muslim society, a safety haven for the spouses, a nurturing shelter for the young.

From this perspective, the Quran gives the man the right of "guardianship" or "superiority" over the family structure in order to prevent dissension and friction between the spouses. The equity of this system lies in the fact that God both favored the man with the necessary qualities and skills for the "guardianship" and also charged him with the duty to provide for the structure's upkeep. In any human organization, power and authority belong to the most qualified candidate—how much more so here. Both man and woman are God's creatures, and neither is to be oppressed. However, each was fashioned for a special task—the woman to bear and raise children and the man to provide for her necessities and protection—so that she can devote herself to her important task without worry about "work" or her safety and that of her child.

Equity lies in the specific physical, mental, and psychological qualities with which each sex is endowed beyond the other. For the woman, this means tenderness, a swift and unconscious positive reaction to the demands of the children, while for the man it is hardness, sternness, and the use of consciousness and thought before moving and reacting. "Oppression" would be to burden the woman with this "guardianship" for which she is not prepared. To be assigned such a task would mean that she loses the abilities to perform her primary task, that of motherhood. Whenever these rules of sound original nature (*fitra*) are violated, human life breaks down and destruction threatens. Children raised in families where the "guardianship" lies with the mother (because the father is weak or there is no lawful father) are usually perverted in some way. Man's "guardianship" is not about quashing the woman's personality or her civic rights; rather it is an obligation to direct and protect the family.[25]

Sura 4:34 and The New Epistemology

Modernity has meant a number of new and different approaches to the problematic of the Quran's eternal nature versus its day-to-day cultural specificity, most often now written in the form of theoretical treatises rather than Quranic commentary. The Pakistani scholar Fazlur Rahman, one of modernism's most thoughtful spokesmen, stipulated that "objective knowledge" of the past is possible through rational discovery of the Quran's value system in its extrahistorical, "transcendental" dimension; that value system can then be infused into the equally rationally researched sociohistorical context of the present "in order to determine priorities afresh . . . and implement the Quranic values afresh."[26] Past interpretations and applications (legal, theological, and philosophical) are of limited use:

> With the passage of time and the rise, growth, and hardening of different points of view and preconceived notions, subjective interpretations have multiplied. The historical tradition will therefore be more an object of judgment for the new understanding than an aid to it, although this historical traditional product can undoubtedly yield insights.[27]

Rahman, then, sought to establish a theoretical model that distinguishes between the Quran's "literal," situation-specific laws on the one hand and the eternally valid "reasons," *rationes legis*, behind those laws on the other. To Rahman, the Quran was "the divine response, through the Prophet's mind, to the moral–social situation of the Prophet's Arabia." To apply this divine truth to all later ages, including our own, requires scripturalist interpretation in the form of "a double movement, from the present situation to Quranic times, then back to the present."[28] For Rahman, the first movement consisted of "understanding the meaning of the Quran as a whole as well as in terms of specific tenets that constitute responses to specific situations"; it was "to generalize those specific answers and enunciate them as statements of general moral–social objectives that can be 'distilled' from specific texts in light of the sociohistorical background and the often-stated *rationes legis*. . . ."[29] Whereas the first movement occurs:

> from the specifics of the Quran to the eliciting and systematizing of its general principles, values, and long-range objectives, the second [movement] is to be from this general view to the specific view that is to be formulated and realized *now*. . . . The general has to be embodied in the present concrete sociohistorical context . . . [after careful assessment of the present situation] so we can determine priorities afresh in order to implement the Quranic values afresh.[30]

Decrying the error of the Muslim legal tradition, "which essentially regarded the Quran as a lawbook and not *the religious source* of the law,"[31] Rahman attributed that error to traditionalist adherence to the letter of the law, while in truth the *ratio legis* is "the essence of the matter," so much so that "when the law fails to reflect the *ratio*, the law must change."[32] Thus, for example, men's superiority over women in 4:34 to Rahman is not inherent but purely functional. If a woman is economically self-sufficient and contributes to the household expenditure, "the male's superiority would to that extent be reduced, since *as a human*, he has no superiority over his wife."[33]

Other modernist, reform-minded Muslim thinkers have dealt with the problem of the Quran's inner structure and the nature of its legislation in related ways. Ismail Ragi al-Faruqi emphasized not only the necessity of getting at the motive, intent, or purpose behind Quranic passages, but also the need to discover a "hierarchy" in the Quran's value system; this is reminiscent of the process by which the Quranic values were first applied to the newly encountered social situations in the formative period of Islam. Such "hierarchization" involves a differentiation of textual "levels" in scripture, the identification of the timebound from the eternally valid, or specific socioeconomic laws from the underlying principle.[34] Applying the method of "hierarchization" of Quranic values, al-Faruqi and other modernist scholars then argue that the moral and religious equality of men and women "represents the highest expression of the value of equality,"[35] and therefore constitutes the most important aspect of the Quranic paradigm on this issue. Sura 4:34, stipulating men's qiwama over women, would be an example of a Quranic law specifically revealed for the patriarchal Arabian society of the Prophet's time. In the social context of the twentieth century, when many women are no longer dependent on their husbands for protection and maintenance, the concept of "priority" of husband over wife in the socioeconomic sphere is subject to change. What prevails is the "higher" principle of ethico-religious equality of women with men, amply legislated in the Quran, which is independent of social circumstances.[36]

An Islamic feminist example of this mode of argumentation is expressed in *Qur'an and Woman* by Amina Wadud-Muhsin.[37] This author's theoretical stance consists of the differentation between two textual levels in the Quran, the historically and culturally contextualized "prior text" and the wider "megatext" of essential or culturally universal relevance. In the latter, gender distinctions (based on early Arabian precedent) are superceded by the Quran's emphasis on gender equality.[38] Wadud-Muhsin distinguishes three categories of Quranic interpretation: the traditional, reactive, and holistic. "Traditional" exegesis is faulted for its atomistic methodology and lack of recognition of the Quran's structure of thematic unity; the main fault, however, is that all traditional Quran interpretations were written by men. "Reactive" interpretation is largely the use of the Quran by feminist and other ideologically motivated individuals who "vindicate the position of women on grounds entirely incongruous with the Quran's position on women." Finally, the "holistic" category, chosen by Wadud-Muhsin herself, involves consideration of the context of a Quranic revelation, the grammatical and semantic composition of its given text, and also the overall Quranic worldview.[39]

Every "reading" reflects, in part, the intentions of the text, as well as the "prior text" of the one who makes the "reading," that is, the reader's own perspectives, circumstances, and background. While a large variety of readings can thus coexist, mere relativism is prevented by the permanence and continuity of the Quranic text itself on which all readings converge; "it is not the text or its principles that change, but the capacity and particularity of the understanding and reflection of the principles of the text within a community of people."[40] No interpretation involving the separation of principles and applicability, however, can ever be final,[41] because to impose a single cultural perspective—even that of the original community of the Prophet—contradicts the essential nature and universal purpose of the Quran.[42]

Within this framework, Wadud-Muhsin's reading of Sura 4:34, the verse on men's qiwama over women, begins with an inner-Quranic context-focused study of essential leximatic terms in this verse. Such a study shows that qiwama (being in charge of), *faddala* (prefer), and *ba'd* (some) have relative meaning in the Quran in general; it is especially so in this verse, which relates to other gender-specific economic legislation such as inheritance shares and specific support obligations. While Wadud-Muhsin follows Sayyid Qutb and others in understanding this verse as legislative of the *functional* relationship between man and husband (protector and provider) and woman and wife (mother of his children), she then extends those other interpreters' principle of "gender equality *qua* mutual dependency in the family" to society at large. Here, in the societies of the modern world, the verse's meaning is revealed as the expression of an ideal (neither biological nor inherent, but valuable) obligation for men to create a better society by bettering their relationships with women, indeed as a part of fulfilling their God-given *khilafa* (trusteeship) on earth.[43]

The hierarchization of disparate levels in the Quranic message has also been employed in different ways. The Sudanese Mahmoud Mohamed Taha (d. 1985) took an "unorthodox, reformist" approach in his book *The Second Message of Islam*.[44] Taha differentiated between the Quran's early (Meccan) message (tolerant and egalitarian) and its later (Medinan) message (seen at least in part as adaptation to the socioeconomic and political situation of the Prophet's Medinan community). Shaykh Taha's student Abdullahi Ahmed An-Na'im has since developed his mentor's general principles into a framework for the radical reform of Islamic institutions, of which gender equality forms an important part.[45] An-Na'im maintains that:

> ijtihad under sharia cannot be exercised in matters governed by clear and definite texts in the Quran and Sunna, [thus] none of the objectionable principles and rules relating to the status of women and non-Muslims [to be examined in his book] can be varied or changed through a modern exercise of ijtihad in the historical sense of the term.[46]

Therefore, in the spirit of his mentor, An-Na'im proposes the adoption of a new "evolutionary principle" of Quranic interpretation, which is to reverse the historical process of sharia positive law formation (which was based on the Quran's Medinan verses) and elaborate a new sharia public law (based on the Meccan revelations),[47] by way of the time-honored theological and juristic principle of *naskh*, the abrogation or suspension of Quranic verses for legal purposes.[48] This puts An-Na'im's methodology beyond that of modernists like Fazlur Rahman; An-Na'im credits Rahman for differentiating the "legal" from the "moral" in the Quran, but he faults Rahman for shirking full consideration of all that this implies, that is, whether the legal should remain legal and the moral should be beyond the realm of legal requirement, or whether the moral should be enacted into law, which would mean the elimination of the corresponding legal principle of the past.[49] In short, to An-Na'im, Rahman's shortcoming lies in failing to transform academic insights into a concise and practical reform methodology.[50]

To An-Na'im, a sharia public law of equal human rights for all, including women and non-Muslims, will only be achieved through "creation" of a new sharia based on the tolerant and egalitarian revelations vouchsafed to the Prophet while he was in Mecca. The sharia in its present form perpetuates discrimination in many areas—such as declaring that women are unfit for full participation in public life, including the holding of public office that would involve their exercise of authority over men. For instance, according to the Shafiite legal school, women may hold no judicial office, while according to the Hanafite legal school they may act as judges in civil cases only. These restrictions are based on Sura 4:34 which was revealed in Medina.[51] That Medinan verse, and its medieval sharia extension, made sense in societies characterized by the dependency of women on men for economic and security reasons. However, such dependence is no longer necessarily true, and thus, in a new sharia, male guardianship over women should be terminated. "Both men and women should now be equally free and equally responsible before the law, which guarantees economic opportunity and security for all members of the community."[52]

From the field of linguistics and textual theory come new approaches as well. Mohammed Arkoun has long applied the epistemology of modern linguistics and semiotics to the reading of the Quran. In his latest book, *Rethinking Islam: Common Questions, Uncommon Answers*,[53] he deals briefly with some of the theoretical problems concerning a rethinking of women's issues; his thoughts culminate in the appeal for "a cultural revolution that would for the first time integrate the emancipation of women into a modern philosophy . . . of the human being." According to Arkoun, however, that modern philosophy is "yet to be written."[54]

Linguistics and literary criticism also provide the theoretical background of the controversial work of Egyptian professor Nasr Hamid Abu Zayd of Cairo University who, especially in his books *The Concept of Text: Study in the Quranic Sciences* and *Critique of the Religious Discourse*,[55] applies theories of modern literary criticism—most especially semiotics—when dealing with the Quranic text from the perspective of "text as cultural product." Abu Zayd skirts the danger of "explaining" the Quran as a product of seventh-century Meccan and Medinan culture by separating its metaphysical being from the historical manifestation.[56] Nevertheless, he dwells on the time-and-place specificity of, especially, the asbab al-nuzul and naskh traditions, whose authenticity traditional Muslim scholarship has long affirmed while simultaneously insisting on the text's word-for-word eternal nature—to Abu Zayd a logical contradiction.

Abu Zayd recently published a small book on women's issues entitled *Woman in the*

Discourse of Crisis,[57] which is a collection of topical articles previously published in the Egyptian press. Here the author distinguishes between the "fundamental" or "core" verses of the Quran that establish gender equality (meaning equal moral responsibility and in divine recompense) and a small number of "exceptional" verses that legislate gender inequality. For Abu Zayd, the latter carry direct historical and social connotations of seventh-century Arabian realities and must therefore be interpreted in light of the Quranic verses establishing gender equality.[58] Instead of engaging in true Quranic exegesis along these lines, the discourse of mainstream Islam to Abu Zayd is resorting to "justification" of its doctrine of gender inequality by emphasizing the biological difference between the sexes.[59] This emphasis reduces the woman to "female" and stipulates her inferiority to "the male" by outmoded labor laws that fail to consider that labor issues have become human rights issues.[60] Woman's enforced veiling and seclusion from larger society amount to her negation—indeed her abolishment and murder—and thus represent the essence of the crisis, the final surrender to defeat.[61]

This book, then, is polemic in nature and presents Abu Zayd's refutation of traditionalist writers, such as Muhammad al-Ghazzali, rather than a new in-depth semiotic analysis of key Quranic passages on women's issues. To Abu Zayd the questions of scripture, gender, and their interrelationship in a new religious discourse require another study, one which he plans to do independently in the future.[62]

Abu Zayd, Arkoun, and other similarly secularist Muslim scholars are thus now using theories on scripture and hermeneutics that derive at least in part from extra-Islamic models of textual criticism. While gender issues are rarely the focus of such theoretical studies, they are directly affected by the implications of such studies. Such scholars are saying that solving the crisis of the contemporary Muslim world requires a break with the past, both in the type of scholars who do the reassessment and also in their approaches to the sacred text.

In the ever increasing Muslim debate on how to achieve both an authentic modernity and an authentic Quran-centered Islam, gender issues continue to hold center stage. The protagonists in the debate now are modernist Quranic scholars, (many of whom still have a grounding in past tradition), feminists, linguists, cultural anthropologists, philosophers, and sociologists. The number and variety of textual approaches and concomitant scripture-based paradigms on women's issues are a sign of the pluralism that characterizes contemporary Islamic thought.

Notes

1. J. Jomier, "Quelques Positions Actuelles de l'Exegese Coranique en Egypte: Revelées par une Polemique Recente," *Melanges* 1 (1954): 70–71.

2. An example is the Moroccan sociologist Fatima Mernissi's *Le Harem Politique*, English translation: *The Veil and the Male Elite: A Feminist Interpretation of Women's Rights in Islam*, trans. Mary Jo Lakeland (Reading, Mass.: Addison-Wesley, 1991), in which the author stipulates that although the Prophet Muhammad's vision of Islamic society was egalitarian, he eventually had to sacrifice this vision for the sake of communal cohesiveness and the survival of the Islamic cause. In this reading, the Quranic verses are related so closely to the historical events surrounding their revelation that a "causal" relationship between the two would logically follow. This book was banned in Morocco by theological fiat (*fatwa*). Cf. Barbara Freyer Stowasser, *Women in the Qur'an, Traditions, and Interpretation* (New York: Oxford University Press, 1994), pp. 132–134.

3. Abu Ja'far Muhammad ibn Jarir al-Tabari, *Jami' al-Bayan 'an Ta'wil 'ay al-Qur'an*, ed. Mahmud M. Shakir and Ahmad M. Shakir, vol. 8 (Cairo: Dar al-Ma'arif, 1972) pp. 290–317.

4. Abd Allah ibn Umar al-Baydawi, *Anwar al-Tanzil wa-Asrar al-Ta'wil*, vol. 1 of *Reproductio Phototypica Editionis 1846–1848)*, (Osnabruck: Biblio, 1968), pp. 207–208.

5. Known as *Tafsir al-Manar*; given form during a lecture course at al-Azhar University, it was first published in the monthly review *al-Manar* which was then edited by Abduh's friend and disciple Rashid Rida (d. 1935). Abduh's commentary, which ended with Sura 4:125, was transcribed and augmented by Rida, and when Abduh died, Rida continued the Tafsir until Sura 12:25.

6. Barbara Freyer Stowasser, "Women's Issues in Modern Islamic Thought," in *Arab Women*, ed. Judith E. Tucker (Bloomington: Indiana University Press, 1993), pp. 8–9.

7. Muhammad Abduh, *al-Islam wa-al-Mar'ah fi Ra'y al-Imam Muhammad Abduh*, ed. Muhammad 'Imara (Cairo: n.d.), p. 117.

8. Ibid., p. 118.

9. Ibid., p. 96.

10. Ibid., pp. 136ff.

11. Ibid., pp. 83, 105–106, 57.

12. Ibid., pp. 58–59.

13. Ibid., pp. 105ff.

14. Ibid., p. 69.

15. Ibid., pp. 75ff.

16. Muhammad Rashid Rida, *Tafsir al-Qur'an al-Hakim al-Shahir bi-Tafsir al-Manar*, vol. 5 (Beirut: Dar al-Ma'arif, 1973), pp. 66–80.

17. Kate Zebiri, *Mahmud Shaltut and Islamic Modernism* (Oxford: Clarendon Press, 1993), p. 139.

18. Cf. Ibid., p. 140ff.

19. Cf. Mustansir Mir, "Tafsir," in *The Oxford Encyclopedia of the Modern Islamic World*, vol. 4, ed. John L. Esposito (New York: Oxford University Press, 1995), p. 174.

20. Zebiri, *op. cit.*, p. 150.

21. Ibid., pp. 150, 161–162.

22. Ibid., p. 168.

23. Muhammad Ahmad Khalafallah, *Al-Fann al-Qasasi fi al-Qur'an al-Karim.* (Cairo: Maktabat al-Nahda al-Misriyya, 1958). Cf. Stowasser, *Women in the Qur'an*, pp. 18–20.

24. Ibid., pp. 62–63.

25. Sayyid Qutb, *Fi Zilal al-Qur'an*, vol. 2 (Beirut: Dar al-Shuruq, 1982), pp. 648–657.

26. Fazlur Rahman, *Islam and Modernity* (Chicago: Chicago University Press, 1982), p. 7.

27. Ibid., pp. 6–7.

28. Ibid., p. 5.

29. Ibid., p. 6.

30. Ibid., p. 7.

31. Fazlur Rahman, *Major Themes of the Qur'an* (Minneapolis: Bibliotheca Islamica, 1980), p. 47.

32. Ibid., p. 48.

33. Ibid., p. 49.

34. Ismail Ragi al-Faruqi, "Towards a New Methodology for Qur'anic Exegesis," *Islamic Studies* (March 1962): 35–52; and John L. Esposito, *Women in Muslim Family Law* (Syracuse, N.Y.: Syracuse University Press, 1982), pp. 105–107.

35. Esposito, *Women in Muslim Family law*, pp. 107–108.

36. Ibid., p. 108.

37. Amina Wadud-Muhsin, *Qur'an and Woman* (Kuala Lumpur: Penerbit Fajar Bakti Sdn., Bhd., 1992).

38. Vincent J. Cornell, "Qur'an," in *The Oxford Encyclopedia of The Modern Islamic World*, vol. 3, ed. John Esposito (New York: Oxford University Press, 1994), p. 392.

39. Wadud-Muhsin, *Qur'an and Woman*, pp. 1–4.

40. Ibid., p. 5.

41. Ibid, p. 10.

42. Ibid., p. 6.

43. Ibid., pp. 69–78.

44. Published in Arabic in 1967. English edition: Mahmoud Mohamed Taha, *The Second Mesage of Islam*, trans. Abdullahi Ahmed An-Na'im (Syracuse, N.Y.: Syracuse University Press, 1987).

45. John O. Voll, Foreword to *Toward an Islamic Reformism: Civil Liberties, Human Rights, and International Law*, by Abd Allahi Ahmad An-Naim (Syracuse, N.Y.: Syracuse University Press, 1990), pp. IX–XII.

46. Ibid., p. 58.

47. Ibid., p. 56.

48. Ibid., pp. 56–58.

49. Ibid., p. 65.

50. Ibid., p. 66.

51. Ibid., p. 88.

52. Ibid., p. 180.

53. Mohammed Arkoun, *Rethinking Islam: Common Questions, Uncommon Answers*, trans. and ed. Robert D. Lee (Boulder, Colo.: Westview Press, 1994).

54. Ibid., p. 62.

55. *Mafhum al-Nass; Dirasah fi 'Ulum al-Qur'an* (Beirut: al-Markaz al-Thaqafi al-'Arabi, 1990); and *Naqd al-Khitab al-Dini* (Cairo: Sina lil-Nashr, 1994).

56. Here reminiscent of the Mu'tazila whose rationalist approach to Quran interpretation Abu Zayd analyzed in his *al-Ittijah al-'Aqli fi al-Tafsir: Dirasah fi Qadiyat al-Majaz fi al-Qur'an 'inda al-Mu'tazila* (Beirut: Dar al-Tanwir lil-Tiba'ah wa-al-Nashr, 1993). Indeed, the Egyptian literary critic Gabir Asfour wrote a thoughtful essay on Abu Zayd's *Mafhum al-nass* which bears the subtitle "al-i'tizal al-jadid" [Gabir Asfour, *Hawamish 'Ala Daftar al-Tanwir* (Kuwait: Dar Su'ad al-Sabah, 1994), pp. 47–82].

57. Nasr Hamid Abu Zayd, *al-Mar'a fi Khitab al-Azma* (Cairo: Dar al-Nusus, 1994).

58. Ibid., p. 76.

59. Ibid., pp. 75–77.

60. Ibid., p. 90.

61. Ibid., p. 103.

62. Ibid., p .101.

Islam, Social Change, and the Reality of Arab Women's Lives

For more than a hundred years, Arab women have been engaged in the public debate on their role in a rapidly changing society. Both women and men have conducted the debate within an Islamic framework; they have turned to the Quran, the sharia (Islamic law), the sayings of the Prophet Muhammad, and the lives of his companions to define women's rights in the modern age. While modernists have argued for the most liberal interpretation of Islam possible, the conservatives have used the same sources to argue for restrictions on women's roles.[1]

Social Change

The debates make frequent references to the centrality of Arab women in maintaining family ties and community solidarity and in transmitting cultural values across generations. This was best captured in the document prepared by the Economic and Social Commission for Western Asia for the 1985 United Nations World Conference on Women, which was held in Nairobi. The document declared:

> Constitutions, charters, and legislation in the region have asserted the role of the family as the nucleus of social organization in Arab societies. It is necessary, therefore, to make available to the family the economic, social, cultural, and psychological conditions that would ensure its stability and satisfy its needs.[2]

Therefore, the document accorded "priority to the work of women who devote their time to family and home affairs and hence ensure the continuity of generations, the cultivation of values, and the transmittal of knowledge and expertise from one generation to another."[3]

Hitherto, Arab women themselves have assigned a great deal of value to their traditional roles within the family. This is partly because they are accorded a great deal of respect. As the social scientist Nadia Haggag Youssef noted, women's status can be seen as having two different components:

> the *rights* given to women and the *respect* given to them. Confusion ensues because the two distinct factors are erroneously used interchangeably, when in reality they are often

inversely correlated. Thus, women receive great respect in certain societies that give them few rights; they receive equality of rights in societies in which they compete with men but have relatively low respect.[4]

Today, Arab women are in the unenviable position of having to choose between rights and respect. Neither women nor men want to lose the warmth and security that the extended Arab family traditionally provided, particularly at a time of rapid social and economic change. However, modernization efforts by the state have steadily eroded traditional support and mediation systems, and women now are increasingly reliant on state legislation and institutions to protect their rights. Yet in the crucial area of relations within the family, the law in the Arab world does not provide for equal rights between men and women. This has occurred because the debate on women's roles has been conducted within the Islamic framework.

Law and the Islamic Framework

The constitutions of the Arab nations, in those countries that have them, provide for nondiscrimination based on race, sex, or creed as called for in international law and United Nations conventions. Thus they provide equal political rights for Arab women, who can vote and stand for election in all the Arab countries that have parliaments (except in Kuwait). Arab labor laws that have been legislated during this century also compare well to international standards.

However, family laws, which regulate rights and responsibilities in marriage, divorce, child custody, and inheritance, do not provide for equality between the sexes because they have been developed within the Islamic framework in all Arab countries. Because the legislation has been developed independently, there is a wide range in interpretation. While Tunisia has almost achieved equality between men and women within the Islamic framework, Egyptian law provides for "equivalence" rather than equality. In Bahrain, which has not passed a state law regulating family relations, the disposition of legal opinion has been delegated to the judges to interpret the sharia directly as they see fit.[5]

Thus, in effect, most family laws, as they currently stand, contradict the provisions of the constitutions and labor laws that have been decreed. For instance, in some Arab countries the constitution may guarantee the right to work and the labor law may be fair, yet the family law may allow a husband to stipulate that his wife must have his consent to work outside the home.

Egypt is one of the Arab countries that has ratified the United Nations Convention on the Elimination of All Forms of Discrimination Against Women (CEDAW), which is the most far-reaching international instrument providing for equality between men and women.[6] Such ratification of a United Nations convention is seen as the governments' commitment to bring their national laws into line with the convention, unless they have stipulated reservations to specific articles. As was the case with many other countries around the world, Egypt had reservations. These included the following reservation to Article 16:

> concerning the equality of men and women in all matters relating to marriage and family relations during marriage and upon its dissolution. This must be without prejudice to the Islamic sharia provisions whereby women are accorded rights equivalent to those of

their spouses so as to ensure a just balance between them. This is out of respect for the sanctity deriving from firm religious beliefs which govern marital relations in Egypt and which may not be called in question.[7]

The reservation explained that, in the Egyptian context, the husband was obliged to support the wife financially and to provide support in case of divorce, while the wife had no such obligation; "the sharia therefore restricts the wife's rights to divorce by making it contingent on a judge's ruling, whereas no such restriction is laid down in the case of the husband."[8] Thus, on the one hand, women should be entitled to full equality with men since Egypt has ratified the Convention. On the other hand, when it comes to the detailed application of the Convention, women's rights are restricted on grounds that no one "may call into question." In effect, the fact that family law has evolved within an Islamic framework means that Arab women can be equal outside the home but not within it.

This is being increasingly questioned by Arab feminists, who hold Tunisia up as a model, noting that it has evolved its family law within an Islamic framework, but has interpreted sharia law in such a way that it provides for equality between men and women.

Islam and Identity

It is clear that the Islamic framework continues to be of great importance and to have a strong hold when it comes to defining women's roles within the family. This attitude is reinforced by the fact that the region is still engaged in shaping its identity vis-à-vis other parts of the world, an exercise that has proven to be quite painful because memories of Western colonialism in the region are still fresh. In many Arab countries, independence was only won in the 1950s or 1960s—and in the case of the Palestinians it has yet to be achieved. The quest for independence was charged by the desire to express national identity without external interference. Thus the contentious question of what constituted an authentic Arab identity surfaced after independence. To date, it has not been satisfactorily resolved, nor have other questions that were a by-product of colonialism, such as how independent Arab state systems should relate to non-Arabs living within their societies.

The effort to define an authentic identity in postcolonial societies gave culture and heritage a more important and prominent role than they might otherwise have had. The extreme example is Algeria, perhaps one of the most harshly colonized Arab countries, where the French sought to stamp out Islamic religion and culture. After independence in 1962, therefore, there was great emphasis on defining Algerian identity in terms of the country's "Arab–Islamic heritage." This had an appreciable impact on defining women's rights and responsibilities. Indeed, one reason why it took the country nearly twenty years to pass a family law at all was because of the complexity (if not impossibility) of forging consensus on what an "Arab–Islamic heritage" is and how this translates into rights and responsibilities for men and women. The family law that was eventually passed was much closer to the conservative interpretation of Islamic law than the liberal one enshrined in Tunisian law.

The question of identity is thus complicated by the need to define "the self" in opposition to the former colonialists, which is, in the final analysis, a defensive position. As Leila Ahmed has pointed out:

the Islamic civilisation is not only a civilisation unambiguously on the defensive, emphasizing and reaffirming old values, but also a civilisation that finds itself reaffirming them the more intransigently and dogmatically and clinging to them perhaps the more obstinately because it is reaffirming them against [an old enemy—the West].[9]

What makes the challenge even more acute is the fact that, in the postindependence era, many Arabs feel that economic and cultural colonialism has replaced political colonialism, and that there is all the more reason to adhere to indigenous culture and tradition in response. Efforts to redefine women's roles in society are often seen, rightly or wrongly, as an extension of Western efforts at cultural domination. During the Lebanese civil war (1975–1990), a Lebanese woman writer, Mona Fayyad Kawtharani, argued strongly that the *hijab* (Islamic headcovering) was a form of resistance to cultural and by extension economic domination. In an article in the daily newspaper *As Safir* in 1985, she said that the West had found that:

[the] best way to control us was by destroying our cultural and religious beliefs, so that the believer came to be defined as a "fanatic." And this was done to enable the West to invade our lands and to penetrate with its consumer commodities, to transform our countries into markets. This led to political and economic dependency, and to loss of cultural identity, which was replaced by "modernisation." The Easterner would not buy these diverse commodities—clothes, cars, electrical appliances, processed foods, furniture, etc.—unless he was convinced that he was in need of a culture other than his own, and that this culture represented "modernity" whereas his own represented backwardness.[10]

Kawtharani went on to defend the veil as a symbol of opposition to political, economic, and cultural domination. In fact, the notable increase in the use of the veil over the last decade is a multifaceted phenomenon. Some people support it for reasons of cultural authenticity, others for reasons of piety, and still others because it enables them to study and work outside the home without fear of harassment.

The search for an authentic (Arab–Islamic) identity, the incomplete separation of religion and state (particularly when it comes to family law), and the sense that the West continues to dominate cultural and economic development, all mean that it is wiser—indeed safer—to articulate proposals for change in Islamic rather than Western terms. This is why, as Ahmed pointed out:

reformers and feminists repeatedly try to affirm (with remarkable tenacity and often too with ingenuity) that the reforms they seek involve no disloyalty to Islam, that they in fact are in conformity with it, and if not in conformity with the letter and actual text of the culture's central formulation, then in conformity with what nevertheless is still there somehow, in the spirit not quite caught by the words.[11]

Thus, the debate on women's roles in the Arab world is not only a debate about women's roles within the family. It is also linked to the debate on the role of Islam in the state, and is closely bound with the Arab search for political independence, economic self-reliance, and an authentic identity. These are some of the reasons why the debate has remained fixed within the Islamic framework, like an old-fashioned phonograph needle stuck in a groove, etching the contradictions ever deeper.

Moving Beyond the Framework

By the 1980s, there were some tentative calls for a change in the framework of debate on Arab women. As noted by Maha Azzam during a seminar on Arab women:

The Quran does have something to say about women, something that may be valid for many women, but if the [modernists] seek the ideals of Western provenance, and even if they manage to assert that they exist in the Quran, they will nevertheless not experience those ideals that are part of a liberal and secular milieu

because the Quran had been specific on men's authority over women except in the spiritual sphere.[12]

She continued, "So long as religion remains an inherent criteria of reference in Arab Muslim countries, then we can expect to find the question of Islam and women coming up again and again." She argued for moving the debate beyond the Islamic framework:

This would not necessarily undermine the importance of Islam, but it would allow us to analyse the role of Arab Muslim women with the use of analytical frameworks that, for example, draw on the sociology of religion and on the political and economic dynamics of nationalism and dependency. . . . By showing some of the contradictions that arise from remaining solely within the Islamic discourse, perhaps we can begin to answer some of the questions relating to Arab women.

There are current signs that the proverbial phonograph needle has at last been unstuck and is moving on. A major step forward was taken at an Arab regional meeting held in Jordan in November 1994 to prepare for the United Nations' Fourth World Conference on Women (held in Beijing in September 1995). As with other such international conferences, preparatory meetings were held in each of the five United Nations regions: Asia and the Pacific, Latin America and the Caribbean, Europe, Western Asia, and Africa. The Western Asia region groups thirteen out of the twenty-two members of the League of Arab States, and is served by the United Nations Economic and Social Commission for Western Asia (ESCWA).[13]

These countries held their regional preparatory meeting in Amman, Jordan, on November 6-10, 1994.[14] However, because ESCWA cosponsored the meeting with the League of Arab States, invitations were also extended to the Arab states of North Africa.[15] The participation of Arab North African countries, some of which are more progressive on these issues than Western Asia countries, added to a dynamic for change at the meeting.

The meeting was held in two parts. The first part of the meeting debated and amended the draft plan of action; participants included national delegations (which grouped governments and, in some delegations, representatives of national nongovernmental organizations or NGOs), independent experts, representatives of United Nations agencies, and NGO representatives as observers. There was an interesting dynamic between these different groups, which led to a watershed in the way women's issues in the region are discussed. NGOs learned how to "lobby" governments to get their views reflected. Thus, while the second part of the meeting, which formally adopted the amended plan of action, was restricted to ministerial delegations (as is the practice in the United Nations conferences), NGOs were responsible for introducing several new sections.

For a sense of how the region has moved forward, it is worth looking back at the document the ESCWA region adopted for the 1985 Nairobi women's conference, which marked the end of the United Nations Decade on Women. At that time, the ESCWA document began with a cultural definition of the region that none of the other United Nations regions had felt necessary to provide: "The Strategy for Arab Women in Western Asia to the Year 2000 is based on the heritage of Arab–Islamic civilization and the religious and spiritual values of this region, the cradle of the messages of God which affirm the dignity and freedom of all human beings in this universe".[16]

The fact that, in 1985, the region felt it important to assert its heritage so categorically indicated an uneasy awareness that this ideal was under threat. Moreover, the statement immediately defined the framework for any discussion of women as "the heritage of Arab–Islamic civilization." As noted previously, the Islamic framework provides women with equivalent rather than equal rights within the family in all Arab countries except Tunisia.

Further on in the 1985 document, ESCWA dedicated an entire section to the family. Other regions mentioned the family, but they did not go as far as ESCWA. This showed the extent to which the Arab region valued women's roles in the family and wanted to preserve them. This led to some contradictions within the document itself, given that it was supposed to promote the advancement of women in all spheres. On the one hand, the recommendations supported "the right of women to choose their roles in and out of the family" (p. 46), yet priority was accorded to women who chose family roles (quoted at the start of this chapter).

Initially, it appeared that little had changed by the November 1994 regional preparatory meeting. ESCWA had prepared a draft plan of action to serve as the basis for discussion, based on the national reports submitted by governments on the status of women in their countries. This paper, like its 1985 predecessor, made many references to culture and tradition. To take just one example, the 1994 draft called on Arab governments that had not ratified CEDAW to do so—but it did not insist on removal of any reservations, which is what the international women's movement calls for. On the contrary, it suggested that Arab countries should lobby at the international level to change the Convention itself to bring this more into line with Arab culture and tradition.

The delegates proved to be much more forward looking than their national reports had apparently been. There was extensive criticism of the draft text, and a drafting committee was established to overhaul it. The first decision of the meeting was to change the draft Plan from being an ESCWA region document to an Arab one, because of the participation of North African Arab countries. It was renamed the "Plan of Action for the Advancement of Arab Women to the Year 2005."

A key decision was to draw on the global ten-point agenda of the Fourth World Conference on Women as the basis for the document, instead of grounding it in the regional documentation of the past decades. Another important decision was to base the text on the recommendations of recent United Nations conferences "of relevance to women and children," in particular, the Children's Summit (New York, 1990), the United Nations Conference on Environment and Development (Rio de Janeiro, 1992), the World Conference on Human Rights (Vienna, 1993), and the International Conference on Population and Development (Cairo, 1994).

The effect of these two decisions was a major shift in framework—from the ethos of the Arab–Islamic heritage to that of the international arena, and from the prescriptions of an Islamic perspective to that of a secular one. The 1994 document has only one reference to heritage. In the fourth paragraph it states: "The Arab plan of action draws on the features of Arab civilization, the values of revealed religions, and human civilization."[17] This is a far cry from the binding cultural framework of the 1985 document, particularly as the 1994 final document continues, "which respect woman's rights as a human being and her participation in development and its benefits as a condition for comprehensive and sustainable development." The words "rights" and "equality" had been missing from the 1994 first draft of the document.

Unlike the 1985 document, which conveyed the sense of a region unsure of its identity—because it had to state it so forcefully, starting at the beginning of time—the absence of such rhetoric from the 1994 document conveyed the impression that participants were at ease with themselves and their identity.

The delegations most active in bringing about substantive change in the document included Egypt, Jordan, Lebanon, Morocco, Palestine, Tunisia, and Yemen, many of whom participated in the drafting group to amend the text. The Sudanese delegation was the only one to protest—frequently—on cultural and religious grounds. Eventually, the Sudanese delegation had to be content with registering some reservations about the final text. For example, it registered reservations concerning the reference to the International Conference on Population and Development held in Cairo in 1994. The documents produced by the Cairo Conference contained a strong statement on family planning, among other forceful messages on women's rights, which had generated strong objections from several Muslim and Christian countries, as well as from the Vatican.

The reservations on religious grounds by the Sudanese delegation were balanced by the Algerian delegation, whose delegates spoke forcefully and movingly against the misuse of Islam as a tool of terror against women. The Algerian minister, who received a standing ovation on more than one occasion, described how fundamentalists were seeking to impose the veil and to prevent women from participation in public life, going so far as attack schools and schoolgirls.

Part of the credit for introducing new issues into the text goes to the NGOs, which lobbied strongly against the initial draft. Indeed, it is worth noting that, in a forum held just prior to the official meeting, NGO participation far exceeded the planners' expectations. They had expected some 300 participants; 900 came. This is a reflection of the increased interest in and activism on women's issues (although not all NGOs were equally outspoken). The NGOs ranged from welfare and charitable institutions, to family planning associations, to legal rights groups and human rights groups. The issues of employment, legal rights within the family, and health issues featured strongly in the workshops they held. Given the emotions raised about real or perceived Western cultural domination in the region, it was interesting to note that many NGO representatives were able to participate because of funding by Western donors.

The new issues that NGOs lobbied to have included in the official text covered how women are represented in the media and their role in bringing about change in that representation, women's role in conserving and regenerating the environment, and violence against women. This included not only violence suffered by women during times of war and conflict but also domestic violence. Indeed, the issue of domestic violence, which has rarely been discussed in the Arab region, is attracting increased attention in the area, as well as worldwide.

The final text called for women's right to participate in decision-making structures and authority; lifting the burden of poverty on women; increasing access to education, health, employment, and self-reliance; protecting women's rights in situations of armed conflict; recognizing and supporting women's roles in the environment; condemning violence against women, including domestic violence; and calling for better reflection of women's roles in the media. It is interesting to note that there was no special section on the family, as there had been in the ESCWA document for Nairobi.

This Plan of Action is a major step forward in terms of enabling the debate on women to take place within a secular, international framework, rather than that of narrowly defined culture and traditions which are often far removed from the reality of people's lives. However, to have real impact on the lives of women, the Plan needs to be translated into a document that can be implemented at the national level. Countries need to assign priorities to areas of the Plan, set baselines and targets, cost the targets in terms of material and human needs, and establish mechanisms for implementation, monitoring, and evaluation.

Women's Role in Changing the Framework

It is interesting to reflect on the causes for the shift in framework. There was no indication at the meeting itself that the delegations were participating in revolutionary change. Throughout, the atmosphere was businesslike, and there was a sense of people wanting to get on with the job and to produce a useful, relevant document. Some participants suggested that the shift in emphasis came about as a consequence of the questioning some governments are engaged in concerning their previous alliance with conservative religious movements. Threatened by radical fundamentalism and no longer in need of a bulwark against communism, governments increasingly are stepping away from formerly close relations with religious conservatives. Others noted the changed dynamic precipitated by the increased presence of NGOs with their active constituencies, while still others ascribed the change to the more progressive positions of the North African participants.

It could also be argued that the major reason for change is rather the cumulative effect of work on women's issues at the national level, as well as increased participation in international forums during the United Nations Decade on Women, as well as in the ten years since the Nairobi Conference. There has been a qualitative change in the way women activists work at the national level. Many have moved beyond the elites in the capital city to undertake outreach activities at the grassroots level, where they are in contact with the reality of women's lives. And many Arab women participate in international conferences, where they learn from and contribute to the international debate, and they have therefore gained confidence and expertise in articulating the issues they face in international terms.

This evolution can perhaps best be illustrated through the experience of the Palestinian women's movement. It began, as did many other Arab women's movements, as a nationalist response against colonialism, in this case to resist Zionist efforts to dominate Palestine at the turn of the century. Palestinian women became involved in organizing and establishing many charitable activities, initially as a response to the need for education, health, and shelter, and later to help deal with the successive tragedies that befell the Palestinian people after the loss of the greater part of Palestine in 1948.

By the late 1970s, a change in approach was discernable. Several young Palestinian women under occupation in the West Bank and Gaza established grassroots committees that sought to combine a nationalist, socialist, and feminist agenda. These grassroots committees heralded a new, politicized generation of women and new organizational techniques. Their contribution was vital in sustaining and directing the popular uprising (the *intifada*) against the Israeli occuption. However, their efforts suffered from fragmentation of the women's committees along party political lines. Moreover, women activists complained that their own agenda was always pushed to the bottom of the mainstream political agenda, regardless of their party affiliation.

Partly in response to these problems, there was a move in the 1990s to set up independent women's research centers. Five centers have been established that articulate a frankly feminist agenda and that are intent on keeping a distance from the political fragmentation that affected the women's committees. For example, the Women's Studies Center in Jerusalem describes itself as an "independent, nonprofit organization which emerged in 1989 from the grassroots movement with the aim of developing both feminist consciousness and a feminist agenda which responds to the needs of Palestinian women." Such centers are tackling hitherto undiscussed issues related to women's social, legal, and economic status. Their agenda includes such topics as violence in the family, inequity in inheritance, school drop-out rates for girls, and women's economic activities in the informal sector.

Similar organizations with a sharper feminist focus have been established in other Arab countries in recent years, adding to the efforts by longer-established academic centers like the one at the Lebanese American University in Beirut. Examples include women's research networks in North Africa, the Tunis-based Center for Arab Women's Training and Research, which cosponsored the November 1994 regional preparatory meeting, and an independent Arab women's publishing house, Nour, established in Cairo in 1993.

The Reality of Women's Lives

As noted earlier, during the late 1980s and 1990s many of these groups undertook research on the reality of women's lives, and how women were faring now that modernizing economies were shifting production from a home and community base to work outside the home and community. Moreover, studies began to reveal the importance of women's traditional productivity, particularly in agriculture and animal husbandry. Indeed, government data collectors also began to reflect a better understanding of women's actual economic roles in the Arab region, as they have in other parts of the world.

For example, in India, the use of new International Labor Organization definitions of work raised women's labor force participation from 13% to 80%. In Syria, male respondents in a labor-force participation survey were initially asked if their wives worked, and a large proportion replied that they did not. More gender-sensitive data collectors rephrased the question, "If your wife did not assist you in your work, would you be forced to hire a replacement for her?" The overwhelming majority answered "yes."[18] In Egypt, an innovative Labor Force Sample Survey was published by the national statistical agency in 1990. The data revealed that women accounted for 53% of the labor force in agriculture, whereas men accounted for 47%. Of those undertaking unpaid work, 70% were women and 30% were men.

A combination of underestimating women's work in agriculture and in the informal sector and insufficient planning for women has given the Arab region the lowest female labor-force participaton rates in the world. The percentage of women in the labor force varies greatly. It ranges from 4% in Algeria, to 10% in Jordan, to 27% in Lebanon, and 29% in Sudan. The United Nations Development Programme's figures for 1993 published in *Human Development Report*, show that, on average, women account for 29% of the labor force in the countries that it qualifies as enjoying high human development, 39% in countries scoring medium human development, and 26% in countries with low human development.

The recognition of the reality of women's lives and work is critical to expanding their opportunities. Often, attempts to serve women through development projects have done more harm than good, by offering training believed to be suitable for women—handicrafts, cosmetology, typing—but rarely related to real market needs. Access to development opportunities such as credit, training, and new technology was, by and large, restricted to men as the householder and provider. Therefore, better understanding of women's productivity is important for women as well as for the overall economic development of the Arab region.

Moreover, despite the progress in education and health in those countries with small populations and sufficient resources, most of these nations still have a long way to go in the area of women's education. For example, 90% of females in Jordan and 98% in Qatar are enrolled in primary and secondary schools, but only 60% in Egypt and 30% in Sudan. The fact that countries with sufficient resources plan for both females and males indicates that culture is a much less important factor than money in restricting women's opportunities.

Nor is culture the key determinant in women's access to the labor force. Where there was a pressing need for additional labor—for example, in Jordan when a large number men migrated for work in the Gulf during the 1970s, or in Iraq during the war with Iran in the 1980s—governments took specific steps to bring women into the workforce outside the home. When the government need for additional workers matched the financial need at the family level because of the higher cost of living, women rapidly took advantage of work opportunities. However, once the need for extra manpower was over and unemployment worsened, women were expected to go back to traditional roles within the home, and government planners concentrated on generating employment for men.[19]

The fact is that Arab women cannot afford to view income-generating work outside the home simply as a step toward personal fulfillment, just as they can no longer rely on traditional support systems in lieu of their legal rights. The changing economy and the high cost of living, together with the increasing number of female-headed households because of war and labor migration, means that women need to work for income outside the home. In Jordan, the Business and Professional Women's Club was among the first to draw attention to women's pressing need for wage employment. As one counselor explained, "At one point, 600 graduates came to us wanting work, so we organized a conference on female unemployment in 1985, which we followed up in early 1989 with a conference on women and work." Today, that same counselor estimated that women represent 50% of those people seeking work and not finding it. In times of economic crisis, women are far less likely than men to receive the attention of government planners.

The conditions of Arab women in terms of health, education, and employment have been described and discussed at dozens of seminars and conferences in the region over the past decade. Understanding and awareness based on research in the field, rather than on religious texts, was a major reason for the drive by women to articulate the situation frankly and without cultural frills at the Arab regional preparatory meeting in November 1994. At last the debate on women is catching up with the reality of women's lives.

Notes

1. See Leila Ahmed, "Early Feminist Movements in the Middle East: Turkey and Egypt," in *Muslim Women*, ed. Freda Hussain (New York: St. Martin's, 1992); Nadia Hijab, *Womanpower: The Arab Debate on Women at Work* (Cambridge: Cambridge University Press, 1988); Albert Habib Hourani, *Arabic Thought in the Liberal Age, 1798–1939* (Cambridge: Cambridge University Press, 1983); Fatima Mernissi, *Islam and Democracy: Fear of the Modern World* (London: Virago, 1993); Barbara Freyer Stowasser, "The Status of Women in Early Islam", in Ahmed, *Muslim Women*, pp. 11–43.

2. United Nations, *Report of the Secretary General: Recommendations of Regional Inter-Governmental Preparatory Meetings*. A/CONF.116/9, February 5, 1985, p. 46.

3. Ibid., p.43.

4. Nadia H. Youssef, "The Status and Fertility Patterns of Muslim Women," In *Women in the Muslim World*, ed. Lois Beck and Nikki Keddie (Cambridge, Mass.: Harvard University Press, 1978), p. 76.

5. See Hijab, *Womanpower*, pp. 9–37.

6. The Arab countries that have ratified the Convention include Egypt, Iraq, Jordan, Libya, Morocco, Tunisia, and Yemen.

7. Quoted in Hijab, *Womanpower*, pp. 4–5.

8. United Nations, *Status of the Convention on the Elimination of All Forms of Discrimination Against Women*. A/CONF.116/BP1, June 4, 1985.

9. Ahmed, *Muslim Women*, p. 122.

10. Quoted in Hijab, *Womanpower*, pp. 54–56.

11. Ahmed, *Muslim Women*, p. 122.

12. Quoted in Hijab, *Womanpower*, pp. 60–61.

13. The countries included are Bahrain, Egypt, Iraq, Jordan, Kuwait, Lebanon, Oman, Palestine, Qatar, Saudi Arabia, Syria, United Arab Emirates, and Yemen.

14. As in the past, Saudi Arabia did not attend, and Syria did not participate for political reasons.

15. Participants attended from such countries as Algeria, Djibouti, Mauritania, Morocco, Sudan, and Tunisia.

16. Report of the Secretary General, A/CONF.116/9, p. 40.

17. It is interesting that the change to the term "Arab–Islamic heritage" was proposed by the Lebanese delegation, on the grounds that there were other religions in the Arab region. This was accepted by the delegates without any difficulty, and resulted in the language quoted here.

18. Hijab, *Womanpower*, p. 73.

19. See Hijab for a full discussion of women and work.

PART TWO

ISLAM, GENDER, AND SOCIOPOLITICAL CHANGE: CASE STUDIES

Feminism in an Islamic Republic

"Years of Hardship, Years of Growth"

Negative news about women's daily lives in Iran continues unabated. Seemingly trivial matters, such as the shape and color of a woman's scarf or the thickness of her stockings, continue to be contested daily, largely among men.[1] Women are far from legal equals of men. Despite many years of hard work by a remarkably active group of women, inside and outside the Majlis (the Iranian parliament), many discriminatory laws passed within the first few months and years of the new regime remain on the books and in full force. Secular feminists, if not repressed or exiled by the government, often feel silenced by the dominant cultural climate.

Yet the past decade has also witnessed an incredible flourishing of women's intellectual and cultural productions in Iran. Almost two decades after the 1979 Islamic Revolution in Iran, against the deepest fears of many of the secular feminist activists of that revolution, not only have women not disappeared from public life, but they have an unmistakably active presence in practically every field of artistic creation, professional achievement, educational and industrial institutions, and even in sports activities. It would be tempting for a secular feminist to claim that Iranian women have achieved all this despite the Islamic Republic, against the Islamic Republic, and even against Islam as the dominant discourse in the country.[2] As Haideh Moghissi, for instance, insists:

> They [women's activities and activism in the Islamic Republic of Iran] . . . signify only one thing: women's determination and their enormous efforts to escape the prisons of the femininity and sex-roles defined and guarded by the guardians of sharia. The Islamic regime has not opened the gates. Women are jumping over the fences.[3]

Indeed, for some women this deep existential sense of proving themselves against all odds has become the creative energy of their productions. This is reflected, for instance, in some of the poetry of Simin Bihbahani and expressed in the interviews of Shahrnush Parsipur.[4] Others have turned the restrictions and limitations imposed by the government and by the dominant ideas about gender roles and ethics into wedges to open up new arenas for their creative energies. The most glaring example has been women turning to the production and directing of film, given the restrictions at the level of acting.[5] In such fields as photography, painting, sculpture, literary production, and publishing, women have established themselves on an unprecedented scale in recent years.

This creative outpouring cannot be accounted for as only oppositional reactive energy. The rise of the Islamic movement in the 1970s in Iran signified the emergence of a new political sociability and the dominance of a new political discourse, within which woman stood for culture, occupying a central position. In this new Islamic political paradigm, imperialist domination of Muslim societies was seen to have been achieved not through military or economic supremacy, as earlier generations of nationalists and socialists had argued, but through the undermining of religion and culture. Woman was made to bear the burden of cultural destruction. As an editorial in a weekly women's journal published in Tehran described it:

> Colonialism was fully aware of the sensitive and vital role of woman in the formation of the individual and of human society. They considered her the best tool for subjugation of the nations. . . . women serve as the unconscious accomplices of the powers-to-be in the destruction of indigenous culture. . . . woman is the best means of destroying the indigenous culture to the benefit of imperialists.[6]

The editorial went on to conclude that "the glory and depth of Iran's Islamic Revolution" was in its recognition that in order for a revolution to occur woman must be transformed. The centrality of gender to the construction of an Islamic political discourse thus changed that which had been marginal, secondary, postponed, illegitimate, and discredited into that which was to be central, primary, immediate, and authentic. Whereas any attention to "the woman question" had been previously relegated from the here-and-now of politics to the unspecified future, the woman question now acquired immediacy and urgency, not only for the discontented, but even more so for the supporters of the new order and for women and men of power. In particular, women in sympathy with and as supporters of the Islamic Republic were placed in a position to take responsibility for its misogyny: to deny it, to justify it, to challenge it, to oppose it—but not to ignore it.

The Islamic Republic's claim that its kind of polity is the ideal solution for all societal problems has put it in a continuous contestation with feminism as far as women's issues are concerned. It exists under the pressure of outdoing feminism.[7] During the reign of the Pahlavis (1926–1979) women's activism and feminism had been scripted by the opposition, secular or Islamic, as a discredited venture at the service of the state or as foreign colonial importation; now, however, activism and feminism have become authenticated, ironically opening new possibilities for growth of all kinds of feminisms—including secular. New configurations of Islam, revolution, and feminism are now emerging.

The Early Setbacks and Struggles

In the first months and years following the overthrow of the Pahlavi dynasty in February 1979, the symbolism crafted in the previous decades between woman and culture was translated into the most horrific meanings: "revolutionary purification and cleansing campaigns" targeted dismissal of secular women professionals as "remnants of the old regime." Having located the site of "social sickness" on the bodies of women, eradication of "Westitis"[8] from Islamo-Iranian culture translated into repeated waves of attacks against unveiled women and the eventual imposition of the veil and an elaborate "code of modesty."[9] The continued resistance of some women against the strict enactments of the dress code was likened to a sickness— a willful sickness or a sickness of the will—against which the rest of society needed to be inoculated through veiling of women:

> This [proper veiling] is a kind of social vaccination, vaccination of the Muslim man and woman, vaccination of our pure and virtuous sisters. One cannot say that there should be no microbes in the world, that there should be no diseases. . . . What shall we do against diseases? We must preserve ourselves. We must quarantine ourselves.[10]

As vaccinations are compulsory for the sake of public health, so veiling must be enforced and not be a matter of individual choice.

On February 26, 1979, barely two weeks after the overthrow of the old regime, the Family Protection Act, first promulgated in 1967, was scrapped as un-Islamic.[11] Women were dismissed from the judiciary and subsequently barred from many positions and disciplines of higher education.[12] Over the next months and years, incontestably misogynous interpretations of Islamic notions of gender set the political agenda of the new government. Against these attacks, the resistance of secular women, though providing a cherished memory, proved feeble and was easily dispersed, defused, and defeated. Acts of defiance and resistance by women became instantly named as counterrevolutionary, a label that not only made these women easy targets of repression, but also cut off any possibility of building alliances with Islamic women activists of the Revolution, many of whom were shocked into silence, frozen in disbelief at this unforeseen turn of events. Islamic women activists had been political supporters and active organizers of the mass Islamic movement that overthrew the old regime. For many of them, their activism had been formed by different notions of Islamic womanhood, as expounded, for example, in the writings of Ali Shariati.[13] Yet the revolution they fought for and the government they supported was proceeding to put into effect some of the most misogynous policies imaginable. With the defeat of secularists, they found themselves acting as critics of the new government on women's issues, and they began to organize for alternative policies.[14] It was thanks to their efforts that universities were once again opened to women, and a new set of family laws virtually reintroduced the Family Protection Act of the Pahlavi period.

Reflecting on these earlier years of struggle under the old regime and the new government, Mihrangiz Kar expressed the confidence of these women activists in these terms:

> Iranian women have gone through a difficult test. During the past decade, they have experienced difficulties and dangers that were unprecedented in their individual and social lives. Prior to the Revolution, Iranian women, accused of benefiting from rights royally granted to them, of consumerism mixed with exhibitionist vulgarity, were expected to be grateful to the government and were dismissed and denigrated, simultaneously from left and right. Eventually they gave up on any privileges [from the old regime] and joined in the great battle. Now a decade has passed within which they have had an effective presence in shaping the new era of Iran's history. Women have come out of these testing times, without owing any debt to any one's propaganda machinery, registering themselves from the margins to the center of social text. . . . Now women, who have fulfilled their obligations, demand, not beg, their rights.[15]

The Women's Press

Out of these early years of Islamic women's activism also emerged the drive toward rethinking gender in Islam in more radical ways. A number of women's organizations and institutes, as well as a variety of women's journals now published in Iran, attest to the significance of this rethinking. These journals are distinct in their respective constructions of womanhood, ranging from *Nida'*, a rather ideologically rigid organ of a quasigovernmental organization, to *Zanan*, a journal that explicitly defines itself as feminist.

Nida' [The Call], edited by Zahra Mustafavi, is perhaps the only women's journal that could be categorized as quasi-official, and waxes praise of the Islamic Republic. In some ways its anti-image is *Payam-i Hajir* [Message of Hagar].[16] Edited by A'zam Taliqani, *Payam-i Hajir* produces a discourse of woman as the suffering victim. Thus the significance of its name, both as the female figure of sufferance and the segment of a Quranic verse they use for their byline:

> And their Lord answers them: "I waste not the labor of any that labors among you, be
> you male or female—the one of you is as the other. And those who emigrated, and were
> expelled from their habitations, those who suffered hurt in My way, and fought, and were
> slain—them I shall surely acquit of their evil deeds, and I shall admit them to gardens
> underneath which rivers flow."[17]

From its early days, *Payam-i Hajir* has acted as a dissident voice, as a call to the conscience of the Islamic Republic on matters to do with women. It publishes reports and commentary on the problems of daily lives of working women, rural women, women state employees, and "other suffering sisters." It describes admiringly these women as persevering, hard working, simple, obedient, and with few expectations. Its own mission is the protesting voice of woman's victimhood, hoping that "God will help and that Islamic justice in the Islamic Republic will take care of all these deprivations and soothe all these discordances."[18]

The other three journals, *Zan-i Ruz*, *Farzaneh*, and *Zanan*, are intimately connected to each other both by past history and current ideological self-definition and location.

Zan-i Ruz [Today's Woman] is part of an important publishing conglomerate, Kayhan, that goes back to the time of the Shah. Benefiting from the financial, human, and political resources of Kayhan, it was taken over by a group of Islamic women activists in the postrevolutionary period. They turned it into a successful campaigning platform of resistance to some of the onslaughts against women's positions in the early postrevolutionary years and for improving women's rights in the new Republic within an Islamic framework.[19] Published under the editorship of an anonymous "editorial council" in its early years, later it identified its editor as Shahla Sherkat through no. 1318 (June 29, 1991). In the next issue, with no explanation, Sherkat's name was replaced by that of Ashraf Girami'zadigan, who remains its current editor. Some seven months later (February 1992), Sherkat launched a new journal, *Zanan* [*Women*], and in its first editorial referred to some of the tensions that accounted for that editorial transformation.

Farzaneh [The Wise Wo/man] is a more recent venture. Its first issue was published in the Fall of 1993, as a "Journal of Women's Studies and Research," under the editorship of Mahboobe Ommi. It is a publication of The Center for Women's Studies and Research headed by Moneer Gorgi, the sole woman representative in the 1979 Assembly of Experts that drafted the constitution of the Islamic Republic. In the English editorial of its first issue, Ommi argued that

> [I]n every corner of the globe women's studies is presently a well recognized necessity and
> an essential component of social, cultural, and economic development. Women's studies

emerges as an important area of academic research not only as a solution to women's issues themselves but as a key to many socioeconomic predicaments.[20]

At the same time, the editorial firmly distanced itself from feminism:

> Encountering women's issues with a biased inclination toward women as a particular social strata, has proven to be inefficient. Feminism, now branched and divided according to various tendencies, seems to face a serious crisis as a natural consequence of the course it has embraced. Instead of isolating women's issues from the mainstream of human life and societies, and dealing with her from a prejudiced, woman-centered, woman oriented, viewpoint, feminism could have chosen to consider the woman in the context of her natural identity and role, to lay emphasis on the rapidly disintegrating family and her central part in that institution and finally to balance her dynamic relationship with her society both male and female.[21]

To appreciate the tension in this editorial, between arguing for the necessity of a women's studies center and journal on the one hand, and the rejecting of the woman-centeredness of feminism on the other, it is helpful to look to an earlier discussion of feminism. Two years earlier, Ommi had authored a series of mildly polemical articles in *Zan-i Ruz* shortly before *Zanan* began publication and in the months after Sherkat's departure from that journal. With hindsight, the articles, entitled "Feminism: From Its Beginning to the Present Time," read as a polemic against *Zanan*'s feminist project.[22] Nevertheless, unlike the common dismissals by both Islamic and secular political thought in Iran of feminism as sign of "social deviation of Western women" and their "Weststruck" counterparts in the "non-West," Ommi's rhetoric in these articles centered on accepting the historical validity and positive contributions of feminism for "the West." It defined feminism as "a set of philosophical, economic, political, and social solutions which enables women's liberation movement to emancipate women from the injustices arising from discriminations between men and women."[23] At the same time, it emphasized that "feminist thinking is only compatible with the intellectual climate of the West," where it grew as a reaction against beliefs, laws, and practices that treated women as inferior to men in Western misogynous religious and secular thought.[24] By abandoning Islamic universalism, that is, by accepting that in "other" times and "elsewhere" other solutions to problems of social injustice had validity, Ommi thus introduced tensions she seemed unwilling to resolve. Throughout the articles she raised a number of significant questions, which she left unanswered. For instance, after pointing out that it was necessary to deal with issues raised by feminism now that "feminism has some supporters in Iran and there are even attempts afoot to Islamicize it," she asked rhetorically, if not unambiguously, "But is an Islamic feminism indeed a realizable/unavoidable matter?"[25]

An implicit answer suggested by the rhetoric of Ommi's articles would be that since Islam did not share the misogynous underpinnings of Christianity and Judaism, there did not seem to be any grounds for feminism in an Islamic country. Yet, significantly, despite the author's promise to deal with these questions in the final installment of the articles, she never addressed them.[26] One can conjecture that this might very well have been a time of disputes and uncertainties, since the editorial of the first issue of the new journal registered an important shift. Whereas, in the earlier essays, the differences between the "West" and "us" had been emphatically constructed so as to exclude the desirability of feminism on the basis of its Western identification (constructing the West as the land where feminism has an abode), the same differences in the editorial were now largely employed to convince a presumably skeptical reader of the necessity of developing local, nationally sensitive research and solutions to the "woman's question" in Iran.[27]

This shift may in part be related to the establishment of *Zanan* as a powerful and articulate new voice, challenging the earlier presuppositions and changing the terms of the debate. Nonetheless, feminism continues to be projected as an unacceptable option in the pages of *Farzaneh*, suggesting the limits of the new journal's identity. In the editorial of its second issue, Western individualism came under attack for its destructive repercussions on the structure of the family, causing the alarming growth of single-parent households.[28] The author argued that the search of Western women for emancipation, shaped by notions of humanism and individualism, had produced various feminisms that had led the Western woman's search for freedom into disarray.[29] More ominously, in a critical book review, feminism was used to define the limits of acceptability.[30] The book was criticized for "mixing valuable historical research with feminist proclamations," for being "influenced by extremist feminist writings," and for offering solutions that are "translations of feminist literature."[31]

It is in the context of such discourse that the emergence of the journal *Zanan* marks an important watershed. In its first editorial in 1992 one can read of the turmoils in *Zan-i Ruz* that led to Sherkat's departure.[32] She describes her years as editor of *Zan-i Ruz* as a decade of enthusiasm, pain, and turmoil [she uses the sufi terms, shawq, dard, and khurush], one in which "our efforts were directed toward breaking down *Jahili* [literally meaning ignorant—an Islamic designation of pre-Islamic world] traditions and lighting a flame in the dark tunnels of stagnation and reification."[33] Continuing her usage of sufi metaphors, she proclaims that "the coldness of those seeking redemption did not cool off our enthusiasm, the cynicism of the times did not dull our pain, and the threats and bribes did not incline our turmoil to submission and abjectness. Our present independence is the sweet fruit of those days."[34]

Her appropriation of sufi language is highly significant. It locates her Islam in the sufi tradition, which is popularly considered as more spiritually religious than the Islam of the clergy—which is considered to be more concerned with formal and rigid observance of rules and regulations. Her years of struggle in *Zan-i Ruz* are thus scripted as efforts to find the true path of reaching one's ideal. The ideal, however, is not the sufi ideal of union with God. What she reaches at the end of these efforts is independence. The faith that resolutely keeps her going despite "the coldness of those seeking redemption" is the righteousness of her cause. But her cause is not seeking the unmediated Truth of the Almighty, but the cause of improving women's rights:

> Now we are determined to continue the path, with a backpack of experience, accumulated out of a decade of struggle against superstitions and ill thoughts, and centuries of oppression. Aware of the wisdom that one hand alone cannot produce sound . . . we call on our friends for help. . . . we make a pact of awakening. For this awakening, we need to go back to the depths of history to uncover the grounds for social beliefs, to find the beginnings of the painful discriminations between the two genders, and the factors that have consolidated what constitutes our social unconscious—which neither comes from religion nor is humane.[35]

The editorial reviews how womanhood is constructed negatively from misogynous stories of creation onward and how women are imprisoned by superstitious traditions or enchained through false promises of liberty. The piece then points to the absence of women in present accounts of history and the undesirability of present models for women; it also emphasizes the necessity of a change in women's own consciousness, which "is not possible except under the conditions of being in a state of—not granting of—freedom. The first pillar of freedom is autonomy and choice."[36] The introduction of individual woman's choice and autonomy into an Islamic discourse is one of the significant innovations of *Zanan*, and as we shall see, various authors in the journal carry this notion into their reinterpretations of Islamic sources. It is this move, moreover, that opens up a new discursive space for conversations between secular and Islamic feminists in Iran.

During the first four years of publication analyzed in this study, *Zanan* embarked on a project of thorough and radical interpretations of Islamic sources concerned with women's rights. Although there is a history of interpretive attempts within Islam to deal with questions posed by modern transformations of Islamic societies, including the "woman question" (even going back to the mid-nineteenth century), *Zanan's* interpretive venture is novel in a number of ways, which promises to make the journal's overall interpretive strategies productive of cultural change and social power for women. It is thus worthwhile to look at the authors' interpretive strategies more closely.

Reinterpreting Islamic Soures

The dominant method of reformist interpretations on women's issues has been to use more woman-friendly sources from an already existing set of authoritative exegetical texts. This confined the reinterpretive attempts to a highly misogynous canon, producing an endless array of contradictory positions for reformers. With rare exceptions, *Zanan's* authors do not use this technique. They engage in direct interpretations in their own right. As Mihrangiz Kar in no uncertain terms declares: "It is time for *ijtihad*."[37] It is this assertive move to take charge of the canon and thoroughly reinterpret it from a woman's perspective that has brought the fire of the more traditional Islamic advocates upon them. In response to Kar's challenge, for example, Muzhgan Kiani Thabit declares such a venture impossible, stating categorically that:

> All laws of the Islamic Republic of Iran are derived from Ja'fari [Shii] rules and jurisprudence, the sources of which are the four grounds [of The Book (Quran), the sunna (traditions of Prophet Muhammad and the Imams), . . . ijma' (Consensus) of the jurisprudents, and reason (and reason of course means reason of jurisprudents not of the common people).] . . . Therefore, any criticism of the Islamic laws weakens the faith and belief and religion of Islam.[38]

Further, Kiani Thabit argues, "What constitutes the majority or consensus opinion of the clergy . . . is impossible to revise or oppose. Opposing these laws constitutes opposition to the holy lawmaker, that is, God Almighty."[39] Despite such threatening warnings, the journal continues to engage in reinterpretation and to defend it as a right not only for every Muslim but even for non-Muslims. In response to Kiani Thabit, another writer of the journal, Muhsin Sa'idzadah, defends the right of interpretation in these terms:

> Reason cannot be divided according to that of a jurisprudent and nonjurisprudent, especially if we believe in ijtihad as an obligation of any responsible adult. . . . Moreover, in the life histories of men of wisdom [*siarah-'i 'uqala'*], we do not see any discrimination

between believer and nonbeliever. . . . If a person, following the existing methodologies of jurisprudence, arrives at correct conclusions, even if s/he were not a Muslim her/his opinion is accepted.[40]

Such a radical expansion of the domain of interpretation is further insisted upon when another author suggests that not only does Islam need to be reinterpreted and new laws deduced according to the needs of the time—which is a well-established ground for reformist currents in Islam—but that such revisions should be carried out in the light of "contemporary schools of philosophy and thought."[41] This level of openness to influences from "the outside," so to speak, contrasts with the usual hostility toward all that is branded as foreign to Islam, an attitude obsessively cultivated by most ideologues in the government and Islamic leaders of the country.

Another way in which *Zanan*'s interpretive work departs from previous attempts is the way in which they expand the domain of reinterpretation to new linguistic constructions of the Arabic language.[42] Arabic as the language of the sacred in fact became codified in syntax, grammar, and vocabulary through the writing of commentaries on the Quran in the first centuries of Islam. The journal is therefore reinventing this interpretive tradition, this time carried out by insisting upon "reading the Quran as a woman." We can see the results of this linguistic venture in their readings of a Quranic verse that has been particularly troublesome for Islamic reformers, namely Sura 4:34 *Nisa'* [Women], which reads in its entirety:

> Men are the managers of the affairs of women for that God has preferred in bounty one of them over another, and for that they have expended of their property. Righteous women are therefore obedient, guarding the secret for God's guarding. And those you fear may be rebellious, admonish; banish them to their couches, and beat them. If they then obey you, look not for any way against them; God is All-high, All-great. And if you fear a breach between the two, bring forth an arbiter from his people and from her people an arbiter, if they desire to set things right; God will compose their differences; surely God is All-knowing, All-aware.

In an article, entitled "Man: Partner or Master?!," discussing obligations and prerogatives of husbands and wives toward each other, the authors argue against the common usage of this verse to make people, including women themselves, believe that men are essentially superior to women, and that women are deficient in their mental faculties and religious credentials.[43] They argue that the meaning of the Arabic root word appropriate to this verse is not q–y–m, related to guardianship of one over the other as commonly accepted; rather it is q–w–m, related to rising up, standing for [thus being supportive of] some one. In particular, they argue this reinterpretation is necessitated by and is more in tune with the capabilities of women today, "who have a prominent presence and social role in all spheres, including employment, education, politics, economy, even war," whereas the older interpretations "resulted from the imposed conditions on her in history and from deficiency of law."[44] They argue further:

> If a woman who is easily an excellent manager on the family and social level is forced to accept probably illogical and unwise opinions of her husband, when they differ, solely on the basis that he is the boss, we have undermined the general goal of family formation— that is perfection and uplifting of woman and man.[45]

Another author takes up the challenge of redefining the Arabic word d–r–b in "beat them," arguing that the verb d–r–b has a variety of meanings in Arabic, beating being only one definition. Others include: to turn one's face away, to move to put an end to, to go along with, to stay at home, to change, to have intercourse with. He proposes that a preferred interpretation for the last part of S. 4:34 would be that women who are rebellious are of three types: those who will turn around through reprimand, those who will become disciplined when one distances oneself from them, and those who need more caressing from their husbands including sleeping together.[46] This interpretation, of course, continues to remain locked into a discourse of obedience and rebellion, but it does give us a glimpse of the kind of possibilities that linguistic control of Quranic verses could offer for feminist reinterpretations.

Claiming Equality: Irrelevance of Difference

Whereas dominant Islamic discourses on women—misogynous or reformist—have grounded their case for differences of rights in the differences of women and men in creation, writers of *Zanan* overturn these accepted connections between differences-in-creation and social responsibilities and rights of women.[47] In response to traditionist Muzhgan Kiani Thabit who says that, "Common sense is enough to see the [physical] differences between man and woman,"[48] and that differences in rights and obligations ensue from such differences, Muhsin Sa'idzadah retorts, "The question is whether or not physical differences can effect inequalities."[49] The Quranic verse "The noblest among you in the sight of God is the most godfearing of you" (S. 49:13) is often used to explain away the social and legal inequalities of women and men—in particular women's exclusion from many domains and professions—as unimportant compared to their worth in God's eyes and compared to the spiritual position comparable to that of men that women can acquire through proper religiosity. In contrast, *Zanan*'s authors use this well-known verse to argue that women's and men's positions in God's sight are unrelated to their differences-in-creation, and that their respective social responsibilities and rights have no connection to these differences. Instead, they argue for equality of rights of women with men. If some people want to insist on differences in rights, it is up to the advocates of such inequalities to demonstrate in each case the reasons for the differences. Insisting on the distinction between equality and sameness, Zuhrah Zahidi, in an article entitled "Rehabilitating Eve," notes in passing some of the physical and temperamental differences attributed to men and women. Nonetheless, she asks:

> But do such differences . . . mean privileging one over the other? Difference does not mean superiority. It just means difference. When we talk of equality, we mean equality of rights of human beings. Discrimination on any basis, whether racial, gender or class, is counter to this concept of equality.[50]

This move, similar to and informed by the discussions on social construction of gender differences, has enabled these writers to draw conclusions vastly different from those generally accepted about gender relations in an Islamic society.

Woman: The Individual

Instead of beginning with creation as a narrative of origins for women's rights and responsibilities, *Zanan*'s authors place individual woman, in her contemporary social concreteness, at the center of their arguments. In an article entitled "Obedience," Shukufah Shukri and Sahirah Labriz begin by citing article 1105 of the Iranian Civil Code that defines the husband as the master of the family.[51] Questioning the logic and wisdom of this ordinance, the authors begin by reviewing the discussions around the marriage contract in Islamic law and jurisprudence, then move to the most controversial aspect of obedience, what is referred to as "special obedience" [*tamkin-i khass*], namely that the wife should submit sexually to her husband whenever and wherever he desires. They challenge this notion on legal and religious grounds, using new criteria that are outside the present Islamic legal and theological discourses. In particular, the authors argue that:

> In a human relationship that depends on the feelings and state of the minds of individuals for its formation, one cannot reduce the woman to just an instrumental creature that has to be at all times under control and available for exploitation. . . . It is the height of injustice, if a woman—who carries social, economic, . . . and family responsibilities and has a delicate and gentle temperament—would be required, regardless of her own emotional and affectionate state of mind, to always submit to the sexual demand of her husband, just because she receives provisions.[52]

Neither the traditional religious discourse nor the legal discourse (grounding itself on the former) is based on any notion of "feelings of the woman." Rather, the justice of women's sexual servility is derived from the notion of marriage as a legal contract between a man who pays and provides for his wife, thereby producing a set of obligations upon her. These obligations include satisfaction of his sexual needs.[53]

The authors challenge the justice of such a contractual notion by introducing "what a woman feels at the time" as a competing criterion. The grounds for justice are shifted from what is exchanged in the contractual agreement (sex for provisions) to what the state of mind and feelings of the contracting individuals are at the time of the exchange:

> The health of a relationship, which according to psychologists is not a one-sided satisfaction but fulfills the inner happiness of and builds mutual trust between the two, is dependent on the physical and mental readiness of both. Such considerations should be taken into account for the woman as much as for the man.[54]

The authors further conclude that, if the state of the mind and body of the female individual constitutes a just ground for refusing the husband's sexual demands, then if the wife refuses to obey her husband sexually, "not out of rebelliousness, but because she is physically or emotionally unprepared," such refusal does not constitute "disobedience" and should not be used as grounds for the husband to refuse to provide for her.[55]

Zanan's discussion of justice, oppression, and disobedience in marriage shifts the ground of these concepts from the marriage contract's definitions of what constitutes justice according to sacred revelation, to what constitutes justice in a woman's lived experience. Yet the concept of justice continues to remain embedded in the notions of obedience and disobedience pertaining to the relationship between husband and wife. This is perhaps related to their continued use of "justice" as a relevant category. Notions of oppression (*zulm*) and justice (*'adl*) pertain to relations of hierarchy: one expects justice from a superior and wise power, as humans from God, as subjects from Sultan or Master, and as citizens from modern state authorities. Continuing to argue from grounds of oppression and justice in gender relations inadvertently reproduces the superiority of man over woman. For instance, the well-known Islamic reformist argument against polygyny— that no man can fulfill the criterion of being just toward many wives—continues to constitute the one husband in the position of authority vis-à-vis all his wives who are entitled to expect him to act justly among them. This is equivalent to an insistence on justice as a necessary qualification for becoming a king—which may severely limit the pool of qualified applicants for the job, but clearly does not nullify the hierarchy of power of the king over his subjects. Even the more radical woman-centered proposition that it is up to the wife or wives to judge the justice of the husband reproduces the position of the wife or wives as the subject(s) of the husband, despite the fact that it introduces the idea of accountability of the superior to the subjects.

The introduction into the Islamic discourse on marriage of woman as a sovereign individual has thus produced new tensions as well as possibilities for feminist interventions. The writers of *Zanan* use the reinterpretations drawn from these three considerations to offer new visions of women's rights in the domains of the judiciary, family law, and political rights.

In a series of articles, *Zanan* takes up controversial issues, such as whether a woman could become a judge, exercise power of interpretation, or become a ruler or jurisprudent.[56] Needless to say, the authors give a positive answer to these queries. What is important, however, is how they arrive at the answers. Mina Yadigar Azadi challenges the various kinds of proofs—from the Quran, the traditions, consensus, and reason—through which women are considered unfit to become judges, interpreters, and rulers. The author begins with Quranic verses frequently used in such arguments, verses that are interpreted either as proofs of innate superiority of men over women (which would therefore exclude women from such positions as judgeship, in which they could exercise authority over men), or verses that are interpreted as grounds for exclusion of women from public positions.

Beginning with the famous verse Sura 4: 34,[57] the author argues that this verse cannot constitute a justifying ground for considering all men superior to all women. That would imply a natural or innate superiority, whereas the preference (*fadl*) accorded to the husband in this verse is constituted in terms of what he "has expended of his property" for her. Moreover, the preference indicated in this sura refers to man as husband versus woman as his wife; it does not refer to man in general versus woman in general. The preference in question gives man the position of standing by and being supportive of his wife and does not pertain to innate superiority of men over women. Using this well-known reformist method of contextualizing and historicizing Quranic verses the author argues against the usual interpretations of Sura 2:228 and Sura 33:32–33 to limit occupational categories for women.[58]

It must be pointed out that *Zanan*'s interpretive work is a discourse-in-formation. For instance, another essay on wife-beating, entitled: "Wife-battery: One of the Consequences of Considering Husband as Master," begins with article 1105 of the Civil Code and is again centered on Sura 4:34 of the Quran. After a detailed discussion of this verse in various commentaries and narratives attributed to Muhammad, rejecting those interpretations that allow a husband to beat his wife, the author further rejects the use of this verse as the religious grounding of article 1105 with the following argument. This verse is a descriptive statement about the state of husband–wife relations for its time and place. For instance, it does not say that women ought to be obedient to their husbands, but, rather, that women are obedient. As such it is not a normative statement, and cannot be used for extracting normative or ethical statements about gender relations.[59] In other words, the author reverses the usual method of Islamic jurists who draw normative–ethical statements from particular Quranic verses, proclaiming them to be historically specific statements about there-and-then rather than morally relevant verses for here-and-now.

Yadigar Azadi also deals extensively with various religious narratives that are used for exclusion of women, using more traditional theological reasoning either to declare these narratives as weak, hence not binding, or to limit their applicability (employing analogical reasoning) as grounds for pronouncement of a general prohibition on women being barred from becoming judges or rulers. The author also contends that, due to the passage of 1,400 years, the historical circumstances of these narratives are unclear and uncertain, and so it is difficult to know where and how these statements are applicable. Moreover, things that are naturally determined, such as maleness and femaleness, cannot be used as conditions for general qualification. For instance, women do not become barred from praying in general and at all times because of their gender, but menstruating women, during that period, face particular restrictions. To the extent that some of these narratives have any particular validity, the historical context limits it to a particular case.

In a subsequent issue, the author continues these arguments by covering the grounds of consensus and reason.[60] Regarding consensus, the author argues that while there is agreement that the qualifying conditions for a judge are knowledge, justice, and perfection [kamal], there is disagreement among jurisprudents on the meaning of perfection. Some consider maleness as one of the conditions of perfection, while others do not.[61] The author argues that if there appear to be certain disabilities that reason tells us should constitute grounds for barring women from judgeships, these disabilities should be seen as the result of women's deprivations, of their having lived behind closed doors cut off from society. The consequences of such circumstances have been used as arguments that women are naturally weak and inferior.

Another argument used against women is that no prophets or *imams* have arisen from the ranks of women. This is no grounds at all, Yadigar Azadi argues; if no woman has acquired a particular occupation or position so far, it does not mean women can never acquire such position. Even if they cannot become prophets and imams, why can they not become judges? Moreover, our sources of information about prophets and imams are narratives. If a woman had become a prophet, how do we know that men, in writing the narratives, have not denied her that role? We know from the Quran that women, such as the mother of Moses and Maryam, did receive revelations demonstrating that women are qualified to receive revelation, which is the ground for prophethood.[62]

Yadigar Azadi uses such reasoning to argue not only that women are appropriate to be judges, rulers, family court mediators[63] (if not imams and prophets), but that they also have the right to become *mujtahids*, since this position does not even require women leaving their homes![64] Indeed many more theologians accept women as mujtahids than as judges and there is a living tradition of women actually occupying such a position.[65] Most important, men and women are considered equal in their ability as well as their obligation to seek and pursue knowledge. They are also declared equal in the following arenas: in taking up any profession, in implementation of justice, in seeking spiritual perfection, in reward and punishment, and in their obligation toward social improvement. All of these cases are supported by Quranic verses and rational principles [*usul-i 'aqlani*].[66]

These moves toward declaring women equal to men allow other writers subsequently to expand the domain of equality to such positions as membership in the Council of Guardians (that checks all legislation passed by the parliament to ensure they do not contravene Islamic precepts), Commander of the Armed Forces, and Ruler or Jurisprudent, the highest position of political power in the new Iranian state, first occupied by Ayatollah Khomeini and since his death by Ayatollah Khaminah'i.[67] Zaynab al-Sadat Kirmanshahi, in another series of articles, has expanded the domain of equal rights to the controversial laws of retribution in the Islamic Republic, insisting that: "We accept the condition of parity [*takafu'*] in religion and then we will critique the conditions ensuing from gender and free/slave situations."[68]

Some of these interpretive moves may sound like rather timid experimentations that only occasionally go beyond the common reformist strategies. While they generally use the same historicizing and contextualizing argument in order to delimit the effective field of these verses to particular time, place, and circumstances (instead of the dominant method of extracting timeless normative legal and ethical pronouncements from them), the authors of *Zanan* have introduced some new interpretive strategies, as already pointed out. Most notably, however, the authors not only assume the position of Quran commentators, but they do so in a different social space: in the printed pages of a women's journal, that is, in a public space, as opposed to the private chambers of a religious scholar. They speak as "public intellectuals" rather than as private teachers. Their audience is other women (and men) as citizens, rather than theological students in a seminary training to become religious scholars and clerical leaders. They write not in order to command the believers into obedience, but, as they put it, in order "to awaken women" so that they will proclaim their rights.[69]

This new public space for interpretation of canonical theological texts is in part produced as an unintended consequence of Khomeini's doctrine of rulership of jurisprudence which became encoded into the new Iranian constitution. Where the jurisprudent is granted the power of political rule and the constitution is said to be derived from canonical texts, every citizen by virtue of rights of citizenship becomes entitled to take charge of these texts and exercise power of interpretation. That women interpreters have now positioned themselves as public commentators of these texts promises that a future process of democratization of politics may not remain an exclusively masculine preoccupation.

At the center of *Zanan*'s revisionist approach is a radical decentering of the clergy from the domain of interpretation, and the placing of woman as interpreter and her needs as grounds for interpretation. For example, a law student asked about the Islamic grounding of article 1179 of the Civil Code, which gives custody rights of sons up to the age of two and of daughters up to the age of seven to mothers, and thereafter to fathers and paternal family. In response, the journal's "legal expert" writes:

> The Iranian Civil Code, at the time of its passage corresponded to the views of influential Islamic jurists of that time, which approximately is the same as the view of many of Imami Shii jurists. What was in the mind of legislators was to satisfy the Islamic jurists not to take into account the conditions of women or the needs of children, and this constitutes a central weakness of this Code. . . . One can thus deduce that the conditions of the time in that article are open to jurisprudential and legal dispute and the article will of necessity be revised.[70]

With this argument, the author detaches the Civil Code from its grounding in sacred revelation through the consent of the jurisprudents, and argues for women's experience and children's needs to be used as grounds for revision of the law.

Zanan and Feminism

Iranian women's response (secular or Islamic) to attacks against feminism has often been one of gender conservatism and "Westophobia": they distance themselves from any identification with feminism as threatening and Western. *Zanan*, on the contrary, has claimed itself in affiliation with feminism. In its first issue it ran a translation of Gilman's "The Yellow Wallpaper;" in succeeding issues it published a translation of an interview with Simone de Beauvoir, articles by American feminists, a translation of Virginia Woolf under the title "The Angel in the House," and more recently a translation of an article by Susan Faludi in defense of feminism. It freely translates from Western feminist journals whatever it judges useful to its readership. Breaking with reactive gender conservatism and Westophobia, *Zanan* has embarked on connecting itself with Western feminism and weaving new textual connections between Muslim women and Western feminism. Unlike most Iranian women activists and writers, secular or Islamic, who have shied away from the label feminism, *Zanan* has explicitly proclaimed itself in solidarity with feminism. In an editorial marking the end of its first year of publication, titled "A Year of Hardship, a Year of Growth," they state:

> Some people in our society generally speak of feminism as some kind of deviation from a feminine essence—a femininity crafted by sons of Adam in the creation story.
>
> Because of the permanent presence of masculinism and the culture engendered by it in Iran, feminism has remained an unknown, yet unacceptable, phenomenon. To the extent that there is an image and analysis of it, it is a negative one. It is fascinating to see that recently one journal has defined feminism in these words: "The Latin word feminist is given to a system of thought in which women rebel against men, without any sense of commitment and responsibility toward their families and dependents, and engage in various jobs and professions outside the home." Misogynous thought has so seeped into the soul of our men that they consider women taking up jobs outside the home as rebellion against men and as a sign of lack of commitment to the family.
>
> It is not the purpose of this article to expound on feminism, but this kind of writing about a school of thought that is a relevant one, is an indication of the kind of severe hardship women are currently up against. More importantly, it aims to conceal the depth of ignorance and darkness that the same male-centered thought has condemned women to, because any rethinking of traditions and limitations that surround women threatens its interests. To refuse this truth is in fact a way of declaring illegitimate and unnecessary the movement of Eastern women, and consider such movements only for Western women, and even there of an illegitimate type.
>
> But the bitter and unforgettable truth is that women in all corners of our country continue to live under pressure of social and family oppression. . . . And yet awakening and struggle of Iranian woman is considered a deviation and imitation of the condemned (!) [exclamation mark in original] Western woman?
>
> . . .
>
> We hope that continuation of publication of *Zanan* will serve as a preliminary step toward formation of a measured movement by women centered on human equality of

women and men, for achieving women's innate and divine rights and for elimination of gender discrimination in all dimensions of social relations.[71]

The editorial closes by breaking down yet another dichotomy: that between Iranian women in Iran and Iranian women residing abroad. It expresses its pleasure at the "serious presence of women intellectuals both inside and outside the country who are quietly engaged in serious study of women's issues and struggle to overcome obstacles to women's growth."[72] This is an important departure from the dominant state of suspicion and hostility between women who reside in Iran and those who, in the aftermath of the 1979 Revolution, either left or were forced to emigrate. The dominant Islamic writings continue to mark Iranian women abroad as corrupt women, "escapees" of the old regime, monarchists and leftists, in a word culturally inauthentic, morally corrupt, and politically alien. Secular women who continue to reside in Iran consider their counterparts abroad as women who have chosen the easier option of exile to the hardships of staying and struggling inside; they see the exiles as cut off from and ignorant of the realities of daily oppression experienced by those inside. For their part, most secular Iranian women abroad consider those inside as either supporters of the regime, or as those who have subsequently compromised themselves in order to survive, or as silenced victims who need a voice outside. *Zanan*'s approach opens up the possibility of productive cooperation between Iranian women across the borders of their current residences.

The text of a talk given by Zuhrah Zahidi on December 19, 1993, in a seminar sponsored by *Zanan* was printed in the journal with the title "Rehabilitating Eve." The speaker began with Islamic and Zoroastrian stories of creation, grounded her brief history of emergence of patriarchal societies in the later development of the division of social labor and gender organization, and offered a few positive words on the emergence of feminism in nineteenth-century Europe. Quoting affirmatively Susan Faludi and Rebecca West's remarks about feminism, she adopted as a definition of feminist "a woman who has the potential of struggling for independence."[73] She brought her talk to a close by reiterating Faludi's statement, but this time without quotations or references to her, as if accepting her definition as her own, collapsing the two voices into one—momentarily.[74] But only momentarily. She then ended by one last Quranic verse that emphasizes male–female parity: "I waste not the labor of any that labors among you, be you male or female—the one of you is as the other." (S. 3:194)

Feminism, Secularism, and Islam

Finally, *Zanan* has broken down the dichotomy between secular and Islamic women in Iran itself. Not only are its pages open to contributions of well-known secular and non-Muslim women, it has also embraced and made its own the tradition of secular women writers and poets of the previous decades. This includes the controversial poet, Furugh Farrukhzad, who has been labeled by a critic of the journal as:

> that corrupt poetess, who participated in pleasure-seeking parties of the *taghuti* times [the devilish time of the old regime]. Her naked [meaning "immodestly" dressed] pictures were portrayed in the press of those times. Her corrupt and sexual poetry is a condensation of inner collapse, filth, and forbidden thoughts that turn away any chaste and authentic woman.[75]

The journal has published favorable articles about Farrukhzad's life and poetry,[76] and Shahla Sherkat, the journal's editor, interweaves her writings with that poetry. In an editorial she describes the first year of the journal's publication as "A year of growth, growth of green hands that pressed our hands of desire with wondrous warmth."[77] The allusion is to a widely known poem of Farrukhzad, "Another Birth," and the title of a 1963 collection of her poetry, the last published before her tragic death in a car accident at the age of thirty-two. The title poem as well as the entire collection became a celebration of "the birth of a female character who rejoices in her new options, a warrior who has fought for every step in her path to freedom. She becomes her own model and gives birth to a self in the image of her own liking and aspirations. Her rebirth is indeed a self-birth."[78] This sentiment of a new beginning, a self-birth, expressed in the poem and in Milani's appreciation of it, has resonated with a whole generation of Iranian women who embraced Farrukhzad's poetry as their own voice. The title of this collection (and of this poem) has been used in a variety of book titles and journal names, in a similar way that Virginia Woolf's title, *A Room of One's Own*, has echoed through its appropriation and repetition in new combinations in writings of later women.

The metaphor of "growing/greening hands" is used repeatedly in Farrukhzad's poetry, as in the title poem, where she says: "I plant my hands in the garden/they will grow green [I will bloom], I know it, I know it, I know it."[79] In another poem, "Dawning of a Cold Season," she says:

> Perhaps the truth was those young pair of hands
> those young pair of hands buried beneath the falling snow
> and next year, when Spring
> mates with the sky beyond the window
> and stems thrust from her body
> fountains of fragile green stems
> will blossom, o my love, o my dearest only love.[80]

Sherkat's appreciation of her journal's work as connecting with "greening hands" thus projects her efforts as a response to Farrukhzad's yearnings, and by extension to aspirations of that generation of women who identified with her. She causes the wall that has been laboriously built by both sides of the secular/religious and the traditional/modernist divide to crumble, and she reaches for connections with secular women of a previous generation. She thus begins to construct a combined genealogy for Iranian feminism. It is precisely this gesture of connecting hands that is deemed dangerous by critics of the journal.

In a letter to Sherkat, Asadallah Badamchian, Adviser on Social Issues to the Head of Judiciary, chides her: "It is a pity that an intelligent sister like you would use her pen in this manner." To speak of Farrukhzad as a progressive Iranian woman, as a creative and brave figure, as a woman conscious of her values and struggling against the ill values of society, as the authors in that journal have done, he argues, is a historical travesty. The martyrs of Revolution, he continues, "shed their blood so that . . . true Islam will survive . . . and colonialists would no longer be able to introduce corrupt and loose women . . . as symbols of free and progressive women."[81]

Another critic, Nasir Haqju, takes the journal to task for having reprinted the full text of a paper that was partially presented by Mihrangiz Kar at the fifth annual conference of the Iranian Women's Study Foundation, held in Los Angeles (June 24–26, 1994). Does the journal not know "what a deep chasm separates today's responsible Iranian woman from the woman of yesterday who was favored by a monarchical society?" He further asks, "Do the people in charge of *Zanan* deny the fundamental and principle differences between women of our society today and women of prerevolutionary society that they seek to use the well-known feminist ideas of the time of the monarchy?"[82]

The alarming tone of these two attacks against *Zanan* speaks to an ideological panic. What is perceived as threatening by Badamchian and Haqju is the reversal of an important historical trend within which the West and the East, modernism and Islam, feminism and cultural authenticity, have been constructed as exclusionary categories, forcing Iranian women to choose between claims to a cultural self and a feminist self.[83] What has proved so useful to ideologues of the Islamic Republic, however, has been anything but empowering to Iranian women. It has become almost a self-evident truth to consider Iranian (and Middle Eastern) feminism as born, originated, and formed under the ideological influence, if not colonial tutelage, of "the West." In response, there has been a rejection of "the Western-oriented" feminism of "the elite" and a search for a more culturally authentic genealogy for women's rights, thereby authorizing one tendency against another.

But Iranian women who raised their voices for women's rights from the late nineteenth century onward did not define themselves in these late-twentieth century categories. They made rhetorical use of any available position to invent a female-friendly discourse. When pointing to "advances of women in other countries" (and these other countries included not only Europe and America, but also China, India, Japan, and the Ottoman Empire), they were not the "blind imitators" and "inauthentic apers of the West" into which they were later made. Employing the widespread acceptability of "new sciences" as the alchemy of civilizational progress, they argued for education of women, using modernist and Islamic justifications to inscribe and constitute their new selves as literate citizens. Though there were contested positions on these issues among women of this generation, they were not considered as incompatible and contradictory positions, one negating the other.

Not only Islamicist feminists, but also some secular feminists have projected a similar dichotomous trajectory for Iranian women. Afkhami, for instance, considers that:

> the politics of women's liberation was closely allied with the politics of secularization, which gained momentum during and immediately after the Constitutional Revolution of 1905–6. To achieve a modicum of freedom and equality, women leaders found it axiomatic that religion be separated from government, as the small sphere of activity they had so laboriously carved out for themselves could be safeguarded only by government protection.[84]

This is a reading back of a much later development into this earlier period. In the early years of the Constitutional regime in Iran, that is, in the first two decades of the twentieth century, and in the pages of the Constitutionalist press and the early women's journals of the 1910s and 1920s, we have a wide spectrum of positions coexisting and arguing with each other on issues related to women. While the anti-Constitutionalist forces, headed by Shaykh Fazlallah Nuri, grounded their political opposition in their interpretations of Islamic precepts, and, for instance, argued that having new schools for girls was an example of abrogation of the laws of God, the advocates of the new schools also drew from the same sources, using, for instance, prophetic narratives to argue for female education. In other words, the clerical voices were not allowed to hold a monopoly of Islamic Truth. While Shaykh Nuri saw "the opening of schools for women's education and elementary schools for young girls," along with "spread of houses of prostitution," as breaches in Islamic law by Constitutionalists,[85] other clerical leaders supported establishment of new schools for girls, and their own female family members were active educationalists. There was also no clear break between women who advocated education and unveiling and those who opposed these measures. Muzayyan al-Saltanah, a tireless educationalist (she established four girls' schools in Tehran within a span of three years, 1912–1915, and was appointed as inspector of girls' schools in Tehran), publisher and editor of Shukufah (1914–1918), one of the most important early women's journals, vehemently opposed unveiling and wrote in her journal against women's abandonment of hijab. At the same time, she published essays and poetry by women known for their secular views, such as Shams Kasma'i and Shahnaz Azad.

The rift between traditionalist and modernist women, though an important part of the modernist and countermodernist discourses on women from the mid-nineteenth century, became consolidated into negating categories during the Pahlavi period. It resulted largely from particular sets of state policies initiated by Riza Shah, and the reaction of the clerical establishment to those policies, demarcating mutually hostile territories by both sides. In the early 1930s, establishment of a single state-sponsored organization, *Kanun-i Banuvan* (Ladies Center), under the supervision of the Ministry of Education, and the closing down of all independent women's journals and organizations, brought efforts for women's rights under state control. This was followed by the compulsory unveiling order imposed from early 1936. It is these later political and cultural developments that consolidated clerical monopoly over sacred truth and the state's claim to be the sole patron of women's rights.

Afkhami' makes the political conclusions that, "The fact is that a 'modernizing' state in a traditional society is usually an ally of the women's movement against a majority in the society," that "without the support of the modernizing state and its political organs . . . women's rights are unattainable in an Islamic society," and that "There was no practical alternative to this model [of using the modernizing state to achieve women's rights]." These conclusions proclaim what were the effects of fifty years of coercive state policy as the only (past or future) model for Iranian women.[86] How can one declare that no other alternative but "the modernizing state" could ever exist on the basis of a historical experience in which all other alternatives were systematically eliminated by the modernizing state? Twice, once in the 1930s and once again in the 1950s and 1960s, the Pahlavi state closed off all possibilities for independent women's initiatives and took over "the woman question" as a domain of state policy. In response, in each period, the clerical faction opposed to any changes in women's social conditions constructed women's liberation as un-Islamic, as illegitimate, and as corruption perpetuated by the state. Thus, Afkhami's "modernizing state" and the Shiite clergy constructed each others' domains of authority[87] and produced Islam and feminism as mutually exclusive, so much so that many of us continue to find the category "Islamic feminism" difficult to imagine, and a "feminist Muslim" an impossible identity.

Emergence of *Zanan* as a vocal women's position is a radical break from this past. The writers have opened up the domain of interpretation to nonbelievers and non-Muslims, insisted on equality of women and men in all domains, and disconnected "nat-ural/created differences" between women and men from cultural and social constructions of womanhood and manhood. In doing so, *Zanan* has opened up a new space for dia-logue between Islamic women activists and reformers and secular feminism that begins to reverse a sixty-year-old rift during which they treated each other with mutual antagonism and constructed the two categories as mutually exclusive. This move also has the possi-bility of reaching across yet another divide: between women of the Muslim majority in Iran and women of other denominations. The kind of interpretive strategies and work that authors of *Zanan* are engaging in has precedents in Jewish and Christian feminist reread-ings of the Old and New Testaments and other Biblical and Midrashic sources. These al-ternative feminist traditions could build a new space for dialogue among women of these communities with Muslim and secular women in Iran.[88]

What will come about from these new possibilities is of course not predictable. It would in part depend on how secular feminism relates to and takes part in these remap-pings, and whether it reacts to it defensively or engages with it constructively. *Zanan* has begun to construct an Iranian feminism that does not draw its identity from counterposi-tion of an Islamic traditional authentic genealogy against a secular modern Westernized one. By inventing new visions and re-visions of Islam, and simultaneously constituting it-self as the "greening hands" of secular feminism, *Zanan* has audaciously messed up our comforting categories of Islamic and secular. By echoing Woolf, Gilman, de Beauvoir, and Faludi while speaking at once Quranic verses, Zoroastrian texts, and 'Attar's sufi writings, it has made West and East speak in a new combined tongue, in dialogue with rather than as negation of each other. Iranian secular feminism needs a similar boldness of vision and generosity of imagination to redefine itself. Current fears among many secular Iranian feminists outside the country that Islamic appropriation of feminism will further reduce their already precarious space continue to project these spaces as mutually exclusive rather than possibly constituting a reconfiguration of the political and cultural space in the pro-duction of which women of different outlooks can have a common stake.

In Iran, however, there are signs of cooperation and a new recognition that the old exclusionary categories need to be abandoned. Within the pages of *Zanan*, known secular feminists and Islamic feminists contribute with no worry about crossing the old bound-aries. Efforts are now afoot to initiate independent women's studies programs oriented to cultural change as well as policy determination on women's issues. A recent investigative report on the position of women in academia ended with a number of policy proposals; among them: (a) setting up women's studies programs in all universities and institutions of higher education, (b) instituting courses on women's studies in all university depart-ments, (c) formation of a society of university women, (d) expanding educational possi-bilities for women, (e) providing legal and economic support (such as flexible work-time, daycare, increased paid maternity leave, and decrease in teaching load for nursing moth-ers) for women in universities, and (f) ending gender discrimination in university ap-pointments and promotions. On a societal level, the report recommended making women's contributions more visible, forming women's organizations, encouraging women's skepticism of existing conditions for women, changing women's and men's per-ceptions of women, ending inequalities not only at the level of laws but in actual social practice through provision of equal opportunities for women. Finally, it called for a cul-tural transformation of concepts about men and women.[89] This is a very tall order indeed.

Notes

Acknowledgments: A shorter version of this paper was presented at the Conference, "Transitions, Environments, Translations: The Meanings of Feminism in Contemporary Politics," cosponsored by The Institute for Research on Women (Rutgers University) and The Institute for Advanced Study (Princeton), April 28–30, 1995, and will be published in the proceedings of that conference, edited by Cora Kaplan and Joan W. Scott (Routledge, 1996). The work on this paper was carried out in 1994 and 1995 while I was a visiting fellow at the Institute for Advanced Study (Princeton). Critical suggestions by members of the "Feminisms and Environmentalisms" seminar at the Institute—Tsehai Berhane-Selassie, Rosi Braidotti, Yaakov Garb, Evelynn Hammonds, Cora Kaplan, Anastasia Posadskaya, Joan W. Scott, and Anna Tsing—were of great help in revising this paper. I am thankful to them all. I would also like to thank Barnard College for supporting this work. An earlier version was presented on February 18, 1994, at the School of Oriental and African Studies (London University). My thanks to the Iranian Community Centre in London and Deniz Kandiyoti of London University, who made that occasion possible. I have also benefited immensely from critical remarks by a number of friends and colleagues whom I would like to thank here: Mehrzad Boroujerdi, Abdi Kalantari, Natalie Kampen, Deniz Kandiyoti, Kanan Makiya, Naghmeh Sohrabi, Mohamad Tavakoli, and last but not least, Parvin Paidar (Nahid Yeganeh), a long-term friend and colleague, conversations with whom over the past fifteen years have profoundly shaped this paper. To her it is dedicated.

1. By emphasizing this contest as one among men, I do not mean to imply that no woman supports the currently enforced "code of modesty" for women in Iran. Aside from political support, one of the enforcing agencies, "Gasht-i Zahra," is an all-female, state-sponsored, vigilante-style task force in charge of inspecting and scrutinizing women on the streets in order to enforce the "code of modesty." However, the whole notion of honor and its protection, which is the purported aim of the code, is a male preoccupation and a location of constitution of masculinity. Female modesty constructs male honor. See the witty essay by Fatima Mernissi, "Virginity and Patriarchy," *Women's Studies International Forum* 5 (2) (1982): 183–191. This point is also recognized in women's jokes. In one recent anecdote, a friend recalled that when she and her mother were visiting an exhibition in Tehran on local cultures of Iran, a group of men suddenly appeared marching through the exhibition grounds and chanting, "Brother! Brother! Where is your honor? Where is your wife's hijab?" A fearful silence replaced the noise and movements of exhibition visitors; many visitors, particularly women, including my friend and her mother, decided to leave the grounds for fear of being accused of "mal-veiling." As they were departing, a contingent of Revolutionary Guards, who probably had been informed of possible trouble brewing at the exhibition, pulled in. One of them inquired what the noise was about. My friend's mother shrugged her shoulders and answered, "I don't know. One group of Brothers are looking for the honor of another group of Brothers."

2. For some recent secular feminist perspectives on women in postrevolutionary Iran, see Haideh Moghissi, *Populism and Feminism in Iran* (London: Macmillan, 1994); Mahnaz Afkhami, "Women in Post-Revolutionary Iran: A Feminist Perspective," in *In the Eye of the Storm: Women in Post-Revolutionary Iran* ed. Mahnaz Afkhami and Erika Friedl (London: I. B. Tauris, 1994) pp. 5–18; and Valentine M. Moghadam, ed., *Gender and National Identity: Women and Politics in Muslim Societies* (London: Zed, 1994), particularly chap. 6, pp. 110–147, "Modernity, Islamization, and Women in Iran," by Nayereh Tohidi.

3. Moghissi, *Populism and Feminism*, p. 183.

4. For a discussion of Bihbahani's views and poetry, see Farzaneh Milani, "The Birth of Neotraditional Feminism," chap. 10 in *Veils and Words: The Emerging Voices of Iranian Women Writers* (Syracuse: Syracuse University Press, 1992); and *Nimeye Digar* 2 (1) (Autumn 1993), special issue on Bihbahani, guest edited by Farzaneh Milani. On Parsipur, see her interview with Farzaneh Milani, "Payi Suhbat-i Shahrnush Parsipur," *Iran Nameh* 11 (4) (Fall 1993): 691–704.

5. See Hamid Naficy, "Zan va 'Mas'alah-'i zan' dar Sinima-yi Iran ba'd az Inqilab," *Nimeye Digar* 1 (14) (Spring 1991): 123–169; and his "Veiled Vision/Powerful Presences: Women in Post-Revolutionary Iranian Cinema," in *In the Eye of the Storm: Women in Post-Revolutionary Iran*, ed. Mahnaz Afkhami and Erika Friedl (London: I. B. Tauris, 1994), pp. 131–150.

6. "Jaygah-i zan dar Jumhuri-yi Islami," *Zan-i Ruz* (961) (April 7, 1984): 3 and 58; the quote is from p. 3. For a fuller translation of this editorial and an expanded discussion of it, see Afsaneh Najmabadi, "Power, Morality, and the New Muslim Womanhood," pp. 366–389, in *The Politics of Social Transformation in Afghanistan, Iran, and Pakistan*, ed. Myron Weiner and Ali Banuazizi (Syracuse, N.Y.: Syracuse University Press, 1994).

7. Headlines from the government-supported English-language journal, *Mahjubah: The Islamic Magazine for Women*, published in Tehran by the Islamic Thought Foundation, provide an expression of such contested claims: "Zimbabwe Women in Uphill Fight for Equality" [*Mahjubah* 13 (12) (December 1994): 25] reports that "Of ten state-appointed governors who run the country's eight provinces, only one is a woman." (Never mind that there are none in Iran!) Other headlines from 1994 issues of this journal include: "Sexual Harassment at the United Nations," and "Combatting Sexual Harassment at Work," (4) (April 1994): 5 and 6 respectively; "Violence Against Women," (5) (May 1994): 23–24; "Discrimination Against Woman Persists Despite Progress," (6) (June 1994): 29; "Women and Development in the EROPA Conference," (7) (July 1994): 20; "Female Genital Mutilation in Southern Nigeria," (8) (August 1994): 27.

8. Gharbzadigi, variously translated as "Westoxication" or "Westitis", is a concept popularized through a work of Jalal Al-e Ahmad bearing that title. See its English translation by Paul Sprachman, *Plagued by the West* (Delmar, N.Y.: Coward, McCann, and Geoghegan, 1981). Al-e Ahmad wrote:

I speak of being afflicted with "westitis" the way I would speak of being afflicted with cholera. If this is not palatable, let us say it is akin to being stricken by heat or by cold. But it is not that either. It is something more on the order of being attacked by tongue worm. Have you ever seen how wheat rots? From within. The husk remains whole, but it is only an empty shell like the discarded chrysalis of a butterfly hanging from a tree. In any case, we are dealing with a sickness, a disease imported from abroad, and developed in an environment receptive to it. Let us discover the characteristics of this illness and its cause or causes and, if possible, find a cure. (p. 3)

9. For a translation of some of the regulations concerning codes of dress and public appearance for women, see Najmabadi, "Power, Morality, and the New Muslim Womanhood," Appendix A, pp. 383–386.

10. From the speech by Dari Najafabadi, given during a four-day seminar on "The Veil and Women's Rights in Islam," held in Karaj (Iran), January 4–7, 1986. Full text published in *Ittila'at* (17829) (March 3, 1986): 13.

11. For a survey of changes in family law in the 1960s and 1970s in Iran, see Behnaz Pakizegi, "Legal and Social Positions of Iranian Women," in *Women in the Muslim World*, ed. Lois Beck and Nikki R. Keddie (Cambridge, Mass: Harvard University Press, 1978), pp. 216–226; and Gholam-Reza Vatandoust, "The Status of Iranian Women During the Pahlavi Regime," in *Women and the Family in Iran*, ed. Asghar Fathi (Leiden: E. J. Brill, 1985), pp. 107–130.

12. For a description of some of these events see the Chronology section, in *In the Shadow of Islam: The Women's Movement in Iran*, ed. Azar Tabari and Nahid Yeganeh (London: Zed, 1982), pp. 231–239. For women in higher education, see Shahrzad Mojab, "The Islamic Government's Policy on Women's Access to Higher Education: 1979–85," Office of Women in International Development, Working Paper No. 156, Lansing: Michigan State University, December 1987; and her article (in Persian), "Kunturul-i Dawlat va Muqavimat-i Zanan dar 'Arsah-'i Danishgah'ha-yi Iran," in *Nimeye Digar* 1 (14) (Spring 1991): 35–76; see also Patricia F. Higgens and Pirouz Shoar-Ghaffari, "Women's Education in the Islamic Republic of Iran," in *In the Eye of the Storm: Women in Post-Revolutionary Iran*, ed. Mahnaz Afkhami and Erika Friedl (London: I. B. Tauris, 1994), pp. 19–43.

13. Ali Shariati, *Fatimah is Fatimah*, trans. Laleh Bakhtiar (Tehran: Shariati Foundation, 1980). For a discussion of various Islamic positions on women in recent Iranian writings, see Nahid Yeganeh, "Women's Struggles in the Islamic Republic of Iran," in *In the Shadow of Islam*, ed. Tabari and Yeganeh, pp. 26–74, particularly pp. 41–54. See also Marcia K. Hermansen, "Fatimeh as a Role Model in the Works of Ali Shari'ati," in *Women and Revolution in Iran*, ed. Guity Nashat (Boulder, Colo: Westview, 1983), pp. 87–96.

14. For an early appreciation and discussion of the activities of these women, see Yeganeh, "Women's Struggles," pp. 54–58. For some of the early statements by a number Islamic women leaders in postrevolutionary period, see Documents 20–29, in *In the Shadow of Islam*, ed. Tabari and Yeganeh, pp. 171–200.

15. Mihrangiz Kar, *Firishtah-'i 'Adalat va Pardah'ha-yi Duzakh* (Tehran: Rawshangaran, 1991), p. 11; see also her article on women's political rights in Iran since the Revolution, "Huquq-i Siasi-yi zan dar Iran az Bahman-i 57 ta Imruz," *Zanan* 3 (20) (October–November 1994): 18–25. For a valuable sociological study of middle class women in the Islamic Republic of Iran, see Shahin Gerami, "The Role, Place, and Power of Middle-Class Women in the Islamic Republic," in *Identity Politics and Women: Cultural Reassertions and Feminisms in International Perspective*, ed. Valentine M. Moghadam (Boulder, Colo.: Westview, 1994), pp. 329–348.

16. Though there are important substantial differences between *Nida'* and *Payam-i Hajir*, common impressions that *Nida'* is quasi-official, whereas *Payam-i Hajir* is oppositional and (in part) patrilineally, if not patriarchally, informed. The former is edited (and linked to an organization headed) by Ayatollah Khomeini's daughter, the latter by Ayatollah Taliqani's daughter. Our understanding of the daughters' enterprises is influenced by our conceptions of their fathers' work.

17. *The Koran Interpreted*, trans. A. J. Arberry, vol. 3 (New York: MacMillan, 1955), pp. 194–195. I have used Arberry's translation throughout this paper.

18. For a collection of reprints from *Payam-i Hajir*, see A'zam 'Ala'i Taliqani, *Masa'il-i-Zanan* (Tehran: Mu'ssisah-'i Islami-yi zanan-i Iran, 1991); the quote is from p. 10.

19. See Manijeh Saba, "Tahlili az Dibachah'ha-yi *Zan-i Ruz* dar Dawrah-'i Ba'd az Inqilab," *Nimeye Digar* 1 (14) (Spring 1991): 8–34.

20. Mahboobe Ommi, "Women's Studies: The Indispensible Cultural Factor," *Farzaneh* 1 (1) (Fall 1993): 1–4; the quote is from p. 3.

21. Ibid., p. 2.

22. Mahboobe Ommi, "Fiminizm az Aghaz Ta'kunun [Part 1]," *Zan-i Ruz*, (1342) (December 14, 1991): 10–11 and 58; [Part 2], (1344) (January 4, 1992): 12–13; [Part 3], (1345) (January 11, 1992): 24–25; [Part 4], (1346) (January 18, 1992): 32–33; [Part 5], (1347) (January 25, 1992): 28–29.

23. Ommi, "Fiminizm [Part 1]," p. 11.

24. Ommi, "Fiminizm [Part 5]," pp. 28–29.

25. Ommi, "Fiminizm [Part 1]," p. 11.

26. The repeated use of this rhetorical technique, posing questions and then not answering them, points to the instability of the position *Farzaneh* currently occupies—having abandoned the solid grounds of Islamic universalism, yet being ambivalent, if not hostile, toward any concept of feminism. The first issue of *Farzaneh* contains an article by Moneer Gorgi on the rulership of Sheba as explicated in the Quran ["Zan va zimamdari," *Farzaneh* 1 (1) (Fall 1993): 9–34]. It opens with this question: "Does the prohibition of women's rulership by Islamic political jurisprudence result from innate and physical weakness of women, or is it rooted in social considerations?" (p. 9). The article never explicitly answers this opening question and ends by posing yet another question: "If the Quran, in its brief discussion of rulers, has chosen to include a woman ruler, on what grounds does Islamic political jurisprudence include maleness as a condition for *vilayat* [leadership/rulership of the Islamic community]?" (p. 29). In another essay, Massoumeh Ebtekar ends her review of *And Sara Laughed*, a book by John H. Otwell, by raising a number of significant questions:

Finally, if we accept the validity of Mr. Otwell's hypotheses and despite all contradictions accept that the Torah or the Old Testament scripts woman as a human being on a par with and equal to man, this question remains that at the end of the Christian and Jewish twentieth century, how can masses of women who consider themselves at least formally belonging to these religions benefit from the Old Testament? Can the decrees and rulings of the Old Testament and the present Torah solve the ever growing social, moral, legal, and political problems of women in these societies? Can the Old Testament offer a practical model for emancipation and happiness of the twentieth century woman? . . . Which book can carry the huge burden of such a mission?" ("Va Sara Khandid," *Farzaneh* 1 (1) (Fall 1993): 121–130; the quote is from pp. 128–129).

It is tempting to say that the implicit answer to the author's closing question would be "the Quran," but by refusing to answer her own question, she is giving the option to the reader to extend the negating logic of her initial rhetorical questions to the last one and say "No book." Massoumeh Ebtekar served as the coordinator of the Women's NGO Coordinating Office for the Fourth World Conference on Women, which held an international conference in Tehran in May 1995 on the theme "Woman and Family in Human Development." See *Mahjubah* 13 (12) (December 1994): 54, and *Mahjubah* 14 6 (June 1995): 7–8. Positions held by such figures as Gorgi and Ebtekar have marked The Center For Women's Studies and Research and the journal *Farzaneh* as "mainstream," in contrast to Sherkat and *Zanan* that have become voices of dissidence.

27. One could also imagine she might be trying to counteract official lack of sympathy for, if not hostility toward, the Center for Women's Studies and Research.

28. Mahboobe Ommi, "Chigunah bayad raft?," *Farzaneh* 1 (2–3) (Winter–Spring 1993): 159–162; the quote is from pp. 159–160.

29. Ibid., p. 160.

30. Sa'id 'Uryan, "Dar Sayah [Review of *Shinakht-i Huviyat-i Zan-i Irani dar Gustarah-'i Pish'tarikh va Tarikh* (Tehran: Rawshangaran, 1992) by Shahla Lahiji and Mihrangiz Kar]," *Farzaneh* 1 (2–3) (Winter–Spring 1994): 305–312. Shahla Lahiji is a writer and a publisher of books largely on themes related to women. Mihrangiz Kar is a lawyer and a regular contributor to *Zanan*.

31. Ibid.; quotes from pp. 306, 307, and 308, respectively. The usage of "feminism" for marking off political boundaries of acceptability is not limited to Islamic currents. Here is an example of a socialist paper's similar usage: "The Iranian women's movement in exile suffers from dispersion, passivity, and the penetration of feminist influences. We should struggle for the formation of independent women's movements geared towards concrete goals and programs, devoid of feminist tendencies." From *Payam-i Kagar* (81) (March 1991), as quoted by Moghissi, *Populism and Feminism in Iran*, p. 187.

32. Shahla Sherkat, "Chashmah-'i Agahi Agar Bijushad . . . ", *Zanan* 1 (1) (February 1992): 2–3.

33. Ibid., p. 2.

34. Ibid.

35 . Ibid.

36. Ibid.

37. Mihrangiz Kar, "Jaygah-i zan dar Qavanin-i Kayfari-yi Iran", *Zanan* 2 (11) (June–July 1993): 16–25; the quote is from p. 16. "Ijtihad: individual inquiry to establish the ruling of the Shari'ah [the body of rules guiding the life of a Muslim, in law, ethics, and etiquette] upon a given point, by a *mujtahid*, a person qualified for the inquiry." Marshall Hodgson, *The Venture of Islam*, vol. 2 (Chicago: University of Chicago Press, 1974), p. 583.

38. Muzhgan Kiani Thabit, "Naqd-i Sukhanrani-yi Khanum Mihrangiz Kar," *Zanan* 2 (14) (October–November 1993): 42–49; the quote is from p. 42. The part in square brackets is from a footnote to the main text, appearing on p. 49.

39. Ibid., p. 44.

40. Sayyid Muhsin Sa'idzadah, ". . . Va Amma Pasukh-i Ma," *Zanan* 2 (14) (October–November 1993): 50–57; the quote is from pp. 52–53.

41. Zaynab al-Sadat Kirmanshahi, "Jaygah-i Zan dar Fiqh-i Kayfari-yi Islam [Part 1]," *Zanan* 2 (13) (September 1993): 56–60; [Part 2], 1 (15) (December 1993–January 1994): 52-55; [Part 3], 3 (16) (February–March 1994): 38–44; the quote is from Part I, p. 56.

42. A similar attempt is engaged in by Amina Wadud-Muhsin, *Qur'an and Woman* (Kuala Lumpur: Penerbit Fajar Bakti Sdn., Bhd., 1992).

43. Shukufah Shukri and Sahirah Labriz, "Mard: Sharik ya Ra'is?!", *Zanan* 1 (2) (March 1992): 26–32; see p. 26 for their argument.

44. Ibid., p. 27.

45. Ibid., p. 28.

46. Muhsin Qa'ini, "Kutak Zadan-i Zan: Yiki az Athar-i Riasat-i Mard [Part 1]," *Zanan* 3 (18) (June–July 1994): 54–59; [Part 2], 3 (19) (August–September 1994): 68–72; see Part 2, p. 71.

47. The differences between reformist and misogynous uses of differences-in-creation argument are important, despite their common ground. Whereas misogynous positions use these differences-in-creation to argue for superiority of men over women, the reformist positions argue that in God's view, superiority only arises from superior piety and religiosity. Gender differences should thus not be used for giving more social worth to men compared to women. They should be taken as value-neutral differences. For a critical review of these positions, see Yeganeh, "Women's Struggles," pp. 41–51.

48. Kiani Thabit, "Naqd-i sukhanrani," p. 43.

49. Sa'idzadah, ". . . Va amma," p. 56.

50. Zuhrah Zahidi, "I'adah-'i Haythiyat-i Havva," *Zanan* 3 (16) (February–March 1994): 2–6; the quote is from p. 4.

51. Shukufah Shukri and Sahirah Labriz, "Tamkin," *Zanan* 1 (1) (February 1992): pp. 58–63.

52. Ibid., p. 59.

53. These sources are extensively quoted and critically discussed in this article. For an English source, see Shahla Haeri, *Law of Desire: Temporary Marriage in Shi'i Iran* (Syracuse, N.Y.: Syracuse University Press, 1989).

54. Shukri and Labriz, "Tamkin," p. 59.

55. Ibid.

56. Mina Yadigar Azadi, "Qizavat-i zan [Part 1]," *Zanan,* 1 (4) (May 1992): 20–26.

57. See the section "Reinterpreting Islamic Sources" for the text of this verse.

58. These latter verses read, "Wives of the Prophet, you are not as other women. If you are godfearing, be not abject in your speech, so that he in whose heart is sickness may be lustful; but speak honourable words. Remain in your houses; and display not your finery, as did the pagans of old." These verses are usually used to argue that it is preferable for women to stay at home. The author rejects this interpretation on the grounds that, first, these verses are directed to wives of the Prophet. As a special category of women, they had to follow more strict rules and accept certain deprivations that do not apply to all women. Second, the verses are in the nature of recommendations, not of requirements. And finally, if these verses could be used to bar women from position of judgeship, they could also be used to bar women from any other job that takes them out of the house, but clearly no one is arguing for absolute exclusion of women from all occupations.

59. Muhsin Qa'ini, "Kutak zadan-i zan [Part I]," p. 58. In this issue, there is also a long investigative report, "Sir, Have Your Ever Beaten Your Spouse?" ["Aqa: Ta Hala Shudah Hamsaritan ra Bizanid?", *Zanan* 3 (18) (June–July 1994): 6–21], by Parvin Ardalan and Furugh Kakhsaz. The bulk of the report is presented as conversations between the reporters (two women) and men who were asked if they had ever beaten their wives, under what circumstances, why, and to what ef-

fect. A supplement discusses the legal issues arising from wife-beating in an interview with Mihrangiz Kar, a woman lawyer.

60. Mina Yadigar Azadi, "Qizavat-i zan [Part 2]," *Zanan*, 1 (5) (June–July 1992): 17–25.

61. Ibid., p. 19.

62. Ibid., p. 21. The author also deals extensively with the argument that woman is a deficient person. The most frequently Shii narrative quoted on this issue is that attributed to 'Ali, the first Shii imam, presumably said after the battle of Jamal, in condemnation of 'Ayisha's role in that battle. Again, here the author argues that even if one can trust such a narrative, this concerns the behavior of one woman in one particular instance and cannot be used as a statement about womanhood, because that would imply something intrinsic and natural, something to do with deficient creation, which would contradict the Quran's statements repeatedly testifying to the intrinsic and natural equality of all human beings. Even if women were considered deficient beings over 1,400 years ago, this testifies to their sociohistorical deprivations, not to their natural limitations. Such claims would indeed point to deficiency in the creative power of God! For a thorough and insightful discussion of 'A'isha, the Battle of Camel, and its uses, see Denise A. Spellberg, *Politics, Gender and the Islamic Past: The Legacy of 'A'isha Bint Abi Bakr* (New York: Columbia University Press, 1994), chap. 4, pp. 101–149.

63. Mina Yadigar Azadi, "Davari-yi zan dar Ikhtilafat-i Khanivadigi [Part 1]," *Zanan*, 1 (6) (August 1992): 22–28; [Part 2], 1 (7) (September–October 1991): 25–29. What is interesting about these articles is that not only are previous arguments reinforced, but the Family Protection Act of the old regime is discussed in a positive way—as a law that was the fruit of half a century of legislative experience and which contravened existing fatwas only on a few minor points. The articles explain that, by removing and modifying these minor problems, the law could be reconsidered, whereas its abrogation constituted a regressive move towards the 1939 civil code.

64. Mina Yadigar Azadi, "Ijtihad va marja'iyat -i zanan," *Zanan* 1 (8) (November–December 1992): 24–32.

65. Most recently, Fatimah Amin (1886–1983) acquired the status of a mujtahidah. See Ahmad Bihishti, *Zanan-i Namdar dar Qur'an, Hadith va Tarikh*, vol. 1 (Tehran: Sazman-i Tablighat-i Islami, 1989), pp. 122–26; and *Zan-i Ruz* (1372) (August 15, 1992): 6–9, 57. Not only have there been many women *mujtahidahs*, but some men have had their permission of *ijtihad* issued by their female teacher mujtahidahs.

66. This is one of the few articles in which the author falls back on the authority of Ayatollahs Khu'i and Najafi, to support some of the arguments and specifically notes this in a footnote by saying that if skeptics would hear this argument from the author, they may not believe it, but hearing it in the words of Ayatollah Khu'i, they will take it seriously.

67. These issues are tackled in Muhsin Sa'idzadah, "Zan bah Didah-'i 'aql va Kamal," *Zanan* 2 (9) (January–February 1993): 29–34, which reviewed a book by Ayatollah Javadi Amuli, *Zan dar Ayinah-'i Jalal and Jamal*. The article was the first open challenge of *Zan-i ruz* by the magazine of its former editor. This book was serialized uncritically in the pages of *Zan-i ruz*. Whereas Ayatollah Javadi Amuli had argued against women qualifying for rulership, the critic, using much of the same arguments as Yadigar Azadi, argues for it.

68. Kirmanshahi, "Jaygah-i zan dar Fiqh-i Kayfari-yi Islam [Part I]," p. 56.

69. Zaynab al-Sadat Kirmanshahi prefaces her article on the criminal code with these words: "This essay is a critical discussion in order to help legislators to revise laws; it is not meant as a discussion pertaining to religious opinions [fatwa] and innovations [bid'at]." ("Jaygah-i zan dar Fiqh-i Kayfari-yi Islam [Part I]," p. 56.)

70. "Pasukh bah Su'alat-i Huquqi-yi Shuma", *Zanan* 2 (15) (December 1993–January 1994): 52.

71. Shahla Sherkat, "Sal-i Usrat, Sal-i Ruyish," *Zanan* 2 (10) (March–April 1993): 2–3.

72. Ibid., p. 3.

73. These are translated from Susan Faludi, *Backlash: The Undeclared War Against American Women* (New York: Crown, 1981), p. xxiii.

74. Zahidi, "I'adah-'i Haythiyat-i Havva," p. 6.

75. Asadallah Badamchian, "Bidun-i sharh . . . ", *Zanan* 3 (19) (August–September 1994): 9–11; the quote is from p. 11. These categorizations and evaluations of Farrukhzad go on for another half a page. For an alternative feminist reading of Farrukhzad's poetry, see Milani, *Veils and Words*. On Farrukhzad's life and poetry, see also Michael C. Hillmann, *A Lonely Woman: Forugh Farrokhzad and Her Poetry* (Washington, D.C.: Three Continents, 1987).

76. See Suhayla Sarimi, "Va in Manam/Zani Tanha . . . ", *Zanan* 3 (16) (February–March 1994): 18–21; and Nahid Farkhundah, "Shi'r-i Furugh bah Almani tarjumah shud, vali . . . ", *Zanan* 3 (18) (June–July 1994): 22–23.

77. Sherkat, "Sal-i 'Usrat," p. 2.

78. Milani, *Veils and Words*, p. 135.

79. Furugh Farrukhzad, "Tavalludi Digar," in *Tavalludi Digar* (Tehran: Murvarid, 1963–1964), pp. 164–169; the verse is from p. 167.

80. Milani's translation, in *Veils and Words*, pp. 135–136. For the Persian text, see Amir Isma'ili and Abu al-Qasim Sidarat, eds., *Javdanah Furugh Farrukhzad* (Tehran: Marjan, 1968), pp. 345–354; the verses are from p. 354.

81. Badamchian, "Bidun-i Sharh . . . "; all quotes are from p. 11.

82. Nasir Haqju, "In Qafilah ta Bah Hashr Lang Ast," *Kayhan-i hava'i* (1113) (December 28, 1994): 8. In many quasi-official papers in Iran, the label "monarchical" is regularly used to dismiss Iranian emigre communities. Though initially this move had succeeded in preventing cultural cooperations between these communities and Iranian writers and artists residing in Iran, fear of reprisals has progressively been replaced by an eagerness on both sides to work together. Wary of this cooperation, *Kayhan-i hava'i* and some other journals published in Tehran consistently attack writers and artists from Iran who participate in events sponsored by Iranian communities abroad.

83. For an eloquent presentation of dilemmas and difficulties of claiming a feminist room of one's own, faced by an Iranian secular feminist, positioned at the cross-fires of Iranian socialist antifeminism, Islamicism, anti-Orientalist ethnocentrism, Western feminist cultural relativism, see the Introduction, to Moghissi, *Populism and Feminism in Iran*, pp. 1–20.

84. Afkhami, "Women in Post-Revolutionary Iran," pp. 9–10.

85. Huma Rizvani, ed., *Lavayih-i Aqa Shaykh Fazlallah Nuri* (Tehran: Nashr-i tarikh-i Iran, 1983), pp. 28, 62.

86. Afkhami, "Women in Post-Revolutionary Iran," quotes from pp. 13, 14, 15, respectively.

87. It is not accidental that the centralization of the state and the clerical hierarchy occurred as twin social processes in these two crucial periods and around important gendered themes—the first around woman's veil, and the second around woman's vote. See Michael Fischer, *Iran: From Religious Dispute to Revolution* (Cambridge, Mass.: Harvard University Press, 1980), especially "The Religious Establishment and the Expanding State," pp. 108–123.

88. Perhaps the single most difficult divide to cross would be recognition of the Baha'i and Babi traditions, both denied status of religious minorities in the Iranian Constitution, banned, and persecuted. Whereas the journal has dared to embrace Furugh Farrukhzad, it is unlikely that it could risk embracing Qurrat al-'Ayn, the female leader of the Babis. On Qurrat al-'Ayn, see Milani, *Veils and Words*, pp. 77–99; and Abbas Amanat, *Resurrection and Renewal: The Making of the Babi Movement in Iran, 1844–1850* (Ithaca, N.Y.: Cornell University Press, 1989), pp. 295–331.

89. Shams al-Sadat Zahidi, "Muqi'iyat-i Zanan dar Jami'ah-'i Danishgahi," *Zanan* 3 (21) (December 1994–January 1995): 2–12; recommendations are from pp. 10–12.

Secularist and Islamist Discourses on Modernity in Egypt and the Evolution of the Postcolonial Nation-State

Both the opponents and the supporters of Islamism in Egypt recognize that its political triumph will have important implications for the operation of the postcolonial nation-state. In an important debate entitled "Egypt Between the Religious and the Civil State" that was held as part of Cairo's (1992) annual book exhibit, the representatives of the secularist and the Islamist discourses presented their different views of a key feature of the postcolonial states that have ruled Egypt since 1952. The Islamists were very critical of the state's circumscribed articulation of cultural difference (represented by both Islam and gender) and its acceptance of the universal character of the economic and the political arenas. The Islamists suggested that the choice that Egypt is asked to make is not between a civil and a religious state, but between an Islamic and an un-Islamic state. The goal of an Islamic state will be to give expanded cultural representation of the Islamic nation (*umma*) in the operation of the political (legislative and bureaucratic) and legal systems.[1] This does not signal the Islamic state's wholesale abandonment of the modern measures of societal strength, that is, the rule of reason, science, and economic development.[2] These will be part and parcel of the concerns of the new state. Women have an important role to play in this cultural–political project. They will simultaneously represent cultural difference (through the Islamic mode of dress and an Islamist definition of femininity) and the exercise of full and universal political rights to vote and run for office.[3]

In response, the secularists argued that in a civil society with a civil government, religion had a role to play, one that is restricted to the spiritual domain. The rise of an Islamic state will spell the end of the universal political and economic projects of modernity which gave all members of the nation the right to self-determination, that is, equal (formal) economic and political standing.[4] By reintroducing religious and gender divisions in the operation of the political and economic institutions, the Islamic state will challenge the modern (nonreligious and nongendered) bases of citizenship rights.[5]

Polemical interpretations of these two discourses have exaggerated the differences between them in the attempt to make them stand for tradition versus modernity. This chapter attempts to develop an appreciation of the common national history of the different secularist and Islamist discourses, and their different strategies on how to reconcile cultural nationalism with the pursuit of the universal project of modernity and the role that gender plays in it. While the secularist wants to localize cultural difference in the home/spiritual/inner domains, the Islamist wants to extend the reach to the definition of the roles that men and women play in the public/material/outer arenas. At the same time, the Islamist discourse has gone a long way in its embrace of the modern regimes of power whose goal is to discipline and normalize the relations of power between men and women of the middle classes within and outside the nuclear family.[6]

The Cultural and Universalist Dialectic in the Development of the Colonial and Postcolonial States

Partha Chatterjee suggests that the history and operation of the colonial state contributed contradictory definitions of the national project of building a developed society. The colonial state instituted the bases of a modern regime of power that sought, through its institutional system (the courts, the bureaucracy, law, education, health, the police, and the military) to use social regulation as an aspect of the self-disciplining of normalized individuals and in this way make power more productive and efficient.[7] These institutions produced new forms of consciousness, and through them novel and universal forms of control that were inherited by the postcolonial state. The early history of these institutions relied on the rule of colonial difference for their success, that is, an "essentialist" definition of the local culture as both inferior and backward, with the consequent political and economic exclusion of the natives from power. As a result, the colonial state, with its alien ruling group that began the regime of modernity, was destined to fail in completely normalizing its power relations as part of creating the modern state.[8]

The development of the nationalist discourse attempted a particular resolution of the contradiction between the universalist credentials of modernity and cultural difference. This discourse retained the discussion of the marks of "essential" cultural difference as a means of both keeping the colonizer out of the inner, spiritual domain of national life and exercising sovereignty over it. It also internalized the presumed backwardness of its indigenous culture to justify the embrace of the economic and political projects of modernity as part of its quest for development. In the process, the nationalists became paradoxically committed to celebrating cultural difference in the spiritual domain and erasing its marks from the outer, public domain (of law, administration, economy, and statecraft) where members of the middle class were previously excluded.[9] The universality of the modern regime of power and its normalizing mission occupied a central place in the postcolonial state's developmental program.

This nationalist formulation, produced by the middle class in colonial societies, became an apt description of its "middle" position (between the indigenous culture and that of modernity, between the colonial ruling class and the indigenous classes). This "mediating" role among the different cultural projects and internal and external groups distinguished the consciousness of the middle class as a subject. Its goal was to work upon and transform one term of the relation into the other. Their primary social preoccupation was with that "vital zone of belief and practice that straddles the domain of the individual and the collectivity, the private and the public, the home and the world, where the new disciplinary culture of a modernizing elite has to turn itself into an exercise of self-discipline."[10] In this exercise, the middle class was simultaneously placed in a position of subordination in one relation and a position of dominance in another. It is a subordinate of modernity but represents its dominance in the indigenous cultural arena and vis à vis other hostile classes.

The Islamists reject this minimalist secular strategy to representation of cultural difference, but without questioning the legitimacy of the mediating mission of the postcolonial state. The Islamist discourse, produced by another segment of the Egyptian middle class, does not challenge the middle position of the developmental project described here. It seeks to expand the expression of cultural difference in the modern (universal) arenas whose fundamental modes of operation and forms of control it does not challenge.

The next section traces the recent genealogies of these two discourses as parts of the history of the postcolonial state under Gamal Abdul Nasser (1952–1970) and Anwar al-Sadat (1970–1981). The Nasser regime developed a nationalist/secularist discourse on gender that was more universalist than culturally specific. In reaction to the organized middle-class women's agitation from 1952 to 1956, the new discourse presented a developmental strategy that used gender to divide and control women in different classes in some novel ways. Because the Sadat regime developed an alliance with the Islamist groups in the 1970s, it tolerated the development of an Islamist discourse that demanded expanded articulation of the culturally specific roles of women in the hitherto neutral economic and political domains.

The First Republic and the Production of a Secularist Discourse on Gender

During the period from 1952 to 1954, the intense activism of professional women (lawyers, university professors, reporters, and teachers) and their organizations convinced the Nasser regime that the issue of gender rights would not go away.[11] In response, the regime incorporated the demands and the gender agenda of middle-class woman as part of its socially progressive agenda. The result was a package of new economic and political measures described elsewhere as state feminism.[12] It gave Egyptian women new rights and, in the process, established the universal character of the modern political and economic arenas. In 1956, the political rights of citizenship (such as the right to vote and to run for public office), which had been given to men in 1920, were now extended to women. In 1959, Labor Law 91 upheld women's right to work by providing them with fifty days of maternity leave, providing daycare services where there were more than one hundred workers, and protecting women from unfair termination of work following the birth of a child.[13]

While the theorists of modernization[14] stress these measures as part of their discussion of the progressive implications of modernity, they do not examine how these universal rights were also associated with the development of new forms of discipline and social regulation that produced a subordinate gender consciousness. Middle-class women were the real beneficiaries of the policy of state feminism. They were also the targets of new forms of social regulation through the system of state education and the modern professions. Access to the gender-neutral general education (al-ta'lim al-'amm), which allowed women expanded professional opportunities, did not overlook the study of home economics and sewing as new and old skills associated with homemaking. While these were no longer primary subjects, their inclusion in the curriculum served to remind women of a different calling. Women were theoretically free to choose any area of study, yet the edu-

cation system continued to channel many middle-class women into the feminine professions, such as medicine and nursing.[15] Both of these professions represented extensions of
women's family roles into the public arena. Within the teaching profession, women were
more likely to be primary-school teachers where child care was still key. Men were the
preparatory- and secondary-school teachers who taught history, science, logic, and philosophy. In many ways, this organization of the modern education system reproduced old
dichotomous definitions of masculinity and femininity in the public arena. While modern
masculinity remained identified with abstract reason and social regulation, modern public femininity was associated with the emotional needs and familial role of caretaker.

Secretarial work was added to these feminine professions in the 1950s and the
1960s. In the secretarial and nursing professions, women transferred some of their familial caretaking functions to men in the public sphere. Here, there was greater social realization of the danger of reproducing women's familial roles in a public arena, where men
were dominant and could abuse their power over their female subordinates. By withholding social prestige from the professions where women worked close to men, there was a
recognition that the public domain was not a particularly safe place for some women professionals.

Despite the relative increase in the number of women in many other different professions, women continued to be underrepresented in the top executive positions. Despite
the emphasis on merit as a criterion of occupational mobility, most women professionals
spent much of their work lives as subordinates of men. The regime celebrated the success
of a few token professional women who reached prominent political positions, like Hikmat Abu Zeid, the first woman nominated to a cabinet position in 1962 as Minister of Social Affairs. Karima al-Said rose to the position of the Undersecretary of the Ministry of
Education in 1965.[16] In general, however, only a small number of women were promoted
into leadership positions. Most reach these positions when they are close to retiring.[17] In
this way, the normalization of women's professional roles included the experience of being
subordinate to men in their professional careers. In other words, despite the multiplication of the number of professional women in the public arena, their professional consciousness did not routinize or internalize relations of equality or empowerment. These
modern professional identities associated authority and leadership with maleness. Femininity was defined in opposition to masculinity as a subordinate status.

Official commitment to women's universal access to work, education, and political
participation aside, the new roles of middle-class women did not leave a major impact on
the lives of the rural working class, who represent the majority of Egyptian women. The
land reform laws were more significant as an indicator of the new forms of control of rural
working-class women. Land reform primarily benefited rural middle-class men and only
some rural working-class men; it excluded women from its benefits. Land was only distributed to male heads of households. In some very rare cases, female heads of households, especially widows, were given access to some land as guardians of their young sons.
These cases did not include female heads of households who were divorced mothers with
sons, which led some of them to protest in 1952 that the law was particularly unfair to
them.

Rule 23 of the law, which was aimed at the prevention of fragmented agricultural
property, would control women's economic fortunes in yet another way. It recommended
that in cases of land fragmentation through inheritance, the courts should rule in favor of

those whose main occupation was agriculture. If there were many women who shared this qualification, then married males should be privileged in these cases, followed by sons. In other words, this rule was to circumvent Egyptian sunni inheritance rules that guaranteed women some direct access to agricultural property. This part of the law faced overwhelming resistance and was not put into effect.

Still, land reform, as a modern economic and legal instrument of change, did not guarantee universal or equal access to land. For the most part, it excluded women as an economic group. It accepted old rural definitions of women as marginal economic actors and introduced new definitions that promised to reinforce their economic dependence on men.

In terms of agricultural labor laws, the Minister of Agriculture, in a resolution passed on November 17, 1952, to implement the land reform law, specified that the minimum daily wage for a male worker was 18 piasters and 10 piasters for working women and children. In justifying that decision, he stated the reason for this inequality was that women workers and children performed tasks that were complementary to those performed by men. Where men and women performed at the same level and circumstances, the custom was for the two to be given the same wages.[18] Not only was women's work equated with child labor, but both were described as secondary to men's primary work. The basis for economic equality in the agricultural labor market was predicated on such ambiguous categories regarding the "same level of work" and, more important the "same circumstances"! It explained how and why the rural labor laws carried old disparities into the present[19] and also contradicted the modern constitutional commitment to equality irrespective of religion and gender.[20]

Official labor statistics that underreported women's economic participation contributed a new subordinate consciousness for rural and urban women. The statistics did not take into account the substantial amount of agricultural work that women did in the fields and at home, which was unpaid because it was family work. As a result, the labor statistics during this dynamic period reported a drop in women's contribution to the labor force from 6.8% in 1947 to 4.8% in 1960 and 4.2% in 1966.[21] These statistics played an important role in shaping rural and urban women's consciousness. They explained why peasant women did not classify the considerable work that they did as "work."[22] These statistics were also used to persuade urban women of the generosity of the postcolonial state to women as a group in spite of their negligible contribution to the economy. In this way, it discouraged continuing activism and the demand to deepen these rights.

In all these definitions of women's subordinate public (economic and political) roles, religion did not play any role. The only aspect of women's lives that was left in the hands of the religious establishment were the personal status laws that regulated marriage, divorce, and custody of children. It was the family that represented the sovereignty of the nation and its culture. In this arena, the very active modern state played a very minimal role. In contrast to a public domain which, in theory, supported the universal rights of all citizens, personal status laws were left to bear the marks of cultural difference and gender inequality. The National Charter, which served as a blueprint for the socialist transformation of society in 1962, described the "family, [as] the basic nucleus of society. It should be provided with all forms of protection to preserve national customs and to reproduce its [social] fabric."[23]

In the 1950s and the 1960s, the family denied women equal right to divorce and tolerated polygyny. While in Egypt polygyny was at best a marginal practice and institution, its legal retention served to highlight an important cultural sign of male privilege. The denial of women's equal right to divorce served to emphasize women's subordinate legal status in the family. The roles given to men and women in the familial arena were intended to represent the marks of cultural difference. When representatives of middle-class women approached Abdul Nasser in 1967 regarding the change of these laws which seemed anomalous in the new modern society, he suggested that they needed to approach the religious establishment, which had final say.

This laissez-faire attitude to the personal status laws was a major contrast to the way the secular state developed its own economic interpretations of Islam, incorporated in the National Charter. The Charter declared that material and spiritual forces were essential for the building of a healthy society. Religion provided a sense of social balance within the new Arab socialist society. On the whole, the Charter was opposed to those interpretations of religion used to block change and supported the progressive message of all religions especially Islam. It also declared itself committed to guaranteeing a belief in God common to all religions.[24]

In short, while the state did not hesitate to put religion in the service of its developmental project, it refrained from any similar effort in the area of personal status. It asked women in different families to bear the burden of representing the culturally specific social rules that established the autonomy of the nation.

The Challenge of the Secularist Discourse and the Politicization of Religion in the Public Arena (1967–1968)

The military defeat of Nasser's regime in the 1967 Six Day war represented a major turning point in the political legitimacy of the government's modern social and economic relations of power. The earliest and most dramatic signal of that change came in 1968 when the country was gripped by a very special religious event: the appearance of the Virgin Mary in a small church in the lower-middle-class suburb of al-Zaytun. Some secularists viewed the event as an irrational manifestation of mass hysteria.[25] The goal here, however, will be to discuss this event as part of Egyptian social and political history and how it represented the beginning of an important political development that paved the way to the evolution of the counter hegemonic Islamist discourse.

The reported sightings of the Virgin Mary took place a month after the regime had issued an important political document, *Bayan 31 Maris*, in which it reaffirmed its commitment to the building of a modern state where scientific planning, technology, the rule of law, and scientific socialism prevailed.[26] This was how the state was going to prepare to liberate Egyptian territories occupied by Israel.[27]

Yet the regime did not dissociate itself from the political spin given to it by the officials of the Coptic church. In a major press conference, the pope of the church, Kirolos VI, declared that the appearance of the Virgin Mary was a sign of divine support for the Egyptian public during its time of crisis and also for the effort to liberate Arab territories including Jerusalem.[28] In offering such a political interpretation of this special religious event, the pope was clearly giving religion and the religious establishment an expanded political role. True to form, the state was silent on matters that pertained to the spiritual domain. At the same time, it used its infrastructure for such activities as directing traffic and maintaining order in the area where people gathered to witness this religious event.

In many ways, this event marked the beginning of a new trend toward the politicization of religion in public life. Not a single analyst commented on the fact that the return to religion, as a source of political and social inspiration, took the gendered form of the Virgin Mary. There were two aspects of the gendered persona of the Virgin Mary which had resonance for the Egyptian public then. First, the representation of the spiritual well-being of the nation through a feminine figure was consistent with the way the National Charter highlighted the way women's role in the family helped the building of the nation.[29] For a wounded public that had lost 10,000 soldiers in the war, the appearance of this mother figure had a soothing and a consoling effect.

Second, most of the reports of the event did not refer to Mary as a "mother," but as "the virgin." In the relatively permissive heterosexuality that had developed in Egypt during the 1960s, the Virgin highlighted an older definition of femininity that some were afraid was being undermined by the rapid economic and social integration of women in the public arena. In support of this interpretation, I want to refer to an important exchange between President Nasser and Shaykh 'Ashur, a shaykh of an Alexandria mosque, during an emergency session of the Congress of the Arab Socialist Union. (The session was held in December 1968 to deal with the renewed student protests that demanded the court-martial of key figures responsible for the defeat in the 1967 war.) In this exchange, Shaykh 'Ashur demanded that the state use religion and women as markers of cultural difference in the public arena to correct its gendered public policies.

Shaykh 'Ashur argued that religious laws needed to regulate social behavior in public. As an example, he pointed out that women dressed in miniskirts had recently entered his mosque in Alexandria.[30] He was critical of both women's un-Islamic mode of dress and the fact that they were allowed into mosques. Nasser responded that he was not interested in limiting the [personal] liberties of Egyptians in the public arena. If he passed a law outlawing miniskirts, then the police would be interfering with women in the streets. This he found offensive. Instead, he suggested that the male heads of households lay down the social rules for their women.[31]

It was clear, however, that the secularist strategy employed by the postcolonial nation-state for sixteen years was under attack. Both the pope of the Coptic Church and Shaykh 'Ashur expressed a desire for a more active public role for religion. The pope suggested that the state use the appearance of the Virgin for the political mobilization of demoralized population. For Shaykh 'Ashur, the problem was not that religion was absent, but that its rules were not implemented by the state in the public arena or in the way women dressed and behaved publically. While Nasser remained adamantly opposed to these demands, later the Sadat regime allowed them greater public expression.

Second Republic and the Production of the Islamist Discourses on Modernity

The development of a political alliance between the Sadat regime and the Muslim Brotherhood in the 1970s distinguished his regime from that of his predecessor. As an expression of this political alliance, the regime amended the constitution twice: in 1976 to state

that the *sharia* (Islamic law) was one of the sources of legislation, and then in 1981 to declare that it was the *only* source of legislation. Because the latter formulation was turned
down by the High Constitutional Court in the 1980s, few civil laws were changed and no
new ones were passed that restricted or changed the universal rights of citizens in the public arena. It has been argued elsewhere that, in this way, the Egyptian state politically de-
mobilized the use of Islam as an oppositional tool and continued the practice of what
'Abdel Baki Hermassi described as de facto secularism.[32] Under both the Nasser and the
Sadat regimes, most economic and political policies were formulated without any reference to Islamic concepts and perspectives. Religion remained marginal to legislation, decision making, and adjudication — with the personal status laws as the only exception. In
other words, the postcolonial state, under Anwar al-Sadat, did not abandon Nasser's definition of the relationship between religious and cultural difference and the operation of
the nation-state.

A major political difference between the Nasser and Sadat regimes was that the latter
created a relatively legitimate institutional space for the Muslim Brotherhood and its political supporters. It freed its members from state prisons.[33] It gave their journal, *al-Da'wa*
(The Call) permission to be reissued.[34] Finally and most important, the state called on
members of the Brotherhood to challenge the Nasserist elements in all institutions of civil
society: student governments at different universities, faculty clubs and professional associations.[35] In this way, the previously discredited wing of the Egyptian middle class represented by the Brotherhood was politically rehabilitated.

The Brotherhood and its Islamist thinkers used the official tolerance of their activities
and views to develop a competing Islamist–modernist discourse that sought to address
this new middle-class audience whose consciousness had already been shaped by a modern educational system and professional training. This new discourse succeeded in persuading a majority of middle-class college women and working women to adopt the Islamic mode of dress as a visible sign of this attempted synthesis of Islam and modernity.[36]

Two other examples will illustrate the Islamist discourse on modernity. The first is
the earliest televised presentation of Shaykh Muhammed Metwali al-Sha'rawi, the religious television star and later minister of *Awqaf* (religious endowment) during the Sadat
years. The second example is shown by some of the published writings of Zeinab al-
Ghazali, the prominent and elderly Islamist figure. During the 1970s, both al-Sha'rawi
and al-Ghazali began a conscious use of the family institution to redefine the private and
public roles of men and women. They sought to make the very modern (middle-class)
nuclear family, with its stress on heterosexual intimacy, also Islamic. They addressed
themselves to the question of how men and women could manage this social institution,
whose limited social and financial resources presented them with new sources of pressure.
In the 1970s, women in these families were expected to work and also to take care of children, their households, and their husbands without the assistance of spouse or kin. Because men were no longer the sole breadwinners, they lost authority within the family,
leading to considerable confusion, tension, and conflict.

In response to these changing roles and pressures, Shaykh al-Sha'rawi and Zeinab
al-Ghazali suggested a return to domesticity. In their discussions of this institution, there
was a clear convergence of modernist and Islamic values and definitions of femininity and
masculinity that were used to socially regulate the behavior of men and women and to internalize discipline as part of a new Islamist–modernist consciousness. The strategy was to

give the modern, nuclear, middle-class family Islamic content in the definition of the private roles of men and women. This was very consistent with the nationalist discourse and its middle position between modernity and indigenous culture. It also still privileged the expression cultural difference within the family. Its goal, however, was to use the family and its private roles to redefine the roles that men and women played in the public economic and political spheres.

In one of his earliest appearances on state television in a popular TV program in 1973–1974,[37] Shaykh al-Shaʻrawi outlined to a largely secularist audience his view of women's status in Islam. As a starting point, he asserted that the human species was divided into two genders whose functional roles were different. Within each gender, members were equal (*mutasawun*) with one another.[38] While the differences between the two genders did not imply opposition or contradictions, the two could not be compared to one another. In other words, while men and women shared common preoccupations and tasks as members of the same species, they had different pursuits that set them apart.[39]

What were some of these common preoccupations? Freedom of belief, reason, and judgment were some of the concerns that women shared with men.[40] The female figures of the Quran offered good examples of these concerns. Balqis, queen of Sheba, demonstrated mature reasoning, plus political and diplomatic skills, in her negotiations with King Solomon. God chose women, just as he chose men, for religious inspiration. The Virgin Mary and Moses' mother were given important religious roles to play and they, in turn, became free believers in God. In contrast, the wives of Noah and Lot refused to believe in the religious messages of their time. Finally, Islamic law gave women freedom of property and freedom to choose important decisions that affected their lives.[41]

These shared tasks aside, the Quran clearly discouraged men and women from crossing the gender boundaries that separate them or the activities that distinguish one from the other. Those men who mimic women and those women who mimic men transgress gender boundaries, and for that reason they were damned by God.[42]

In his earliest formulation of an Islamist discourse that targeted secular middle-class women (who had TV sets then), Shaykh al-Shaʻrawi appealed to his audience by using the familiar language of individual liberties and rights, suggesting that they made important decisions and judgments about what to believe and why. The concept of and the right to equality, however, were deemed more problematic. One could speak of equality among members of the same gender, but not equality between genders. Yet, if women had an equal capacity for reason, why should they not be equal to men? In this demand for equality with men, women transgress divinely sanctioned gender boundaries and deserve God's wrath and damnation. Men, who transgress these boundaries by imitating women—a euphemistic reference to homosexual identities—were also damned.

Instead of dwelling on God's damnation, Shaykh al-Shaʻrawi chose to elaborate on the reasoning behind these gendered arrangements and order. As part of this discussion, he presented a romantic ideal of domesticity that was designed to appeal to the tired working women of the middle classes. According to his reading of the Quran, God created men for hard work[43] and struggle.[44] Women were created to minister to these tired hardworking men, providing them with rest, affection, and support.[45] This was their primary task. In fact, this care of men was more primary than their reproductive task.[46] Shaykh al-Shaʻrawi argued that this was not an easy task, but a full-time one.[47]

This argument represented a convergence between Islamic and modern discussions of the sexual division of labor that assigned women to the private (family) sphere and men to the public sphere. It presented an unflattering characterization of the public sphere in which men were engaged, hoping to discourage women from demanding integration. What was rather startling was the Islamist embrace of heterosexual (emotional) intimacy. Some analysts have argued that Shaykh al-Sha'rawi's views "concerning women and the family [were] strictly traditional and [were] actually quite representative of medieval Islamic thought".[48] But his discussion of Islamic heterosexuality was clearly not medieval. The medieval views treated heterosexuality as a powerful religious and social distracting force that distracted men and needed to be controlled and undermined.[49]

In al-Sha'rawi's reading, men needed to turn to women as the source of nurturance (*li taskunu 'ilayha*). Women have this gender-specific skill. He did not relate these skills to child rearing because that would have made men seem infantile. His discussion of heterosexual intimacy was premised on the loss of women's autonomy, as they addressed the needs of their husbands first and foremost and then to those of their children. This discussion of heterosexuality, and its definition of femininity as loss of autonomy were clearly modern. Shaykh al-Sha'rawi's presentation of both concepts as culturally Islamic, reinforced by Quranic verses, served to underline the Islamist (unconscious) preoccupation with the mediating function of his discourse. While he might not recognize heterosexuality as particularly modern, the characteristics he underlined in the discussion were different from medieval Islamic views and were part of the postcolonial modern culture that prevailed in Egypt in the 1970s.

Next, Shaykh al-Sha'rawi turned to child rearing as the other major gendered task of women. While the Quranic verses he referred to described child rearing within extended families with both spouses, children, and grandchildren present,[50] his discussion assumed that a mother was the single caretaker and, therefore, the model was a nuclear family. A mother's preoccupation with any other kind of work was described as leading to dependence on hired help (not a grandmother or other female kin, as would be the case in an extended family) and the loss of proper care during the crucial years. Because the public world was one in which men were preoccupied with objects that could be put in the service of the species, they were not fit for this role. In contrast, the female world was built around people, establishing its superiority.[51] This private world of the home also gave women these important skills. If you add to this the dependent nature of the human infant following birth, child rearing emerged as an important and noble task performed by women.[52]

While Islam did not forbid women to work, it required those who did to be motivated by necessity. Aspiring to a better living standard than that provided by the husband's income did not qualify as necessity. Devout women were those who accepted their husband's incomes as a basis for their lifestyle. They should not pressure their husbands to seek ways that would provide them with this alternative way of life, and they should not abandon their roles as wives and mothers in search of that goal. If they think they could perform this difficult juggling act (of being wife, mother, and working woman), they could take on public work provided it was framed by Islamic principles.[53] Their behavior in the public arena should be governed by the boundaries that Islam set for women and men, that is, women should not behave like men. They should be mindful of their temporary and subordinate role in these activities. They should also veil the marks of their gender difference.[54] In this way, Islamic society sought to protect men from temptation. In protecting men from seductive younger women, it secured the interest of men in their tired older wives.[55]

In short, numerous strategies of control were used to discourage women from public roles. Child rearing was presented as a valued activity in a hierarchy of work activities women could choose. Public work was ranked lowest and was largely a question of necessity, defined as providing basic needs—not bettering one's life. Not only should women not work for that purpose, but devout women should not pressure their husbands to provide them with more than what their incomes offer. If all this failed to discourage women from working, then let women take on public work provided they acknowledge their subordinate role in that arena. Outwardly, they should cover physical signs of their sexual difference. Curiously, this established the universal masculine character of the public arenas. The public expression of women's gender difference transformed them into what the medieval writers described as the temptresses of men. Finally, while public work was seen as degrading to women, Shaykh al-Sha'rawi described the housewives who spent their lives serving their husbands and children as an equally degraded (and old) lot whose husbands needed protection as a guarantee against desertion.

Zeinab al-Ghazali pursued similar themes in the articles she published in *Al-Da'wa* in the 1970s. Like Shaykh al-Sha'rawi, she concerned herself with heterosexual intimacy and especially what contributed to a "happy [Muslim] home." Her discussion was different from his in its very detailed discussion of the specifics of the relations between husband and wife. In this way, she opened these private relations to intense and close scrutiny as part of an Islamist–modernist domesticity: What should women share with their husbands? What should they not share? What should they wear? Where? Who should determine it? The result was at best an old-fashioned Egyptian ideal of heterosexual relations, and at worst a repressive heterosexuality that is very modern and controlling.

As part of her discussion of the building of a Muslim family, al-Ghazali emphasized the relations between husbands and wives as being central to a happy home. She offered her sisters the following advice that contributed to a stable and a secure family. If a woman was tired, she should not express those feelings. It was better to let your husband notice and come to the realization of how hard you work for him. A woman should also learn to minimize her own pain and not exaggerate its extent to a husband. In this minimal expression, you will get his consolation. At the same time, a woman should take into account all her husband's feelings (especially jealousy) to avoid conflict.[56]

A woman's home was the place where her personality was given expression. To earn love and respect, she should look after her house and take care of her responsibilities, which include cooking, child rearing, cleaning, and creating a beautiful environment. A wife was also responsible for her husband's comfort, serenity, and the good financial management of his income.[57]

A woman should select her female friends carefully. They should be respectable, virtuous, and well behaved. Their visits should be planned and useful. For example, one could use these visits to discuss religious readings on the family, male–female relations, and religious rituals. These were worthwhile and useful occupations for groups of women.[58]

If a wife had a secret or a problem, she should share it with her husband. Honesty and clarity were the guiding principles in relations between the spouses.[59] The affairs of the couple and their marital disagreements should not go beyond the couple. Any problems should be settled by the two and one should think a thousand times before consulting others. In the final analysis, a woman should stand by her husband. Any complaints a wife might have about her in-laws were unacceptable.[50]

Finally, a woman's dress at home should be determined by both the woman and her husband. Outside the home, a woman's mode of dress was totally up to the husband, provided it was within the boundaries set by God.[61]

This advice represented a serious attempt to preach the return to the old patriarchal family of al-Ghazali's youth in the 1930s. Women were to repress their feelings and minimize any pain they might feel and not share them with a husband. Al-Ghazali suggested that this was the best route to the approval of the spouse. This silent daily struggle for male recognition was a key part of a feminine consciousness. Conversely, a husband's feelings and needs were given full expression and attention. A woman's creative potential was invested in the home and especially in the service of a husband's desires.

This focus on the couple and their privacy was, of course, very modern and part of the operation of the nuclear family. Women in these families were isolated even from their women friends, with whom they were not supposed to share any secrets. The husband was the party with whom to share these secrets or problems. If the husband was the problem and wives were not supposed to burden their husbands with their feelings, then one had the familiar alienated middle-class wife.

The final symbol of this repressive Islamist–modern femininity was the role that men were to play to determine women's dress. Even in this area, men determine what women wear within and outside the house. The support of these patriarchal rights stops when a husband opposed the adoption of the Islamic mode of dress outside the home. This was the only instance in which al-Ghazali encouraged Muslim wives to disobey their husbands.

In another article, entitled "The Mother and the Building of a Good Human Being," al-Ghazali extended the same social logic to the discussion of mothering. She argued that the creation of a strong and solid basis upon which Islam could prosper required the cultivation of mothers who absorbed the costs (both personal and social) of this process and who knew their boundaries as part of nurturing the orders of God. In learning God's message and following in the footsteps of the Prophet, a mother set the basis of a strong household. Because a mother was a central figure in the lives of children and also their earliest love object, she could instill in their hearts the love of Islam and its rituals. She was also responsible for guiding their development into good and well-behaved Muslims.[62] For that reason, the development of a correct Islamic pedagogy and training designed to prepare Muslim mothers in the faith, its understanding, and its practice was a serious matter. It should be the primary concern of schools and colleges that provide highly qualified experts and contribute to the understanding and knowledge of the process.[63]

This, al-Ghazali informed her readers, behooves us to reconsider the basis of education and training in our schools, especially in girls' schools. Our imitation of the West had left us unconscious, without goals and understanding. A mother who grew up alienated from and ignorant of Islamic teaching could not provide the right education for the development of good children.[64]

The emphasis in this discussion of women's education was on another important role that they play in the family: child rearing. The starting point was a Muslim woman's desire to take on this difficult task as a service to her faith. Women were asked to absorb the personal and social costs of this process for the goal of a strong household. While women had been engaged in child rearing since the beginning of human society, al-Ghazali wanted their child rearing to be guided by scientific knowledge and training. Since girls' schools only existed at the primary, preparatory, and secondary levels, al-Ghazali wanted young girls to start this training for mothering very early. In this way the education system would be put more explicity and actively in the service of internalizing these gender roles. Science and professional knowledge were to be put in the service of an Islamic upbringing. This suggested the development of an education that was both Islamist and modern. Here, the mediating character of the nationalist secularist discourse was also a concern for that of its Islamist challenger. What they advocated in the educational arena was an attempt to represent gender and cultural difference and, in this way, influence some aspects of the kind of education young girls have in that public arena.

Conclusion

In this chapter, an attempt was made to examine the different strategies that the secularist and the Islamist discourses offered the postcolonial nation-state. Many secularists argue that an Islamist political triumph will spell the end of modernity. In addition to the polemical character of this claim, it ignores the fact that their dominant interpretation of modernity is not the only one available in public debate. The Islamists have their own interpretation of modernity. Conservative modern views of gender sit well with conservative Islamist views. For polemical purposes, they may not want to admit their acceptance of these modern views and definitions—especially in dealing with the family, where they claim to valorize the expression of cultural difference. In their discussion of an Islamic society, Islamists are unequivocal in declaring the importance of science, reason, professional education, and technology in the building of the new society. Since the Islamist groups and their discourses have been part of the historical development of modern society in Egypt, it is not surprising that the Islamist, oppositional, discourse is very modernist. It accepts the nuclear family and the modern systems of education and training as the basis of its alternative Islamic society.

Notes

1. Muhammed al-Ghazali, "Al-Janib al-Islami I," in *Munazarat Misr bayn al-Dawlah al-Diniyah wa al-Madaniyah* (Cairo: al-Dar al-Misriyah lil Nashr wa al-Tawzi', 1992), p. 14; Ma'mun al-Hudaybi, "Al-Janib al-Islami II," in *Munazarat Misr bayn al-Dawlah al-Diniyah wa al-Madaniyah* (Cairo: al-Dar al-Misriyah lil Nashr wa al-Tawzi', 1992), pp. 17–20.

2. Al-Hudaybi, p. 21.

3. Ma'mun al-Hudaybi, "Al-Janib al-Islami X," in *Munazarat Misr bayn al-Dawlah al-Diniyah wa al-Madaniyah* (Cairo: al-Dar al-Misriyah lil Nashr wa al-Tawzi', 1992), p. 73.

4. Muhammed Khalaf Allah, "Al-shu'ub wa al-'umam hiya masdar al-sulutat," in *Munazarat Misr bayn al-Dawlah al-Diniyah wa al-Madaniyah* (Cairo: al-Dar al-Misriyah lil Nashr wa al-Tawzi', 1992), pp. 25, 28.

5. Farag Fuda, "al-Janib al-'Almani IV," in *Munazarat Misr bayn al-Dawlah al-Diniyah wa al-Madaniyah* (Cairo: al-Dar al-Misriyah lil Nashr wa al-Tawzi', 1992), p. 39.

6. Michel Foucault, *Power/Knowledge* (New York: Pantheon, 1977).

7. Partha Chatterjee, *The Nation and Its Fragments: Colonial and Postcolonial Histories* (Princeton: Princeton University Press, 1993), p. 17.

8. *Ibid.*, p. 10.

9. *Ibid.*, p. 26.

10. *Ibid.*, p. 36.

11. Duriya Shafiq, *Al-Mar'ah al-Misriyah* (Cairo: Matba'at Misr, 1955), pp. 255–261; "Ta'lif al-Itihad al-Misri al-'Amm lil Hay'at al-Nisa'iyah," *Al-Ahram* (January 1, 1956), p. 3.

12. Mervat Hatem, "Economic and Political Liberalization in Egypt and the Demise of State Feminism," *International Journal of Middle East Studies* 24 (1992): 231–251.

13. Markaz al-Abhath wa al-Dirasat al-Sukkaniyah, *Al-Mar'ah al-Misriyah fi 'Ishrin 'Am: 1952–1972* (Cairo: Markaz al-Abhath wa-al-Dirasat al-Sukkaniyah, 1972), p. 77.

14. Elizabeth Warnock Fernea and Basima Qattan Bezirgan, "Introduction," in *Middle Eastern Muslim Women Speak*, ed. Elizabeth Warnock Fernea and Basima Qattan Bezirgan (Austin: University of Texas Press, 1977), p. xxxiii; Nikki Keddie and Lois Beck, "Introduction," in *Women in the Muslim World*, ed. Lois Beck and Nikki Keddie (Cambridge, Mass.: Harvard University Press, 1978), pp. 16–17.

15. Hekmat Abou Zeid, Fathia Soliman, Karima al-Said, and Ahmad Khaki, *The Education of Women in the U.A.R during the 19th and 20th Centuries* (Cairo: National Commission for UNESCO, 1971), p. 39.

16. Ahmed Taha Muhammad, *Al-Mar'ah al-Misriyah bayn al-Madi wa-al-Hadir* (Cairo: al-Matb'at al-Dar al-Ta'lif, 1979), p. 82.

17. Majmu'at al-Muhtamat bi Shu'n al-Mar'ah al-Misriyah, *Al-Huquq al-Qanuniyah lil Mar'ah al-Misriyah bayn al-Nazariyah wa al-Tatbiq* (Cairo: n.p, 1988), p. 16.

18. Wizarat al-Irshad al-Qawmi, *Dawr al-Mar'ah fi al-Jumhuriyah al-Arabiyah al-Muttahidah* (Cairo: Maslahat al-'Isti'lamat, n.d), p. 33.

19. Amina Shafiq, *Al-Mar'ah Lan Ta'ud 'ila al-Bayt* (Cairo: Dar al-Thaqafah al-Jadidah, 1987), pp. 17–18.

20. Hatem, "Economic and Political Liberalization in Egypt," p. 232.

21. Wadad Morcos, *Sukkan Misr* (Cairo: Markaz al-Buhuth al-'Arabiyah, 1988), p. 42.

22. Mona Abaza, *The Changing Image of Women in Rural Egypt* (Cairo: The American University in Cairo, 1987), p. 60; Soheir Morsy, "Rural Women, Work and Gender Ideology: A Study in Egyptian Political Economic Transformation," in *Women in Arab Society*, ed. S. Shami, L. Taminian, S. Morsy, Z.B El Bakri, and E. Kameir (Paris: UNESCO, 1990), pp. 122–123.

23. *Al-Mithaq wa-Taqriruhu* (Cairo: Dar wa-Matabi'ah al-Sha'b, 1968), p. 106.

24. *Ibid.*, pp. 160–162.

25. Sadik Jalal al-'Azm, *Naqd al-Fikr al-Dini* (Beirut: Dar al-Tali'ah, 1982).

26. 'Adil Hamoudah, *Al-Hijrah 'ila al-'Unf* (Cairo: Sinah lil Nashr, 1987), p. 100.

27. *Ibid.*, p. 100.

28. *Ibid.*, p. 99.

29. *Al-Mithaq*, p. 217.

30. Hamoudah, *Al-Hijrah 'ila al-'Unf*, p. 101.

31. *Ibid.*. p. 102.

32. Mervat F. Hatem, "Egyptian Discourses on Gender and Political Liberalization: Do Secularist and Islamic Views Really Differ?," *The Middle East Journal* 48 (4) (Autumn 1994): 664–665.

33. Omar al-Tilmisani, *Dhikrayat . . . La Mudhakkarat* (Cairo: Dar al-Tawzi' wa al-Nashr al-Islamiyah, 1985), p. 223.

34. *Ibid.*, p. 189.

35. *Ibid.*, p. 126.

36. Mervat Hatem, "Egypt's Middle Class in Crisis: the Sexual Division of Labor," *The Middle East Journal* 42 (3) (Summer 1988): 407–422.

37. Ahmad Farrag, "Introduction," in Shaykh Mohammed Metwali al-Sha'rawi, *Al-Qada' wa al-Qadar* (Cairo: Dar al-Shuruq, 1974), pp. 5-7.

38. Shaykh Mohamed Metwali al-Sha'rawi, "Makanat al-Mar'ah fi al-Islam," in *Al-Qadh' wa al-Qadar* (Cairo: Dar al-Shuruq, 1975), p. 157.

39. *Ibid.*, p. 160.

40. *Ibid.*, p. 165.

41. *Ibid.*, p. 169.

42. *Ibid.*, p. 161.

43. *Ibid.*, p. 170.

44. *Ibid.*, p. 171.

45. *Ibid.*

46. *Ibid.*, pp. 171–172.

47. *Ibid.*

48. Barbara Freyer Stowasser, "Religious Ideology, Women and the Family: The Islamic Paradigm," in *The Islamic Impulse*, ed. Barbara Freyer Stowasser (London: Croom Helm, 1987), p. 284.

49. Fatima Mernissi, *Beyond the Veil* (New York: Schenkman, 1975), pp. 4, 14.

50. *Ibid.*, p. 172.

51. *Ibid.*, p. 173.

52. *Ibid.*

53. *Ibid.*, p. 179.

54. *Ibid.*, p. 183.

55. *Ibid.*, p. 186.

56. Zeinab al-Ghazali, "Al-Tariq 'ila al-Sa'ada," in *Al-Da'iya Zeinab al-Ghazali: Masirat Jihad wa Hadith min al-Dhikrayat min Khilal Kitabatiha*, comp. Ibn al-Hashimi (Cairo: Dar al-I'tisam, 1989), p. 75.

57. *Ibid.*

58. *Ibid.*

59. *Ibid.*, p. 76.

60. *Ibid.*

61. *Ibid.*

62. Zeinab al-Ghazali, "Al-'Umm wa Bina' al-'Insan al-Salih", in *Al-Da'iya Zeinab al-Ghazali: Masirat Jihad wa Hadith min al-Dhikrayat min Khilal Kitabatiha*, comp. Ibn al-Hashimi (Cairo: Dar al-I'tisam, 1989), p. 77.

63. *Ibid.*, p. 78.

64. *Ibid.*

Women and the State in Jordan

Inclusion or Exclusion?

The modern state of Jordan has made great development strides since the days of the Amirate (1921–1950), the second Palestinian influx (1967), and the oil boom (1973). When placed in regional context, and when viewed against the background of the resources with which Jordan is endowed, the development is all the more impressive. Nonetheless, the country still faces severe poverty and unemployment—increasingly so since the economic crisis of 1988–1989. One set of problems concerns the status and development achievements of Jordanian women.

Jordanian women's discussions of their status often begin with, "The Jordanian woman has made great strides in the last several decades." The analysis that follows does not dispute that statement. Nor does it dispute that, when placed in regional context, Jordanian women exceed some of their other Arab counterparts in various achievement categories. The intent here is to examine the development of the status of Jordanian women over the years as a function of the state and societal context in which it has taken place. This chapter will argue that the historical evolution of the Jordanian state has played a central role in shaping the political, economic, and social opportunities and constraints Jordanian women face. One of the major constraints is the fact that existing national legislation and societal practice continue to reinforce women's exclusion from certain spheres, thus underpinning a general condition of second-class citizenship.

First, a short history of the kingdom will present some of the key developments and factors that have shaped state formation. The discussion will then proceed to sketch a brief picture of Jordanian women's status in the *badia*,[1] rural, and urban areas. It will then turn to considerations of Islam and the state, women's place in legislation, women's participation in the workforce, and their access to education. These sections provide concrete examples of the impact the country's specific development path has on women. They also reveal implicit assumptions that underlie the government's policy (or lack of explicit policy) toward women. The final section reviews the history of the Jordanian women's movement as a case study of the relationship between women and the state. Throughout the paper it will be argued that the state has pursued policies of inclusion and exclusion of various types which, whether consciously so constructed or not, have nonetheless served to maintain various forms of patriarchal control.

The Development of the Jordanian State

Transjordan was established as a link in the British imperial defense line, an arc that extended from Egypt across the Fertile Crescent to Iraq and into the Persian Gulf. Britain was responsible for placing the first monarch, the Amir 'Abdallah, on the throne and then, through substantial yearly subsidies, keeping the state apparatus solvent.[2] Transjordan's role in regional security was further reinforced as a result of the Palestinian–Israeli conflict and the outbreak of the Arab–Israeli war in 1948. The fact that the war ended in separate armistice agreements and not a full peace settlement meant that, thenceforth, Jordan faced the ongoing possibility of war from the west. This new national security concern provided an additional reason for the leadership to continue to focus on the development of a strong military force. The importance of the security forces was reinforced by the reality that Western nations (as well as some Arab states) counted on Jordan to serve as a buffer between Israel and the rest of the Arab East and, by extension, the Gulf. These states depended on Jordan to insulate them from the forces of "revolutionary" pan-Arabism or Palestinian nationalism. Thus, depending on the time period, the United States, Saudi Arabia, Kuwait, and others have provided military and budgetary assistance to the kingdom to support its buffer function.

The role of the military in the evolution of the Jordanian state takes on additional importance if one considers the patterns of armed forces' recruitment.[3] The basis for the earliest forces established by the British were the powerful Bedouin tribes of the southern part of the country. Such recruitment filled the ranks of the military and security apparatus and provided a key means by which these tribes were incorporated into the state. This cooptation, or establishment of patron–client ties between the tribes and the leadership, was a central element in building a legitimacy formula for 'Abdallah.

Numerous studies have shown women to be adversely affected by state policies that underpin or reinforce a strong military. Peterson and Runyan write:

> Most male-dominated societies have constructed elaborate sanctions and even taboos against women's fighting and dying in war. As a result, men have gained almost exclusive control over the means of destruction worldwide, often in the name of protecting women and children, who are either discouraged from or not allowed to take up arms to protect themselves.[4]

In Jordan, as in other Middle Eastern countries, women have been recruited into the security services, but in clerical, not fighting, roles. More important than this marginal female presence in the security forces is the fact that the military as an institution plays a role in reproducing gendered notions of the two sexes. This means that men must act as "men"—meaning being willing to kill and die on behalf of the state and thus prove their manhood. But the structure also demands that women behave as "women." This requires that they be properly subservient to the needs of the military and the men who serve in it, thus reinforcing traditional notions of appropriate gender roles.[5] While the Jordanian state has provided well for the men who serve in its military, including offering benefits that improve the lot of the entire family, there is no question that the focus on the military over the years has led to less of an emphasis on investment in crucial social welfare projects, projects that generally tend to benefit women.[6]

With an average of more than 50% of state spending directed toward the military and public security over the years, it is clear that Jordan's security role has been a major factor shaping its economic development, whether in terms of attracting subsidies from abroad or in determining patterns of domestic spending and investment. One key result has been the development of a reliance on external sources of income, rather than a vibrant domestic economy, for sustenance and growth. Some of the subsidies that Jordan received for its regional buffer role were not specifically earmarked for the military; even those that were not, however, went directly to the state, leading to a bloating of the state sector. This focus on the state sector had additional import for women, for the lack of attention to developing the private sector has been one factor that has retarded the development of industry. In other regions, such as Latin America, the emergence of industries has been an important step in drawing women into the workforce outside the home. While it is understood that such incorporation has often led to wage exploitation, it has, nonetheless, made women frequent and accepted actors in the public sphere.

There is yet another negative implication of this kind of development for women. Beginning with 'Abdallah and continuing with Hussein, state subsidies as well as state employment (often in the army) were used as a means of cooptation or reinforcing loyalty, and they were generally directed at Jordan's tribes. In addition to building support for the state, such practices by extension strengthened the role of the shaykh, tribal structure, and tribal law. As we shall see, the continuation of the state's support for the tribes and its tolerance of traditional law (*'urf*) as opposed to civil law, has had a negative effect upon women's inclusion as full citizens in the kingdom.

Turning to the other communal group in Jordan, the large post-1948 Palestinian population, some Palestinian elite families threw their lot in with 'Abdallah and came to constitute an important political and commercial basis—as opposed to security force basis—of the regime. There was no parallel attempt by the state to develop a clientalistic relationship with the vast majority of Palestinians as there was with Transjordanians.[7] However, it is worth noting that the Palestinians who lived in the refugee camps of the East and West banks generally related to the state through a network of village headmen (*mukhtars*), the traditional authority structure transplanted from Palestine. Similar to the impact state patronage had on tribal shaykhs, these leaders' positions were further reinforced by the services that were channeled to the camps (food rations, health care, education) by the United Nations Relief and Works Agency for Palestine Refugees in the Near East (UNRWA).[8] Thus, agents external to the communities (whether the state or nongovernmental organizations, NGOs) used existing (or reconstituted) authority structures that strengthened the positions of these traditional leaders and structures regarding matters implicitly deemed to fall outside the realm of state concern. In other words, the structures that had prime influence and control over women were kept in place and not made accountable to the state on issues concerning the sphere most closely associated with women.

There are several final points to be made about state formation that have relevance to the discussion of the status of women in the kingdom. The first is that, given the circumstances of the Palestinians' forced inclusion into the Jordanian state, they (and particularly the refugee camp dwellers) were often regarded as a potential internal security threat. This fear was confirmed in 1970 with the outbreak of fighting between the Jordanian army and the Palestinian guerrillas. Following the civil war, Palestinians argue (and there is reason to believe it), the government initiated a policy of preferential recruitment of East Bankers into the bureaucracy. What developed as a result was an intercommunal division of labor, with the Transjordanians even more closely associated with the state, and the Palestinians therefore left to the private sector.[9] This certainly reinforced and gave additional structure to the sense of second-class citizenship felt by Palestinians, thus rendering female Palestinian citizens the second-class among the second-class when it came to dealing with the state.

Second, with the exception of a brief period of political liberalization in the mid-1950s, Jordan's history until 1989 was one of continuing, if varying, levels of repression against political organizing and expression. In this regard, women's activity was subject to the same harassments as men's activity (although we shall explore the differential impact later). During most of this period, the state consciously fought the emergence of or gradually coopted what are generally referred to as civil society institutions: political parties, labor unions, professional associations, women's unions, and the like.[10]

To sum up, within the context of an embattled civil society and an expansive bureaucratic apparatus, the state reinforced preexisting authority structures, which were clearly patriarchal in nature, and left them to deal with the issues of the so-called private sphere. Given the nature of Jordanian society with its limited participation by women in activity outside the realm of the family, this meant that issues related to women (and children), were largely left to the realm of the personal status law, derived from *sharia*, or 'urf. Most of the remaining legislation that affects women applies only to those who have entered the work force as we shall see, a small number indeed. This exclusion of women's concerns from the areas in which the state directly interferes through legislation has led to their exclusion from many of the rights and much of the protection afforded men.[11]

Women and Society

Even though Jordan is a small country, it is not possible to discuss Jordanian women as a single, undifferentiated category. As in other societies, women may be divided according to socioeconomic status, region of origin, religion, place of residence (town or village), communal affiliation, and so on. Because so little published work deals with Jordanian women, what follows is a brief sketch of some of the salient differences, based largely on the only complete book available on Jordanian women, authored by writer, social researcher, and activist Suhayr al-Tall.[12]

al-Tall divides her analysis into three categories: Bedouin women, village women, and urban women. While the proportion of Bedouins is small in comparison with Jordan's total population, al-Tall begins with a discussion of them, perhaps because Bedouin society constitutes a mythical ideal for many Arabs. Bedouin culture stresses the concepts of honor and gallantry. It also calls for the protection of women, on the one hand, because they are seen as weak and, on the other, because they bear the offspring. A woman's status is in part a function of the tribe to which she belongs and her lineage in it, but in the end her position derives from her production of male children. Only boys "count" as children,[13] and women who do not produce male offspring are subject to divorce.

In customary law, a woman does not have the right to accept or refuse a proposed suitor (except in rare cases related to her socioeconomic position). Her dowry, usually money, land, or animals, goes entirely to her father. Women can be easily divorced for reasons of appearance or personality. On the other hand, they cannot demand divorce, although they may flee the house of the husband and may be able to secure a divorce if an appeal is made to a shaykh. In the event of divorce the father is awarded the children and the mother may be forbidden access to them.[14]

Perhaps the most central concept associated with women is that of honor or *sharaf*. Maintaining sharaf requires that a woman be a virgin at the time of her marriage and that there never be any hint of impropriety in her behavior with men.[15] While it is the woman's behavior that maintains sharaf in the first instance, nonetheless, preservation of family honor is seen as a male responsibility, which requires that a woman whose honor is questioned be killed by a male family member. Such a murder, aimed at restoring family honor, is called an honor crime (*jarimat al-sharaf*) and generally results in a light prison sentence. On the other hand, if a woman should be killed in a non-honor crime, the blood money (*diyya*) is four or eight times what it would be for a man. And if, while she is pregnant, she is exposed to injury that triggers a miscarriage, the diyya for the fetus is that of a full man. Again, these practices involve several implicit assumptions about women: their primary worth as deriving from their reproductive power; their presumed weakness; and that their families and not they themselves bear responsibility for their actions.[16]

In the rural areas, women are a critical element in the agricultural workforce, but, like their Bedouin counterparts, they generally lack decision-making power. In rural society responsibility for supporting the family and making decisions belongs to men. In the villages, most women—married and unmarried—engage in unpaid labor for the family, often in the fields. As elsewhere, this activity is neither acknowledged by most rural dwellers as constituting "work," nor is it computed as such in national statistics. Instead, a woman's worth derives from two things: her chastity and her production of male children. Here again, honor is critical: a father, husband, or brother has the right to kill a woman if there is a hint of dishonor or improper behavior. Fathers also have a great deal of control over their children's lives in other areas. Young women often have no say in the selection of a marriage partner, while a boy may have some say. Marriages are usually arranged between the families, often at the time of a child's birth.[17]

Finally, there are the urban areas, and Amman in particular, in which more than half the population lives. It is difficult to generalize about the cities, for they contain members of all social classes as well as recent arrivals from the badia and the countryside. Nonetheless, one can say that while the badia and the rural areas are Jordan's poorest and often most overlooked in terms of basic services such as schools and health clinics, in general women in the cities have access to a range of services that nonurban women do not. The percentage of girls and young women in all levels of schooling is higher, infant survival rates are greater, and the percentage of women in the paid labor force outside the home is higher. Having said that, despite the very modern and even Westernized feel to the capital in particular, al-Tall stresses that the many economic and social changes Amman and its residents have undergone have not altered the basic importance of tribal (*'asha'iri*) values discussed at the beginning of this section.[18]

Islam and the State

Jordan's population is more than 90% Sunni Muslim and, as a result, Islam has been responsible for shaping certain aspects of Jordanian society and the Jordanian state. As with any religion, however, the nature and practice of Islam varies from country to country, and in Jordan several factors have been central in shaping Islam's role. The first is that the royal family traces its lineage to the prophet Muhammad. This has helped to legitimize Hashemite rule and to lead the Islam practiced by the royal family to "set the tone" for Islam in the kingdom more broadly. Perhaps the result of the philosophy of King Hussein and the family members themselves, perhaps partly in reaction against religious practice in Saudi Arabia, Jordan's powerful neighbor to the east, the kingdom has been characterized by an Islam of tolerance and moderation. Hussein himself has long demonstrated what one may call a quiet but clear piety in his personal style and behavior.

This approach has then been reflected more broadly in state behavior and policies. The Christian minority has traditionally been disproportionately represented among the circles of advisors and have generally viewed the monarchy as a protector of their position. Throughout the years of his reign, Hussein has also maintained a relationship of peaceful coexistence with (and at times outright encouragement of) the Muslim Brotherhood. This relationship has been unique in the Arab world: the Brotherhood was allowed relative freedom to engage in its sociopolitical work in exchange for not challenging the regime. Not until the beginning of peace talks with Israel in the fall of 1991 did the regime and the Islamists have serious political disagreement, and even on this issue, most Islamists have preferred to behave as loyal opposition.

On occasion, when the image or practice of moderation has been challenged, the king or, by extension, his government, has stepped in. The king himself was instrumental in preventing the notorious Toujan Faysal apostasy case from going to trial,[19] and the cabinet or parliament has turned back a number of attempts to implement more conservative policies championed by the Islamists in parliament, including laws aimed at sex segregation in various educational and recreational institutions and programs, and laws outlawing alcohol. Institutional expressions of the moderation of the Hashemites may be found in the establishment of Al al-Bayt University, which is intended to promote a tolerant Islam and encourage interfaith understanding, and the Royal Institute for Interfaith Studies, under the patronage of Crown Prince Hasan.

In this context, and given that women's status in the Arab world is generally attributed to Islam, how should one then interpret the present status of women in Jordan? The discussion here does not deny the importance of Islam to legislation and to more general societal mores in the kingdom which affect women and their status. Nevertheless, understanding the place of women in any Islamic society requires an examination of the interaction of a complex set of factors, of which Islam is only one. Over time, any religion is interwoven with or conditioned by the structures and traditions of the society into which it is introduced. As will be noted in the discussion of law, not just sharia, but also 'urf (traditional tribal or village law) plays a key role in Jordan. The state's reliance on the tribes, and its cultivation of them through the provision of various forms of patronage, has strongly reinforced the importance of tribal values and norms in Jordanian society, whether they are actually codified in law or not. Neither the state nor the Islamists have sought to exorcise the impact of 'urf from Jordanian law. Indeed, many average Jordanians do not distinguish between sharia and 'urf, instead believing that all current practice is demanded by Islam. In the case of women's status this conflation or confusion is most dangerous on the question of sharaf and honor killings, which, contrary to many people's beliefs, have no basis in Islam.

A number of scholars today, some of them Muslim feminists, have attempted to reconstruct through historical and textual analysis an original Islam by stripping Islam, as it is presently practiced, of the influence of external factors and developments that occurred following the life of the Prophet. The argument is that Islam has been hijacked by patriarchy to oppress women and that the earliest Islam in fact represented progress for women.[20] Another trend argues for reopening the "door of independent interpretation" (*bab al-ijtihad*), clearing the way for reinterpreting the Quran's message in light of present-day considerations. Such writers are by no means all feminists, but one area that would certainly be affected by the possibilities of a contextual rather than unchanging interpretation of the sources of Islamist law would be women's status.[21] To date, however, proponents of both trends continue to represent a small minority, and their potential for greater influence is highly uncertain. Moreover, given the importance of patriarchy in influencing religion's view of the role of women, such innovations in religious interpretation alone would likely be insufficient to force major change.

Women and the Law

Legislation (and its implementation) is the instrument through which intended state policy on most issues is most clearly revealed, and gender is no exception. The Jordanian constitution states that all citizens are equal under the law in terms of rights and responsibilities. Nevertheless, it bars only race, language, and religion as bases of discrimination; sex is not mentioned. Women have witnessed[22] some important changes in recent years; indeed, The National Charter (issued in 1991) made explicit reference to equality before the law regardless of sex. Nevertheless, in numerous laws women's rights are unprotected or underprotected. Relevant provisions of these laws are reviewed here, followed by an overall analysis.

The Citizenship Law states that all Jordanian men and women are entitled to citizenship; nonetheless, only a man can automatically pass his citizenship on to his children. A foreign woman who marries a Jordanian national can obtain citizenship after three years if she is an Arab and after five years if not; however, there is no provision for a non-Jordanian male to obtain citizenship as a result of marrying a Jordanian woman. In a similar vein, women have no automatic right to a passport of their own. They, along with children, may obtain separate passports only with the agreement of their husband (or father).

In the realm of social security, the retirement age for men is sixty years and for women fifty-five years, and widows and widowers have different rights to the pension of a deceased spouse. For a man to receive his wife's pension he must be no longer working (incapable of work), but for the woman there is no such condition.[23] Similar themes may be found in the Retirement Law. A man may retire after twenty years of service, a woman after fifteen. A woman who resigns can withdraw what she has put into her pension, but a man cannot. A retired woman receiving a pension who then loses her husband cannot receive two pensions: she will receive only the larger of the two. In the same way, the payment of a retirement pension to wives or daughters of a deceased employee stops if they marry, but can begin again if they are widowed or divorced. If they subsequently remarry, the pension stops permanently. If a woman employee receives a pension for her own work, she does not lose it if she marries; however, if she dies, her dependents can continue to receive her pension only if they can demonstrate need and that she was directly responsible for them.[24] In a related field, health insurance, it was not until a late 1993 change in the law ordered by the Minister of Health that children were eligible for health insurance through their working mothers. Before the approval of this amendment, children could be insured only through their fathers, despite the fact that their mothers worked and were insured.[25]

The Labor Law, before it was amended in 1995, was singled out for special criticism by women. In general, and as will be discussed in a later section, there is wage discrimination between men and women in the private sector (the state sector has established levels and ranks) and there is no minimum wage. There is also differential application of laws depending upon whether one is employed in a regulated establishment (one with five workers or more) or an unregulated one (those with less than five workers). In these latter institutions, many protections afforded by the law are not applicable.[26]

The law forbade women and children to work in certain jobs, but there were no comparable provisions for men. The labor law also ruled out certain work hours (7 P.M. to 6 A.M.) for both women and children, in the absence of special circumstances. In benefits, women were entitled to three weeks of leave before and after childbirth. The first three were at her discretion, but she was not permitted to work until three weeks after childbirth, and this time was taken at half pay. Any institution with more than thirty female employees had to provide a child-care room for children under age six, but the law gave women no nursing time. Again, these laws applied only to regulated institutions, thus leaving many women without such benefits.[27] Certain positive changes were introduced into the law in 1995 that dealt with the right to nursing time and extended maternity leave, but it has not been enforced.[28] However, despite the improvement that some of the proposed changes represent, there continues to be no clear statement regarding wage or employment equality between men and women. Nor is there an affirmation of a right to equal or comparable wages.

The Civil Status Law is perhaps the most *implicitly* sexist law. Important parts of this law relate to the family book (*daftar al-'a'ila*), which is needed for almost all official state transactions. At her marriage a woman is transferred from her father's daftar to that of her husband. However, if she is divorced or if her husband should leave and take the document with him, there is no possibility of her being issued a daftar even if she has become the actual head of household. This is a major problem for a number of reasons. Without the family book one cannot vote or be a candidate (and with it, a husband can register the entire family in whatever district he chooses). Without the daftar, women cannot obtain food assistance to which their families are entitled, nor can they register their children in school, in the university, or for civil service jobs. For a woman who, through death or divorce, is "separated" from a daftar, the only solution is for the woman to reregister on the daftar of her father or brother. However, sometimes this is not practical (if the family members are living and working overseas) or possible (if the male family member is deceased).[29]

The Personal Status Law, on the other hand, is perhaps the most *explicitly* sexist. It continues to allow polygamy and arbitrary divorce as permitted by long-standing interpretation of the sharia. It makes it much easier for men to obtain a divorce than for women—women must request a special clause in their marriage contract for such a right—and the law requires men to pay support to divorced wives for only one year, which can cause great hardship. However, the real problem here is that what few protections are included in the law are often not realized in practice. Indeed, many women complain bitterly about this law, but insist that its proper implementation, sexist as it is, would nonetheless improve their lot. This is especially true when it comes to arbitrary divorce (women often cannot obtain the compensation their contract provided for, including support for children), or inheritance cases (in which women are generally coerced into giving up their rightful shares to their brothers).

Finally, there is the Punishments Law. This piece of legislation is generally not mentioned by women's groups in their discussions of the need for legal reform. The most blatant discrimination between men and women according to tradition lies in crimes related to honor. While men who catch their wives or female family members committing fornication or even illegally being with men, and react by killing them, are entitled to sentences lighter than for murder under other circumstances, the reverse is not true for a woman who finds her husband in such a situation and reacts in the same way. However, Jordanian law stipulates that a woman (and her partner) found guilty of fornication can be sentenced to between six months and two years. The same sentence applies to a husband who has a girlfriend (that is, if he has been committing adultery publicly and regularly). The girlfriend receives the same penalty.[30] (These last two sentences for women are predicated, of course, upon their not being killed by their families for such honor violations).

This cursory examination of Jordanian legislation reveals several clear themes in the relationship between women and the state. One is that of the need to protect women, presumably because they are weaker or more easily exploited, but certainly because of their central childbearing role. Exemplary of this theme are the provisions that women may retire at an earlier age and after having worked fewer years than men, that women can always take out of the pension fund whatever contributions they made, and that women and children are forbidden from working at certain jobs and during certain hours. A second, more cynical interpretation of these laws, as well as several others, is that women are in effect being treated as minors, as if they belonged in the same category as children. For example, women, like children, cannot obtain a passport of their own unless they have their husband's (or father's) permission. Moreover, they must always be carried on the daftar of a male family member and they, like unmarried children, must be included in a family with a male as head of household.

This point leads into the third clear message of these laws: that economic, political, and social control rests with male family members and that only men can be recognized as heads of households, responsible for supporting the family. The failure to guarantee even in the text of the Labor Law (as opposed to implementation) a woman's right to equal pay for equal work derives, as others have pointed out, from the implicit assumption that a woman does not need to work or does not need as high a salary because she is also being supported by her husband. The corollary to this is that men need higher salaries because it is assumed that they support an entire family and women do not.[31] There is also inheritance law practice, which fails to enforce the sharia stipulation that a woman receives half of her brother's share. The sharia provision certainly presumed that women would be taken care of by their male relatives and therefore did not need as much inheritance. That alone puts women at the mercy of their male relatives and leaves them at a disadvantage in accumulating an independent source of savings. Worse is the fact that in practice women often inherit nothing at all, persuaded or intimidated by family members not to let the wealth "leave the family" (that is, potentially go to *her husband's* children—note the irony of the phrase). Judges in Jordan were all male (until the appointment of the first woman judge in May 1996) and, according to oral testimony, are unlikely to examine a woman's verbal or written statement regarding relinquishing inheritance and questioning whether it resulted from coercion or insufficient information regarding her rights.

Some of the provisions of these laws may be viewed from another angle as well. By taking the philosophy that "only a male can be head of household and provider" to its logical conclusion, the state saves money. (How much, is not clear.) This is accomplished through the construction of many of the provisions of the Retirement Law and other social welfare laws, which are then applied based on a citizen's personal status, not his or her employment service status. For example, a man cannot automatically receive his wife's pension. Women and children lose the pension of the husband or father if they (re)marry (thus transferring responsibility for their care to another man). Until 1993, children could not receive health care through their mothers. In all these cases, not only is the implicit assumption of male as provider upheld, but in so doing citizens of both sexes are also deprived of the right to funds that should have been theirs on the basis of years served. Given Jordan's heavy dependence on external sources of income and perennial budget balancing woes, this aspect of these laws cannot be coincidental and should not be overlooked.

Another more basic theme found in some of the provisions mentioned here and explicit in others is that women are not full citizens in Jordan. Unlike men, women cannot give their nationality to their children and, as already noted, they have no right to separate passports without the approval of their male "guardian," be he husband or father. A woman also has no right to a daftar, even if it is clear that she is in fact head of household. Women simply cannot be considered heads of household in Jordan, no matter what the reality of the family situation is. The fact that the husband or father holds the daftar may very well impinge on their access to state services, not to mention ability to vote or vote freely. Moreover, women's access to state justice is severely circumscribed, since in matters of greatest sensitivity and importance—divorce, child support, inheritance, equality in the work place, and protection from family violence—they face male judges who are overwhelmingly committed to the discriminatory status quo.

Finally, and bluntly, women cannot be considered full citizens in a country in which, regardless of the number of such incidents, they can be killed with relative impunity, and with little or no evidence, simply on the grounds of suspicion of loss of honor. Male family members who are underage are often chosen to commit the honor crime—the murder—of their female relative because the family knows they are even less likely to receive severe sentences. In many cases, these women are victims twice: first they are victims of rape or incest, then they are made the ultimate victims to "cleanse the family honor."[32] It is a practice shared by both Palestinian and Transjordanian communities, and while it tends to be concentrated in the lower socioeconomic strata it is by no means limited to them. More important, however, those who are educated and in a position to outlaw such practices are reluctant to "intrude" into this "private" sphere of family life through legislation which would implicitly challenge some of the most basic forms of societal control over women.

Women and Work

Participation in the labor force is often used as an important indicator of women's status. In Jordan, the statistics show a small but growing percentage of women working outside the home. In 1972, the number of women in the labor force was 27,000 (out of 369,000 of working age); in 1979 it was 31,000 (out of 456,000); and in 1990, 113,000 (out of 846,000). The number of those actually employed was 25,000 in 1972; 27,000 in 1979; and 79,000 in 1990.[33] On the other hand, unemployment among women was 5.9% in 1972, 11.7% in 1979, and 30.6% in 1990, the last figure indicating both a general increase in unemployment in the country and the large numbers of women attempting to enter the workforce.[34] Clearly, women's labor force participation rates are low in the kingdom, but, the official statistics are problematic as well. For example, most statistics do not include women's work in agriculture, particularly if it is non-wage labor on a family farm. In keeping with the prevailing "liberal" economic view of what constitutes "work," such women—as well as others who engage in nonremunerative labor in the home—are generally viewed as unemployed.[35] Moreover, official statistics do not include establishments with fewer than five employees, thus excluding another group of working women; the statistics also do not include the informal sector.

One study argues that the availability of foreign labor has helped maintain a low female participation rate.[36] But there are contradictory forces at work. It may be that the low-paying jobs that women might have been offered have been taken by foreigners. On the other hand, the availability of foreign labor, especially domestic help, has enabled some women to ease their work burden. This is primarily true for upper-middle-class and wealthy women who can afford to employ someone to do the housework for them and stay with the children while the Jordanian woman goes out to work. There are also many women who have such domestic help but do not work.

Despite the changes in women's labor force participation since the mid-1960s, there has not been a great change in the way that women's work is viewed, although there is probably a difference in the degree to which it is tolerated. In other words, the increase in the number of young women entering or seeking to enter the labor force is more an expression of economic need, rather than a manifestation of a qualitative shift in the way a female's participation in the labor force is valued.[37] A range of factors is at work here. First, what is seen as positive in the Jordanian context may be regarded differently elsewhere. As one study points out, low female participation in the labor force may be viewed as indicative of improved status (women have the luxury *not* to work) or low status (women do not have sufficient independence or impact on family decision making).[38] One finds both attitudes in Jordan, with variations explained by class, education, regional background, and so on. Some families push their daughters to enter the workforce at a young age for economic reasons, thus forcing them to leave school. In a society in which female activity outside the home is generally restricted, the need for additional income is an acceptable justification for loosening these restrictions. On the other hand, some young women go out to work to escape the excessive restriction of the home or problems at home.[39]

al-Tall finds that there is a tendency for employers to hire very young women, especially in manual labor jobs. They do not receive high salaries, and they are generally not conscious of their rights, so it is easy for the employer to break the labor law, which is discriminatory enough. At higher skill levels, women also tend not to be promoted to upper management, particularly at times of high unemployment, because of the belief that the male is the breadwinner and that therefore he should have priority in appointment. There also appears to be a disinclination on the part of employers to send women on training programs to improve their skills.[40] Women's job opportunities and promotions are also negatively affected by the demands of the home and the conservative constraints on their mobility.[41] Most women prefer manual (clerical) work, not work with equipment, because of the societal view of what tasks are appropriate for women (and therefore what they are trained to do). Teaching is also attractive, due to segregation of the workplace by sex, hours that do not conflict with home responsibilities, and a large number of vacation days.[42] Not surprisingly, many women have difficulty combining a job with their house-work, and therefore they prefer to quit when they marry. The paucity of child-care facili-ties—and the high cost of those that do exist—further burden working mothers. Many women who work have no choice but to leave their children with female relatives.[43]

In addition to all this is the fact of clear wage discrimination, noted earlier. Despite prohibitions in the state sector, a 1987 survey indicated that men receive 27.9% more than women given equal education, age, and experience. This is difficult to trace in the public sector, although there is no dearth of stories of unequal promotion. The sex-based wage differentials are most clearly found in agriculture and industry, where women receive only about two-thirds of what a male counterpart makes.[44]

Nor does the state appear to have had a strategic plan of any kind to encourage female employment, although an examination of the last two development plans (1981–1985 and 1986–1990) reveals certain employment goals. In the 1981–1985 plan, produced at a time when Jordan was actually facing labor shortages in some sectors because of migra-tion to the oil states of the Gulf, both the sections on social development and labor dealt with women's employment in one way or another. The plan notes that a Department of Women's Affairs was established in the Ministry of Labor in 1977 "to deal with problems relating to Jordanian women and to encourage greater participation by women in the so-cioeconomic development process." This plan also explicitly stated its intent was "to in-crease the labor force participation rate, particularly of women." A number of the projects proposed were aimed specifically at women (such as the Vocational Training Center for Girls at Na'ur and the Nursing College and Ancillary Medical Services Institute). How-ever, the vast majority of projects were not, and the total state contribution to all the pro-posed programs over the five-year period was only JD 4.5 million (approximately $12.4 million).[45]

The 1986–1990 plan was the first to have a separate section on women. Fifteen in-dividual projects were mentioned, a few of which involved vocational training while oth-ers encouraged local income-generating projects. The total state commitment to the pro-jects was again approximately JD 4.5 million.[46] In addition, there was state financing for upgrading several medical facilities, including developing institutions to train nurses and midwives under the health section of the plan, so that this figure by no means represented the total contribution to projects that might prepare women for employment.

Nonetheless, it is probably not coincidental that a specific commitment to increasing women's participation in the labor force was omitted from a development plan that was is-sued as unemployment in Jordan was beginning to increase. In such an atmosphere the only commitment to women's employment was through the traditional forms of largely ru-rally based income-generating projects. It seems clear that the state's primary concern is not unemployment in general, but male unemployment. Here, again, the issue of women's full citizenship is relevant.

Women and Education

Along with participation in the workforce, education is viewed as a major determinant and indicator of women's status. Greater access to higher levels of education, it is argued, will generally increase women's decision-making roles, make them more likely participants in the labor force, and enable them to make informed decisions about fertility and health care. Education is also critical to increasing women's awareness of their economic, political, and social rights. Nevertheless, the mere presence of women (even large numbers of them) in school and in the workforce could lead the casual observer to erroneous conclusions about the position of women.[47]

There is a wide difference in societal attitudes toward this issue: in the badia and the countryside, some regard girls' education as a luxury, whereas in other places it is viewed as necessary preparation for the labor market. In rural areas in particular, girls may be taken out of school to help with harvesting, both out of the family's need for her labor and from the view that a girl's education is not really important. Among other groups education is viewed positively, but mostly because it enables women to find good husbands and makes them better homemakers and mothers, not because it prepares them to enter the workforce or become professionals in their own right.

One key indicator of advancement on the education front is the level of illiteracy. The first statistics on illiteracy are for 1961 and showed that 84.8% of women and 49.9% of men were illiterate. By 1974, of those aged twelve and above, 48% of women and 22% of men were illiterate. In 1980 it was 35% of women and 15% of men. In 1990, among women fifteen years of age and older, illiteracy had fallen to 28.1%. The percentage of women holding high school degrees was 6.8% in 1972 and 13.4% in 1990. Not surprisingly, the capital enjoys the highest achievement levels in all categories. The percentages of illiteracy clearly increase if one goes to the rural areas, to the badia, and among certain socioeconomic sectors in the cities.[48]

Women have certainly made great progress in education, but illiteracy—and one of its primary causes, attrition from school—continue to be major problems in the kingdom. Education did not become compulsory until the promulgation of the amended constitution of 1952 called for nine years of obligatory schooling—primary and middle school. While the institution of such a policy was a positive step, it is insufficient. "Compulsory education," at least in Jordan, simply means the provision of seats, not forcing families to put or keep their children in school. In practice, there is no real enforcement by the authorities, so the decision about a child's education is left to the family, usually the father, who often holds very traditional ideas about the value of a girl's education. On the other hand, in some villages, there are no schools for girls after a certain level, and families are less likely to send daughters outside the home village for school even if there is a facility nearby. This may be for social (female mobility) or financial (travel costs) reasons.[49] Again, generally, if such expenses are going to be borne, the family is more likely to support a boy's education. Education becomes costlier the further along one goes in school: this includes actual costs such as uniforms, books, and travel, as well as opportunity cost (what other remunerative activity the child might engage in instead). Attrition continues to be a particularly severe problem for girls because, if it occurs at a relatively early age, they are left functionally illiterate.

The level a child reaches in school is often closely related to the family's socioeconomic status: the more privileged the background, the more likely a child is to remain in school. Secondary education is not obligatory, and the percentage of girls enrolled in school drops markedly at this level, especially in rural areas. Moving up to the next level, for a long time there were only two universities in the kingdom: Jordan University, established in 1962, and Yarmuk University, started in 1976. As a result of the insufficient number of seats, many students, most of them male, went abroad for university study. Over the years there has been a gradual increase in the number of women enrolled in universities: 32% in 1972, 38% in 1978, and 40% in 1988, although these figures do not take into account the number of students abroad, most of whom are male. Although boys and men in the sciences outnumber girls and women in high school, at the college level the enrollment is balanced. However, given the labor market, this sets women up for greater unemployment in the future, because there is already substantial unemployment among engineers and doctors, and because men are more likely to be hired for jobs demanding such skills.[50]

In general, credit must be given to the Jordanian state for its focus on developing educational institutions and for the marked drop in the illiteracy levels over the past three decades. Nonetheless, there continue to be social and economic pressures that lead to higher rates of female attrition from education institutions than those of males at each stage. Much more could be said about societal pressures that channel women into certain professions and not others and that create different expectations between young men and young women about the meaning and value of an education. Here, we will conclude by saying that the patterns found in Jordan do not distinguish it from other developing countries, nor, sadly, from many countries of the so-called developed world, where "traditional" ideas about women's roles continue to shape young females' expectations and opportunities.

History of the Women's Movement: Women versus the State

No discussion of the role and status of Jordanian women would be complete without an examination of the women's movement in the kingdom. The first prominent Jordanian women's activist traces what she calls the renaissance of Jordanian women to the 1940s with the establishment of women's solidarity societies in 1944 and 1945.[51] The first society, founded in 1944 and named the Women's Social Solidarity Society, had the mother of King Talal as its honorary president. The society's goals were limited to caring for children and providing assistance to the poor and needy. The princess was also made honorary head of the organization founded the next year, the Society of the Jordanian Women's Federation, although the active head was Princess Zayn Sharaf (wife of Talal and the mother of Hussein). These organizations differed from their predecessors[52] in that they were concerned with the social condition of Jordanian women, raising their educational level, and improving child health care. The two Jordanian societies combined in 1949 as the Hashemite Jordanian Women's Society, but the joint organization was dissolved in the same year.[53]

The establishment of the Arab Woman's Federation (Ittihad al-Mar'a al-'Arabiyya) (AWF) on June 17, 1954, marked a qualitative change in the type of women's organization found in Jordan. In Jordan, as in other Arab countries, women were caught up in the general political ferment of the 1950s and in helping the Palestinians who had been displaced. Hence, the atmosphere that preceded the establishment of the federation was one of political party and opposition activity. At the AWF founding in Amman, attended by more than one hundred women, Emily Bisharat, the first female lawyer in Jordan, was elected president. Among AWF's goals were: fighting illiteracy, raising women's socioeconomic level, preparing her to exercise her full rights as a citizen, and developing bonds of friendship and understanding between Arab women and women around the world to improve the situation at home and to strengthen peace. The federation had a fully developed constitution and institutional infrastructure.[54]

Branches of the AWF spread beyond Amman to Irbid, Zarqa, Kerak, and Salt, and the membership grew to thousands of women. Activity focused on increasing women's political, economic, and social awareness throughout the country from the cities, to the badia, and the refugee camps. Women presented and published and lectured, held conferences and seminars, and participated in numerous Arab and international conferences. The political parties and the professional unions supported this work in what was a relatively open political atmosphere.

In early November 1954 the AWF presented its first memorandum to the prime minister requesting a change in the Elections Law to give women the right to run for office and to vote in municipal and parliamentary elections. Women were supported in this quest by the political parties and professional associations. The government took the matter under advisement and the Legal Committee in the Parliament recommended that an amendment be discussed. However, when the proposed changes were published, they stipulated that only educated women be given the vote, something that caused great outrage (since any male illiterate had the right to vote as well as sit in Parliament).

The women also demanded changes in the Personal Status Law, specifically, the outlawing of arbitrary divorce and polygamy.[55] In the realm of more socially acceptable demands and political activity, women were in the forefront of demonstrations in support of Palestine, against Zionism and the Baghdad Pact, for the Arabization of the Arab Legion, against the French, British, and Israeli invasion of Egypt, protesting French treatment of Algeria, and supporting Nasir's nationalization of the Suez Canal Company. In the context of the nationalist surge of the spring of 1956, the federation waged a media campaign demanding that women receive weapons and first-aid training. The authorities agreed and officers from the Jordanian army trained female volunteers.

In the meantime, the women continued to send memos each time there was a cabinet reshuffle, and finally the government agreed to reexamine the issue of amending the electoral law. In cooperation with other women's societies and with the political parties on both banks, AWF held a historic festival on February 5, 1956. At its conclusion, telegrams were sent to the king, the prime minister. the president of the Senate and the speaker of the lower house about the meeting.[56] Unfortunately, the timing could not have been worse, as a coup attempt in early April led to a political crackdown which counted AWF among its casualties.

Thereafter, some of the women continued to work, hold meetings, and send memos to the relevant authorities about changing the law and resuming the dissolved society's activities. But not until nearly a decade had passed was the issue of the franchise raised again, when on April 21, 1966 the king sent a letter to the prime minister on the subject. But political circumstances intervened yet again to delay action.[57] No swift action was taken and, after the June 1967 defeat by Israel, most attention turned to the question of Palestine and the newly occupied territories.

At this point, those interested in political activity, men or women, began to gravitate to the constituent factions of the Palestinian resistance movement, which was based in Jordan until 1970–1971. The renewed possibility for political organizing was a direct result of the 1967 war. As a result of Jordan's defeat, the regime, its military, and the security services were, to a certain degree, discredited. Shortly thereafter, the Palestinian guerrilla organizations began to take advantage of the consequent political "opening" to expand their operations. Particularly after the Battle of Karameh in March 1968 (at which Palestinians along with Jordanian army forces turned back an Israeli incursion onto the East Bank) enthusiasm for the guerrillas surged in the region.

Their popularity brought new recruits, among them young women primarily (but not exclusively) Palestinians, many (but not all) from the refugee camps. All the factions eventually developed their own women's activities, which often took rather traditional forms. A women's committee emerged in Fateh, but was not acknowledged until 1969,[58] and not really activated until 1970, at which point, in addition to its other functions, it operated workshops and vocational training centers. In addition, the General Union of Palestinian Women, founded in 1965 but forbidden from opening an official branch in Jordan before the 1967 war, also took advantage of the opportunity to offer such facilities as literacy classes, first-aid and civil defense instruction, embroidery workshops, and sewing courses. Again, even though the women were working in the framework of a political organization, the activities were largely traditional. Very few women were integrated into the decision-making frameworks of the resistance organizations. Much of their work ended up resembling that of a women's auxiliary group.[59]

Just as important, the focus on the "national problem" meant that "women's concerns" were not addressed. As male cadres were (and are still) wont to argue, women's and other issues (implicitly less important in their view) had to take second place to the national problem lest energies be diluted. Only once the homeland was liberated could attention be diverted from that central concern. It was an argument common to third-world "revolutionaries" at the time, and it was an argument that most women accepted, if grudgingly. Unfortunately, as case after case across the developing world indicated, triumphant revolutionary regimes rarely rewarded women for their sacrifices, and once the revolution was over, the door was often closed on addressing women's issues, this time in the name of the exigencies of independent national development. In the final analysis, the Palestinian resistance interlude in Jordan, like the experience of other male-run movements, only diverted women from work on issues of everyday concern to them as women.

But even more serious setbacks were on the horizon. In September 1970 major violence broke out between the Jordanian army and the resistance. By July 1971 the remnants of the resistance had been driven from the country and its institutional infrastructure, including that of the women, had been destroyed or closed down. The lack of preparation socially and intellectually for such developments in Jordanian society led to a multifaceted backlash. One manifestation was on a communal level, as suspicion and dislike between Palestinians and Transjordanians soared. On another level, there was a reaction against what had been viewed as the greater social freedom exercised by resistance members—both men and women. But, of course, the response was aimed at women and involved new "protective" measures in the form of a resurgence of "weapons of virtue" and sharaf. This was part of a broad reaction, a revival of traditional values and practices, intended to recover the conservatism (and the identity perhaps) that resistance days had temporarily submerged. It then led to an increased caution in raising women's issues.[60]

For several years, activist women had limited options: to work with one of the underground political parties or to bide their time working with the charitable society of their choice. The first sign of impending change came in a March 5, 1974, letter from the king regarding the franchise for women. The king's letter, which included a royal decree finally amending the Elections Law to give women the vote, came against the backdrop of preparations for the United Nations Decade for Women, scheduled to begin in 1975. At about the same time, a group of women, many of whom had been active in AWF, met in anticipation of the UN conference to form a preparatory committee to celebrate the women's year in the name of what they called the National Women's Grouping in Jordan. In addition to their work on the upcoming UN meeting, one of their most important goals was to reestablish a women's federation in the kingdom. As a result of intensive activity (seminars, memoranda, and as well as support from the popular organizations), on August 13, 1974, the Society of the Women's Federation in Jordan (WFJ)[61] was licensed by the Ministry of the Interior as a recognized popular organization that would include all sectors of women. Before the end of the year, on November 17, 1974, the women announced the official establishment of the federation and on November 19 the first meeting of its general council elected Emily Bisharat president.[62]

In the six years of the WFJ's activity, its membership grew from 100 to some 3,000, with 1,500 in the capital.[63] The federation opened branches in Amman, Irbid, Salt, Zarqa, Madaba, and Aqaba, as well as committees (potential future branches) in Kerak, Ramtha, Fuhays, Rusayfah, Samakiyyah, Ribbah, Dahiyat al-Iskan, and al-Wihdat. WFJ operated training and literacy centers, and sponsored support services for children, including nurseries. It also briefly published a magazine, *al-Ra'ida*, until the state publications department closed it without explanation and all attempts to resume publication proved futile. Among the federation's regular programs were weekly seminars, lectures, story or poetry readings, trips, fundraising dinners, and annual charity bazaars to sell the products of the various training centers. In the political realm, WFJ demanded the right to participate in discussions of the Labor Law, the right to attend seminars and conferences to offer better presentations on women—whether in education, labor, or political rights—and the adoption of international and Arab resolutions regarding discrimination against women. It also published a number of studies on women and their rights as well as on the Palestine question. While the federation played an active role domestically and internationally, with the Parliament inactive there was no opportunity to mobilize women to exercise their newly granted right to vote.[64]

On the surface, the appointment in 1979 of the first female cabinet minister in the kingdom seemed to mark another important milestone and to bode well for an increasing role for women. In'am al-Mufti, a woman with long experience in education in the West Bank and who headed the first Woman's Bureau in the Ministry of Labor, was appointed the first minister of the newly created Ministry of Social Development. Yet, in this case, appearances were deceiving, for a new tendency soon became clear: the desire to incorporate all women's activities into a single organizational framework directly under the control of al-Mufti's ministry. Shortly after her appointment, she began working for the establishment of a new women's union.[65]

Beginning about the time of al-Mufti's appointment, the state authorities began to harass WFJ delegates to Arab and international conferences, claiming that the federation took positions antagonistic to the country.[66] Rumors began to circulate that the Ministry of the Interior intended to close WFJ, and finally, on December 18, 1981, the federation received a letter from the Ministry dated October 26, 1981, ordering its closure. According to the Charitable Societies Law, the Minister of the Interior is empowered to close any organization if it is demonstrated that it has contravened its constitution; however, a close review of WFJ's activities revealed that it had committed no such violation. Hence, the real explanation had to lie elsewhere. After discussions with WFJ subsequent to the arrival of the closure letter, the Minister of the Interior seemed to scale down his objections to the federation, stating that the problem was in its name, which was similar to that of the new union. The foundation responded by changing its name to al-Rabitah al-Nisa'iyyah fil-Urdunn, the Women's League in Jordan, in order to continue its work.[67]

In the meantime, the General Federation of Jordanian Women (GFJW) was established under official auspices, shortly before the WFJ dissolution letter was written and without an attempt to include WFJ women as members. After their receipt of the closure letter, WFJ activists decided to fight the order. Not surprisingly, however, in the battle of bureaucratic wills during a period of martial law, the Ministry of the Interior succeeded in blocking the implementation of the High Court's ruling.[68] The name change had not saved the federation. The activity of the former WFJ was "frozen."

The effective closure of the WFJ left Jordanian women without an independent, unified institutional framework that was near where they lived, took an interest in their health needs, sought to raise their educational level, and strove to raise consciousness about women's rights. The new federation was of a very different nature.[69] It was intended to serve as the official representative of Jordanian women in Arab and international gatherings, and to coordinate from above the women's special clubs and societies under the purview of the Ministry of Social Development. These groups formed the basis of the GFJW, while each maintained its own structure and program. Not surprisingly, then, since its founding the GFJW has remained isolated from the vast majority of Jordanian women.[70] That is clear from the nature of its leadership and its limited membership and branches.[71] A union that has few real branches and minimal organizational structure of its own is certainly not in a position to implement a creative program. In the case of GFJW, there simply has been no such program.[72]

This then briefly outlines the evolution of the organized women's movement in Jordan. There are numerous criteria according to which this experience may be evaluated; however, in keeping with the focus of this chapter, the following discussion will look specifically at what some of the themes in the movement's history reveal about the relationship between Jordanian women and the state.

First, and perhaps most basic, for the historical reasons outlined at the beginning, civil society in the traditional sense has normally occupied a very small sphere in Jordan. Not in a position through most of the kingdom's history to pose its own challenge to the state, civil society was forced, in effect, to accept the openings the state allowed it. At the same time, the societal restrictions on women's movement and activity outside the home served as a further broad constraint on the possibilities for women's participation in the civil society institutions that were permitted to operate. That said, it is clear that women's activity in the form of traditional charitable societies was generally tolerated (although during some periods it was easier to register new charitable societies than others, and societies that were Palestinian in composition if not in name were always scrutinized more carefully).

On the other hand, women's activity that implied the real or potential development of kingdomwide structures appears to have been much more problematic. The successes of AWF may be attributed to the political organizing "space" that the period of relatively greater freedom (1954–1957) allowed Jordanian society in general. The same may be said of the activities of the unofficial branch of the General Union of Palestinian Women, which operated openly throughout the country in the period between the 1967 war and the civil war of 1970.

When the political crackdowns came ending these periods, these two women's unions met the same fate as all other non-state-sponsored political actors: closure or destruction. Again, this was a different response than that encountered by the women's charitable societies. The lesson of these experiences seems to be that what the state, and the men who run it, generally think of as "women's work" is viewed as apolitical and nonthreatening. Indeed, not only does such work reinforce traditional women's roles and activities, it also encourages a welfare rather than an empowerment approach to the poor— a status quo rather than a transformational strategy, which is certainly more acceptable politically to the upper echelons of the state and society, both men and women.

A second lesson from the experiences of the Jordanian women's movement appears to be, "if not outright repression, then control." It is quite possible that had there not been a UN Decade for Women on the horizon, WFJ would not have been established, certainly not in 1974. The argument that the kingdom needed a representative of its women to attend the meetings to launch the decade, lest it be embarrassed in an international forum, appears to this writer as a convincing reason for the state to permit the reemergence of a national women's union after the passage of nearly twenty years. That the award of the franchise came during the same period can also be explained plausibly by the upcoming UN meeting and Jordan's position at the time as the only non-Gulf Arab state that had not granted women the vote. Both developments certainly were allowed largely as internationally directed public relations statements. It was "just a women's union" after all and, at the same time, since the Parliament had been largely inactive since the occupation of the West Bank in 1967 and the holding of new elections was not contemplated for the near future, extension of the franchise was largely meaningless on a national level.

However, as the decade unfolded WFJ expanded its numbers, operations, and branches. Several factors then came together to lead to the freezing of WFJ's activity. The first appears to be a minister—unfortunately, a woman—who was intent on reining in WFJ's activity so that all women's organizational work would come under her ministry's control. But it is unlikely that al-Mufti acted alone, for ministers rarely have such power in Jordan. Rather, it is more plausible that, as a result of WFJ's grassroots activity or because of its prominent and regular support of the Palestine problem in international forums, the Ministry of the Interior became interested in imposing greater controls on the federation's activity as well. The Jordanian state is rarely merely complicit in such measures; the whole episode smacks of a state apparatus heavily involved in effective demobilization of women. The preceding discussion of the structure and the nature of membership in the state-sponsored GFJW that replaced WFJ only reinforces this argument.

The same is true of the GFJW leadership. Over the years "acceptable" women have in effect been designated by the powers that be. These women have come from prominent families, members of the elite who are close to the regime, and who have little understanding or awareness of the conditions of everyday life for Jordanian women of less privileged sectors. Perhaps not surprisingly, since the beginning of the political liberalization in 1989, GFJW has floundered and lost the limelight to a new set of more activist women's NGOs.

Conclusions

November 1993 appeared to herald the "year of the woman" in Jordan. In parliamentary elections, former TV journalist Toujan Faysal became the first Jordanian woman elected to the lower house. When the government was formed following the voting, a new position, Prime Ministerial Consultant for Women's Affairs, was created. A woman was appointed Minister of Trade and Industry, and the king appointed two women to the upper house. There is no question that these developments engendered a great deal of excitement among a certain sector of the Jordanian populace, men and women alike.

However, the prime minister's consultant on women's issues resigned after only a short time in her job and the position has now been abolished, reportedly due to pressures from the office of the King's sister, Princess Basma, who has assumed for herself the role of leader of the Jordanian women's movement. Since 1993 she has begun to push for a number of legislative amendments and for a more prominent political role for women. While she has certainly raised the profile of women's issues, her involvement has also placed the regime back in a position of direct control of women's organizations. The verdict is still out on how serious the princess is about more extensive reforms. Powerful social forces and cultural traditions that are, at best, skeptical of a woman's role and worth in nontraditional activities continue to exert tremendous influence in the kingdom. Suspicions about the propriety of a woman's activity outside the home, family, village, or tribe are compounded when such activity could mean—as it may in labor union or other political work—imprisonment (because of possible honor violation), exile, prohibition from work, and so on. But the lack of acceptance of a full civic role for women extends beyond the family to the state and its policies. Women were not given the vote in general parliamentary elections until 1974 and did not have the chance to exercise that right fully until 1989. State budgeting and funding patterns have reinforced patriarchal leadership that has not been sympathetic to improving women's legal, political, or economic status. The focus on the military has reinforced traditional gender roles and led to a diversion of spending from social welfare to defense. The focus on the state sector has led to bureaucratic expansion and tertiary sector development, not broader industrialization, which in many other developing countries has drawn women into the paid labor force—for better of for worse. At the same time, national legislation both implicitly and explicitly relegates women to a citizenship status inferior to that of men and similar to that of children, supported by clear mechanisms of control. Outside the bounds of the state, the long years of political repression severely narrowed the possible range of civil society activity for all citizens. And, among the illegal political parties, the factions of the Palestinian resistance which operated in Jordan, or the relatively powerful professional associations, the primary focus was traditionally the struggle against Israel, not daily economic or social concerns.

Women's concerns were always argued to be secondary (at best) in importance to the needs of the national movement. Worse, testimonies of some activist women suggest that the "progressive" nationalists often manipulated and threatened women with honor issues just as their mukhabarat counterparts did.[73]

The picture that emerges is one of women who, because of traditional mores and wider historical patterns of state formation (which have in turn heavily influenced regime practice), continue to be largely excluded from empowered or empowering activity outside the home. The story inside the home may be very different, and the argument here is not intended to imply that women in Jordanian society are powerless. Quite the contrary. But it is a power of a different sort, generally exercised within certain limits, and always within the framework of or deriving from broader societal structures that are overwhelmingly patriarchal. While one may argue that this is a question of cultural differences, as long as it is in the public sphere that many of the issues affecting women's daily lives are decided, women's exclusion from the decision-making process in this sphere will continue to render them "less citizen" and, hence, more potentially vulnerable, than their brothers, fathers, and husbands.

The current political liberalization, while encouraging, is still managed from above. Given the recent peace and its lukewarm reception by the population, the Jordanian leadership is unlikely to propose legislative changes that might create further dissatisfaction among its support base by challenging traditional notions of gender roles and patriarchal control. Nor does the peace seem to indicate that the kingdom will make any substantial cutbacks in the funding to the military. Indeed, the austerity measures dictated by Jordan's agreements with the International Monetary Fund to reschedule its debt have led to cutbacks elsewhere, in areas that generally negatively affect women. Positive developments like peace, and the appointments of women to a variety of political posts notwithstanding, there is little to suggest that the situation and status of Jordanian women is likely to change substantially in the near future.

Notes

The fieldwork on which this paper is based was conducted during numerous research trips to Jordan undertaken over the last twelve years supported by grants from: Fulbright; The School of International Relations, University of Southern California; The American Center for Oriental Research, Amman; the Council of American Overseas Research Centers; and the Social Science Research Council.

1. The *badia* refers to the desert/Bedouin areas; they include much of the eastern part of the country, from north to south.

2. A. Konikoff, *Transjordan: An Economic Survey* (Jerusalem: Economic Research Institute for the Jewish Agency for Palestine, 1946), p. 94. See also Mary C. Wilson, *King Abdullah, Britain and the Making of Jordan* (New York: Cambridge University Press, 1987), chaps. 5 and 6, for details on budget subsidies.

3. For a detailed study of the Jordanian military, see Panayiotis J. Vatikiotis, *Politics and the Military in Jordan, A Study of the Arab Legion, 1921–1957* (New York: Praeger, 1967).

4. V. Spike Peterson and Anne Sisson Runyan, *Global Gender Issues* (Boulder, Colo.: Westview, 1993), pp. 81–82.

5. Peterson and Runyan, *Global Gender Issues*, pp. 83–84, citing Cynthia Enloe, *Does Khaki Become You?* (Boston: South End, 1983), p. 212.

6. From 1955 to 1970, defense and public security accounted for an average of 52% of central government expenditures. From Hanna Odeh, *Economic Development of Jordan, 1954–1971* (Hashemite Kingdom of Jordan: Ministry of Culture and Information, 1972), Appendix 8.

7. While the distinction is by no means a clear one and becomes increasingly complicated as time goes on, the term "Palestinians" refers to those who trace their fathers or grandfathers origins to West of the Jordan River. "Transjordanians" refers to those who are descendants of native East Bankers.

8. See Avi Plascov, *The Palestinian Refugees in Jordan, 1948–1957* (London: Frank Cass, 1981), pp. 16–26.

9. For more information about the role of such institutions see Laurie A. Brand "In the Beginning was the State: The Quest for Civil Society in Jordan," In Augustus A. Norton, ed., *Civil Society in the Middle East*, vol 1 (Leiden: Brill, 1994), as well as Laurie A. Brand, *Palestinians in the Arab World: Institution Building and the Search for State* (New York: Columbia University Press, 1988), chaps. 10 and 11.

10. Ibid., chaps. 10 and 11.

11. For a full discussion of this and related issues see, Carole Pateman, *The Sexual Contract* (Stanford, Calif.: Stanford University Press, 1988).

12. Suhayr Salti al-Tall, *Muqaddimah Hawla Qadiyat al-Mar'ah wa-al-Harakah al-Nisa'iyah fi al-Urdun* (Beirut: Al-Mu'assah al-'Arabiyah lil-Dirasat wa-al-Nashr, 1985). To the best of my knowledge, this is the only full-length study of Jordanian women, which is a major reason for my heavy reliance on it. Others studies are far shorter and often careless with detail.

13. It is interesting here to note that the idea of a female being important at birth—because she will one day be a woman key to continuing the family line—does not seem to exist. It is as if there is a break in the logic. The male is viewed as key to maintaining the line from his birth, the woman not until puberty or marriage.

14. al-Tall, pp. 28–29.

15. Ibid., pp. 25–27.

16. Ibid., pp. 25–27, 30.

17. Ibid., p. 41.

18. Ibid., p. 50.

19. Toujan Faysal was a former television personality who ran for Parliament in 1989. As a result of a newspaper article she wrote criticizing the Islamists and women's support of them, she was charged with apostasy by the *mufti* of the army, who therefore insisted that her marriage be dissolved (since she was no longer a Muslim); the mufti also sanctioned her death. Reportedly, thanks to the intervention of the king, the charges against her were ultimately dropped.

20. Most notable here are Fatima Mernissi in, for example, *The Veil and the Male Elite: A Feminist Interpretation of Women's Rights in Islam*, trans. Mary Jo Lakeland (Reading, Mass.: Addison-Wesley, 1992); and Leila Ahmed, *Women and Gender in Islam* (New Haven, Conn.: Yale University Press, 1992).

21. One feminist representative of this trend is Amina Wadud-Muhsin, *Qur'an and Woman* (Kuala Lumpur, Penerbit Fajar Bakti Sdn., Bhd., 1992).

22. The use of a verb implying lack of initiative is not coincidental. These changes have been granted from above, not demanded from below by any numerically significant or well-organized and active sector of the population.

23. Nasrin Mahasanah, "Wad' Al-Mar'ah al-Urduniyah fi Tashri'at al-Qanuniyah," unpublished study sponsored by the General Secretariat, National Assembly, Hashemite Kingdom of Jordan, 1994, p. 19.

24. Ibid., p. 22; al-Tall, *Muqaddimat*, p. 105.

25. See *Jordan Times*, July 11, 1993.

26. See *al-Dustur*, May 19, 1996.

27. Ibid., p. 5; al-Tall, *Muqaddimat*, p. 98.

28. Mahasana, "Wad," pp. 6–7.

29. Ibid., p. 18.

30. Ibid., p. 26.

31. This point is also made in Pateman, *The Sexual Contract*, chapter 5, in her discussion of American, British, and Australian women.

32. Beginning in early 1994, Rana Husayni, a young female reporter for the English-language *Jordan Times* began reporting details of honor crimes. In the past, there was generally only a brief line or two in the Arab press about a killing. Husayni, on the other hand, began visiting the neighborhoods in which the crimes took place and then reported on the contextual details. According to Suhayr al-Tall, who has completed a number of studies on violence against women, these crimes are on the increase.

33. Husayn Shikhatra, *Al-Mar'ah al-Urduniyah: Haqa'iq wa-Arqam* (Amman: Nadi Sahibat al-A'mal wa al-Mihan, 1992), pp. 21–22

34. Ibid., p. 36; Nadia Takriti Kamal and Mary Qawar, "The Status and Role of Women in Development in Jordan," Manpower Division, Ministry of Planning, Hashemite Kingdom of Jordan, 1990. Unpublished paper presented at the ILO meeting on "Women in the Jordanian Labor Force" held at the Royal Scientific Society, December 1990, p. 16.

35. See Paula England, "The Separative Self: Androcentric Bias in Neoclassical Assumptions," in *Beyond Economic Man: Feminist Theory and Economics*, ed. Marianne A. Feber and Julie A. Nelson (Chicago: University of Chicago Press, 1993).

36. Takriti and Qawar, "Status," p. 15.

37. al-Tall, *Muqaddimah*, p. 26.

38. Takriti and Qawar, "Status," p. 2.

39. al-Tall, *Muqaddimah*, p. 77.

40. Ibid., p. 76.

41. Takriti and Qawar, "Status," p. 29.

42. Ibid., pp. 3–4.

43. al-Tall, *Muqaddimah*, pp. 76–78.

44. Takriti and Qawar, "Status," Table 4.

45. National Planning Council, Hashemite Kingdom of Jordan, *Five Year Plan for Economic and Social Development, 1981–1985* (Amman: Royal Scientific Society Press, n.d.), pp. 295, 297, 307.

46. Ministry of Planning, Hashemite Kingdom of Jordan, *Five Year Plan for Economic and Social Development, 1986–1990* (Amman: National Press, n.d.), pp. 203–207.

47. Takriti and Qawar, "Status," p. 4.

48. Shikhatra, *Al-Mar'ah*, pp. 19, 23–30; al-Tall, *Muqaddimah*, p. 65.

49. al-Tall, *Muqaddimah*, pp. 53–54, 63.

50. Takriti and Qawar, "Status," p. 4.

51. Emily Bisharat, "Muhattat Mudi'a fi Tarikh Masirat al-Mar'ah al-Urduniyyah" *Al-Dustur*, June 29, 1993. Bisharat is the matriarch of the Jordanian women's movement.

52. al-Tall exempts two groups from this general characterization: The Women's Society to Fight Illiteracy and the Society of Arab Women. She argues that the first really did focus its efforts on the poorest in the villages and the refugee camps, setting up more than fifty centers to fight illiteracy. The Ministry contributed the teachers and allowed them to use schools in the evening. They also held parties and fundraisers of various kinds to collect money to expand their activities. al-Tall, *Muqaddima*, p. 124.

53. It should be noted that since Bisharat and al-Tall are the only two I am aware of who have written about this period, I have combined their accounts. Unfortunately, they do not always agree.

In cases of lack of conflict, I have relied on al-Tall. She is a careful researcher and it is a critical account. Bisharat has clearly omitted many things, presumably for political reasons.

54. al-Tall, *Muqaddimah*, p. 126.

55. Ibid., p. 129.

56. Bisharat, "Muhattat."

57. Ibid.

58. al-Tall, *Muqaddimah*, p. 115.

59. Brand, *Palestinians in the Arab World*, pp. 199–200.

60. al-Tall, *Muqaddimah*, p. 58.

61. The name is significant: the Women's Federation in Jordan, rather than the Jordanian Women's Federation, or some similar formulation. It allows for both Transjordanian and Palestinian women to participate without a feeling of compromising their communal identities. There was a conscious effort at this point—when the memories of 1970 were still quite strong—to bring together women from both communities to work together in a common framework.

62. Da'd Mu'adh, "Tajribat al-Ittihad al-Nisa'i (1974–1981)," *Al-Urdunn al-Jadid*, (7) (Spring 1986): 60; al-Tall, *Muqaddimah*, pp. 117 and 130.

63. al-Tall, *Muqaddimah*, p. 134; Mu'adh, "Tajribat," p. 61. While Mu'adh cites the same total numbers, she attributes only 800 members to the capital. In most respects, however, her presentation follows that of al-Tall quite closely.

64. al-Tall, *Muqaddimah*, 141–142.

65. Ibid, p. 161; and Mu'adh, "Tajribat," p. 63.

66. Mu"adh, "Tajribat," p. 64.

67. al-Tall, *Muqaddimah*, p. 157.

68. It is interesting to note that in her long newspaper article on the history of the women's movement Bisharat simply notes that the union was closed; no comment nor explanation is offered.

69. It is worth noting that the regional Arab Women's Federation refused to recognize the GFJW, maintaining that the WFJ was the legitimate union.

70. The only exception to this demobilizational strategy came in 1991, when, to counter an attempt by Islamist women to take control of the union, the federation leadership, in conjunction with some of the traditional leftist activists, worked to turn out the vote.

71. Majida al-Masri, "al-Azmah al-Rahinah li al-Harakah al-Nisa'iyyah fi al-Urdun," *Al-Urdunn al-Jadid* 7 (Spring 1986): 66.

72. al-Masri, "Al-Azma," pp. 67, 69.

73. Author's interviews and discussions with female activists over the years.

The Slow Yet Steady Path
to Women's Empowerment
in Pakistan

The status and position of women in Pakistan and their subsequent access to power have undergone substantive change since the onset of the twentieth century. Muslim women in nineteenth-century India faced uphill struggles in easing some of the extreme restrictions on women's activities associated with *purdah*, restricting polygamy, ensuring women's legal rights under Islamic law which Muslims perceived had been taken away under British civil law, and in introducing female education. In the 1870s, Sir Syed Ahmad Khan advocated modern education as the only means for emancipation of Muslims under the British. In 1880, he developed the Mohammedan Educational Conference to propagate his message, now referred to as the Aligarh Movement. However, it was not until 1896 that the Conference formed a women's section, and three years later opened its first girls' teacher-training school, which laid a foundation for the education of Muslim girls. Progress was slow; by 1921, only four out of every thousand Muslim females had enjoyed the benefits of formal education.[1]

In the ensuing struggle for independence from Britain, the Muslim League—and indeed, Islam itself—was popularly perceived as supporting the empowerment of women. The Muslim League was founded in 1906 by thirty-five elite men (lawyers, merchants, and large landowners) who wanted to ensure that Muslims received a fair share in the upcoming constitutional reforms. Indeed, the majority of these men and their followers were recipients of the education system promoted by Sir Syed Ahmad Khan, and many were graduates of the Mohammedan Anglo-Oriental College which Sir Syed's group had founded. Their views on women's social and political participation was relatively progressive, especially when compared to the views of Islamist parties such as the Deoband School.

An early victory for Muslim women was the enactment of the Muslim Personal Law in 1937. Muslim groups had convinced the British that this law was vital for the integrity of their community, because it enabled Muslims to live—marry, inherit property, and so on—under Islamic principles. Muslim women regained the right to inherit property and other rights guaranteed under Islamic law which had been taken away under British civil law. Nearly all Muslim groups, secularists and Islamists alike, hailed the enactment of the new Muslim Personal Law as a victory for Muslims in British India.

The unanimity among Muslim groups that prevailed in 1937 is long gone in today's Pakistan. Somehow, it appears that the social goals of the inheritors of Khan's education movement have come to be diametrically opposed to those of the Islamist parties. However, long-standing popular support for secular democracy has waned since 1988 as the two major political parties' leaders, Benazir Bhutto and Nawaz Sharif, have battled each other publicly while virtually ignoring the dramatic decline in the quality of economic life and social norms throughout the country. By the mid-1990s there was growing popular support for Islamist parties, in large part as a reaction to what is often considered to be opportunist political squabbling at the higher echelons of government within the country and the popular sentiment that Western governments are anti-Islamic.[2] This support has enormous implications for women's lives in the current political climate.

This chapter begins with a discussion of traditional relations between men and women in Pakistan as derived from both South Asian and Islamic influences. Specific concepts of family and female separation have long-standing bases in South Asian cultural norms. Using the old Walled City of Lahore as an example, we see that architectural structures accentuate how the gendered division of space correlates into a marked separation of male and female spheres. We move on to an analysis of the ways in which Pakistani state policy has affected gender relations and the expansion of the women's movement in the country. We conclude by looking at recent efforts by the state to engineer reforms, and the parallel rise in support for Islamist parties given the heightened public disillusionment with the state.

South Asian Muslim norms have historically placed extensive restrictions on women's actions. The idealized woman stays at home, serves the men in her family, raises children, and leaves any and all involvement with the outside world to men. She neither physically intrudes into that male domain, nor even symbolically intrudes by inquiring about non-family matters. This purdah—the practical as well as figurative curtain separating the everyday worlds of women and men—remains powerful symbolically. Various political figures periodically intimate the need for separate women's bank branches, separate seating areas on buses, and even separate universities. The reality, however, is that many women have already crossed the lines: they bank wherever they want, sit wherever they can, and freely enroll at all major universities. Therefore, a conflict exists in the roles women are encountering and the ways in which women and men think of accommodating them. An ongoing reallocation of responsibilities is occurring both within homes and in the workplace, resulting in a redistribution of gender-based rights and obligations that is not acceptable to everyone.

An example of this can be seen in changes in gendered perceptions among residents of the old, predominantly working-class Walled City of Lahore. Anchored in centuries-old traditions while being forced to confront the challenges of contemporary life, their experiences are typical of changing gender attitudes among non-elite women and men in Pakistan.

When one walks down the thin lanes of the Walled City of Lahore, all we can see is the public space of the male world.[3] Men are active in all spheres of economic activities. The layout of the city, which was built hundreds of years ago, lends itself to this perception: the constricted streets and alleyways lined by high buildings provide cooling relief to the inhabitants below, who are seemingly perpetually bathed in shadows. Buildings are usually occupied by a shop or workshop on the ground level, with two or three levels of family living quarters above, and are topped with a latrine and a flat roof. Windows face inward, onto central courtyards. The few outward-facing windows, for those who look, are small and tend merely to frame electric wires. Minimum space exists for movement along the narrow walkways. In the inner sanctum of some neighborhoods, it is difficult to recognize people in the darkness of the alleyways.

Most women spend the bulk of their lives physically within their homes; they go outside only when there is a substantive purpose. Only a small percentage of women desire to move out of the Walled City so as to escape the dirt and crowds and perhaps raise their status by becoming residents of areas with higher socioeconomic demographics. Instead, most women are happy to be in close proximity to relatives, goods, and services, and they are resigned to the Walled City's shortcomings.

Beneath this public face lies a significant amount of social confusion, particularly regarding changing gender roles, expectations, and possibilities. Characterizing traditional society as patriarchal, patrilineal, and patrilocal tells us little about the actual relations between men and women in this poor urban area. In the idealized past, purdah was an essential element of everyday life. Of course, women would often interact with closely related men often throughout the day. Their relationship, however, was one of servitude: women were to ensure a clean home, tasty cooked food, obedient children, and to maintain social relations. Maintenance of social relations included attending the many functions associated with marriage, birth, and death, plus the performance of certain rites identified with Islam expected of a woman in that particular family. Wives were less friends and confidants than partners. Best friends may never have met each other's wives—and certainly not their friend's sisters (postpuberty).

The gendered division of labor within the family is due to a unique combination of economic and status concerns. Invariably, the institution of the family plays a principal role in the Walled City. Access to many opportunities is often contingent on the connections that one's family has with others. Family interpretations of religious and social values, as well as their own preferences, are the greatest factor in whether or not daughters are sent to school, parallel cousin marriages are preferred, or women must wear a veil. In fact, women can come from similar socioeconomic backgrounds and some will wear a veil, others will not. Some families will allow a daughter to enroll in a college for higher education while others will not. Until recently, these decisions were based more on family traditions than on external factors.

Families provide a nearly complete package of economic and social support, provided that members abide by its norms. Men do not necessarily have complete authority over household economics; in a sizable minority of families, women have traditionally heen responsible for daily decision making and often have input in determining major purchases.[4] Where is it then that men wield power? It is in their absolute control over women's actions and mobility, because women are considered the repository of their family's respectability. Male elders overlook minor transgressions of social norms committed by boys; the same minor transgressions are absolutely forbidden for girls.

Gender roles and expectations have been undergoing substantive change in the last decade with the introduction of new kinds of technology that free up women's time (such as running water from taps, gas connections for cooking, covered drains for more hygienic conditions, and accessible low-cost transportation), the availability of waged labor for women (albeit generally in the informal sector where they receive lower pay than men), women's increased exposure to higher education, and their growing attentiveness to mass media. For example, a woman I have interviewed used to live within Kashmiri Gate. She was born in the Walled City, married just after her first menstrual cycle, and has never earned any income on her own despite the severe financial need of her family. Whenever I met with her, she was invariably washing dishes or clothes using a neighborhood hand-pump. She only spoke her regional language, Punjabi, because she did not know the national language, Urdu. In our later encounters, she was very apprehensive about her family's future because they were faced with the imminent destruction of their home; developers sought to expand a nearby wholesale bazaar. The opinions she voiced regarding local political matters invariably were those of her husband or sons.

In contrast, her daughter has grown up with other expectations about her life. Despite being from a poor family, she has benefited from the Pakistani government's successful program over the past two decades of providing basic medical care in urban areas. She had her first inoculations when she was a year old, followed by injections against measles and smallpox a few years later. Her life also reflects changing views on purdah; she wears a loose-fitting *chador* instead of the fitted *burqa* (body veil) worn by her mother. She attended the Anjuman Khudamuddin Banaat Girls Public School, a small school with ten rooms for some 300 girls a short walk from her home inside the Walled City. Most of the girls studying there are young and from poor families. As the girls grow older, their families try to transfer their daughters to English medium schools, which ascribe greater status and enables preferable marriage options with wealthier men.

This girl's goals and values are very different from her mother's; she expects to take initiatives to affect some aspects of her future which women rarely did in the past. When I asked her what was the best day in her life, she told me it was "the day that I passed my matric [tenth class] exam." She chose not to continue in a secondary school but rather to attend a government-run sewing and embroidery center. During this time, she and her sister began to do intricate *salma sitara* embroidery on a piece-rate basis for a local shopkeeper. Some of this money eventually went toward her dowry, and the remainder went toward her family's daily expenses.

She was an avid supporter of Benazir Bhutto. She saw Benazir as an important role model for women in Pakistan. The confidence this young woman had gained from her independent experiences is reflected in her other attitudes. Aside from having her own political opinions, she wanted to have a say in whom she would marry, where she would live after marriage, whether she would have to earn an income, and the number of children she would have. She hoped to have a small family consisting of only four children, as is increasingly becoming the norm in Lahore. I am not saying that this young woman eventually had a say in determining who she would marry or in any of these other desires, but her *desire* to have a say is revolutionary in this cultural context.

This young woman, however, does not see herself as being in a *better* position than that of her mother when she was young. While their lives are very different, she considers that her mother was more emancipated because her mother did not have to contribute to the family's income as she must by doing embroidery. There was minimal expectation in the past that women would do such work in their homes. Indeed, both out of necessity and by choice, women today are forced to renegotiate traditional norms, values, and power relationships.

In fact, we can see that the multifaceted system of norms and controls that has served to constrain female activities and mobility in traditional Muslim society does not exist mainly out of concerns regarding female promiscuity. Instead, the notion of what is accepted as *respectable* and what is not—perhaps initially tied to matters of sexuality but no longer—has become a form of social control. It is the fear of losing respectability that drives most people to suppress their women's freedoms. This results in a general consensus that any activity in which a woman engages outside of the home needs to be monitored. This also explains why conditions of high density in places like the Walled City—as in other poor urban areas in Pakistan—have become factors in strengthening the power held by families over their members, particularly power held by males over females.

Traditionally, a girl was placed into seclusion before the onset of puberty. This decision was usually made by a close male relative who, at a certain point, decided that the girl's interactions with males should be limited. One older woman in the Walled City recounted to me how one day her grandfather decreed that she was no longer to go outside and play with the other children in the neighborhood. From age nine onwards, she was only to observe social life on the streets from the roof of her home; she was no longer to partake of it. I was often told that a woman's father, brother, or mother's brother had put her into purdah.

In field research, I observed that while both boys and girls needed to be obedient in front of their elders (particularly in front of older men), I never saw an instance when mobility restrictions were placed on boys. Social pressure was instead applied to boys in three arenas: school attendance, choice of career, and marriage selection. Even then, it seems that parents and other elders were rather relaxed about enforcing the first two activities. I heard many accounts that a boy stopped going to school because he "wasn't interested in studying" or he "didn't like to study." Career options became available through informal networks that often did not require an independent decision on the part of a boy. It was only in the third kind of pressure—to marry a spouse chosen by one's family—where it seems that both men and women generally submitted to the will of their family. While it was possible for a boy to suggest a potential spouse, this was unheard of in the case of a girl—who would have disgraced herself and her family just to have voiced an opinion. Once the decision was made as to who would be married, however, it seems that both sons and daughters were generally unable to break the engagement without severe discord and antagonism within the family.

However, gendered power within the family is in the midst of flux. The renegotiation of gender images and expectations appears to fall into three categories: (1) women being allowed—and in some cases, encouraged—to study beyond the stage of simple literacy; (2) changes in the perception of gendered work given the existence of expanding labor opportunities for women; and significantly, (3) the renegotiation of personal power and mobility within the family. The first two of these arenas are direct reflections of what women now are doing differently from the past, resulting in men relinquishing some of the powerful control they have held over women while also expecting women to hold different roles. The last category, the renegotiation of personal power and mobility within the family, is a direct result of the first two. Due to women's increased competencies, men are also realizing that women do not need them as much as in the past, and that it is possible for women now to be self-reliant. Needless to say, this creates a great deal of confusion in a society where social norms still revolve around honor and respect. There is a discernible increase in men's fears of what *uncontrolled*, qualified women might do.

Increasingly, parents are allowing their daughters to acquire a higher education, even though such mobility for a postpubescent girl is antithetical to traditional mores. That girls from this working class area are completing secondary education is, therefore, no small event. Indeed, men's diminishing ability to control the mobility and activities of women within the family is due in large part to the increase in female education and related access to mass media and other forms of information. It may not be what is actually learned in school but the experience of *leaving one's home after puberty and attending classes*—mixing with people from a wide socioeconomic spectrum—that exposes a woman to other students and teachers and, in effect, to the larger society from which she was once hidden and uninformed.

The lifestyles and status of elite women have not changed as dramatically as have those of most poor women, who are the majority in the country. The former, especially "super-elite" women such as prime minister Benazir Bhutto and former ambassador Sayeda Abida Hussain, generally enjoyed greater degrees of freedom to begin with. Most adults living in the Walled City would contend that certain activities that elite women have come to see as norms (such as, entering a non-female domain profession, joining a women's political movement, or selecting her own husband) are outside the purview of female respectability, and that elites have become too Westernized for their own good. Yet these same working-class parents aspire for their daughters to attend Islamia College for Women (Cooper Road) or the newer Government College for Women in Bilal Ganj, both of which are close to the Walled City.[5] Idealized norms have not yet caught up with the pragmatics of daily life, which often require college degrees to arrange a good marriage or survival strategies for poor girls who may someday need to earn an income.

I have found that the kinds of changes in perception once associated with elites are gradually making their way into those of girls enrolled in colleges, despite their class background.[6] At one point, I had a discussion with some fifty girls at Islamia College (Cooper Road), all of whom were from the Walled City. They had heard from their college principal that I had written a book about women's lives in that area. They expressed to me a dilemma they were facing. On the one hand, their college was exposing them to a great deal of nationalist ideology and propaganda. This included the increased emphasis on Islamic and Pakistani studies in the curriculum, campaigns to collect clothes and raise money to help flood victims in rural areas, support of autonomy in Indian Kashmir, and other issues to make them strive to do something for the larger society. It embedded in them the sense that they were Pakistanis and that they could make a difference in these matters. Given their new level of educational attainment, they also expected that they would eventually experience a significant rise in class and status.

On the other hand, they expressed a real frustration in not knowing what they could actually do with their newfound knowledge, their new awareness, and their sense of nationalism. When I formally questioned the female students (in a written questionnaire format) about their occupational aspirations, the vast majority wrote that they wanted to become teachers. Later, in more informal discussions, other professions surfaced (such as, journalist, shop owner, and banker) which culturally lie in the male domain. These girls were confused as to what other avenues might be available to them. One girl from the Walled City said that she wanted to become a freedom fighter to help her Muslim brothers and sisters in Kashmir; however, the Pakistani military does not accept women into combat positions nor is it actively engaged in any skirmishes at the Kashmir border. This goal, of course, was antithetical to the mores and norms of what was most likely in store for her future.

I found two different kinds of responses among men studying at colleges in Lahore regarding the merit of educating women. The majority from upper-class families found it to be a good thing and would prefer a highly educated wife, while most men from working-class families (similar to those found in the Walled City) told me that there was no reason why women should occupy places in colleges that men could take or jobs that men needed. Despite the fact that women studied alongside them in their classes,[7] they would not approve if it were their own sister or wife studying in their college. Clearly, the latter group felt more threatened by the prospects of educated women than the former.

There also seems to be another significant change occurring within the family. We can see this in the loss of will to maintain the extended family, which has repercussions for women who become victims of domestic violence. The system of arranged marriages fits in well with the structure of the extended family. While the desire by men to control their wives has a long-standing basis, domestic violence was contained by the intervention of other family members in resolving conflicts. While extended family members continue to intervene despite the shift to nuclear families in urban areas, the physical absence of others within the household leaves open the possibility of escalated domestic violence.

When the earnings from a woman's labor is combined with those of other family members in joint work, the gendered division of power within the family only changes slightly. Such work has minimal effect on increasing a woman's decision-making power within the family or requiring its members to renegotiate gender roles. While a woman gains a stronger voice in influencing important family events when she becomes the primary economic support of her household, she is still not an independent agent. For example, a widow I met who strings flowers to support her son and daughter must ultimately defer to the choices of her late husband's brother when arranging marriages for her children; she must also secure his permission before travelling anywhere or applying for any government programs. Men still seem able to exert fundamental control over women's mobility and in their access to instruments of social change.

This leads to the third category in which gender images and expectations are being renegotiated, that of personal power and mobility within the family. Men and women have very different visions of the important changes that are occurring. While men view women as being more capable now than in the past, they also feel threatened by the potential of uncontrolled educated or economically independent women who may compromise their honor and therefore their status among other men. Interestingly, they tend to regard women as more honest than men in economic matters. Men no longer have the same level of genuine trust in other men, including kin and friends, as they had in the past. This is due to the acute rise in corruption in recent years which has, in the eyes of many of these working-class men, favored unscrupulous actions over integrity and has promoted an unprecedented regard for crass materialism.

Many women expressed to me that they feel they can no longer rely on the men in their family with as much confidence as they had in the past. They have seen men abandon their wives, go abroad to work leaving a wife on her own, and use drugs more than ever before. One woman from the Walled City told me that the most viable survival strategy now for daughters is for them to acquire a good education, because gold and property can always be taken away by someone else. She is afraid for her daughters because she has

witnessed many extended families break down and people relinquish traditional obligations.[8] She and many others feel that the education and work opportunities now available
to women can help them take a tentative step toward independence.

The most noticeable change seems to be in women's expectations of other women.
Women realize that they are now more capable to conduct necessary worldly activities
(such as pay an electric bill, take a child to a doctor, and get a prescription filled). They
are raising their expectations of the arenas of life in which women can be active and responsible, and of what they can achieve—especially what their educated daughters might
achieve—and they are taking these expectations to unprecedented levels.

Changes in gender relations will continue to accelerate; this is reflected in the opinion voiced to me by many women that no women in the Walled City will be wearing a
burqa by the end of the century, even though it is still common today. However, while the
physical restrictions on women's mobility by her own family may be lifting, this is being
replaced by a new threat to her mobility: the rise in violence against women by unknown
assailants, especially when women venture outside their own neighborhoods. In the past,
rape was comparatively rare and generally occurred as retribution against the property of
an enemy. This has changed considerably, and horror stories of multiple rapes are no
longer uncommon in the local newspapers. The rise in the number of rapes may be due
to the frustration (political and economic) that many men experience in the larger society,
as well as the desire by conservative men to keep mobile women contained. Later in this
chapter, we will return to the question: does the rise in violent crimes against women indicate that men perceive this as a way of exerting power, or are they punishing women who
are acting outside of traditional norms that emphasize limited mobility?

An important outcome of these gendered changes in perception is that the nature of
restrictions on women's actions have been modified in this rapidly changing urban context. Regardless of this reality, however, people continue to speak about the stereotypical
view of women's place in the family and other traditional notions of family dominion. This
is perpetuated by a number of factors, especially repressive images of women which had
been promoted and perpetuated by the state. The government of Zia ul-Haq, in particular, had idealized the image of women faithful to "*chador aur char diwari*," wearing a veil
and remaining within the confines of the four walls of one's home. The government had
promoted this image while trying to ignore the reality that women's lives were becoming
increasingly integrated into the public realm.

Changing Gender Relations and Gendered Power

Gender relations have undergone their greatest shifts in the last quarter century. Two factors account for these changes more than any others: what has been official state policy toward women, and the subsequent rise in the intensity and power of the women's movement in the country.

In its formative phase, the women's movement was focused on educational reform.
Muslims in nineteenth-century South Asia did not have to struggle with the kinds of legal
issues that Hindu reformers referred to as "social evils," such as abolishing *sati* or promoting legal reforms to allow widow remarriage. Many Muslims did engage in some of
these cultural practices (such as disclaiming widow remarriage and divorce), but there
was no organized movement to keep Muslims from practicing them, because they were al-

ready contradictory to Islamic tenets. Instead, the argument was that the intermingling with Hindu culture and institutionalization of British law had taken away many rights granted to women under Islam. If Islamic family law could only be enforced, women would once again enjoy rights such as inheritance. Few Muslims disagreed with this stance, although it was a few decades before the British administration would also agree.

The uphill struggle lay instead in introducing Western forms of education for Muslim girls, in easing some of the extreme restrictions on women's activities associated with purdah, and in restricting polygamy. The watershed period for the idea that there was a value to empowering South Asian Muslim women was with the Aligarh Movement in the 1870s and 1880s. Its membership included many of the earliest proponents of female education and of raising women's social status in the wider society. As tended to be the case in many other parts of Asia at the time, men were the early advocates for such social reform.

The Muhammadan Educational Conference, the traveling component of the Aligarh Movement, formed a women's section in 1896, about twenty years after the Movement itself became functional. In 1899, they opened the first girls' teacher-training school. The intent was to advance girls' technical knowledge (such as in sewing and cooking) within a religious framework and thereby reinforce Islamic values. What became known as the Women's Reform Movement gathered momentum after 1904 and caused the opening of various Muslim girls' schools by 1911, but the progress was slow: by the time of independence, only about 1% of Muslim women in South Asia had received secondary education.

The promotion of female education was the first step in moving outside the bounds stipulated by traditional views of purdah and contributed to transforming the very concept. To advocate the education of girls became socially acceptable, and this, by extension, enhanced women's rights. Indeed, the promotion of female education remained the focus of the fledgling women's movement throughout the period of the nationalist struggle for independence.

Two important women's groups were established in the early nationalist period, just at the end of World War I. The first was the politically oriented All-India Muslim Ladies Conference, consisting of elite women whose husbands were active in the Muslim League. The second was the social-reform–oriented Anjuman-e-Khawateen-e-Islam, which came to be the precursor for other social-welfare–oriented women's groups. Members of both groups became strong advocates for expanding educational opportunities for girls.[9]

During the Khilafat Movement, which demanded the restoration of the Ottoman Caliphate by the British at the conclusion of the First World War, Abadi Begum (better known as Bi Amman) began to tug further at the purdah curtain. As spokesperson for her imprisoned sons, she would address crowds of thousands of men, calling them her brothers and sons, skillfully using acceptable notions of kinship for a political cause. Although she remained within the boundaries of tradition by her usage of kinship metaphors, she also established a precedent for women to participate openly in a political movement and, in turn, to reinterpret traditional strictures set by purdah. In the gradual buildup of support for a Muslim homeland, elite women continued to question women's roles and link their empowerment to the larger issues of nationalism and independence.[10]

The only pre-independence legal change that specifically affected women was the enactment of the Muslim Personal Law in 1937. In an effort to assuage some of the Muslim demands, the British deemed they would allow religious communities to govern themselves in the sphere of family law. The Muslim Personal Law enabled women to inherit property and regain other rights that the Muslim community felt they had lost with the anglicization of certain civil laws.[11]

After independence, a small group of elite women remained politically active, continuing to advocate women's political empowerment through the passage of specific legal reforms. However, what happened to activist women in Pakistan was very similar to what occurred at a later time in Algeria: after independence was achieved, few found any role to play in the new state. Nearly all elite women in Pakistan shifted their focus toward promoting female education and other social-welfare–oriented activities, specifically the work in which the All Pakistan Women's Association (APWA) was involved. The main focus of APWA was to provide assistance to those in need, followed by a distant second interest in promoting female education, and an even more distant third involvement in promoting legislation to empower women.

There was not a great deal of the latter. Prior to 1979 and the onset of Zia ul-Haq's Islamization program, there had been two major issues around which the state had acted that affected women's legal position in Pakistan: the accommodation between Muslim family law and civil, democratic rights, and women's political representation.[12] The outcome of the first was the passage of the Muslim Personal Law of Shariat (1948) which recognized a woman's right to inherit all forms of property as guaranteed under *shariah*, and the 1961 Family Laws Ordinance, which regulated marriage and divorce. Various efforts were made to secure women's political representation, such as the futile attempt to have the government include a Charter of Women's Rights in the 1956 Constitution and the later successful reservation of seats for women in the National Assembly in 1973. The issue of whether or not a woman could rule the country was first raised in 1965 when Fatima Jinnah contested the national election for the presidency. Islamist groups supporting her issued a *fatwa* condoning her candidacy.[13]

General Zia ul-Haq's assumption of power in July 1977 did not, at the outset, appear to have profound consequences for women in particular. His implementation of an Islamization program in February 1979 unequivocally changed that view. A great deal has been written elsewhere on the various consequences of Zia's Islamization program.[14] What is important to note is that by the end of Zia's regime in August 1988, a set of laws had been put into place *which constructed an image of women as not having identical civil liberties as men* and which justified such laws in the name of Islam.

The Islamization program decisively affected women in three specific ways: (1) in the highly visible territory of law, (2) in affecting women's social and economic positions and options, and (3) in facilitating the mobilization of women to become social activists and defend their civil rights. It is because of the kinds of repressive laws that Zia's government implemented that there was a marked transformation of the women's movement to one that became focused on defending women's fundamental rights. In the wake of the Islamization program, groups formed such as the Women's Action Forum (WAF) and the Pakistan Women Lawyers' Association (PWLA) in response to what their members perceived as a state threat to women's civil rights. APWA also underwent a noticeable transformation as it shifted its focus toward political activism, lending its name in support of the strikes and demonstrations organized by WAF.

WAF organizers decried the scapegoating of women which Zia's policies incited, and the state's lack of attentiveness to women's needs. They cited Pakistan's founding father,

Quaid-e-azam Muhammad Ali Jinnah, in WAF's founding charter: "No nation can rise to the height of glory unless your women are side by side with you; we are victims of evil customs. It is a crime against humanity that our women are shut up within the four walls of the houses as prisoners. There is no sanction anywhere for the deplorable condition in which our women have to live."[15] Throughout the eleven years of Zia ul-Haq's rule, his ideological interpretation of Islam and its role in a modern state became increasingly powerful in Pakistan. He filled the ranks of government ministries with retired army officials, thereby transforming the state institutions from the inside with loyalists who would not question his actions.

Moving Beyond the Zia Period to Democracy

The Pakistan People's Party (PPP) winning platform in the 1988 election included the kinds of progressive assertions that had endeared the party to the masses in the past. It promised to include the needs of previously disenfranchised groups, especially women and the poor. To empower women, the PPP manifesto pledged it would eliminate inequitable practices that handicapped women by promising it would: (1) sign the United Nations Convention on the Elimination of All Forms of Discrimination Against Women, (2) improve working conditions and employment prospects for women, (3) introduce maternity leave, (4) repeal discriminatory laws against women that were passed during Zia's tenure, (5) reform the Muslim Personal Law to bring it in line with the demands of contemporary socioeconomic realities, and (6) take special measures to promote the literacy of women.

Immediately following the 1988 election, the vast majority of people—PPP supporters and adversaries alike—were exuberant about Pakistan's future possibilities. Here was a new government that was affirming democracy and promising to include the voices of all groups into the state. However, disillusionment soon followed, as the ruling party became enmeshed in simply trying to survive in power and did little to follow through on the promises made in the election manifesto. By the time the PPP government was dismissed in August 1990, few raised their voices to protest.

Why did this happen? There are two aspects to this answer: the actual commitment by the government to follow through on the election manifesto, as well as their capacity to do so. Insofar as Bhutto's government did not enjoy an absolute majority in the legislature, there was little her government could do to follow through on its campaign promises. While the PPP government had its own philosophical stance, it still remained formally tied to the former government's weak proposals for incorporating women into Pakistan's development agenda. The People's Party would have had to garner strong support to veer from the Seventh Five-Year Plan (1988–1993), a plan that acknowledged that the results of neglecting women were "an unacceptable cost, both morally and economically," yet only offered vague, indeterminate, and poorly funded solutions.[16] Furthermore, while the platform on which her party had run supported women's empowerment, most individual party members who had won seats in the provincial and national assemblies remained entrenched in patriarchal views of women's place in society. There were few long-term PPP stalwarts in their ranks, because in order to win the election PPP had needed to win at the local levels. Out of this necessity, it transformed itself from the inside by having local popular politicians run on the PPP ticket, but these politicians did not necessarily embrace the party's ideology. The PPP government soon became dependent on these new members for its survival. It would have risked the defection of many of these members over the potentially controversial initiative of empowering women. Indeed, it ultimately took less controversial issues to bring down the government in August 1990.

We return then to the question, that *if* the PPP government *could* have followed through on many of its election promises, would it have done so, especially its pledge to empower women? We must be skeptical in the light of later events.

The PPP government did take some limited action to assist women. As soon as Bhutto came to office, she had many female prisoners released from the country's jails. In July 1989, the government took an important symbolic step when it elevated the Women's Division to become the Ministry for Women's Development and ordered the establishment of a Women's Bank. The full range of women's groups lobbied the new PPP government to follow through on its election manifesto. They hoped it would introduce laws that would empower women (such as, promoting female literacy and the availability of jobs for women in the formal sector of the workplace) and reverse some of the laws decreed by Zia such as *zina-bil-jabr* (rape as a part of the Hudood Ordinance) and the proposed Shariat Bill. Within a few months, however, supporters became disheartened and increasingly disillusioned with the prospects of the party's ability and commitment to deliver on its promises. Indeed, none of the laws that were targeted as discriminatory towards women were reversed during the PPP's first tenure.

While supporters argue that the PPP government did not have the legislative support to reverse those laws, there were a number of minor actions the government could have taken to promote women's empowerment which would not have been deemed overtly controversial. Such actions included releasing the Report of the Pakistan Commission on the Status of Women (whose members had been appointed by Zia ul-Haq), becoming a signatory to the United Nations Convention on the Elimination of All Forms of Discrimination Against Women, and ensuring the continuation of reserved seats for women in Parliament which expired in 1988.[17] But it did none of these.

The government's dismissal by President Ghulam Ishaq Khan in August 1990 is attributed more to its inability to govern than to any of the controversial stances it could have taken on substantive issues, including those specifically affecting women. Following a brief interim period, a fresh election was held in October 1990. Although the electoral process is regarded by many as having been problematic, the victor was Nawaz Sharif's Pakistan Muslim League (PML) party. Nawaz, a member of the industrialist family owning the Ittefaq Group of companies, had been groomed as a political ally in the Punjab by Zia ul-Haq. Nawaz was the natural recipient of support from the Islamist parties (such as the Jama'at-i-Islami) and others that were vehemently anti-PPP. As a consequence of this support, he did not promote the kinds of policies one would expect to be championed by a Western-educated businessman. Indeed, he virtually reinvented himself: the media showed him praying; wearing the traditional modest garb of *shalwar, kamize*, and a waistcoat wherever he went; and pledging as his top priority to continue the process of the Islamization of institutions and laws.

This priority is indicative of the dilemma that faced Nawaz Sharif's government. Similar to the dilemma facing the earlier PPP government, the PML also had to appease its supporters, most of whom had been the previous government's antagonists and many of whom were political conservatives. Nawaz Sharif lent his support to the Shariat Bill (stipulating that all laws must be in conformity with Islamic shariah), which Zia's government had been unable to get passed. Nawaz finally engineered its passage in April 1991, but without the gender-discriminatory clause that had sparked earlier controversy during Zia's regime. Women's groups remained worried, however, that the Family Laws Ordinance of 1961 might be reversed if conservative groups could convince the judiciary that it was antithetical to Islam. Their fears were further raised when the Supreme Court, in 1992, reversed the requirement that a husband give written notice of a divorce to his local union council. This made the husband's declaration of divorce, with or without witnesses, the defining legal step and one that he could confirm or deny at will. A woman, lacking written proof of divorce, remained legally and socially vulnerable.

Other state actions further attest to the ideological stance taken by the PML government. A good example can be seen in the kinds of educational reforms it sponsored. Instead of focusing on improving technical training and female education—recommended by both domestic and international experts for their obvious implications for Pakistan's development prospects—the government's formal emphasis was placed on promoting Pakistan Studies and Islamic Studies throughout the curriculum. The state was now bent upon institutional transformation within an Islamic ideological framework. At this point, the sincerity behind these efforts had become irrelevant; what is important is that the government also expected to gain popular support for this stance, as Zia had anticipated in the past. There was no longer any room for secularists within the PML party or, for that matter, within any political party in Pakistan by the mid-1990s. I believe Mohammad Ali Jinnah himself would not have found the prevailing ideological atmosphere conducive to his own political stance.

Nawaz's government placed a low priority on the activities of the Ministry for Women's Development. In 1992, a high male official in the Ministry boasted to me that women in Pakistan now enjoyed full equal rights with men. He said one could just look at his wife as an example—she was able to go shopping at whatever bazaar she wished to, and everything was available! It was no surprise, then, that the PML government undermined the power of the women's ministry by expanding its role and making it the Ministry of Women's Development and Youth Affairs. Concerns of women and children were collapsed into one unit, which became increasingly ineffective and powerless.

There was some success, however, on the local level as a consequence of the government's Social Action Programme launched in 1992 to ameliorate some of the extreme social inequities. These social conditions had earned Pakistan a great deal of criticism from donors in the international development community; at the same time they were in line with the focus of the Nawaz government on building up the local economy. The Programme created a coordinating body, the Trust for Voluntary Organisations (TVO), to support the establishment and enhancement of nongovernmental organizations (NGOs) throughout the country. The Trust focused on four kinds of activities: human resource development (including improvements in education), community health, poverty alleviation, and women in development.[18] TVO implemented small projects focused on such economically oriented issues as training women entrepreneurs and providing housing to working women in cities. The proliferation of NGOs during this era began to make small—albeit significant—strides at the local level toward improving women's options and opportunities. Other long-standing women's organizations created their own NGOs, which often targeted educating women about their legal rights, adult literacy, or income-generating activities. By the time Nawaz's government was dismissed in 1993, there was a massive proliferation of NGOs that had been a rarity in the country merely a decade earlier.

The PML government also tried to build up support among former adversaries and show that it too championed change in the society. For example, in its deliberations for the Eighth Five-Year Plan (1993–1998), the government enlisted representatives from women's groups for feedback on a range of important areas affecting women; it commissioned the well-known feminist Khawar Mumtaz to write a prescriptive paper on women in development for its momentous "National Conservation Strategy Report" (Government of Pakistan, 1992). However, the political crisis of 1992–1993 intervened and the Eighth Plan was not released. We can only speculate as to the extent to which the PML government would have both included and followed through on the solicited recommendations.

The political turbulence in Pakistan in 1993, which saw the elected government of Nawaz Sharif being dismissed, reinstated, and dismissed once again, exacerbated many of the social problems Pakistan was facing. Violence against women continued to escalate; daily items were reported in the newspapers flaming activists' concerns. Moen Qureshi's interim government arranged for national elections to be held on October 6, 1993. Both major political parties campaigned on platforms that included support for women's rights; both parties argued that each was truly the champion of the cause. This public stance seemed far removed from the reality of state policy existent under each party's respective government when it had held power. Despite all the rhetoric, marked distinctions persist in Pakistan between human rights for men and human rights for women.

Recent Events of the State Engineering Reform, and Corresponding Islamist Responses

In October 1993, it appeared that there was something new and exhilarating on Pakistan's political horizon. Four teams of international observers, as well as a larger domestic team, organized by the Pakistan Human Rights Commission agreed that the election was one of the freest and fairest in the country's history, and that it conformed to most international standards. Bhutto's rejuvenated PPP, holding a greater parliamentary majority than it did in 1988, was invited to form a government. In an ingenious pre-election move, Bhutto is said to have made her party's candidates submit documentation in advance that she could use to authorize any resignations, enabling her to be somewhat immune to the kind of political blackmail from within her own party that supporters claim stifled her efforts during her first tenure.

Bhutto continued to make the kinds of promises that have been the mainstay of the PPP. Shortly after assuming office, she vowed to introduce a new social contract to facilitate her serving the people in the country:

> The core of the government's special attention will go to its social system. This system has been unfair for a long time. The literacy rate is inadequate in the countryside and in several places it is difficult even to get water. There is inequality everywhere. The health sector itself appears to be sick; the rights of women are trampled upon; and minorities do not consider themselves part of the national mainstream. It is clear that all of these evils cannot be eradicated in a day. The government has, however, presented a concept for a

new social contract that calls for the redistribution of rights between the central government, the provinces, and local bodies. The citizens should get justice at their doorsteps.[19]

The Ministry for Women's Development and Youth Affairs, to fulfill its part of this new
social contract, articulated four priority areas for women-oriented development projects:
(1) human resource development on public–private partnership basis, (2) improvement
in educational status, (3) expansion of health-care facilities, and (4) provision of free legal
aid and protection to women. The PPP government pledged 64% more to these areas in
the 1994–1995 budget (to a total of Rs 141 million [US $3.5 million]) than it had allo-
cated in the preceding year. Additionally, as of June 1994, the Ministry had funded a total
of 339 NGO projects involved in education, health, skill training, income generation, and
the like.[20]

The PPP government has also raised the issue in Parliament to introduce a constitutional amendment for the reinstatement of women's reserved seats in the National Assembly, but legislative wrangling with the PML has since delayed its passage. While both parties have given formal support to the idea of reinstating the seats, neither wants the other
to be credited with the legislative victory (and hence possibly gain increased popular support). The measure has also run into opposition from conservative parties such as the Jama'at-i-Islami. A Jama'at member is reported to have said that women should have their
own assembly, and if they are allotted special seats in the National Assembly, they should
not be allowed to contest general elections.[21] This view makes the proposal for reserved
seats appear like a double-edged sword; under such an arrangement, Benazir Bhutto (one
of four women elected in the general election to the National Assembly in 1993) would
not have been able to become prime minister.

Indeed, while the issue of reinstating parliamentary seats reserved for women was a
timely one in late 1993, its importance has waned over time. Substance has been replaced
by form, with one party attempting to outmaneuver the other but neither commanding the
kind of popular support enjoyed only two years earlier, prior to the election. On this and
other matters, there is a growing disillusionment in Pakistan, that while both major parties
use the correct rhetoric, neither is truly committed to the needs of the common people.

Another example of this disillusionment can be seen in the attitudes of many people
toward the PPP's program to open women's police stations throughout the country. In
theory, such an action is commendable, because it finally addressed issues of power.
There has been a serious rise in violence against women in Pakistan in the last decade.[22]
The Pakistan Human Rights Commission has reported that a woman is raped every three
hours, every second victim is a minor, and every fourth is the victim of gang rape.[23] There
has also been a marked increase in the numbers of reports of sexual abuse of women
under detention by police. Some women claim they have been coerced by police officers
to trade sexual favors for their release from detention; other women were simply raped. In
a study conducted in January 1992 by War Against Rape, an NGO dedicated to publi-
cizing the problem of rape and providing victim assistance in Pakistan, police officials
were implicated in nearly 20% of the sixty rape cases reported in Lahore. In addition,
many women are intimidated from going to a police station to register a complaint, given
the prevailing patriarchal attitudes in Pakistan and their fear that a woman's complaint will
not be taken seriously or received properly. Bhutto has also stated that in response to recent episodes of domestic violence, the Law Ministry would organize panels of lawyers to

grant free legal aid to female victims of abuse, and that the Ministry for Women's Development and Youth Affairs would sponsor NGOs to set up protection centers for battered women.[24]

Opening the women's police station, staffed only by female personnel, is a visible effort on the part of the state to reduce police violence towards women. The powerlessness of women becomes aggravated when the agents of the state, who are delegated to enforce the law, become instead the perpetrators of violence. This important step that will affect women from all classes goes back to the renegotiation of power relations that is occurring at a variety of levels in the society, despite the affirmation of Islamist ideologues. The state is asserting that if a woman is arrested, she has certain rights. To receive a penalty, she must first be proven guilty, and the state has the responsibility to ensure her safety while she is in its custody.

As part of this renegotiation, the government chose an unprecedented method to establish the women's police stations. Normally in Pakistan the state just decrees something. In this instance, however, the government consulted with a number of constituent groups, including representatives of the Women's Action Forum and other groups, soliciting their suggestions for what was needed and how these needs might be addressed in the establishment of the women's police stations. The process itself is empowering as women's groups are having a voice in influencing state actions.

At a substantive level, the women's police stations would certainly stop some abuses although they have been criticized as being somewhat ineffective. Their greater importance was at a symbolic level, in that the state recognized that there had been abuses of power and was seeking to correct this. Seeing such abuses in a police station where women are confined is relatively easy. Seeing these abuses elsewhere — as in the inferior facilities provided at girls' colleges compared to those at boys' colleges, the lack of employment opportunities for women who might want to work, the widespread assumption that a woman walking alone down a street is breaking some moral code, the legal reality that a woman who leaves her husband's house can be easily arrested for adultery while in truth she might be escaping a physically abusive environment, and the existence of a law which is still "on the books" that considers a lone man's testimony as being equal to that of two women — is considerably more involved and more formidable to overcome. In the general election in February 1997 — while the reserved seats for women had not yet been reinstated — an unprecedented number of twenty-nine women contested for seats in the National Assembly. While only five actually won (Syeda Abida Hussain, NA-69 Jhang; Majeeda Begum Wyne, NA-123 Khanewal; Tahmeena Daultana, NA-130 Vehari; Nusrat Bhutto, NA-164 Larkana; and Benazir Bhutto, NA-166 Larkana), a foundation has been laid for greater numbers of women to contest elections as viable candidates. This, coupled with the government's continuing promise to reserve 10% of government positions for women — thereby remedying the long-standing problem of the dearth of women in high positions within the bureaucracy — should help the state to see the range of abuses affecting women.

While the opening of the women's police stations may appear groundbreaking to us, the reception in Pakistan has been mixed. Few people were aware of the state's goals for the police stations, and most people were suspicious of the government's intentions. People's attitudes toward democracy had undergone considerable change in Pakistan. The enthusiasm for democracy and Pakistan's future which greeted Bhutto's assumption of office in 1988 had become muted by the 1997 national election, which saw the lowest turnout of registered voters in the country's history. Random acts of violence once confined to metropolitan Karachi have become commonplace in many other areas of the country. People are frustrated with what they perceive as politicians fighting each other for power instead of working for the needs of the average person. The credibility of both political parties and their leaders have suffered. For the first time in Pakistan's history, support for Islamist parties is swelling. They are becoming alternatives for a disappointed, well-intentioned electorate. To counter that upsurge, both Benazir Bhutto and Nawaz Sharif were careful not to take any stance that may be interpreted as anti-Islamic.

Bhutto's participation at the United Nations Population and Development conference in Cairo in September 1994 is a cogent example of the impasse that she had reached. That she intended to go to Cairo personally and participate in the conference at all raised much protest among increasingly important Islamist leaders in the country. However, when she gave her address, she delivered the Islamists' script. Was her performance in Cairo determined by her perception of herself as politically vulnerable, and was she therefore concerned that saying the "wrong thing" would bring criticism from leaders of other Muslim countries? Or was it politically motivated as a means by which she could gain the patronage of supporters of Islamist parties within Pakistan? Or was it an expression of her innermost beliefs and interpretation of Islam?

Bhutto could have presented a more modernist interpretation of Islamic views toward population planning at the Cairo conference. She could have stated that Islam favors nurturing one's children and providing them with a good life. Supporters of this stance in Pakistan have argued that because Islam places so much importance on *haquq-ul-abad* (one's obligations to God's creation), that it in turn places a great deal of importance on the responsibility of caring for one's children. This stance would have lent support to Pakistan's family-planning goals of lowering what is one of the world's highest population growth rates (at least 2.9%). The argument continues that the lack of success in family planning in Pakistan has had less to do with any ideological opposition than with simple bureaucratic mismanagement. Earlier population planning efforts never raised the issue of Islamic teachings and values. For example, the Social Marketing of Family Planning project begun in 1986 under Zia's government tried to use the media as a means to persuade people to think about having smaller families. Advertisements appeared showing how much happier children were when their parents only had to be concerned with the needs of two offspring. At the time, religion was not raised as being necessarily relevant to the immense task at hand.

But Bhutto opened a Pandora's box in Cairo and brought in religious teachings on the issue, stating that Islam is opposed to abortion because Allah has promised to provide for however many children one has. She placed greater attention on the issue of abortion—and her principled stance in opposition to it—than on the need to raise the status of women and thus to lower population growth rates. Her government praised her principled stand on Islam, supporting a woman having as many children as possible:

> Pakistan's effective participation and success in so reshaping the Programme of Action of the International Conference on Population and Development held in Cairo as to meet the religious and ethical values and standards of member states could perhaps be described as the government's most important achievement in the field of population planning in its first year in office. The Prime Minister's decision to lead the Pakistan delega-

tion and address the inaugural session paid the country rich dividends in terms of international goodwill and respect for Pakistan's principled stand on the issue. . . . It was because of her that [the] Pakistan delegation was able, of course in close collaboration with other Muslim countries and in consultation with many other developing and developed states, to bring about important amendments in the suggested Programme of Action, paving the way for its final adoption by the Conference.[25]

I am not arguing that she should have sidestepped Islamic orientations relevant to the Population and Development conference. Rather, there were other interpretations or issues that could have been raised instead, such as placing the need to educate and empower women in an Islamic context. This would have furnished support to women having a say in their own fertility—as the young woman I interviewed in the Walled City of Lahore hopes she will have in the future—and thereby address issues of power. But she did not.

In August 1995, at a meeting of Muslim women parliamentarians, Bhutto declared that Islam was a religion of tolerance and blamed widespread discrimination against women on archaic traditions and ignorance.[26] At the same time, the government of Pakistan became a signatory to the U.N. Convention on the Elimination of All Forms of Discrimination against Women. At the Beijing conference a month later, Bhutto declared that Muslim women have a special responsibility to help distinguish between actual Islamic teachings and those that may popularly be assumed to be Islamic but are instead social taboos spun by the traditions of a patriarchal society. She further declared that Pakistan would do all it could to promote the empowerment of its women.

Islamist interpretations, particularly attitudes toward women in society, have also changed over time. In 1965, Islamist leaders supported Fatima Jinnah's bid for the presidency; twenty-three years later they wanted a fatwa issued to prevent Benazir Bhutto from becoming prime minister. In 1952, the Family Planning Association of Pakistan was established. In the ensuing years, the association and successor organizations have come to realize that the single most important factor involved in lowering population growth rates is the enhancement of the power and status of women. But in Cairo in 1994, instead of raising and standing behind this issue, Bhutto stood up and focused her comments on Islam's views opposing abortion, which is a separate matter.

The dilemma within Pakistan is that there is no one interpretation of Islam that is embraced by the vast majority of people. While an overwhelming majority of Pakistanis (97%) are Muslim, they include the full range of Muslim sects. Are there institutional conventions based on Islam on which all Pakistanis can agree? Pakistan's experience thus far has been that there are very few. For example, Shias and members of other minorities held impassioned protests when the state introduced its *zakat* system, considered standardizing inheritance laws, and introduced certain kinds of punishments all based on *Hanbali* interpretations of shariah. In the past, Islam could play a powerful social role as a unifier, but such a role became problematic once it became standardized into law because, in practice, there are so many "Islams" in Pakistan. Indeed, once the state began to legislate a given interpretation of Islam, its ability to play a superstructural role became problematic.

Where the juncture between Islam, women, and state action will lie in twenty-first century Pakistan must be resolved soon. There is an urgency associated with questions of education, family planning, and women having a political voice. Are there enough physical, capital, and human resources to have the postulate of equal but separate viably work? Can Pakistan's social development goals ever be met if it does not contain its population growth rate? If the status and power of women does not rise, development per se will be compromised, as it has been in the past. At this time, there do not seem to be signs of an Islamist response to this quagmire.

References

Asghar, Raja. 1995. "Moslem Women MPs Vow to Fight Terrorism, Prejudice." BBC/Islamabad, August 3.

Carroll, Lucy. 1982. "Nizam-i-Islam: Processes and Conflicts in Pakistan's Programme of Islamisation, with Special Reference to the Position of Women." *Journal of Commonwealth and Comparative Politics* 20: 57–95.

Government of Pakistan. 1992. "National Conservation Strategy Report." Islamabad.

Jehangir, Asma, and Hina Jilani. 1990. *The Hudood Ordinances: A Divine Sanction?* Lahore: Rhotas Books.

Jilani, Hina. 1994. "Law as an Instrument of Social Control" in *Locating the Self: Perspectives on Women and Multiple Identities*, ed. Nighat Said Khan, Rubina Saigol and Afiya Zia, 96–105. Lahore: ASR Publications.

Mirza, Sarfaraz Hussain. 1969. *Muslim Women's Role in the Pakistan Movement*. Lahore: Research Society of Pakistan.

Mumtaz, Mumtaz, and Farida Shaheed. 1987. *Women of Pakistan: Two Steps Forward, One Step Back?* London: Zed; Karachi: Vanguard.

Pakistan Commission on the Status of Women. 1986. "Report of the Commission on the Status of Women in Pakistan." Islamabad.

People's Government Fulfilling an Agenda for Change: Social Sector. 1994. November.

Planning Commission, Government of Pakistan. 1988. *The Seventh Five-Year Plan: 1988–93 & Perspective Plan, 1988–2003*. Karachi: Manager of Publications.

———. 1992. "Eighth Five-Year Plan (1993–98) Approach Paper" Islamabad.

Sarwar, Beena. 1995. "Women: Muslim Legislators Conference Sets the Tone for Beijing." Inter-Press Service, August 7.

Shaheed, Farida, and Khawar Mumtaz. 1992. *Women's Economic Participation in Pakistan*. Islamabad: UNICEF Pakistan.

Trust for Voluntary Organizations. 1992. *First Annual Report, 1992*. Islamabad.

United Nations Development Programme. 1991. *Human Development Report 1991*. New York: Oxford University Press.

United Nations. 1991. *The World's Women: Trends and Statistics, 1970–1990*. New York.

Weiss, Anita M. 1992. *Walls Within Walls: Life Histories of Working Women in the Old City of Lahore*. Boulder, Colo.: Westview.

———. 1986. "Implications of the Islamization Program for Women." In *Islamic Reassertion in Pakistan: the Application of Islamic Laws in a Modern State*, ed. Anita M. Weiss, 97–113. Syracuse, N.Y.: Syracuse University Press.

———. 1994. "The Consequences of State Policies for Women in Pakistan" in *The Politics of Social Transformation in Afghanistan, Iran, and Pakistan*, ed. Myron Weiner and Ali Banuazizi, 412–444. Syracuse, N.Y.: Syracuse University Press.

Zia, Afiya Shehrbano. 1994. *Sex Crime in the Islamic context: Rape, Class and Gender in Pakistan*. Lahore: ASR Publications.

Notes

1. Mumtaz and Shaheed (1987, 40).

2. Disputes in Bosnia, Chechnya, and Indian-held Kashmir are often cited as examples of this.

3. For further elaboration on details of women's lives in the Walled City, refer to Weiss (1992), on which this section is based.

4. For an extended discussion of gendered decision-making powers in the Walled City, see Weiss (1992, 114).

5. This is based on research conducted in 1987 for *Walls Within Walls* (Weiss, 1992) and followed up on in the ensuing five years.

6. Research for this section was conducted in 1992 at eight colleges in Lahore on a CIES Fulbright Lecturing/Research grant.

7. Coeducation now only exists at the M.A. level in government colleges and universities in Pakistan.

8. For further discussion of women's views on how family obligations are changing refer to Weiss (1992, 121–122).

9. Mirza (1969) and Mumtaz and Shaheed (1987) both include extensive discussions of this period.

10. Refer to Mirza (1969) for further elaboration on women's activism during the Pakistan movement.

11. Jilani (1994) discusses the class basis of this action.

12. For further discussion on Pakistan state policy's effects on women's position, refer to Mumtaz and Shaheed (1987) and Weiss (1994).

13. The issue of this *fatwa* became important in the 1988 elections. In 1965, Fatima Jinnah was supported by the Islamist party, Jama'at-i-Islam, in her bid for the presidency. However, in 1988, the same party contended that Benazir Bhutto could not become president because the office was the equivalent to the Islamic notion of an *'amir*, who must be a male. The dispute was finally resolved with the issuance of another *fatwa* that contended that the Prime Minister is only the head of a political party and not the head of state, and it was therefore acceptable within Islam for the office to be held by a woman.

14. Refer to Carroll (1982), Weiss (1986), and Jehangir and Jilani (1990) for further elaboration.

15. As quoted in Mumtaz and Shaheed (1987, 183).

16. The full text can be found in Planning Commission (1988, 281).

17. The 1973 constitution stipulated that the reserved seats for women were to remain in effect for two national elections, after which the provision for them would expire if it were not renewed.

18. For an overview of TVO's activities, refer to its *First Annual Report, 1992*, and the occasional status reports it has released on particular kinds of efforts.

19. As reported in a BBC news broadcast, October 29, 1993.

20. This is based on information in *People's Government* (1994, 22–24).

21. Reuters News Service (India), April 28, 1994.

22. A valuable discussion is found in Zia (1994).

23. *Sydney Morning Herald*, May 28, 1994.

24. Reuters News Service (India), March 24, 1994.

25. As quoted in *People's Government* (1994, 20–21).

26. The meeting resulted in the Islamabad Declaration (1995), which called on Islamic states to abolish discriminatory legislation and help women combat illiteracy, deprivation, bias, and violence. For commentaries, see Sarwan (1995) and Ashgar (1995).

Changing Gender Relations and the Development Process in Oman

There is growing recognition of the important role women play in the political and socioeconomic development process of their countries. This chapter seeks to redress their neglect as subjects by analyzing gender dynamics and social change in Oman, a country which despite its strategic significance was, at least until 1970, one of the least known countries in the world. The sex/gender system and all that it involves is undergoing profound change in Middle Eastern countries. Women are immersed in diverse socioeconomic, political, and cultural arrangements. According to V. M. Moghadam, "To study the Middle East and Middle Eastern women is to recognize the diversity within the region and within the female population."[1] Thus, an important objective of this chapter is to increase the amount of data on what women do and why.

In Oman, one of Sultan Qaboos' political and social objectives has been to organize new constituencies which were at a disadvantage prior to his coming to power in 1970. Among these groups are women. While Oman appears to be among the most progressive of the monarchies of the Arabian Peninsula in introducing women into the national development process, women were not members of the State Consultative Council (1981–1991), nor are they represented in the more recently created Majlis Al-Shura.

Despite their important contributions, women in Oman continue to face formidable social, economic, and political barriers. Their roles and status are structurally determined by state ideology (regime orientation and judicial system), level and type of economic development, and class location.[2] These factors serve as independent variables in this analysis and will be examined in terms of their impact on a six-dimension framework of women's status adopted from Janet Giele[3]: political expression, work and mobility, family, education, health and fertility, and cultural expression. Due to the nature of the dependent variables, state ideology, economic development, or class location will be more relevant to some categories than to others. Also, the discussion of some of the variables will be more complete than others due both to the state of methodology in the social sciences and the difficulty of finding sufficient and reliable data.

Political Expression

The Formal Aspects of Political Behavior

Politics and public life in Oman appear on the surface to be the exclusive province of men. By the mid-1990s, Oman was one of the few states in the world preserving a system of absolute monarchy. Sultan Qaboos is the source of all authority—not so much head of state as the embodiment of the state itself. There is no constitution, no legislature, and no political parties. All government enactments, laws, and appointments ultimately must be approved by the ruler. A State Consultative Council was appointed in 1981. It was controlled by government members, met infrequently, and had few powers. In 1990, the Sultan announced that Oman would have a new consultative council, chosen through indirect election on a provincial basis, with expanded powers. The initiative came from the top of the political system, not by public demand. Other government institutions on the national level include the Council of Ministers, the National Defense Council, the Development Council, and the Ministry of Diwan Affairs, which supervises the affairs of the royal court. The only woman to serve on any of these bodies before 1994 was Rajiha 'Abd al-Amir, who was Undersecretary for Planning on the Development Council.

The idea of individual rights and democracy are not indigenous to the Arabian Peninsula. There have never been directly elected representative institutions in Oman. Oil substantially altered the relationship between state and society in Oman, resulting in an expansion of state functions. The increased wealth of the general population, combined with the increased power of the state to confer or withhold that wealth, reduced demands for political representation and participation in the 1970s and 1980s. Given the underdevelopment of their country before 1970 under the current Sultan's father, Said Bin Taimur, and the comparatively late discovery of oil in the country (the first exports began only in 1967), most Omanis are still more concerned with simply having a decent standard of living than worrying about any Western notion of modern political rights.

However, as the role of the state in the Gulf countries has grown, some citizens have begun to make demands for representative institutions and responsible government.[4] Citizens are increasingly holding the state accountable for economic conditions and would like to see this accountability institutionalized. The intense ideological pressure felt by the Sultan's regime during the Dhofar Rebellion of the early 1970s, as well as the oil bust of 1985 and the 1990–1991 Gulf War, may have inclined Sultan Qaboos to a loosening of the restrictions on political life by his creation of an elected Consultative Council, the Majlis al-Shura, in 1991. This council, chosen through an innovative selection process, has greater powers than its predecessor. It has displayed a spirit of independence and subjected government ministers to sharp questioning. However, it has no right to review foreign and defense policy issues and produced no major legislative initiative during its first years.

In response to recent census figures, Sultan Qaboos in 1994 increased the number of members on the Majlis Al-Shura from 59 to 80. Women were also granted the right to vote and stand for elections. Given the novelty and embryonic nature of Oman's venture in parliamentary government, the right of women to candidacy to the Majlis al-Shura was confined to the Muscat Governorate. Two women gained appointment to the council: Shukar bint Muhammad bin Salem al Ghamari, representing Muscat, and Tiyba bint

Muhammad bin Rashid al Ma'awali, representing Seeb. Given the conservative, patriarchal nature of Gulf society, this constitutes a breakthrough among the nations belonging to the Gulf Cooperation Council. Sultan Qaboos, with the approval of the Ibadi Mufti of Muscat, took a step along the road to limited democracy and the inclusion of women in the political process. Might the autonomy demonstrated historically in the country's unique expression of Ibadi Islam and independent foreign policy come to be demonstrated as well in the political sphere?

Oman's regime orientation and ideology play an influential role in shaping women's status in the country. Oman is a neopatriarchal state, a monarchy binding religion to power and state authority; it is a state where the family, rather than the individual, constitutes the primary unit of the community. Oman was one of the first countries to embrace Islam during the lifetime of the Prophet, and the religion remains influential in all aspects of life and society in the Sultanate. Omani Islam is unique in that it is principally Ibadism, a branch of Islam that became an integral part of Omani national culture and a political force that shaped the development of Omani history in post-Islamic times. The Ibadis are distinguished from the main body of Muslims over their insistence that the Caliph should not be determined according to genealogical considerations but should be elected on the basis of merit.

Lacking a constitution or a comprehensive civil code, the juridical system is based on Islamic canon law (the sharia), and administered by judges (qadis) appointed by the minister of justice. In remote areas, the law is based on tribal custom. The sharia remains preeminent for all matters of personal and family law. Apart from the sharia, there is a statutory system of law expressed in royal decrees ...id ministerial decisions published in the Daily Gazette and a private international law that applies to commercial and financial transactions. This rounds out the picture of the Omani legal system, but the latter regulations are of slight if any relevance to women's personal and legal status.

Gender dynamics in Oman are affected by the policies of such a neopatriarchal state, which are often pronatalist, emphasize sex differences and complementary roles rather than legal equality, and serve to perpetuate stratification based on gender. The Islamic legal code sustains the illusion of unchangeable gender differences, using women's reproductive function to justify their segregation in public, their restriction to the home, and their lack of civil and legal rights. Oman, along with most other Muslim countries, has not signed or ratified the United Nations Convention on the Elimination of All Forms of Discrimination Against Women. Except perhaps for a few charities, nongovernmental women's groups are missing in the conservative Gulf states, including Oman. (Kuwait is an exception.)

Oman has one woman decision-maker (on the Development Council), and women hold approximately 13% of government jobs. That women should be represented at all in the higher political echelons in a system with no voting rights and no parliament can be explained by elite recruitment, by which women from elite families have access to the limited opportunities for women. Upper-class and upper-middle-class women have access to greater resources and can exercise a greater number of choices than can women from lower classes. Oman became open to the modern world only in 1970. Despite its late entry into the modern world, it has, in the short space of twenty-five years, recognized the significance of women for the task of national development and provided one of the most open climates on the Peninsula for a change in women's roles.

Middle-class women, benefiting from economic development, universal schooling, mass communications, and eventual legal reform, will be at the center of change. As this group emerges and grows in Oman, its members will gain confidence in applying social science skills to investigations of their own society and their position within it. Upper-class women, given their ties to elites and those in power, may also play a particular role, as they have in the Kuwaiti Women's Social and Cultural Society. Due to its membership, this nongovernmental organization worked closely with governmental organizations in calling for and convening the first (1975) and second (1981) regional conferences for Gulf women. These conferences emphasized older modes of thought regarding Gulf women. Yet the studies presented by Arab male researchers, as well as those of Arab and Gulf women, agreed on the necessity of a new goal, that of integrating women into development.[5] For a country that has only recently emerged from an era analogous to the Middle Ages, attitudes cannot change overnight. Change will come slowly for Oman.

The Informal Political Influence of Omani Women

In stressing the formal, public, and institutional aspects of political behavior where women do not appear to have a visible role, the political significance of women in the private and informal arena cannot be overlooked. Traditionally, Omani women were powerful in influencing family decision making. Omani society is based on kinship relationships, meaning that an individual's main social and economic ties are with the family. Society emphasizes the collectivity of the family and the tribe over the individual. Thus, women and their networks play an important, if often invisible, political role.

Traditionally, women marry in their late teens, but with the spread of education the age of marriage has been delayed. A woman begins to gain status when she produces children, especially sons. Ultimate control over the lives of women tends to remain in the hands of their husbands, fathers, and brothers. Even so, women's power is far from negligible. Women with extensive contacts in female society can gather useful information for the male members of their family. Women can observe what is being discussed and done in the homes they visit. They are important political actors because of their significant position in the webs of informal relationships that make up the private domain. Women can also play decisive roles in arranging marriages that can have political implications. Their support or opposition often influences which matches take place. Visiting between households strengthens ties between allied men. Within the family circles, women's opinions often affect men's decisions. The laws of Islamic inheritance have allowed women to amass significant economic power to buttress their political influence.

Kinship also plays an important role in the political process. In the sheikhdoms of the Gulf, the core of the political elite consists of members of the ruling family. Sultan Qaboos is a member of the Al Bu Said family, which has ruled the country since the second half of the eighteenth century. However, due to the small size of the the Sultan's family and the absence of a male heir, his relatives do not have the same political influence or power of many royal families on the Arabian Peninsula. The mother of Sultan Qaboos may have exercised considerable informal authority, given the great loss felt throughout the entire country at her death in August 1992.

Restructuring to Meet Women's Needs as a Political Issue

Sultan Qaboos said in a press release shortly after coming to power in 1970 that his first and immediate task would be to establish as soon as possible a forceful and modern government whose main goal would be to remove unnecessary restrictions under which his people had suffered and to provide a happier and more secure future for all of them. While Oman has certainly come a long way from the equivalent of the dark ages, the state still plays a major role in perpetuating social, economic, and ideological processes that subordinate women. Women are treated as dependents on men in legal and administrative procedures rather than as persons in their own right. State policy upholds patriarchal family forms in which women do not have the same access to resources as men. Equality for women will require a diminution of male privilege. Resources will need to be distributed from men to women. Restructuring to meet women's needs is thus a political issue.[6]

There is an often quoted remark by the Sultan to the effect that his country is not yet ready for Western-style parliamentary democracy and that no purpose would be served by setting up an imitation parliament. The implication is that, gradually, the country will move toward a less personalized system of government. In January 1992, the Majlis al-Shura met for the first time, replacing the appointed State Consultative Council that had existed since 1981. Though by no means a Western parliament, the Council is viewed by many as a first step toward broader participation in government.

Oman has been independent since it evicted the Portuguese in the mid-seventeenth century and has experienced no nationalist movement, which generated activity by women in so many Arab counties under colonial rule. Power is in the hands of Sultan Qaboos who is the ultimate authority. He accepts his own power as justifiable based on the legitimacy of inheritance and tradition. Television, radio, and newspapers are rigorously controlled by the Ministry of Information. No hint of a critical or nonestablishment opinion ever appears. At the end of twenty-five years of what Oman calls its "renaissance," most Omanis seem satisfied with what has taken place. Given that Oman was the last Arab country to begin the process of transition from the constraints of isolation, traditional society, and a social structure that had not changed for years, personal attitudes in Oman are often influenced more by economic concerns than by politics or social conscience.

The country is thus an unusual mixture. On the one hand it is a materialistic society that appreciates the higher standard of living brought by oil wealth, built on deep loyalties to family and tribe, and based on free-market principles for trade and commerce. In contrast to this are statist precepts supporting welfare measures and loyalty to Islam. The outcome is a society that on the surface is highly Westernized, but beneath the surface it is entirely different from Western societies. Relating this to the position of women: if the patriarchal order of the family is seriously shaken to provide a more egalitarian role for women, what will happen to the neopatriarchal order of the entire society? When the changes brought by modernity, among which figure the emancipation of women, challenge the underpinnings of tradition, what will the result be? Furthermore, while massive oil wealth, albeit more modest in Oman, did reduce demands for participation in the early years of the oil boom, according to Gause, the process of state growth and educational expansion have led to a new wave of participatory demands from society in the Gulf Arab monarchies. Women may be among the groups demanding greater participation—

witness the women's driving incident in Saudi Arabia, in which women commandeered their own vehicles to protest their lack of rights.

Employment

The Quran and the Economic Rights of Women

A woman's right to gainful employment has existed since the earliest days of Islam and is guaranteed by the Quran. The Islamic religion bestows economic freedom upon men and women. When a woman is denied the right to exercise this freedom by family members, the blame lies with tradition, not religion. Muhammad succeeded in making great progress in the elevation of the status of women. Equality of the sexes, however, was difficult to incorporate into tribal practices and customs. For example, according to some interpretations, nowhere in the Quran is seclusion and veiling of the face mentioned. Local customs and traditions brought them on and preserved them. Islam, in time, became an integral part of tribal society. Tribal customs, including those that made it difficult for women to exercise their economic freedom, became viewed as a sacred tradition passed down from their ancestors.

Even though the Quran strengthened the economic position of women, due to local traditions forcing women to remain within the confines of the home, it was difficult for them to exercise their economic rights. In the pre-Islamic and early Islamic period, women did enjoy economic freedom. The Prophet's wife, Khadija, was a highly successful business woman. There is much Quranic legislation referring to women's right to inherit as well as bequeath. Daughters are entitled to their share, as are wives and mothers, each according to her position in the family. They are free to invest this money or property as they wish without the approval of the closest male relative. A husband cannot force his wife to give him money. Even among poor couples, a wife usually keeps her money or property separate from that of her husband. There is no shared community property between them. In Islamic practice, there is no concept of matrimonial property, or property jointly owned by spouses. Another example of Islam's support for the economic independence of women is the fact that the bride price (*mahr*) is given to the woman for her own personal use and not to her father. When the bride does receive the mahr for her personal use, she uses it to purchase gold, which serves as a form of security should she ever have to support herself.[7] Women in the Gulf area, unlike most parts of the Muslim East, have always received their assured shares of inheritance as designated by the Quran. For women who needed to provide an income for themselves and their children, opportunities were scarce prior to the discovery of oil.

State Expansion and Political Economy

The major source of social change in the Middle East since World War II has been the twofold process of economic development and state expansion. The economic systems of the region have modernized and grown, affecting social structure, patterns of stratification, and the position of women. Economic modernization in Oman is based on income from oil. Even with its oil reserves, discovered later and more modest than those of other Gulf states, women's role is restricted owing to the country's semiperipheral position in the world economic system. Oman is largely dependent on its oil revenues, and it has limited water and agricultural resources. Hindered by a small domestic market and high transportation costs for exported goods resulting in limited industrialization and manufacturing for export, there have been limited opportunities for women. What capital-intensive industries and technologies do exist in the formal industrial sector tend to favor male labor.

The position of women within the labor market is frequently studied as an empirical measure of women's status. For scholars and policy makers who argue that women's economic dependence on men is the principal cause of their low status, change in the structure of the labor force is the key target. Others argue that employed women have greater control over decision making within the family. Participation in the labor force is thus a key indicator of women's contribution to national development. Moreover, an important measure of women's status is the extent of their integration in the formal labor force.

Women's employment patterns then are largely shaped by the political economy of Oman. In this regard, female employment has been constrained by overall limited industrialization. Oman is a country rich in oil but poor in other resources—including population. It will continue to be almost entirely dependent on oil and any money earned from overseas investments. Countries rich in oil and poor in other resources have usually chosen an industrial strategy based on petroleum products and petrochemicals. A strategy depending on oil, gas, and finance, which is capital but not labor intensive, is not helpful to female employment.[8]

Oman has a small population that depends on expatriate labor (roughly 20% of the workforce). Lessening this dependence and mobilizing the nation for development when Oman's oil wells run dry necessitates making the most of the nation's human resources and employing women, who constitute nearly half of the population (47%). Muslim countries such as Oman rank among the nation-states with the lowest percentage of females. Their low ranking may reflect the tendency of some Muslim countries not to report women. Because the country has only a small income from oil and limited resources, Sultan Qaboos considers it necessary that women enter the labor market as soon as possible. Women's economic status and employment possibilities, however, have been limited by the inability of the formal economy to absorb all the entrants to the labor force, a situation worsened by the financial crisis of the mid-1980s resulting from a sharp drop in the price of oil. Oman's debt increased considerably during this time.

The greatest opportunities for women are available in government, following a global trend. Omani women prefer public sector jobs, given the social stigma attached to private sector employment and to any positions where a woman is on view to the public. Public service is the second largest employer in Oman after the oil sector, which largely hires expatriate men. In government jobs, women receive pay equivalent to that of men for comparable work. Throughout the Arab world, equal pay for equal work has been a long-standing tradition.[9] Government-employed women also receive generous benefits for maternity leave—two months paid leave and one to two years unpaid leave. According to estimates, women make up about 13% of Oman's governmental employees, and they usually work in traditionally female fields. Women from elite and middle-class families are those most likely to be employed, especially in the Gulf, suggesting a relationship between class, income, and work participation. Like other Omani civil servants in senior positions, most of the women were educated outside the country. Women work as police officers and are allowed to join the armed forces.

In the oil sector, which provides 95% of Oman's income and is the largest employer, women constitute 10% of a workforce of 4,500 at Petroleum Development Oman (PDO). Omani women make up 84% of the total number of women working at PDO. Women work on the coast and not in the interior, where about half of the jobs are located, although they may visit if their work requires.

Social attitudes are more conservative regarding employment of women in the private sector. Few women hold positions in administrative and managerial occupations. Yet, Omani women can be found at many levels and in various sectors of the economy. Women have positions as bank officials, hotel managers, entrepreneurs, secretaries, nurses, junior accountants, and receptionists. There are no women's banks in Oman. Women work for a variety of reasons: to replace expatriates, to use their education, to earn extra income, and, perhaps for a very few, to achieve self-fulfillment. As long as oil revenues remain adequate, none of the working women need to work out of economic necessity. If a woman has no male relatives to support her, she may rely on the government welfare system, which allows no woman or man to go without the basic necessities of life.

Omani women presently work out of a sense of duty to their country or self-fulfillment, which should make it easier for them to assume roles of both mother and worker, since they are aware that they are not forced to work. The idea of employment as an alternative to marriage will not easily take root in Oman, due to the high value placed on the institution of marriage in Muslim societies. For Muslim women and men, marriage is strongly recommended in the Quran. Financial constraints may one day require women to work and lower the number of children women choose to have, but the institution of marriage itself will remain strong throughout Muslim societies. Employment for women is made easier in Oman by the availability of domestic help. At present, women working in the private sector form a small percentage of the total workforce, about 8%. All working women in Oman do so with the consent of their husbands.

With ever increasing levels of education and expanded public access, the bases for noticeable and extensive changes in the status of women are being established. Areas of expansion for women in Oman will be the professions, especially medicine, pharmacy, teaching, nursing, and the social sciences, which are occupationally stereotyped as women's fields. Women may be less likely to enter saleswork or even clerical work, because these are occupations with the highest possibility of unregulated contact with outsiders. The merchant class has been typically male, with Hindus and Muslims from the Indian subcontinent and Shia from Iran predominant in Muscat. The commercial elite, consisting of about twelve merchant houses, ranks just below the ruling family and a few expatriates, mainly British, who occupy positions of importance in the military, the oil industry, and the development program and enjoy the Sultan's support. The merchant families control import franchises and are active in various enterprises other than oil. The traditional urban markets have been the province of men. Women in Oman remain an underutilized human resource because of limited industrialization and traditional definitions of women's role.

The Contradictions in Official Ideology

On one plane, Oman is among the more progressive of the Gulf states in supporting an enlarged role for women in the public sector. The initiative for this has come from the

Sultan, and it is hard to imagine that Oman would have taken these steps otherwise. Another development has, perhaps inadvertently, contributed to the process as well. This was the return of East African Omanis to Oman in the early 1970s. Many of them were married (some to women who were not Omani) and had daughters who had been raised and educated in a British colonial setting and had pursued careers. When these women returned to Oman, they sought similar jobs there. As a result, the civil service acquired a considerable number of proficient female personnel. Omanis became more quickly accustomed to seeing women in responsible jobs, and Omani women came to realize that careers were possible and acceptable.

Yet, a gender ideology stressing women's family roles has continued to limit their participation. Oman is among the patriarchal countries characterized by extremely restrictive codes of behavior for women, rigid gender segregation, and a powerful ideology joining family honor to female virtue. Perceptions of the masculine and feminine are embodied in law and custom, defined by a judicial system based on the sharia, and a belief system shaped by Ibadi Islam. Men and women have unequal access to political power and economic resources. Cultural images and representations of women are fundamentally different from those of men. The legal system, the educational system (using textbooks in which nearly half the lessons portray women doing housework), and the labor market are all areas for the construction and reproduction of gender inequality and the continuing subordination of women. Inequalities are learned and taught, leading to a deprived group who do not perceive their own disadvantages—thus helping to perpetuate these disadvantages.

Oman's state managers therefore display some ambivalence toward the integration of women into the economy. On the one hand, they recognize the need for economic diversification and the necessity for making the most efficient use of the country's chief resource: its own population. On the other hand, the state supports a gender ideology based on sexual differences, an ideology that stresses family roles for women and perpetuates a system of stratification based on gender. The government does not take an active role in improving or facilitating women's status and opportunities beyond the areas of education, health, and traditionally female occupations, nor does it have an active and autonomous women's organization, other than a charity or two, to protect and further women's rights and status. Such contradictory aims create role conflicts for women, who find themselves caught between the prospect of contributing to national development through employment and a conception of gender that stresses family roles and distance from males for women.

The Differential Impact of Development on Women's Lives

Economic growth is not gender blind. As economies develop, existing gender gaps persist in the distribution of wealth and in access to resources, and these gaps often grow worse. From the 1950s through the 1980s, worldwide standards of living rose dramatically. Yet women never achieved parity with men, even in the presumed developed countries. Development, consequently, does not always provide benefits to women; women may even fall behind. Unless specific steps are taken, they may fall even further behind. Advances in technology may further erode the status of women, demoting them to less valuable work or even eliminating their jobs. The industrialization that has gone with the globalization of production has meant more employment opportunities, but often these are low-tech, low-wage jobs. Access to a decent income may increase their bargaining power in the household, but as long as women carry the double burden of unpaid work in reproduction and sustenance of human resources as well as paid work, producing goods and services, women will be unable to compete with men in the market on equal terms. Women with high incomes can reduce their disadvantage in the market relative to men by employing household help. Even this, however, does not eliminate their disadvantage, since they still have responsibility for household management. All other women who are not in the highest income groups must undertake a double day of work. Development then has a differential impact on women's lives depending on region, culture, and class.

Family

Family as the Linchpin of Omani Society

Through all these changes, Omani social life both in the city and the village continues to focus on the family. Family loyalty permeates all aspects of life in Oman (and the Gulf in general), with family law being the least modified of all legal codes by modern legislation. It is not uncommon for an Omani to postpone a meeting or other business due to family responsibilities and obligations. Family groupings form the basis of group interaction, with lineage patterns operating as the invisible framework of the community. The typical family has a patriarchal structure, one in which power is held by male heads of households. There is a clear separation between the public and private spheres of life. Sexual segregation is the norm. Most households, poor or rich, have two living rooms (majlises), one for males and the other for females and close family friends. More urbanized young married couples tend to socialize together more and more at home or in restaurants. In the private sphere of the home, the patriarch exercises paramount power over all junior males, all females, and all children. In the public sphere, power is commanded by male patriarchs. Just about every man expects to be a patriarch at some time in his life; no female holds any formal public position of significant power. Although a few upper-class and middle-class women have become employed outside the home, norms dictate that females are not allowed into the public realm of power. Women may influence their male patriarch within the household informally, but this is their only avenue to power.

The traditional Omani family unit usually consists of a man, his wife or wives, his married sons with their wives and children, his unmarried sons and daughters, and possibly other relatives such as a widowed or divorced mother or sister. The preferred marriage is that of a man and his father's brother's daughter. Marriage is a family affair rather than a personal one. Marriage patterns are critical, because they determine the future of the family group. The Omani extended family is patrilineal; a person belongs to the family of the father. Daughters marry into families of their husbands. The family is also patrilocal, patriarchal, endogamous, and occasionally polygamous. According to Germaine Tillion, it was endogamy, the practice of marrying within the lineage, that set the shape for the oppression of women in patrilineal society, long before the rise of Islam. Endogamy kept property within the lineage and protected the economic and political interests of the men.[10] Upon marriage sons bring their brides to live with or near the father, thus strengthening the extended family. Unless the family is prosperous, newlywed couples may live in part of their parents' house. The formation of nuclear households is still rare in Oman. Some nuclear households form parts of extended families, living in adjacent or nearby houses rather than in the same house. The undisputed head of the family is the eldest male of the senior generation. The head of the family is responsible for all family matters. He is recognized as the sole owner of all its property and he makes all decisions of importance.

The honor of the men of the family depends on the conduct of the women, particularly the sisters and daughters. Women are expected to be modest, decorous, and virtuous. Men expect brides to be virgins, but no such expectation exists for bridegrooms. The slightest inference of unrequited indiscretion could irreparably destroy the family's honor. Although family honor resides in the person of a woman, it is actually the property of the men of her natal family. A faithless wife, for example, shames her father and brothers far more than her husband. Enforcement of honor is the obligation of the men of a family and a requisite of any social standing. Control over women is considered necessary in part because women are regarded as the latent source of *fitna* (moral or social disorder). Men traditionally have the unilateral right of divorce and the right to decide whether their wives work outside the home or travel. The sharia does not require women to veil, but certain *hadith* (sayings of the Prophet) do. Social mores in Oman tend to be more tolerant than those in some other Gulf countries in this regard. Women can shop at the *suq* in Matrah, Nizwa, or Ibri without veils and wear brightly colored clothing and shawls. Wearing a headscarf without covering the face is the practice in cities, but type and style of veiling varies according to region in Oman.[11] Women do have the right to drive, but on the whole, Omani women's lives are severely circumscribed. An adverse sex ratio, low female literacy and educational attainment, high maternal mortality rates, and low female labor force participation in the formal sector are demographic facts still characteristic of the country.

The Family Writ Large

Oman is a neopatriarchal state, a general term that has been applied to the various types of regime in the Middle East.[12] Thus, Oman's contemporary political structure, a conservative monarchy or sultanate, is the outward form for a state whose internal structures remain rooted in the patriarchal values and social relations of kinship, tribe, and religious and ethnic groups. Like the family writ large, Omani society is a paternal one characterized by the loyalty found in the relationship between father and son and in the larger family units between fellow tribesmen. In fact, Sultan Qaboos is regarded very much as the father of his people. Most Omanis of this generation appreciate what he has done, taking their country from the "dark ages" into the modern world. They regard him with almost filial devotion. He is a benevolent autocrat, seeking to transform a tribal society into an urban one in harmony with both tradition and change.

Neopatriarchal state procedures reinforce and strengthen normative views of women and the family, often through the law. States that legitimize their own power on patriarchal structures such as the extended family support its perpetuation through legislation that subordinates women to the control of men. These states may also find it useful to encourage patriarchal structures because the extended family performs vital welfare functions.

The joint household system and intergenerational wealth transfers that characterize patriarchal structures provide welfare and security for individuals. The state does not have to assume greater responsibility for the welfare of its citizens—especially for women who attain status and old age security through their sons—as long as patriarchy endures. Change in family law is a significant index of social change in the Middle East, a measure of the debate within Islam, and an indication of the possibility of Islamic reform. It also suggests the role of the state and of state legal policy toward issues of gender and the family. Neopatriarchal systems such as Oman's are beginning to allow women increased public participation in education and employment and to provide options other than marriage and household life. Professional women, the area of least resistance to female employment, have found that their chances of finding a job increase when they wear the traditional *burqa* (the facial covering worn by women in the United Arab Emirates and the Batinah region of Oman) or veil. Yet the Omani regime maintains assymmetrical definitions of gender roles and relations within the family and society at large, definitions non-threatening to its traditional underpinnings and legitimacy.

Education

Access to Education

The expansion of educational opportunities for women in Oman since 1970 has, for the first time, presented women with options other than traditional marriage and household life. Education seems to be a more important variable than employment in changing the position and self-perception of women. Education, while still limited, has been extended to many more women than has formal employment. Though not to the same degree as for boys, educational opportunities for girls and the number of girls enrolled in school at all levels has increased dramatically. There are far more women attending literacy centers in Oman in 1990 than men—74% of students in Muscat, 90% in al-Batinah, 95% in al-Sharqiyya, 67% in Dhofar. In 1970, an estimated 8% of Oman's adult population was considered literate. In 1987–1988, there were 248 literacy centers attended by 10,625 students (8,539 female, 2,086 male). There were also 209 adult education centers attended by 10,926 students (6,305 female, 4,611 male).[13]

Great advances have been made in education since 1970, when Sultan Qaboos came to power and there were only three primary schools in the country. Government spending on education in 1991 was 11.4 % of total spending. Although education is still not compulsory, attendance has greatly increased. Primary education begins at six years of age and lasts for six years. The next level of education, divided into stages (preparatory and secondary), lasts for an additional six years. Schools are not coeducational; boys and girls attend separate classes. As a proportion of the school-age population, the total enrollment at primary, preparatory, and secondary schools increased from 25% (boys 36%, girls 14%) in 1975 to the equivalent of 82% (boys 87%, girls 77%) in 1990. Primary enrollment in 1990 included an estimated 84% of children in the relevant age group (boys 84%, girls 82%). In 1989–1990, Oman had 388 government primary schools, 283 preparatory schools, and 70 secondary schools.[14] In 1990, 31% of the teachers out of a total number of 13,695 were Omani, of which 47% of these were women. Oman is divided into ten educational regions, of which al-Batinah is the largest.

Sultan Qaboos University opened in 1985, admitting students on the basis of academic ability (grade point average). In 1990, 47% of the 3,021 students enrolled were female (1,609 male, 1,412 female). This is a much higher proportion of female students than at other educational levels. Due to the few activities acceptable for young women, they may channel their energy into homework, consequently receive better grades in secondary school, and be more likely to gain university admittance. Within the traditional norms of Omani society, pursuing an education is an acceptable outlet for women, because it will ultimately benefit their families. Women students may also attend local universities because families are reluctant to send them abroad to be exposed to Western influence. If women do go abroad to study, one of the other conservative Gulf states is a likely first choice. Women are more likely to enroll in areas traditionally regarded as appropriate for women-education, medicine (very popular), Islamic sciences, and the sciences. Women are not encouraged to enroll in disciplines that, due to present attitudes and conditions, will provide them with few employment opportunities upon graduation.

In 1992, no women were being admitted to the College of Engineering, although a small number had been in the past. In the College of Agriculture, women are restricted to the area of plant sciences, because it is thought inappropriate for women to work in the fields. In areas where they are represented, women take exactly the same course work and fulfill the same requirements as men. Of the 492 students graduated in 1991, 210 were female. Of these, 60% were in the Islamic sciences (compared to 33% of graduating males), 23% were in literature, 8% in sciences, 4% in agriculture, and 3% in engineering.

Classes are not segregated and women are expected to fulfill the same obligations as men, giving oral presentations in front of the class if necessary. Women students often sit in the back and usually enter the classroom by different hallways. Common facilities such as the library, lecture halls, theaters, and seminar rooms can be entered from different sides from different hallways. The main corridors have an upper and lower elevation for sex-segregation purposes. In theory, the sexes are segregated in their academic activities as they are in their living accommodations. In practice, although formal separation exists, a natural informality has developed. Since the ratio of undergraduate females to males is around 47/53, an acceptable and necessary mix occurs in the educational environment of instruction and seminars. Official university policy does not require segregation of the sexes, and school administrators request that women students do not observe purdah or covering of the face.

Family Influence On Education

Although protection in legal codes is an important basis for women to act as independent persons, the expansion of schooling for girls is critically important. What might motivate girls to pursue an education? Specific data for Oman is not available, but women in developing countries often mention family support as influential in their desire to get an education. Many speak of one or more parents as having influenced them. In general, women perceived that their fathers exerted a predominant influence (supportive or not), on their education. In many cases, the fathers themselves had received an education. Women most often speak of their father's positive influence as having actively encouraged them to break with tradition and pursue an education. The father's influence seems to have been transmitted to the daughters directly, through teaching and encouragement, as well as indirectly, by providing a role model to be imitated. Other women speak of their father's negative influence as having been conveyed by his insistence that education is not necessary for a daughter's future role as homemaker and childbearer.

Educational Aspirations

Whether or not they themselves are literate, women in the developing world generally express the belief that education offers advantages. Women identify education as an aspiration they hold for themselves and for their children. Educational attainment by parents seems to have an effect on their children's aspirations. Students whose father or mother had completed a university education saw a similar goal for themselves. Girls whose mothers were illiterate were more likely to see secondary education as their ambition. Furthermore, girls believe that once a young woman completes her education, she must work. They saw future employment as the principal reason for educating women.[15]

In changing aspirations, education has also had an impact on the age of marriage and is its single most important determinant. The average age of marriage for men and women in most Arab countries has undergone a noticeable increase. The conservative regimes of the oil countries have also experienced an increase in the number of unmarried young people: age at marriage for women is twenty, and for men, twenty-seven. More urbanized youth marry later in all countries.

Mass education has been one of several social forces, along with urbanization, industrialization, legal reforms, and growth in the labor force; the cumulative effect has been the transformation of female roles and an expansion of the range of options available for women. Women in the Middle East and Oman do not represent a homogeneous social category. They are distinguished by region, class, and education. Educated women are moreover divided politically and ideologically. Yet, increasing rates of female education in Oman, along with greater socioeconomic development and employment, will affect women's position in family and their gender consciousness.

Health and Fertility

Illiteracy, Domesticity, and Male Dominance as Correlates of High Fertility

Among the Arab countries, the greatest material differences are between underdeveloped economies endowed with relatively diversified productive sectors, and economies organized completely around plentiful petroleum rents. Oman is among the latter group. These countries have encouraged fertility rates to remain at the highest levels; Oman's was 6.7% in 1991.[16] The states assume many costs of child rearing, and import workers to preempt the entry of women into the national labor market. These states have effectively suspended all reduction in fertility, nullifying factors that encourage demographic change—most important, female education, at the exact moment when the need for them becomes apparent.

Female illiteracy and high fertility are correlated. In Tunisia and Morocco, and for some time now in Lebanon, women who have attended high school or university have no more children than do Europeans.[17] However, in Oman female illiteracy is high and so is the fertility rate. Ongoing high fertility may also be explained by the persistence of the patriarchal household, incomplete industrialization, and pronatalist state policy. For many new states, a large population is associated with national strength. In Oman, very little information on modern contraception (or none at all) is available. The percentage of married women using contraceptives in 1994 is 8%.[18]

The admission of women into the professions and formal labor market is a second aspect of fertility decline. The countries of the Arabian Peninsula have a surprisingly low rate of urban female workforce participation—5%. The rate of female workforce participation is in perfect negative correlation with average fertility.[19]

In all societies, domestic responsibilities that are the responsibility of women increase with the size of the family and, at a certain point, make it difficult for women to practice a profession or occupation outside the home. Another factor, more intrinsic to Arab society, also seems to be operating. A large number, sometimes a majority, of Arab women employed outside the home before marriage leave their jobs upon getting married even before they have children. Husbands, not children, seem to be responsible for women leaving the job market. The correlation then is not between high fertility and the invisibility of women in the urban workforce, but between these two phenomena and a third, the strength and influence of the patriarchal family.

Omani Women's Health and the Challenges to It

Information on women's health in Oman remains sparse. The life expectancy for both men and women in 1987 was fifty-seven years, up from forty years in 1960.[20] The number of Omani women dying each year from pregnancy-related causes has decreased; there has been an improvement in medical care in general. In 1970, health services were limited to one hospital in Muttrah, run by an American mission, and a few simple clinics scattered around the country. By 1993, there were hospitals in all the main centers of population. The National Health Programme (NHP) in Oman has been remarkably successful in reducing infant mortality and preventing disease. The NHP works primarily by the education of mothers. Mothers are instructed when they attend a clinic in any health-care center or hospital in the country. In addition, NHP runs supervisory teams that operate out of health centers and oversee sanitation in the home and villages.[20] Emphasis on the education of the mother in family and child care may contribute to the strengthening of her position in the household and society at large. If, however, women do not wish to have more children, they have minimal or no access to family-planning services.

Women generally live longer than men, but throughout their lives they face many challenges to their health and well-being. Biologically, women may be born with certain natural strengths, but these are often canceled out by social, economic, political, and cultural disadvantages. In Muslim societies such as Oman where the legacy of tribal tradition and custom remains strong, females suffer discrimination from birth to old age. Male offspring are preferred over females. As children, girls are likely to be less well fed than boys, less likely to receive medical attention, and less likely to be allowed to finish their education. As adults, women are denied equal social, legal, and economic status and are excluded from decision making.[22]

Omani Women's Associations

Official policy treats Omani women as a national asset, and a number of agencies and organizations have been established to encourage their social development. The Ministry of Social Affairs and Labor supervises the general mandate for advancing women's issues and affairs. Huda al-Ghazzali, Adviser, and 'Aida al-Hijry, Director-General, of Women's and Children's Affairs, established in 1985, play prominent roles in this capacity. Their work is organized into four departments: women's affairs, children's affairs, research and study, and women's associations.

The women's associations are voluntary organizations that run courses, give training, administer child care and advice, and in general work for the social welfare of women. The women's associations address women's issues in the larger urban areas, while a community development program assists women in the villages. The first women's association—and still the largest and no doubt the most sophisticated—was established in Muscat in 1973. It has the largest number of volunteers, an architecturally elegant building near the Ministry of Foreign Affairs, and a clinic for handicapped children. The women's associations are supported by the Ministry of Social Affairs and Labor, which furnishes buildings. To set up an association requires the signatures of thirty volunteers and the agreement of the *wali* (regional governor). There are now thirteen women's associations. The Center for Women and Children at Taqah and the Center for Women's Education in Marbat were established within the last five years. These centers are housed in hexagonal two-story buildings constructed around an open courtyard filled with children's playground equipment. Rooms for meetings, classes (sewing machines provided), handicraft displays, and lectures surround the inner court.

These centers provide education on health matters and hygiene, child care, and literacy classes. Volunteers make available a wide variety of programs and services, including sports, religious studies, health, public relations, plants and horticulture, and handicrafts. Skills such as typing, computer keyboarding, sewing, cookery, and flower arranging may also be offered. Handicrafts are important as a means of beautifying the home and of earning extra income while working at home. The availability of child-care and daycare facilities means that women can bring their children with them and know that they are provided for while attending lectures or classes. Socially, the centers operate as meeting places; provide support in times of grief or personal crisis; welcome women from abroad; and plan picnics, trips to the mountains, and other activities. Their main problems are operational finance and regular participation by the volunteers who run them.

Women play a critical role in assistance for the disabled in Oman. The Omani Women's Association has established seven centers for the disabled. These are government funded, staffed, and directed. The only nongovernmental organization offering assistance to the disabled is the Association for the Welfare of Handicapped Children. It is entirely voluntary and the premier charity in the country. Rayya al-Riyami, also Director of Girl Scout Activities, is Vice Chair. The program started out as a grassroots organization, meeting outdoors, under trees, beside bushes, with participants sitting on rocks, until members could rent facilities or use donated rooms. The association holds monthly meetings in five cities and villages (Muscat, Bidbid, Medinat Qaboos, Quriyat, Dank). Its primary goals are to promote awareness of the condition and problems of disabled children, provide parental support, and build support for additional services. The association works in cooperation with the medical school at Sultan Qaboos University. In a country with little or no previous understanding of the needs of the disabled—where they were even despised and neglected—these services, organized and staffed by women, provide crucial groundwork for future development.

Omani Women and Community Development

The government's community development program, begun in 1975, reaches out to women in the villages and has thus far opened eight-four centers. Support for women in the villages is crucial, because many of the young people have migrated to the cities and because many men are gone during the week (Saturday through Wednesday) to work in urban areas. Village populations are aging and showing an increasing imbalance between the sexes. On average, males of working age (fifteen–sixty) residing in a village constitute about one-fifth of its total population. Male migration may reduce the expenses of the household, but all too often this reduces household resources even more and leads to a deterioration of the position of women and children. The number of women-headed households depending upon insufficient and unstable remittances is reported to have grown. The increase in female-headed households is not a sign of freedom from male power. Migration may be a euphemism for desertion, a male survival strategy rather than a female survival strategy.[23] The core of gender subordination resides in the fact that women cannot amass adequate resources (both material and in terms of social identity) except through dependence on a man.

At the centers, women receive information on matters of health and hygiene, training in embroidery, poultry rearing, and home economics, with the assistance of social workers. Instruction in traditional local crafts is provided to improve women's skills and to protect this particular heritage from extinction. Marketing facilities are provided for these products by the centers. Children may attend kindergarten at the centers. Naima Hamed al-Belushi, Director of Health for Women, supervises the center in the village of Ja'alan Bani Bu 'Ali. In September 1992, community leaders presented a program of appreciation for women who had completed a sewing course. Although such skills may seem rudimentary, the process of improving women's education and status in the family is a vital first step toward gaining support and laying a foundation for attitudinal changes regarding women's social, economic, and political roles.

Official Policy Supports Women's Practical Gender Needs

Without the strong support of Sultan Qaboos, the progress made to date, in considering women at the early stages of development, would have taken much longer to achieve. Attention to women's needs at this point focuses on education and instruction of the mother in family health and child care. The Sultan's backing of the woman's movement in all areas—education, health, employment, and social and cultural organizations—is expressed within the tenets of Islam regarding the rights of women, helping him gain public support for his policies concerning Omani women. Such policies, however, serve to fulfill women's practical gender needs rather than advance their strategic gender needs, preserving existing gender relations rather than transforming them. Women remain focused on their immediate and pressing, practical needs, especially needs for resources to ensure household survival and a better future for their children. Collective organization by women for self-help is a survival strategy. Such self-help schemes consist of women helping one another to meet their functional immediate needs. They formalize the informal support networks that women everywhere construct, but they perpetuate the idea that unpaid labor for the benefit of others is women's work and they define women's work in community organizing as an extension of their domestic role. Such volunteer organizations enable not just survival but the perpetuation of existing gender relations.[24]

Nonetheless, the fulfillment of these everyday, short-term needs is not entirely disconnected from intentional, long-term gender needs. A satisfactory meeting of women's practical gender needs implies improvement in meeting women's strategic needs, a diminuation of their subordination to men. The need of women for resources of their own to perform their duties as household managers cannot be met without reduction of women's dependence on men, a move toward greater gender equality in the control of resources.

Putting Resources into the Hands of Omani Women

Two reasons help explain the necessity of putting resources into the hands of women themselves. One is that individuals within families do not necessarily, have common interests or work toward common goals, as is often assumed. Development programs have been constructed on the assumption that what is good for men is good for the family. Often, however, this is not the case. First, research shows that women provide the largest share of the family's basic needs, and the incomes of men are often siphoned off by the purchase of alcohol, tobacco, or other consumer products. An increase in the income of a male within the household may not mean an increase in total consumption by family members. Children's nutrition may deteriorate while men in the household acquire wristwatches, radios, or cellular telephones. Second, resources in households are often skewed toward the males. When household income rises, men and boys throughout the developing world prosper much more than do women and girls.[25]

Discrimination against females in families and societies derives from another form of gender gap: the huge disparity that exists between the actual economic and social benefits derived from women's work and the social perception of women as unproductive. Gender bias exists in every country, at virtually every income level, and in every stratum of society, but is especially pernicious in the developing world where most of women's work takes place in the non-wage economy for the purpose of household consumption. Institutions persist in counting women as part of the dependent or "nonproductive" portion of the population. Women's work that does not produce cash directly is heavily discounted. The low estimation of women's work is reinforced by women's lack of control over physical resources. Although Islam itself improved women's status in the seventh century, women in Oman today have few legal rights regarding land tenure, marital relations, income, or social security. Ignoring women's economic contribution hinders efforts to achieve broad development. The ubiquity of this bias is a sign that practically every country is operating below its economic potential.[26] Greater resource availability for women leads to greater equality between men and women and to the empowerment of women.

Cultural Expression

Omani Ibadism: A Vital Force

What images of women and their "place" are prevalent in Oman, and how far do these reflect or determine reality? What can women do in the cultural field? Due to Islam's comprehensive nature (it is concurrently an intellectual system of thought, a religious system of belief, and a sociolegal system for the particular and right ordering of society), it must be studied for an understanding of Gulf societies. The ubiquitious influence of Islam is difficult for Westerners to comprehend, because there is no distinction between the proper spheres of authority for secular and religious institutions. Islam deeply permeates the life of all the societies bordering on the Gulf. The forms of Islam adhered to by religious elites and popular masses are more traditional than those that prevail in the more urbanized and Westernized states, such as Egypt, Lebanon, Syria and Turkey. Thus, in Oman, as everywhere in the Gulf, Islam remains a vital force. It has immense significance in the belief and behavioral patterns of the great majority of people. Most of the people are keenly aware of the religious dimension of human existence and are convinced of the binding character of the sharia.

Most Omanis follow the Ibadi sect of Islam. The sect had its origins in 657, when Ali, the fourth Caliph and the Prophet's cousin and son-in-law, agreed to peace talks with his main rival for the leadership of the Muslim community. The Kharijis ("seceders") were originally followers of Ali but broke with him on the principle that by agreeing to discuss the leadership question he had compromised on a matter of faith. This compromise, they believed, rendered him unworthy of both their loyalty and the leadership itself.

The Ibadis are one of the few Khariji sects which has survived into the twentieth century. They take their name from Abdullah Bin Ibad al-Murri al-Tamimi, a theologian, probably from Najd (in modern Saudi Arabia), but who did most of his important teaching in Basra (present-day southern Iraq) during the late seventh century. His teachings seem to have taken hold in Oman because they offered a compelling political response at a time when the Omani tribes were rebelling against the Damascus-based Umayyad caliphate. Ibadism came to prosper on the edges of the Muslim world. The only other place where a powerful Ibadi state was ever established was in western Algeria in the eighth century.

Ibadi Islam has become an integral part of the national culture. As noted earlier, Ibadis insist that the Caliph should not be determined according to genealogical considerations but should be elected on the basis of merit. For the Ibadis, any believer, as long as the individual is just, devout, and competent, can be chosen as *imam*. If no one meets these requirements, the office can remain vacant. When political conditions require that the existence of an imam be concealed, the Ibadis believe in the practice of *kitman* (secrecy). In one form or another, the imamate continued in the remote parts of Oman's interior until the middle of the twentieth century.

Omani Ibadism remained steadfastly loyal to its sources in the Quran and the hadith, the precepts of the first century of Islam. The results were conservatism, puritanism, and austerity, along with a belief in simplicity, which remain major influences in Oman today. Ibadism tends to be moderate in its requirements from its followers relative to other Islamic sects. The legal system is based on the Ibadi interpretation of sharia, containing precise dictates for virtually every aspect of a Muslim's personal and private life. It is noteworthy, however, that Oman does not apply the strictest sanctions for infringements of the law, such as cutting off the hands of thieves or stonings or beheadings of offenders.

Islamic Law Regarding Women versus Tribal Traditions and Modern Practices

Although Islam, around which life in Oman revolves, is often criticized for the low status it has ascribed to women, many scholars believe that it was primarily the interpretation of jurists, local traditions, and social trends which brought about a decline in the status of Muslim women. In this view, Islamic law as revealed to the Prophet Muhammad granted women rights and privileges in the spheres of family life, marriage, education, and economic endeavors, rights that help improve women's status in society. Equality of the sexes, however, was not a feature of tribal society characteristic of seventh-century Arabia. These Arab Bedouins were dedicated to custom and tradition and resisted changes brought about by the new religion. As time passed, because of the interpretations of various religious scholars influenced by local traditions and social trends, women have not been given the rights due them under Islam. The inequality of Muslim women happened because of the preexisting habits of the people among whom Islam first took root. The economies of these early Muslim societies were not favorable to a comfortable life for women. More important, during Islam's second and third centuries the interpretation of the Quran was in the hands of deeply conservative scholars, whose decisions are not easy to challenge today. This is not primarily the fault of religion.

The Quran is more favorable to women than is generally realized. In principle, except for a verse or two, the Quran grants women equality. For example, Eve was not the delayed product of Adam's rib (as is the tradition for Christians and Jews); the two were born from a single soul. It was Adam, not Eve, who let the devil convince them to eat the forbidden fruit. Muslim women are instructed to be modest in their dress, but only in general terms. Men are also told to be modest. Many Muslims believe that veiling and seclusion are later male inventions, social habits picked up with the conquest of the Byzantine and Persian Empires.

The Quran allows a man to have up to four wives, but it seems to permit it as a reluctant accommodation to man's nature, since it made it contingent on equal treatment. Some think it may have been Muhammad's way of controlling the previously unrestrained polygamy of Arabia. Men outrank women in the Quran in other ways. They can inherit more, and their testimony is worth more in a court of law. But most of the legal discrimination against women began with those early male jurists who gave their interpretation to the Prophet's teachings.

Sura 4, "On Women," verse 34, is a source of controversy. Some interpret S. 4: 34 in a manner that has God saying that men have authority over women, and that women can be beaten if they cause trouble. Others modify the first part to say that men are women's protectors or guardians, partly because in seventh-century Arabia men earned all the money. Sura 4: 34 remains a source of contention as to interpretation.

Many Muslims believe that the disadvantages Muslim women suffer under have nothing to do with the Quran. The problems come from the practical circumstances of time, place, and location. Of all the social revolutions that have come out of the West, that which may endure the longest is the revolution reordering male–female relations. If the Muslim world does not follow, it will be isolated. The change requires stronger economic performance and more educational opportunities. Most of all, this revolution requires a transformation of the group that has done the most to hold Muslim women back, the *ulema*, the scholars of Islam. These are the closely knit, all-male, more or less self-selected coterie of learned men who claim the authority to say what God means. They made a mistake about women centuries ago and continue to make that same mistake today.[27]

In many Muslim countries, where gender inequality exists in its most obvious form, it claims a religious derivation and thus establishes its legitimacy. Few Muslim countries, Oman included, have signed or ratified the United Nations Convention on the Elimination of All Forms of Discrimination Against Women. Yet, the position of women in the Middle East cannot be attributed to the presupposed inherent properties of Islam. Gender ideology as sanctioned by religion remains important, but gender asymmetry and the status of women in the Muslim world cannot be attributed solely to Islam. Islam is experienced, practiced, and interpreted quite differently over time and space. In order to understand the social implications of Islam, it is necessary to look at the broader sociopolitical and economic order within which it is exercised. The status of women in Muslim societies is not uniform, unchanging, or unique.[28]

Nevertheless, Muslim societies, like many others, do hold misconceptions about inalterable gender differences. Women are considered different beings, and this perception intensifies social barriers to women's achievement. It is thought that women do not have the same interests as men and will keep their distance from men's pursuits. Precautions are also taken to make sure they cannot prepare for roles considered unsuitable. Women's childbearing capacity is used to justify their segregation in public, their restriction to the home, and their lack of civil and legal rights. All of a woman's roles are defined by the men in her life. She is rarely seen as an independent person in her own right. Public access for women is restricted, while the roles of housewife and mother are elevated to the highest possible degree. A social system upheld by these beliefs controls and subordinates women, marginalizes them economically, and conceptualizes them as human beings inferior to men.

The Vocabulary Of Human Rights

Most Middle Eastern nations have moved or are moving toward adopting the Western political language of human and political rights—and toward according these rights to women as well as to men. Although the peninsular countries have opened up education to women, in most other ways the old constrictions remain in place. Modern ideas about rights, such as the right to vote, have made no advances, except in Kuwait—and then not for women.

Islamic family law—the laws governing men's and women's rights in marriage, divorce, and child custody—continues to govern the relations between men and women in all but a few Arab countries. In the tenth century, the development of Islamic law was considered complete, and for the following nine centuries family law endured untouched and unchanging. Islam favors patrilineal bonds and instructs men to assume responsibility for the support of their wives and children. In the Arab–Islamic family, the wife's primary duties are to maintain a home, care for her children, and obey her husband. The husband may exercise his authority by controlling his wife's activities and preventing her from showing herself in public. Restriction of a wife resembles the medieval social customs of veiling and seclusion of women, practices meant to protect their honor. The heritage of social and cultural institutions in the Gulf is such that men's honor, pride, and dignity have been inextricably bound to the modesty and chastity of their women.

Family law is the cornerstone of the system of male privilege established by official Islam. That it is still preserved almost intact signals the existence of powerful forces within Middle Eastern societies determined to uphold male privilege and male control over women. Jurists of the early Islamic period were hostage to societies in which misogyny and androcentrism were undisputed and invisible norms. Their descendents, applying laws devised in other ages and other societies, are rejecting contemporary understandings of the definitions of justice and human rights as applied to women, even as they adapt modern technologies and languages in every other sector of life.[29]

Conclusion

Gender dynamics in Oman are affected by the policies of a neopatriarchal state that are pronatalist and emphasize sex differences and complementary roles rather than legal equality; thus these policies serve to perpetuate stratification based on gender. Consequently, existing gender relations are preserved rather than transformed, and asymmetrical definitions of gender roles and relations within the family and society—definitions that are nonthreatening to a conservative regime—are maintained.

The impetus for improvement in women's roles in Oman has come from the top (through the initiative of Sultan Qaboos), rather than from the bottom. Change can come when rulers and the ruling elite decide in favor of it. So far most changes concerning gender relations have been accommodated and absorbed into the existing traditional social patterns. These changes have not posed a challenge to religious authority and have gained approval and acceptance through their grounding in religious doctrine.

Development strategies in Oman, as in all countries, limit the ability of women to achieve their real human potential; as such, these strategies limit the potential of the nation as a whole. Without the participation of about 50% of its citizenry, Oman will remain dependent on expatriate assistance as the crux of its labor force. Furthermore, oil is a nonrenewable resource, which means Oman will not be able to depend on oil income indefinitely. Alternative sources of income must be developed and the economy diversified. This effort will require making efficient use of all the country's human resources. Omanis have experienced almost a quarter century of prosperity; but they and their rulers can still remember the previous centuries of decay and hardship. Conflicts between Islam (as rendered through local tradition) and the requirements of modernization must be resolved. The most difficult of these controversies is the position of women.

Improving the status of women requires a complete reorganization of development efforts by increasing women's control over income and household resources, improving their productivity, establishing their legal and social rights, and increasing the social and economic choices they are able to make. The first step toward achieving these goals, and establishing an environment in which both women and men can prosper, is asking women themselves which needs should be accorded top priority. It is important to get Omani women themselves involved in improving their own status and then persuading men that their support is indispensable. At present, the basic theme of official statements regarding the role of women is that women have a duty to their families and to society. By informing and educating themselves, women raise the status of their family, as well as strengthen Omani society in general. Furthermore, these objectives can be accomplished within the requirements of orthodox Islam.

An emerging feminist movement in Oman may take on characteristics that distinguish it from its counterpart in the West. It will not be based on the concept of the liberation of the individual, a quest for self-fulfillment or self-indulgence, or the definition of one's own identity. The movement will most likely be perceived as an integral part of the overall effort to liberate society from outdated cultural precepts, ill-disposed social customs, and foreign control. The support, promotion, and encouragement of the cause by men will be significant, because as advocates, men will take up the issue of women's condition and find it imperative to convince others. The movement will never advocate sexual liberation; as seen in other Middle Eastern countries, it must repudiate such a goal in order to survive.[30]

Women are at the center of change and discussions of change in the Middle East. As in other Arab countries, middle-class Omani women will come into their own; they themselves are products of socioeconomic development and in turn will engender development and change. This will eventuate changes in patriarchal family and kinship structures. Thus far countries like Oman have demonstrated ambivalence about transforming women and the family. They have pursued the contradictory goals of economic development and strengthening of the family. The latter goal is often an accord concluded with conservative social elements, such as religious leaders or traditional local communities.

Moreover, despite the modern appearance of Muscat's Qurm, Ruwi, and Medinat Qaboos districts, much of the country, including parts of the capital area, remain intensely traditional. Oman has been open to the modern world only since 1970. The day-to-day life of the average Omani, living in a town in the interior or a fishing village on the coast, is close to what it was centuries ago. Omanis seem to be adept at assimilating what they want or need of modern life, experiencing its benefits without letting the new technology adversely affect their own lives and values. On a broader scale, traditional social institutions and cultural patterns in the Gulf have proven to be highly flexible capable of incorporating vast changes, while at the same time denying that any change has in fact taken place. Most changes in Oman have been accommodated and absorbed into the existing traditional social patterns. The result so far has been persistence and stability. Changes in women's position may thus come about gradually and nonviolently. The smaller Gulf states are further behind than other Arab states in experiencing the overall changes introduced by European influence. Oman, like the others, is undergoing a transition from rule by a sheikh family, in cooperation with merchant families, to more technically trained elites. Traditional habits, including those shaping gender relations, have great staying power and are firmly embedded in Omani society. Tradition maintains the separation of the sexes, which is one of the main characteristics of Arab and Omani society.

Since the discovery of oil in the 1960s and the coup of 1970, the country has modernized very quickly. Development that took over 200 years to accomplish in the West has happened in Oman within the past 25 years. It is not surprising that, underneath all this, the traditional system of social organization and political structure has continued relatively unchanged. Of course, fundamental change and even instability cannot be ruled out; as more drastic changes more deeply affect an increasing number of social groups, the accommodating institutions will be strained to the breaking point.

Notes

1. Valentine M. Moghadam, *Modernizing Women: Gender and Social Change in the Middle East* (Boulder, Colo.: L. Rienner, 1993), p. 10.

2. Ibid., p. 14.

3. Janet Z. Giele, "Introduction: The Status of Women in Comparative Perspective," in *Women: Roles and Status in Eight Countries*, ed. Janet A. Giele and Audrey C. Smock (New York: John Wiley, 1977), pp. 3–31.

4. F. Gregory Gause III, *Oil Monarchies: Domestic and Security Challenges in the Arab Gulf* (New York: Council on Foreign Relations, 1994), pp. 78–118, 162–163.

5. Mervat Hatem, "Towards the Development of Post-Islamist and Post-Nationalist Feminist Discourses in the Middle East," in *Arab Women: Old Boundaries, New Frontiers*, ed. Judith E. Tucker (Bloomington: Indiana University Press, 1993), p. 37.

6. Diane Elson, "From Survival Strategies to Transformation Strategies: Women's Needs and Structural Adjustment," in *Unequal Burden: Economic Crises, Persistent Poverty, and Women's Work*, ed. Lourdes Beneria and Shelley Feldman (Boulder, Colo.: Westview Press, 1992), pp. 26–48.

7. Moghadam, *Modernizing Women*, pp. 29–53.

8. Linda Usra Soffan, *The Women of the United Arab Emirates* (London: Croom Helm, 1980), p. 77.

9. Ibid., pp. 19, 66–81.

10. Moghadam, *Modernizing Women*, p. 107.

11. Alain Cheneviere, *L'Oman et les Emirats du Golfe* (Paris: Hachette, 1990), pp. 64–68.

12. According to Hisham Sharabi, neopatriarchy is the outcome of the encounter between modernity and tradition in the setting of dependent capitalism; it is modernized patriarchy. Hisham Sharabi, *Neopatriarchy: A Theory of Distorted Change in Arab Society* (New York: Oxford University Press, 1988), p. 145.

13. "Oman," *The Europa World Yearbook, 1993* (N.p.: Europa, 1993), p. 2194.

14. Ibid.

15. Moghadam, *Modernizing Women*, pp. 124–126.

16. George Thomas Kurian, *The New Book of World Rankings* (New York: Facts on File, 1991), p. 33.

17. Philippe Fargues, "From Demographic Explosion to Social Rupture," *Middle East Report* 24, 5, (September-October 1994): 8–9.

18. Sally Ethelston, "Gender, Population, Environment," *Middle East Report* 24, 5, (September–October 1994): p. 4.

19. Fargues, "From Demographic Explosion," p. 9.

20. Moghadam, *Modernizing Women*, p. 121.

21. Ian Skeet, *Oman: Politics and Development* (New York: St. Martin's, 1992), p. 116.

22. "Women's Health: Tragedy of Gender," in *Third World 94/95*, ed. Robert J. Griffiths (Guilford, Conn.: Dushkin, 1994), pp. 231–236.

23. Elson, "From Survival Strategies," p. 41.

24. Ibid., pp. 26–48.

25. Jodi L. Jacobson, "Women's Work: Why Development Isn't Always Good News for the Second Sex," in *Third World 94/95*, ed. Robert J. Griffiths (Guilford, Conn.: Dushkin, 1994), pp. 231–236.

26. Ibid.

27. "A Survey of Islam," *The Economist* (August 6, 1994): 10–12.

28. Moghadam, *Modernizinq Women*, pp. 5–8.

29. Leila Ahmed, *Women and Gender in Islam* (New Haven: Yale University Press, 1992), pp. 240–242.

30. Yvonne Yazbeck Haddad, "Islam, Women and Revolution in Twentieth-Century Arab Thought," in *Women, Religion, and Social Change*, ed. Yvonne Yazbeck Haddad and Ellison Banks Findly, (Albany, N.Y.: SUNY Press, 1985), pp. 296–297.

Women and Religion in Bahrain

An Emerging Identity

In the tiny state of Bahrain a grassroots antigovernment protest uprising (*intifada*) has been occurring since the summer of 1994. By December of that year, the protestors from the less favored strata of society took to the streets demanding the dismissal of foreign (British) security officials; a reduction of the number of foreign imported laborers; expansion of social, economic, and employment opportunities for Bahrainis; a more equitable justice system; and the appropriation of more democratic practices by the government. This appeared to be the tip of the iceberg, as more disaffected Bahrainis joined to vent their accumulated anger and bitterness in vociferous activities. While initially the conflict seemed to reflect a class dimension, it became apparent that it also expressed sectarian and ethnic differences and animosities.

One common demand from all elements was the return of the short-lived democratic process that had been scrapped by the ruling family in 1975.[1] This created networks of common ground between various currents, groups, and strata of the Bahraini society: Shiis and Sunnis; liberals, leftists, and Islamists; workers, professionals, and intellectuals; men and women. The contacts, exchanges, and relationships forged among these groups in the common endeavor were instrumental in clarifying and exposing ideological differences as well as opening channels of cooperation. From the outset, it was clear that the umbrella under which the largest number of activists—males and females—congregated was that of the Islamic currents.

The protest movement addressed the grievances of the nation and its fears, and it demanded in clear and concrete terms a redress of the deteriorating conditions through basic political reforms. The movement advocated a return to a constitutional democracy as the channel through which all Bahrainis would participate. Soon the popular reaction assumed a two-pronged approach in relaying its message. On one side was the Shii population, especially the village dwellers, who represented the large and more economically depressed elements of society that hold particular grievances against the government and the police. They became associated with acts of sabotage and violence against state and civilian premises. On the other hand, the Sunni population who were generally sympathetic with the underlying causes of the protests and anxious for reforms, refrained from such violent activities.

The other approach to the problem took the form of petition campaigns mounted by the emerging opposition; the petitions reflected the movement's aim to forge changes beneficial to all society and all those in support of the movement. All five petitions raised to the ruler Shaikh Issa Bin Salman al-Khalifa were endorsed by both Sunnis and Shiis, as well as the various interest groups including the religious leaders, the merchant strata, professionals, and women. The petitions expressed the same appeal for reforms and the need to reinforce national unity and justice. While some of these petitions were delivered to the authorities, there has been no direct response, and most requests to meet with the ruler have been denied.

The first petition (October 1994) was signed by approximately 25,000 people (in a country of 350,000). While the leadership came from all elements of the society, the signatories mainly represented the religious movements, including the educated professionals, government employees, and some of the merchants. A tiny proportion of signatories represented leftist, liberal and women's movements. The significance of this petition is the high proportion of women (25% or 6,000) who signed it. They came mainly from the more conservative, rural Shii background known to be of lower economic status, and more religiously oriented than Shii women from the city.

The tone of the petition itself reflected the role and input of religious conservative reasoning. While it expressed concern with the mounting waves of riots that had engulfed the country, precipitating rifts in the society, and grief at the number of deaths and frustration at the official handling of the crisis, it also demanded particular changes in the political system including an end to corruption, favoritism, and permissiveness towards loose moral standards. It stressed the need to reactivate the constitution, thus representing all sectors and strata of society in the governing process. However, when it came to the role of women and their participation in these changes, the petition was particularly silent and only alluded to "take into *consideration* the role of women in these changes" in the most general and undefined terms.[2] It has been reported that opposition to any role for women in the political arena and in future socioeconomic development, even at this hypothetical level, was adamantly insisted upon by both Shii and Sunni representatives of the religious currents.

In view of the role played by Bahraini women in the development and modernization of their country during the past half century, this petition provides a number of indications as to the deep changes women throughout the society, particularly those that the emerging middle and lower classes, have undergone recently. While this group of protesting women seemed to be swayed by religious males, they nevertheless were taking risks and a stand that projected them as women in support of political and social issues. The role of women in this petition must be studied in conjunction with that of women of the liberalization era in the 1960s and 1970s, as well as middle-class and professional women who had recently converted to a strict adherence to the tenets of the Islamic movement. Such a study gives us an overall picture of the changes that have taken place in the role of women in the Gulf generally and in Bahrain particularly during the last decade. While the region had passed through an era of intense socioeconomic and political change in the last twenty years, women have been participants and parties to this process, but the nature of the identity and role Bahraini women express as a result of these changes needs to be assessed and highlighted. But this state of crisis and political turmoil forced the entire society, women included, to face soul-searching dilemmas and act spontaneously, expressing their genuine commitments and beliefs and thus exposing the spectrum of shifting and conflicting identities.

To what extent are these women similar to women in other developing countries in their reactions to conditions of crisis? How similar are they to Palestinian, Algerian, Iranian, Saudi, and Kuwaiti women who pass through intense political challenges? In view of the experience of these Arab women participants in Third World national struggle, are Bahraini women consciously protesting against the patriarchy and subordination of the state or are they part of the male-led political activism? How much of this protest is directed against regional, Western, and international hegemony and exploitation of the Arabian Gulf, and the impact of this hegemony on Bahrain's economic ills? How much does this protest reflect the emerging identity of women especially within the religious currents that have assumed political struggle as a platform?

Theoretical and Methodological Considerations

To answer these questions, it is essential to situate this popular protest experience in Bahrain within the broader historical and theoretical context, and to analyze the extenuating conditions that made it possible for Bahraini women to be heard and their role and contribution to society to be recognized. The political context that prevailed in Bahrain has provided the framework through which the crisis of confidence between the government and the people, as well as the social and economic structures, are exposed. The Bahrain crisis could be compared to the conditions that prevailed for Kuwaiti women during the Gulf War (1991), where the occupation of their country and the repercussions of that occupation subjected women to extenuating conditions that brought about more articulated identifications and confrontations.

Another significant example in the region is that of the Saudi women who, also under crisis conditions during the Gulf War, attempted to wrest some rights and a margin of liberation by driving their cars. Under such conditions, the economic and social categories that define the problems of society are contested and redefined in terms of gender as an index of development, again highlighting the role women have achieved and reflecting the gendered nature of politics. In researching the identity, role, and status of Bahraini women, before and during the current crisis, the gender system and its sociocultural underpinnings (such as class location, state political ideology, and its socioeconomic development strategy) are categories that need to be consciously referenced as part of the dynamics of women's involvement at this juncture.[3] Similar to other Third World experiences, the core issues that the nation and women are protesting are economic, social, and political inequalities as they manifest themselves in class, sectarian, and ethnic differences. As subalterns within an oppressed social system, women need to be alert to the possibility of finding their cause and rights used as a battlefield between the subordinating authorities and suppressed male society bargaining for agendas of their own.[4]

The aim of this chapter is to investigate the emerging identity of Bahraini women influenced by the sociopolitical conditions and the religious revival movement surrounding them. The information was gathered in interviews of liberal and Islamist Shii and Sunni women gathered mainly during 1991–1993 and the summer of 1994. While the original intent was to investigate and determine social and sectarian differences by which Bahraini Islamist/veiled women identified themselves, the eruption of political protests provided a potent and clarifying index to help in this study. Women's participation in the political and social struggle has provided an important dimension to their identity. In addition to the field work, this research is based on my experience in the country during the period 1983–1993, a time of fermentation that has given rise to the conditions we now witness.

Twenty Bahraini women were interviewed during the summer of 1994 as part of this research. All the interviewees were established and known Islamists, Sunni and Shii, many of whom had become part of the revivalist trend in the last ten years. At least half of them, mainly from among the Sunnis, had joined the ranks of the movement while studying abroad (mostly in the West and particularly Canada in the 1980s), thus expressing a strong anti-Western reaction as part of their identity. All the respondents, for that matter, seemed consciously to equate their Islamic commitment in opposition to Western identities and influence. While they all assumed strong identification with the Islamist trend, some were overtly associated with the male-directed religious organizations, and all strongly identified with their particular religious sect. Furthermore, these women felt that they had a mission and duty to proselytize and spread a way of life they considered virtuous and correct. It was clear that all the interviewees came from the emerging lower middle class, from families that had moved up socially and economically in the last decade and who had personally achieved a status through education and their emphatic association with the revivalist movement. A large number of these women were employed, particularly the Shiis among them, and some held professional positions.

In addition to this sample, approximately forty other women were also intermittently interviewed during 1991–1993. These were women who had veiled during the last decade, had come from conservative and veiled backgrounds, or had until this date resisted the Islamist trend.[5] Most of the veiled women studied in this group came from the lower class and the emerging strata within it that had become more socially conscious and better educated; many but not all of them were students at the university. The modern Western-attired women in this group came mainly from the middle and the lower middle class; they were educated (some of them in the West or Western-oriented institutions), and most of them were employed or financially independent. Furthermore, my association with Bahrainis in the course of my residence and work there (1983–1993), and my contacts with village dwellers,[6] city dwellers, students, and citizens, has given me further insight and information on the phenomenon studied here. The ages of the interviewed women were from eighteen to the mid-fifties.

There are, however, deficiencies in the availability of records as well as difficulties in extricating pertinent and cogent information on women. Studies on Middle Eastern women have been confined mainly to Egypt, Iran, and Turkey, and to a lesser extent some areas of the Levant, notably Lebanon. Paralleling wider trends in history, since the late 1980s a trickle of research on Gulf history, particularly the history of women and their role in society, has started to enter the sphere of scholarly consideration. Many publications in the field have given Arabian Gulf women attention in passing as part of larger theses on women of the Middle East in general. However, it is the work of women of the Gulf themselves—those who identify the dilemmas of their changing status and devise solutions within the reality of their politicocultural constraints—that have left the strongest impact on the field; among these writers are Thuraya al-Torki, Aisha Almana', Badriyya al-'Awwadi, and Munira Fakhro.[7]

The study of women, a marginalized and often hidden sector of society, poses a challenge filled with professional minefields and uncertainties to historians. One of the major difficulties faced is in retrieving the voice or identity of women and other subalterns from records, archives, and even from cultural concepts that have been constructed by patriarchal and controlling forces. Written sources do not yield clear pictures of the suppressed and subsumed subaltern voice, because these sources are loaded with influences and nuances from various directions. Even women interviewed who are consciously aware of their identity and the role of societal and cultural biases, unconsciously convey their complex view of reality. It is important to understand these limitations and accept that we are talking about an approximation of reality that cannot be fully confirmed. The difficulty is in extricating woman's pure voice, from the complex web of societal structure, while she remains in her subordinate role. How can information, changing processes, and consciousness be identified in a system that structurally negates and diminishes the part of the subaltern in the public scene?

Despite interest in the field by Gulf intellectuals, records are few and those that exist are often constrained by politics—even more tangible now when, in addition to Bahrain's usual hypersensitivity for security, the fear has precipitated an atmosphere of paranoia. Furthermore, there appears to be a deliberate blackout and cordoning of information coming out of Bahrain and about Bahrain by the international media.[8] It is only recently that some reports about the situation began to appear in some U.S. and European publications and periodicals. As the Bahrain government gained better control of the situation, however, these limited reports have dwindled. Therefore much of the recent information provided here has had to depend on unorthodox channels and sources as well as personal interviews and personal observation and experience. Consequently this study is of an exploratory nature and precludes any clear conclusions.

Historical Overview

For an understanding of women's participation in the events of the Bahrain political crisis today, it is important to reconstruct the dimension of women's role in the nationalist struggle of Bahraini history for the period prior to 1995. It is only by bringing to light the intersection of international, regional, and local socioeconomic developments that the current events could be properly assessed. Internally the impact of this legacy on the class, sectarian, and ethnic makeup of society was tremendous and involved women at every stage and period.

For the last fifteen years, Bahrain's economic and political development had become completely entwined with Gulf regional developments, particularly that of its hegemonic neighbor, Saudi Arabia. The economic and the political alignment and subordination of Saudi Arabia to the world capitalist system and the hegemony of the United States has become clear, an alignment that has also linked the whole Gulf area as well as the Arab world to the same subordination. As a direct result of the Gulf war, Saudi Arabia became deeply indebted to the United States. "In addition to direct contributions to the war effort ($17 billion), the Saudis will have to 'pay' in a different sense: by giving up part of their sovereignty in the field of price and production policies."[9] The more integrated the Gulf political–economic structure becomes in the global economy, the more important it had become to the West to maintain the Gulf's stability, even if at the cost of overlooking its dependency, traditionalism, and authoritarianism.

We can distinguish two distinctive developmental stages in Bahrain, whose economic and social structures were directly affected by the oil industry. The first stage started in the 1950s and culminated in the late 1970s, and the second unfolded in the 1990s. Both stages have been prompted by international as well as regional and local factors. Even though Bahraini oil was discovered in noncommercial, limited quantities, the country is still dependent on oil production and labor; and because of low production, the state benefits mainly from refining and distribution. Economically, Bahrain is the weakest Gulf state and dependent on Saudi Arabia, which provides it with oil, funds, and investment. By the late 1970s, in an attempt to diversify income and create jobs, Bahrain started such industries as aluminum and a dry dock, and in the early 1980s it offered the country as an international banking center. Since the late 1980s the impact of these enterprises have visibly weakened, and more so after the Gulf War of 1991.

The tremendous growth in oil wealth after 1973 has been successful in building up the infrastructure and other manifestations of the state along modern lines; oil revenue has provided citizens with a wide range of services such as education, health, social services, and even entertainment. These have been centralized projects by the state, the supreme employer and provider of benefits. Therefore, the ruling institution plays the major role in creating and withholding opportunities whether from women or any other subaltern. It has also rationalized its legitimacy through these achievements and by building a network of alliances based on tribal, sometimes religious and/or economic, interests.[10] Economic favors in the form of money or land donations, or control of power-generating posts are some of the means by which these alliances were and are cemented.

This system, however, has created superficially modern looking societies without solving the dilemmas that rapid Western modernization has brought. Change has come into conflict with the religiously grounded traditional cultural value systems that control social behavior. The policy has always attempted to find a balance between a commitment to modernization and economic development and a commitment to the internal traditional sociocultural forces. It has also manipulated both perceptions in order to create allegiance to its continued presence and control.[11] All modernization techniques introduced in Bahrain since the inception of this state were tailored to endorse this relationship and confirm these roles. Modernization also meant the creation of departments and apparatus to ensure control and order.

Bahrain differs from other Gulf states in the makeup and origin of its population. According to a December 1991 census the population of Bahrain, including foreign residents, was approximately 500,000.[12] This population has varied origins: Arabs of tribal extraction, Arabs from the settled communities of the eastern region in the Arabian Peninsula, Arabs from Iraq, Persian/Arab tribes (Hawala) coming from coastal and inland regions of the Persian coast, and Iranians from the coast and interior of Iran, in addition to a small number of Baluchis, Indians, and Pakistanis who have lived for generations in Bahrain and have become Bahraini. Each of these groups is large enough to leave an ethnic imprint on the fabric of society.

Shiis are a majority (the official estimate is 35%, the Western estimate is 55%, and the Shiis estimate is 75%), especially in villages. They are either descendants of the original Arab inhabitants and from the eastern quarter of Saudi Arabia, or Persians who have immigrated in the last fifty years. Sunnis are also either Arabs of tribal origin (such as the ruling family) or local Arab families of undefined origin, or people from Persian/Arab tribes who settled in Bahrain at different times since the late eighteenth century or Sunnis of African descent. These ethnic origins can be noted in linguistic differences as well as social attitudes and norms. They belong to the variety of social classes, except that the ruling family is of tribal Sunni origin. The rural villages are almost exclusively Shii and mostly Arab.

Since early in the century, the Shiis of Bahrain—representing the majority of the working class—have taken part in movements against the established authorities. Such a history and tradition of rebellion is associated with Shii demands for economic equality, union protection, and political participation.[13] Even though these activities became associated with Shiis, because they make up the majority of the economically depressed strata, Sunnis also participated in most of these movements. Whether employed in the pearl industry, the oil fields or in government, Shiis have felt victimized and the first to lose their means of livelihood.

Another historical reason for Shii disaffection is their opposition to the ruling (Al Khalifa) family, which Shiis view as a staunch Sunni minority of occupying tribesmen, who are accused of appropriating and misusing the resources of the country. The issue of land appropriation, whether in the early period of the Khalifa family advent or in the more recently reclaimed areas of the coast, have always been a sore issue to the local Shiis.[14] While the main cause of Shii opposition is economic it also has an ideological base, often fomented by outside inciters, mainly Iran.[15] But the Sunni and Shii Bahrainis also have had many causes in common. They participated in the nationalist movement against the British in the 1950s and 1960s, as well as the quest for democratization and popular participation in the government in the 1940s, the 1950s, the 1970s, and now again in the 1990s.[16] It was in the 1950s that women began to support the male-led demands for reform. A few women have reportedly unveiled in public in one of the protest demonstrations against the British.

The Era of Expansion

By the 1960s, regional Arab development, combined with a rapidly growing generation of Bahraini university graduates, further developed and politicized this protest current. The influence of the liberation movements, Arab nationalism, and political confrontations with colonialism in the Arab world in the 1950s, 1960s, and 1970s formed the political orientation of the young Bahraini generation. These included the tripartite attack on Nasser's Egypt in 1956, the Algerian war of independence, the liberation movement against the British in Yemen in 1963, the Arab defeat in the 1967 Six Day War, the Dhofar revolution in Oman in 1971, and the Palestinian struggle against Israel. Whether the reactions were spontaneous street demonstrations, the growth of underground political organizations, or the emergence of civil servants with heightened sociopolitical consciousness, society changed in unprecedented ways. The unrest culminated in the popular movement for a Parliament and political participation following independence from the British in 1971.

Male and female students educated in universities with thriving nationalist and radical political currents (such as those in Beirut, Cairo, Baghdad, and Kuwait) joined political organizations. Whether the organizations were leftist nationalist or procommunist, the women wanted to take part in changing their society. Since the early 1950s, women of the elite classes had organized charitable societies, but in the early 1970s voluntary women's societies sprang up with political orientations and were led by women from the emerging middle class. These women, with a few others from the working class, had benefited from the developing educational system, scholarships provided for university education in the Arab countries, and the need for Bahrainis in the job market. With that came social consciousness and the push to change. This development was similar to that of Kuwait where the earliest women's societies were organized by the socially conscious women and members of the emerging middle class.[17]

Women's earliest political experience was a disappointment. They were excluded from the short-lived liberal experiment with the Parliament in 1975, partly because the traditional tribal orientation was still very strong in both Sunni and Shii society, but mostly because the radical and liberalized men in society did not endorse women's issues. These men had encouraged women to support social change and to contribute to political change; but when it came to women's sociopolitical aims, men turned traditional and conservative. It was unfortunate for males as well, because the entire project was dissolved by the ruler before it really started.

During the 1960s, women made substantial advances in education and employment, which gave fruit in the 1970s. By the mid-1970s women were very visible in Bahraini society. The younger, more educated urban generation discarded the *abaya*, drove cars, took part in political demonstrations, communicated with male colleagues from their student days and from work, were involved in politics, joined the Ba'this, nationalist, and radical leftist groups and organized themselves in civil, nongovernment organizations (NGOs) such as women's societies, female sections of sports clubs, and professional organizations to further social and political aims. With a strong drive to achieve and a nationalist commitment to build, women were active elements in the early years of establishing Bahrain's modern society. The government was also anxious to build the infrastructure of the state, and women figured as an important element in the control of the job market by Bahraini nationals as well as for projecting a modern image abroad. This fact legitimized the more liberal behavior of women in seeking education and socializing outside the home, a behavior not fully condoned by tradition and the conservative society.

Despite these many achievements, Bahraini women still had few personal or civil rights; this was especially so in the villages and among the lower-class population, which had been practically excluded from what was mainly an urban, middle-class social revolution. In rural areas women were unaware of their personal rights. Illiteracy or minimal education, economic depression, and conservative oppressive socioreligious institutions were the overriding causes of this condition. Even among the new urban middle class, change barely touched on the core issues of feminism. The most that women acquired was to establish their right to free education and limited participation in the job market. Activities of these women through societies and personal relations took a political approach that was often elitist and reflected competition between the different political currents and among themselves. These modernized young women had unconsciously distanced themselves from the realities of their society and could not reach all strata of women by traditional mechanisms.

Following the 1975 parliamentary crisis, political activities were banned and women acquiesced. During the 1970s and early 1980s Bahrain experienced economic prosperity. While the 1970s saw the emergence of an urban, largely Sunni middle class, the late

1980s saw these developments reach the village, mostly Shii communities. Educational, health, and other services were built for rural and urban areas, along with high-rise office buildings and other modern outlets. The local economic market expanded as various corporations (monopolies by certain families of established status and wealth) were established and employment in the service sector increased. It was a period of major material expansion, which raised the economic and social expectations of people at a time when signs of economic contraction—as well as class and sectarian differences—were felt.

The 1980s and 1990s

Gradually the Bahraini social structure was coalescing into two economically homogenous classes with a growing gap between them. One was a stratum of glaringly wealthy merchant and technocrat families and high government officials, mostly from traditional merchant families and a few newly elevated families, particularly Shiis from Arab or Persian origins, who found their way to the upper middle class. This prosperous group also included a conglomerate of various ethnic groups that coalesced into a professional salaried and broker merchant stratum whose power depended on income from government-sponsored services or economic opportunities. At the other end was the lower middle class, which had developed from another large combination of most ethnic/religious groups; these were people with minimal education whose standard of living had been forcibly raised and who found themselves constantly in search of more income while anxiously protecting what they had already acquired. Closest to them was the lowest economic stratum that remained in the villages with little substantial difference in their economic or conservative structure. This stratum had benefited from the enlarged education and health services of the state and had acquired more political awareness and expectations for development, with no corresponding opportunities.

Similar to what occurred in other Arab and Gulf states,[18] in Bahrain the oil revolution of the 1970s left a very conservative social order characterized by a laissez-faire, capitalist, open-door economic policy, one that did not democratize opportunity and had no contingencies for the period of reversed fortunes. The business community, the upper classes, and the upper-middle-class merchant strata experienced a boom, with proliferation of visible accumulated wealth (palatial houses, residential compounds, spectacular business centers, and a wealthy life-style). There was also a mushrooming of Western enterprises (Kentucky Fried Chicken, McDonald's, Pizza Huts, Woolworth, etc.). At the same time, the lower middle class was experiencing a contraction in its purchasing power and vulnerability in its employment. It was worse among the lower classes, whose expectations had been whetted through education and through the obvious signs of prosperity at its doorsteps[19]; a prosperity denied to it even at the lowest levels.

These local conditions had been exacerbated by international and regional political and economic reasons. The 1980s saw the physical signs of Bahrain's incorporation into the Saudi sphere of influence through the construction of a 22-km causeway connecting the two countries, plus the Iraq/Iran war and the Gulf war; both conflicts were very close to Bahrain and both affected its population on many far-reaching levels. The final retraction of Arab nationalist ideals as part of normalizing policies with Israel had an effect as well. The reversal in the fortunes of the oil-producing nations brought contractions in the liquidity strength of Bahrain, its off-shore operations, and its banking system, as well as in the available funds for state-sponsored projects. Saudi utilization of Bahraini soil for entertainment purposes, promoted socially and morally laden controversies and elicited the ire of the conservative and religious sensibilities of Bahrainis. Government animosity toward Iran and sometimes toward Iraq hit at a basic chord within the economically depressed strata, mostly the Shiis whose family and religious links with both countries and peoples were restricted and monitored. The quiet endorsement of Western projects, a marked Western presence, and influence by Western officials deepened popular anti-Western and antigovernment feelings.[20] All these conditions translated themselves in the rise of unemployment and pauperization (street beggars had become visible on the streets of the capital city Manama and around the mosques), social unrest due to conceived signs of moral degeneration and social and political inequalities (these were most clearly verbalized in the 'Ashura celebrations, becoming progressively succinct during the 1980s), and a harsh policy of control in order to protect Bahrain's projected image of economic haven and entertainment venue.

Islamic Revivalism

The Islamist movements found adherents and support out of these conditions and the resulting feelings of frustration, defeatism, isolation, impotence, and discontent. The Islamist discourse provided the opposition with refuge and response to its outcry against conceived injustices. With the complete absence of all legal political channels for expressing grievances, revitalized Islam filled the vacuum. Throughout the 1980s the Islamic idiom was slowly entering all levels of life and most particularly among the lower middle classes and the lower strata of society. While the Gulf region generally had always been a more genuinely religious and conservative society, when compared to other parts of the Arab world, this modern return to tradition was shocking in its intensity and assertiveness.[21]

The religiopolitical thrust of these movements stimulated a discourse of hope and redemption induced by the modern crisis on moral, economic, and political levels.[22] In view of the transformations in Bahraini society already discussed, the social implications of revived Islam gradually became pervasive. An important dimension of this movement is the prominence given to the issue of women and their role in its discourse, one that reinforced traditional definitions. While discourses pertaining to gender are clearly used by Islamists as part of their platforms and features of self-definition, it is also the discourse used in the cultural project of the leftists and liberal currents.

Despite basic improvements in the living conditions, education, and politicization of most Bahraini women, the extent and amount of these improvements were neither uniform nor pervasive. In fact, they reflected the sociocultural differentiations that characterized the society in the 1980s and early 1990s. Women are stratified by class, religious and ethnic affiliation, education and age, and are also differentiated by ideological and political alliance and orientation. These differences bear on the consciousness and activism of women which has been clearly shown in the latest political events.

Education and employment have been the main channels that provided women of all classes with mobility and self-awareness, but access to either or both has been constrained by the economic and political system of the country. It is clear that women of the wealthy upper class, similar to women in the same class of other Gulf states and Arab countries, have utterly different concerns than those of the economically less fortunate classes. While education remains an important index of modernization, for women it is not necessarily for the sake of employment. In Bahrain as in Kuwait, a few upper-class women hold high administrative posts, but their limited number makes them symbols rather than the norm. Furthermore, it should be noted that the majority of these women come from the previous merchant and petty bourgeois classes who had benefited from the early economic boom associated with the state. The interest of this strata is aligned with the establishment and its power base.

The concentration and thrust of this study, however, has been primarily on middle-class women, especially those of the lower middle class, as well as those of the lower economic strata. Economic development, state-sponsored projects, and public works have provided opportunities for mobility, especially for middle-class and upper-middle-class women who had taken advantage of the changes during the 1970s and 1980s. Women in that category have become salaried and professional. Despite the constrained economic situation they still find various options and solutions. It is the lower strata of that class and the lower classes who face restricted opportunities of work and economic advancement. They had expectations of improvement by virtue of education, an achievement that has come one generation too late, and to a subaltern within another less favored sector of the society, the Shiis. This has added to the women's sense of social as well as gender inequality and accentuated their vulnerability.

Consciously or unconsciously, these women are activists in all the processes of change their country is experiencing. While they all expressed views to the effect that education and employment has strongly influenced their identification, political idiom and activism was the underlying feature of their consciousness. Those who were interviewed in September 1994, during the first weeks of the crisis, clearly projected an identification with the particular political stand of their class, their religious sect, and (for some) their ethnic origin.[23] Even those interviewed during the two previous years implied and unconsciously identified with particular religious sects and political lines aligned to them. Political conflicts seem to have a defining impact on the way active and educated women view the world around them and reflect on their role in the process of change.

Involvement of Middle Eastern women in the struggle for national liberation and reform is not new; Arab history is dotted with many examples, not the least of which are those of Algeria and the ongoing struggle of Palestinian women. The struggle of Kuwaiti women for democratic rights and participation is a model often cited, and their achievements, however minimal, are applauded.[24] These are issues that Bahraini women are aware of and bring up constantly. It was enlightening to find Bahraini activists who had experienced and lived through the anticolonial demonstrations of the 1960s and the 1971–1975 parliamentary protest movement in Bahrain. These secular nationalists were trained in the school of liberal nationalism of the 1960s and 1970s of the Nasserite era. During the peak of their activism, this brand of nationalists had fought for equal participation and a role in national development but were disillusioned. Twenty years later, it is in the same spirit that Bahraini secular nationalists have again petitioned for parliamentary participation.[25]

Nationalism remains an important category to use in assessing this participation especially since historically it has helped project women into the public arena and has acted as a channel for emancipation.[26] Despite the negative experience of women in the national liberation movement in Bahrain, nationalism remains an idiom of cohesion. It has produced a national culture, which fostered linkages and affinity among the participants despite the dissipation of political nationalism from the 1970s to the present. During the current crisis, these elements have reformulated and reexpressed demands for a progressive role under nationalist platforms. Nationalism is appropriated by all the parties in Bahrain, whether liberal, leftist, or Islamist: each group defines nationalism according to a different agenda. It is obvious that the goal of these women, similar to that of all women in developing countries, remains to end subordination on the international, national, and personal levels. In the final analysis, active, conscious, and politicized women are demanding the restoration of control over their lives and over their ability and power to make life choices.

While the agenda, identity, and commitment of the nationalist women is clear and easy to read as a consequence of their experience, the message of the women identified with the Islamist currents presents a much more complex, diverse, and emerging consciousness. The pervasiveness of the Islamic revivalist movement is more obvious among women because of the dress and behavior required. The young generation of women who have joined it see religion as the solution for dealing with modernization without jeopardizing the cultural and religious legacy of a society with such varied ethnic backgrounds and rapid accumulation of socioeconomic benefits:

> Although modernization resulted in an increase in urban women's access to education and employment, enhancing their potential for self-empowerment and emancipation, the existing structural problems in the character of modernization led the majority of modernized women, as well as men, into an alienating, frustrating, and confusing state.[27]

To the young Bahraini Islamists this confusion and alienation is dealt with through an Islamic accommodation of modernization. Followers of this current are not only from among the economically depressed and youthfully impressed women, but it has also cultivated women of the liberal eras who had considered themselves politically radical and socially liberal. This is a wave that has swept most of the middle class and practically all of the lower, economically depressed, strata. This wave of conservatism and the invoking of tradition and religion affected the view women have of themselves and their role in society.

Why was the Islamist movement so strong, so fast-spreading, and so appealing to women? In the Bahraini context the responses should be sought within the socioeconomic crisis, the crisis of state legitimacy and the opposition to the political system, selective social justice producing inequalities, and the weakening of traditional structures (particularly the extended patriarchal family). Islamists propagate the belief that Islam, tradition, and culture are endangered and their salvation is through a reconstruction of authenticity within the religious identity. Gender is politicized and women are given the roles of upholders of authenticity, propagators of generations, and transmitters of morality and social values. In this active role, women are articulating the identity of Muslim women and an Islamic world view for Bahrainis. Women have an exalted family role, a traditional status, and a gender linked to group identity. This should be given priority to all personal inclinations.

Forms and Channels of Revitalized Islam

By analyzing the positions of both Sunni and Shii women activists concerning a number of vital issues related to their religiosocial perceptions, such as education, the veil, work, Sunni/Shii relations and differences, politics and social change, a framework was formed within which common identifications and differences were identified. It is clear that the approaches and attitudes of these women have been acquired in a similar process that has its roots in their sociocultural background and influenced by their contacts with what they perceive as Western knowledge. The failure of alternative nationalist solutions has given the Islamization programs the chance to influence women of these strata in similar ways. But the obvious difference between Shii and Sunni Islamist orientations is in their structural base and operational philosophy. These in turn are controlled by the political tradition of each and the circumstances governing their history.

The veil and the public demonstration of Islamic behavior in Bahrain are followed mainly by the young educated generation of women who grew up in the 1970s and 1980s and saw the economic constraints on the middle and lower classes. This demonstration of Islamic identity took place at a time when the literacy base had broadened tremendously in the rural communities, mostly among Shiis, along with better health services and education, and when urban contact further politicized this strata.[28] Another factor inducing social change among them is demography; Shiis of the villages have a much higher birth rate and as a result have been instrumental in the altered political equilibrium. Demands for services, facilities, and employment opportunities have created a confrontational platform between the Shiis and the authorities. The fewer Sunni rural areas suffer from similar deficiencies, but to a much lesser degree. Education remains the major inducer for young people, both Sunni and Shii, to join the ranks of the Islamists, and it is both in the schools and at the university where conversion and commitment to the Islamic cause take place.

Education

The National University of Bahrain, a coeducational institution established in the early 1980s, has played a crucial role in the Islamization process by providing the venue for social and political awareness. Both Sunni and Shii Islamists propagate their views and demonstrate in support of their convictions.[29] This new university has become the vehicle for popularizing higher education for all Bahrainis, particularly the Shiis. Until the early 1980s, higher education was sought abroad, only by those endorsed by the state or from among the emerging wealthy strata of the upper and middle classes. For the emerging lower middle class and some members of the lower strata who joined the university, it became the only source of professional education and a means for future employment. Many branches of the university educational and administrative departments have become Islamist strongholds; the Islamist platform and message are issued from here. This trend is the most conspicuous among the more technologically advanced Western-educated staff and faculty.[30] The political, social, and economic constraints and realities have made the Shiis the majority both among the faculty and the students.

The number of women students is much higher than that of men, even though there is a policy of attempting to find a gender balance. Women students are very ambitious and hard working; unlike male university students, the women are usually chosen from the top performing high school students. Also, a very large percentage of university students are from traditional and rural backgrounds.[31] For them the university has been a forum of exposure, education, and political consciousness. In the last twelve years the changes have been quite dramatic in the women student body. Nearly 95% of the women wear the veil. Those who do not are under a constant and persistent pressure to do so.

The Veil

The veil and Islamic dress are the outward obvious signs of women's adherence to the new Islamic trends. However, the veil and formal compliance with tradition do not necessarily mean commitment to all the ideological baggage associated with it. In fact all respondents, both Sunni and Shii, conceded that the veil was used for various reasons, not all connected with religion. While there was a consensus that the veil was a source of affiliation and identification, it also gave these women peace, serenity, and the security of belonging to a group. Most of them also saw it as an affirmation of ethical and social customs. Both Sunni and Shii Islamic activists stressed that appropriating the veil has different significance and meaning than that understood by their parents. Islamism, in their view, does not change their identity but clearly channels it in a more conscious, knowledgeable fashion. To this younger generation the reconfirmed faith is due to an awareness, an understanding, and an educated comprehension of the written word commanding veiling; the veil has been ordained and prescribes what a proper woman's attire should be. In fact, they insist that this new attire is not the traditional abaya, but it does follow particular Islamic prescriptions. In their view it is a modern, educated Muslim woman's choice. It also signified a whole spectrum of life-style, the understanding of which is also modern in its concern with segregation, education, the family, and the role of woman.

While the veil carries religious significance, it is a social symbol as well; women have come to use it to fulfil other needs within this conservative setting. It is a protection from male harassment, in the street and in the work setting where women need to mix with men; it is a source of respectability and social acceptance; it offers nostalgia for the protection patriarchy used to provide; it is also a means to carry on social activities and behavior that otherwise would be condemned.[32] Nevertheless the veil has also been a cause for personal dilemmas to many of those who came to use it and maintained a nonsegregated life-style. Reconciling modern demands of work and the market with this new adherence entailed compromises which some seemed to accept as necessary.

Some of the interviewed veiled women expressed their dilemma as to what extent an observant Islamist should follow veiling and complete segregation. They often found Quranic verses and other religious indicators to justify their work as long as the job conditions did not contradict adherence to a segregated life-style. Paradoxically, a few expressed the wish for adamant observance of full veiling (full face cover, the *burqa*, and gloves) if it were not for official prohibition to do so while driving (a regulation these women considered unjustified). Such suggestions mainly came from women who had been educated in the West and who were completely immersed in the Islamic movement. It was noticeable that these women showed great self-confidence and expressed leadership traits of being assertive, emphatic, and proselytizing.[33] It is clear that to them the veil was the strongest symbol forging their revitalized identity and they went to great pains in asserting its distinctiveness and authenticity.

Sunni and Shii Women Islamists

While there is much common ground between Sunni and Shii women regarding the Islamist currents in Bahrain, differences can be very sharp and instrumental in their identities. While Islamic activism is very common among the emerging lower middle class and the lower strata of both sects, it is more obvious and more widespread among the Shiis. Both Sunnis and Shiis who are involved in the movement are from the younger generation who staunchly defend the veil and stress the importance of the family and the role of the woman in it, and woman's sacred role in creating an Islamic society and the future generations of Muslims; all call for education as being a Muslim duty (some stressing it more than others); all believe that Islam is a liberator and emancipator of woman and has endowed her with special rights.

When it came to the issue of work and women's right to work, Shii women spoke in social and political terms and stressed a woman's right to help the family and support the husband's income. However, whenever the issue of justice and rights came up, Shiis defined justice as a sacred duty that entitled a Muslim to demand and fight in its cause. While they were clearly referring to social justice and equal rights to economic opportunities, they were cautious not to define these issues particularly. Education is integrated into the aspiration and search for employment. While both Sunni and Shii women demanded and pushed for the education of women as a means for mobility and economic independence, they differed on the final results. It was clear that Sunni Islamists were more socialized and accepting of the conservative role of woman that the religious front projects. They made statements such as: "It was the duty of women to leave jobs for the males in society, men have the religious duty of supporting families", or "Women's virtue is better protected in the home, unless working in segregated settings women should not work, etc. . . . "

While Shii women would agree with all these arguments, they still maintained that it is necessary for women to work; because work opportunities for Shiis are limited, it is essential to educate children in order to create better work channels and a more promising future. They would often sidestep the religious argument and forge into social and political reasoning for justifying women's need to work, support the family, and educate their children.

Active Bahraini Islamists have taken a clearly conscious choice to identify with and participate in a formatted project with defined roles and contributions. Organized religious affiliations of both sects are influential because of their appeal to the grass-roots relations of the religious and ethnic communities.[34] Sectarian characteristics are overstressed in order to maintain this linkage and produce cohesiveness among each group.

The organization of Sunni Islamic movements and charitable societies is more formalized and at times has gained official recognition and support. These organizations also have links with other Sunni revivalist groups outside Bahrain. Jam'iyyat al-Islah (Reform Society) has Muslim Brotherhood links and has a strong network of wealthy supporters within Bahrain and many other Gulf states, notably Saudi Arabia and Kuwait. This society has good relations with the authorities and is cautious to maintain them. al-Jam'iyyah al-Islamiyyah (Islamic Society) is endorsed by a family with a number of educated religious *ulema*, with degrees from al-Azhar and links with other reform-minded currents in the Gulf and Egypt. This society is open to Muslims from all directions, including Shiis who have been attracted by its overall humanitarian approach and nonsectarian attitude. One of its main figures, Dr. Abdul-Latif al-Mahmoud, a university professor, was expelled from his professional position for publicly criticizing the ruling institutions in the Gulf and demanding democratization of the political system. Jam'iyyat al-Tarbiyah al-Islamiyyah (Society for Islamic Education) is another society related to the last two, but with more fundamentalist beliefs and a *salafi* orientation. It seems to appeal to the Hawala (Persian-origin) elements of the Sunni community, who are known for being staunch practicing Muslims. This society is also supported by some Hawala clerics and a few wealthy families, and it has links in the United Arab Emirates and Pakistan.

All these societies have very active women's sections and branches in various areas of Bahrain that provide Islamic education and socialization. The participation of women in these activities is confined to the programs of the societies and are directed by male leaders. The role of women as projected in these orthodox societies is more strictly bounded by the traditional, noninnovative confines of classical positions. It is the women associated with these currents who have confirmed this impression through the roles they have assigned to women and themselves.

This situation is not duplicated in the Shii community. While the community had one officially recognized society, al-Jam'iyyah al-Islamiyyah (Islamic Society), originating in the village of Diraz (1975) and representing the fundamentalist direction of Shii Muslims in Bahrain, the organization was outlawed for political reasons in 1984. Members of the society were accused of fomenting an Iranian-inspired coup, and were arrested.[35] When the appropriate government department was approached with the request to authorize a charitable society for rural women, Jam'iyyat Fatat al-Reef, which would have been dominated and led by Shii women from the rural areas, the request was denied. The Shii Islamist currents do not have one set structure of religious reference that binds the whole community under a single umbrella. Religious referrals (*marja'iyyah*) are either linked to Najaf (Iraq), Qum (Iran), or within Bahrain itself. Many of the religious *mullahs* have been educated in Iran at the Bahrain Studies Center in Qum, while others have studied in Iraq, which remains an important center of Shii scholarship. Shiis also have no formal organizations to channel the ideological perceptions of an Islamist orientation or to organize on the social level. Such activities are banned by law.

Therefore Shii women, whether formally or informally grouped in their villages and quarters, through their professional affiliations, in the *Ma'tem/Husayniyyah* (religiosocial gathering-house similar to a mosque), or even in their extended family settings, express innovative, nonconformist platforms of activism. They view their roles in a wide range of options from the militant to the homebound traditional position. This diversification and decentralization of religious controls also expresses itself in more grass-root maneuverability, whereby there is overall cohesive political orientation by Shii women of all strata but a difference in the technique of achieving social justice. While the professionals and middle-class women see their role as catalysts in attaining social cohesion for their community—through education, training programs and self-help projects such as the charitable funds (Sanadiq Khairiyyah)—members of the younger generation express their identity by showing opposition and, increasingly, through public demonstrations. The charitable funds have sprung up as spontaneous projects to help needy families and to support village projects. Again the authorities have cut short their activities by banning them. In a comparable situation during the Palestinian intifada, spontaneous civilian organizations took over from the banned formal structures to help the Palestinian civilian population.[36]

As already mentioned, since the late 1970s Shii women activists have tried to organize charitable organizations similar to societies run by urban women, but they were always denied permits to do so. The official women's organizations organized in the 1950s, have lost legitimacy to the Shiis as part of the loss of confidence in the political system. These societies were always viewed with suspicion, and they did not develop a legitimacy separate from that of the regime.

Because of their particular sociopolitical situation Shii women—as distinct from Sunni women and as significant contributors to the development of the Shii community— unconsciously express radical feminist views. In times of crisis and perceived oppression that generate feelings of distress and coercion, their Shii religious heritage—or what they called intrinsic communal religious characteristics—come to the fore and express a rejection of oppression. These women try to express this distinctiveness in symbolic terms such as the difference in the form of the veil used, mannerisms acquired, and salutation given. These symbols are endowed with religious content by associating them with particular Shii beliefs.

It has been reported by both groups of active Islamist women that feminist issues such as birth control, the importance of education, and the role of women in the family are under debate, discussion, and education. Among Sunni women's societies, these activities are organized in the form of lectures or internal group meetings with a preference for religious discussions and interpretations of the Quran. For the Shiis, the ma'tam is an important venue where formal and informal gatherings often take place, and where these issues are debated as current problems and concerns. Furthermore, the month of Muharam is a period of continuous education for women when such teaching is intensified. During that month it is an accepted social behavior for women to congregate, listen to male preachers in the village squares and in front of mosques, and go to the ma'tam for social and religious education.

Conclusion

In a rapidly developing society, Bahraini women have undergone tremendous changes in the idiom and form they project in order to express their particular gender identity, autonomy, and subjectivity. While in the 1960s and 1970s the idiom was one of national liberation, constitutional democratization, Western dress, and political radicalization, in the 1980s and 1990s the idiom of Islam is used. This is accompanied by activism to fulfill Islam's message for a proper Muslim life; the veil is the symbol of its triumph. In both phases it has been women from within the rapidly changing social classes who have expressed these roles. In the earlier period it was the urban middle-class woman, who had traveled, become educated, and broken the barriers of tradition. She had become a salaried, independent, assertive, and politically aware citizen, hopeful for national development and salvation. In this more recent generation, it is also a movement of the middle-class women (mainly from the lower middle class) and the lower classes of rural backgrounds who continue to be attached to conservative and traditional ideologies. Islam has found fertile ground in a class still in transition and vulnerable to economic and political pressures of the 1980s. In some measure this explains the division and gaps between these two generations of activist women. While the liberal, pro-secular, first generation also belongs to a conservative religious background, various reasons impeded their ability to break through the class/ethnic/religious barrier to reach the rural, mainly Shii women.[37] It took another generation and Islam to activate the Shii.

Now, following the Gulf War, the region as a whole, and Saudi Arabia, Kuwait and Bahrain in particular, are facing the repercussions of policies binding the region to Western hegemony and economic controls. These states are confronting a serious backlash in the form of opposition/revivalist politics. Saudi Arabia must contend with an ultra-right-wing religious opposition (now based in London) criticizing and inciting against the regime, as well as an active (albeit suppressed and muted) opposition from the substantial minority of Shiis in the oil-producing Eastern region. In Kuwait, since the elections of October 1992, the sweeping parliamentary victory of the Islamist groupings has sharpened and redirected the tones of social and political development in the country and broadened the margin of future strife. As for Bahrain, the grass-roots, popular uprising has been continuing, accelerated since December 1994 by the alliance among the liberal professionals and intellectuals, a wide range of Islamist structures (both Sunni and Shii), the lower middle classes, and the economically depressed lower stratum of society. In Bahrain as well as Kuwait there are clear indications of the involvement of women in these reactions, whether within the organized frameworks of the Islamist groups or from the liberal intellectuals and independent elements. The demands of all opposition platforms is for a larger margin of democratization and a more equitable distribution of the state wealth.

In the latest events in Bahrain, women were given media exposure due to their contributions in the protest activities, in the negotiations, and in giving the crisis a gender dimension. Whenever the situation has been reported in the international press or in the underground press of the leftist and Shii Islamist opposition fronts, the issue of women's demands for democratization and participation is given prominence. Women in Bahrain have been part of events, and reports of actual physical involvement have been circulated. Women have participated in demonstrations, mainly at the university. Amnesty International has reported on cases of men and young girls, as well as cases of women being arrested and subsequently disappearing, and women being denied medical attention while in detention and being denied visits by family and lawyers. A significant contribution is the all-woman petition of protest demanding political reforms, as well as the first popular petition, which had the signatures of at least 6,000 women. This is indicative of the class dimension of the uprising and the depth of women's involvement in it. Women students at the university suddenly became the only family breadwinner when brothers, fathers, and husbands were arrested. Their academic life and their family life were disrupted by these disturbances and by the official backlash against their villages and communities. The issue of arrests and long internment with no legal action and no recourse to humanitarian aid has added to the feelings of anger, frustration, and bitterness.

Whether these activities will lead to an immediate change in the condition of women is doubtful, but this is one more step in the path for women's struggle to social liberation and to a better awareness of their capabilities, justifiable rights, and a significant role in national development. In a manner similar to Palestinian women responding to the intifada, their social and political consciousness and their identity have been accelerated and defined through political activism.

Notes

1. Several articles, appearing in periodicals with different policies, have generally reflected similar analytical approaches. See *Rose al-Yusif,* January 16, 1995; *Crescent International,* January 16–31, 1995; *Le Monde Diplomatique,* March 1995; *Al- Sharq al-Awsat,* last week of April 1995 (series of five articles by Fouad Matar); *The Wall Street Journal,* June 12, 1995; *The Washington Post,* June 13, 1995.

2. These petitions have been widely circulated in Bahrain and published by the opposition press in England and Syria.

3. See Valentine Moghadam, *Modernizing Women: Gender and Social Change in the Middle East* (Boulder, Colo.: L. Rienner, 1993), pp. 14–16.

4. See Florencia E. Mallon, "The Promise and Dilemma of Subaltern Studies: Perspectives from Latin American History," *AHR Forum* (December 1994): 1510. The example of the Kuwaiti women's struggle for political participation in the elections in 1993 should be kept in mind, as well as that of Bahraini women in the early attempt to share in the elections of 1973.

5. These data were collected as part of previous, general research on the role of Bahraini women in the development of their country. See May Seikaly, "Women and Social Change in Bahrain," *International Journal of Middle Eastern Studies* 26 (1994): 415–426.

6. I lived in one of the villages for five years.

7. See Badriyya al-ʿAwwadi, *al-Marʾah wa al-Qanun* [Woman and Law] (Kuwait,: n.p. 1990); Munira Fakhro, *Women at Work in the Gulf: A Case Study of Bahrain* (London: Kegan Paul International, 1990); Farida Allaghi and Aisha Almanaʾ, "Survey of Research on Women in the Arab Gulf Region," *Women* (UNESCO) (1991): 16–17.

8. The only indication of official U.S. concern with the disturbances was in a U.S. Department of State public announcement sent for immediate release as a travel advisory and circulated through the embassies and on the Internet on February 3, 1995. It was an advisory to U.S. citizens to consult with their government before traveling to the area. For those already living there, it advised exercising caution about arson and other attacks (to which some American vehicles had been subjected), avoiding public gatherings, and maintaining conservative dress.

9. Paul Aarts, "The New Oil Order: Built on Sand?," *Arab Studies Quarterly* 16 (2) (Spring 1994): 5.

10. Baqir al-Najjar, "Maʿuqat al-Istikhdam al-Amthal li al-Qiwah al-ʿAmilah al-Wataniyah fi al-Khalij al-ʿArabi wa-Imkaniyat al-Hal," in *Conference of Experts on Policies for Arab Labor Mobility and Utilization* (Kuwait: Economic and Social Commission for West Asia [ESCWA] and Kuwait Institute of Planning, 1985); Muhammad al-Rumaihi, "Athar al-Naft ʿala Wadʿ al-Marʿah al-ʿArabiyah fi al-Khalij" in *al-Marʾa wa-Dawruha fi Harakat al-Wahdah al-ʿArabiyah* (Beirut: Markaz Dirasat al-Wahdah alʿ-Arabiyah, 1982), pp. 231–251.

11. See Hisham Sharabi, *Neopatriarchy: A Theory of Distorted Change in the Arab World* (New York: Oxford University Press: 1988); Moghadam, *Modernizing Women,* pp. 11, 14, 99, 112.

12. State of Bahrain, *Statistical Abstracts, 1990* (Bahrain, n.p., 1991).

13. See Fuad Ishaq Khuri, *Tribe and State in Bahrain: The Transformation of Social and Political Authority in an Arab State* (Chicago: University of Chicago Press, 1980) pp. 85–105; Olivier da Lage, "Bahrein Ebranle par une Vague d'Emeutes," in *Le Monde Diplomatique* (March 1995).

14. This accusation against the ruling family has been often mentioned to me during my interviews and conversations in Bahrain.

15. Munira Fakhro, "The Uprising in Bahrain: an Assessment," paper presented to the Third International Conference—Gulf 2000, Bellagio, Italy, July 25–27, 1995, p. 11.

16. For a history of this period see: Khuri, *Tribe and State*, 195, 200, 219, 229–233; also see Rumaihi, "Athar al-Naft" and Fakhro, "The Uprising in Bahrain."

17. The similarity between women's activities in Kuwait and Bahrain is very strong and practically the same type of societies sprang up in both Gulf states. The three major charitable societies in Bahrain, the Society of Mother and Child, Al-Nahda Society, and Awal Society, had corresponding organizations in Kuwait. This has been confirmed by Haya al-Mughni in a lecture on "Women Societies in Kuwait" at Center for Cross-Cultural Research on Women (CCCRW), Oxford, on June 24, 1995.

18. See Leila Ahmad, *Women and Gender in Islam* (New Haven: Yale University Press, 1992), pp. 217–219; Moghadam, *Modernizing Women*, pp. 52–53; Seikaly, "Women and Social Change in Bahrain," pp. 415–426.

19. What exacerbated conditions for the lower classes and rural communities was the encroachment of "garden residential compounds" onto the heart of the villages. Mostly foreign communities resided in those ultraluxurious living compounds, oblivious to the squalor and poverty surrounding them and insensitive to the conservative traditional lifestyle of the villagers. The uprising was ignited by an incident in these villages when some foreign residents were taking part in a marathon and passed through these villages wearing what was conceived as indecent sports clothes.

20. The fact that Ian Henderson—the commander of police and the official responsible for investigations—was still a British citizen, has been a cause of national protest. There was particular reference to him in the protest petitions sent to the Amir in these latest disturbances.

21. From my own personal observation and experience during my stay in Bahrain, the pervasiveness of the movement by women to veil and show outward signs of adherence to Islamic observance was tremendous. Between 1983 and 1993, the number of my students who joined the ranks of the veiled increased from 5% to 95%.

22. Eqbal Ahmad, " Islam and Politics," in *The Islamic Impact*, ed. Yvonne Y. Haddad, Byron Haines, and Ellison Findly (Syracuse N.Y.: Syracuse University Press, 1984), p. 25.

23. The Shii upper-middle-class respondents were cautious with strong sectarian commitment, while those Shiis of the lower middle class expressed anger, bitterness, and frustration. Sunnis of Persian origin identified as Muslim, non-Arabs.

24. See Mai Ghassoub, "Feminism—or the Eternal Masculine—in the Arab World," *New Left Review* no. 161 (1987): 11; Shafeeq Ghabra, "Democratization in a Middle Eastern State—Kuwait, 1993," *Newsletter of the Society for Gulf Arab Studies*, 4 (2) (November 1994): 4–12.

25. In April 1995, 310 women representing a cross-section of the liberal, educated, and professional strata raised a petition to the Amir demanding, among other things, a role for women participation in the political process.

26. Nahla Abdo, "Nationalism and Feminism: Palestinian Women and the Intifada," in *Gender and National Identity*, ed. Valentine Moghadam (London: Zed, 1994) pp. 149–152.

27. Nayereh Tohidi, "Modernity, Islamization and Women in Iran" in *Gender and National Identity*, ed. Valentine Moghadam (London: Zed, 1994), p. 120.

28. State of Bahrain, *Statistical Abstracts 1990*, pp.17–18; 29; 195; 288.

29. In the recent confrontations between student demonstrators asking for political reforms, the police (reported to be mercenary Baluchis, or Saudi national guards) shot two students dead. Women students are also reported to have demonstrated and made very incendiary statements.

30. Islamists are in the majority in the Arabic and Islamic Studies department and are also in control of the computer section and employment of the Administration. Most of those are Sunni Islamists, but the number of Shiis among the teaching faculty is also very high.

31. There are no statistics on these facts, however they are common knowledge among those who work at the university and those who live in Bahrain. Similar conditions exist in other parts of

the Middle East. See Ahmed, *Women and Gender*, pp. 220–222; Moghadam, *Modernizing Women*, pp. 122, 130–131.

32. These reasons for veiling have been observed by myself and reported by other Bahrainis during the last ten years when a large number of my students and acquaintances had started to use the veil.

33. Many of these women had been studying together in Canada, and a few in the U.S., during the 1980s. When I asked a well-known Bahraini enlightened cleric (who has been very influential among women activists) about the reason for their veiling, he responded "To prove themselves and forge an identity."

34. This has been proven historically when sectarian solidarity took a political stand in the 1930s , the mid-1950s, and during the 1970s. See Khuri, *Tribe and State*, 194–217. This has also transpired during the latest crisis in the country.

35. Munira Fakhro, "Non-Government Organizations in Bahrain" (Cairo: Ibn Khaldun Publications, 1995).

36. Souad Dajani, "The Struggle of Palestinian Women in the Occupied Territories: Between National and Social Liberation," *Arab Studies Quarterly*, 16 (2) (Spring 1994): 15.

37. See Seikaly , "Women and Social Change," pp. 415–426.

Gender, Islam, and the State

*Kuwaiti Women in Struggle, Pre-Invasion
to Postliberation*

The ideology and politics of citizenship, democracy, and gender in Kuwait are the central themes of this chapter. Only a fraction of the Kuwaiti population—first-class citizens of the male gender—enjoy the practice of full political rights. Second-class or naturalized citizens have not been granted political rights, nor have those known as *bidun*, people of nomadic origin who cannot prove settlement requirements and are thus classified as stateless.[1] As first-class citizens, women have been granted full political rights by the Constitution, but an electoral law has prevented them from exercising these rights.[2] If rights guaranteed by the Constitution are curtailed in practice, the duties spelled out in the highest law of the land are expected to be fulfilled. Moreover, Kuwaiti citizenship passes down through the male line; a Kuwaiti woman married to a non-Kuwaiti cannot pass her citizenship to her children, while a Kuwaiti man with a foreign wife may do so. While the indigenous population is divided into three unequal categories, and made more unequal by repressive gendering practices, national loyalty is expected by all segments of the population.

From the very start of parliamentary life in Kuwait, women protested the withholding of their constitutionally granted suffrage rights. Women's associations began in the 1960s, simultaneous with the birth of their suffrage campaign. If women's calls for the vote and the right to be elected could be ignored before the invasion and occupation of 1990–1991, in the postliberation era they could not be so cavalierly dismissed. Women had demonstrated the ability to defend their country through a sustained resistance struggle. In most democracies, defending one's country and the ability to vote are interconnected. Women (and second-class citizens and biduns) defended their country on all levels during the invasion and occupation. This defense, and the loyalty and practice of citizenship it displayed, has made women's demands for their full political rights more compelling, as well as claims of second-class citizens and biduns—and the withholding of them more egregious.

Women in Kuwait have been able to achieve a broad genuine solidarity only once. This was during resistance, when conventional gender rules did not apply. Defense of the nation and people legitimized all behaviors. The abnormal as normal in Kuwait under the occupation freed women to perform as citizens and to prove their abilities. Drawing on women's resistance narratives, the central section of this chapter looks at women's resistance experiences to demonstrate how their performance as citizens under national duress exposed fallacies of conventional gender ideology and contradictions at the core of the construction and practice of democratic citizenship in Kuwait.[3]

The first section of this chapter, focusing on women's association activities from the 1960s to 1990, demonstrates how women's societies were positioned in a patriarchal class and clan-grid that "froze" them in place and inhibited the enactment of a broad gender solidarity, thus subverting their suffrage cause.[4] The last section looks at women's resumed suffrage discourse in the early aftermath of liberation and analyzes women's suffrage within the politics of postliberation Kuwait. Women's gender consciousness enhanced during resistance could not preserve the solidarity women achieved under occupation and redeploy it during reconstruction.[5] In postliberation Kuwait, patriarchal gender ideology, patriarchal politics, regional politics, and an Islamist threat all conspired to enable a pre-invasion model of state and society to be reinstalled.

Pre-Invasion Gender Activism

Women had integral roles in the political economy of premodern Kuwait. They were active in the premodern pastoral economy and in the pearling, fishing, and trading communities. During the long periods of the year when the men were at sea, women ran their communities.[6] The memory of this self-sufficiency and of taking charge of the community has been evoked by women as part of a proud past.[7] Women who were the backbone of the resistance in Kuwait during the Iraqi occupation linked their resilient selfsufficiency and community activism to this early heritage.[8]

In the transition to a modern state and society, which accelerated after the discovery of oil, women gained access to education and to work relatively simultaneously with men (which is not to minimize the obstacles and limitations women have experienced). By now, women are found in nearly every profession.[9] However, women have not kept pace with men in enjoyment of their political rights. To this day, despite the high posts they hold in government ministries, institutions of higher learning, and at the head of foundations and enterprises in the private sector, Kuwaiti women cannot vote or be elected to Parliament.

In 1963, when the first Parliament was inaugurated, women protested the withholding of their political rights in a public demonstration where they burned their *abayas* (black wraps), as symbols of their seclusion from society. This signaled the beginning of Kuwaiti women's call for suffrage.[10] In Egypt forty years earlier, women protested the withholding of their suffrage rights in a demonstration when the first postindependence Egyptian Parliament was inaugurated (they also had removed their veils the year before, signaling the beginning of their feminist movement and the call for their political rights).[11]

The same year that women went out in this suffrage demonstration they also formed their first associations.[12] A young high school graduate, Nuriya al-Sadani, formed the Arab Women's Development Society (AWDS), hoping to attract a cross-class membership, but she succeeded only in drawing other newly educated middle-class women like herself. AWDS focused on the education and development of all women, including trying to work with bedouin women.[13]

Meanwhile, women of wealthy merchant families ("blue bloods" who came in the eighteenth century from what is now Saudi Arabia) under the lead of Lulua al-Qitami formed The Cultural and Social Society, renamed the Women's Cultural and Social Society (WCSS) in 1966. This elitist society devoted itself to philanthropy and to members' recreational activities. Although both of these organizations took a pro-suffrage stand, there was no interaction between the two societies, which expressed the class and kin cleavages rife in Kuwaiti society. From the start, this adumbrated the enormous difficulties in forging a broad gender solidarity among women in Kuwait.

Expressing and enhancing its women's liberationist thrust and an affinity with Arab nationalists, AWDS, not long after its establishment, joined the Arab Feminist Union (formed in Cairo by Arab women from fertile crescent countries two decades earlier).[14] By the early 1970s, as a more feminist agenda was crystalizing, AWDS began to attract a larger constituency. The association organized the first Kuwaiti Women's Conference in 1971 which drew women from both the middle class and merchant elite. The call for women's political rights was placed at the top of the list of demands at this conference and at a second conference AWDS convened in 1975.

For a brief moment, from 1974 to 1977, the two women's organizations, AWDS and WCSS, under the initiative and presidency of Nuriya al-Sadani, combined forces in creating the Kuwait Women's Union to further women's rights. The Girls Club established in 1976 by another group of women from the merchant elite (from Jinna'at Merchants with Iraqi roots) joined the Kuwait Women's Union, offering a counterpoint to WCSS. However, the fragile union, encumbered by internal strife among women and creating alarm with its women's rights agenda, was closed by the government in 1977. AWDS survived, but not for long. Persistent rivalries among members created enemies within the ranks; in addition, the government was troubled by president al-Sadani's association with the Free Democrats, a male Arab nationalist political group, and the society's staunch adherence to women's rights. All these factors appear to have led to the government shutdown in 1980 of AWDS.

The 1980 witnessed the birth of Islamic women's organizations as Islamism itself began to spread in Kuwait. State encouragement of Islam to counter growing concern over Arab nationalist forces in Kuwait has been credited with the growth of the Islamic movement from this time. If AWDS was a casualty of Arab nationalist politics and a growing feminist assertiveness, Islamic women's associations could provide an alternative. One example is Bayader al-Salam, a sufi-type organization founded in 1981, under the tutelege of a Syrian woman invited into Kuwait for the purpose. This organization, which appealed to a rising generation of middle-class women, preempting a gravitation towards feminism, gained many adherents. This, in turn, posed a threat to other Islamic forces. The Muslim Brotherhood, observing the growing appeal of Bayader al-Salam, responded by organizing a women's committee. The Muslim Brothers, concerned with expanding, were alert to the instrumental importance of women in political struggle. Indeed, they supported the vote for women, but not the right to run for office. (Women's votes had helped Islamist forces gain control of the Kuwait National Student Union in the late 1970s.)

It was not long before an initiative came from government quarters to provide its own Islamic alternative. In 1982, Shaikha Latifa, the wife of the Crown Prince and prime minister, founded the Islamic Care Society (ICS). This association attracted an older membership, mainly relatives and friends of its founder. The society broadcast the importance of a domestic-centered existence for women and encouraged a heightened sense of piety. This was coupled with a firm stand against political rights for women.

In the first half of the 1980s, with the dissolution of AWDS, it was left to WCSS and the Girls Club to promote the suffrage cause. Neither organization was able to mount an effective campaign to persuade deputies to vote affirmatively when a bill to grant women political rights was put to the vote in the National Assembly in 1982.[15] Three years later when elections to the National Assembly were held, WCSS women attempted to place their names on the registration lists without success; this tactic was tried again in 1992, also to no avail. The Girls Club, meanwhile, supported Arab nationalist men running for election, expecting in return that successful candidates would support the women's suffrage cause. An end was put to the matter of women's political rights, for the time being, when the Department of Jurisprudence and Legislation issued a *fatwa* claiming it was not permissible for a woman to vote or to run for office. (This department, al-Fatwa al-Tashri, was headed by a jurist from Egypt where a fatwa endorsing women's rights to vote and to be elected had been issued three decades earlier.)[16]

The history of women's associations from the 1960s through the 1980s reveals the difficulties of women to form a broad united front. Kuwaiti scholar Hayat al-Mugni has pointed out that women replicated societal divisions along class and kin lines.[17] When women began to breach these barriers in the attempt to organize around a women's rights agenda, they met a counterthrust. The state, National Assembly, and Islamic groups, themselves composed of class and kin factions, each in their own way, operated to undo the nascent broadening gender base of feminist. Meanwhile, women themselves allowed their old antagonisms and rivalries to be rekindled.

By 1990, still dispersed in their associations reproducing the grid of class and kin, and dividing them as "secularists" and Islamists (or Islamics more attuned to the state), women remained far from achieving a broad gender solidarity around the common cause of voting rights for their gender. This was the situation on the eve of the Iraqi invasion of Kuwait in the summer of that year. If, after three decades, women still did not have their formal political rights, they were about to play unprecedented, de facto nationalist political roles during the seven-month Iraqi occupation and Kuwaiti resistance. During this time, women would forge the gender solidarity that until then had eluded them.

Armed Occupation and Gendered Resistance

In the early hours of August 2, 1990, Iraqi troops crossed the border into Kuwait and, after meeting resistance and inflicting bloodshed, imposed themselves on an unwilling population. A young woman resister told how she and other women went to the center of town the day of the invasion to see how they could help. She and her friends were raped by Iraqi soldiers. A middle-aged man who had accompanied them stood by powerless to prevent this. In the midst of this violation and violence, Iraq announced to the world that it was responding to calls from within Kuwait to rescue the country from oppressive rule. That same day the Amir and Crown Prince of Kuwait fled the country for Saudi Arabia, where they set up a government in exile.

Iraq, after initial vacillations and contradictions about the temporary and limited nature of its entry into Kuwait, announced the annexation of the country as its nineteenth province and the end of Kuwait as a sovereign state. All Kuwaiti symbols such as photographs of the ruler, the flag, and national insignia—indeed any signs of national identity (including vehicle license plates)—were outlawed. Iraq took over government offices, the media, schools, hospitals, and public utilities. Iraq's Republican Guards, the standing army, the popular army (which also tried to impress non-Kuwaiti locals), and members of the intelligence service (*mukhabarat*) were sent in increasing numbers to subdue and control Kuwait. At their peak these forces were reported to have outnumbered Kuwaitis two to one.[18]

Women were at the center of the seven-month resistance to the Iraqi occupation. They came from all classes and backgrounds. Women also created one of the first resistance groups abroad, the Women's Joint Resistance Committee in Cairo, and set up resistance committees elsewhere as well. The government in exile and external resistance committees assisted and coordinated with the resistance inside Kuwait. Women resisters inside Kuwait were called the *samidat*—the steadfast.[19]

The first collective action of women was a political statement in defense of their nation and its sovereignty. This took place three days after the invasion. Between 400 and 500 women participated in a demonstration which began at the 'Adailiyah Mosque.[20] Women, young and old, some pregnant and some with babies, many cloaked in abayas (which most had ceased to wear but resumed at that time) marched down the street affirming Kuwait's rejection of Iraq. They chanted the slogans: "God, Country, and Amir," and "Saddam, keep your hands off Kuwait. The people don't want you." After the demonstration the women returned to the mosque and in the sanctuary of this safe (and, in normal times, exclusively male) space they exchanged names, addresses, and telephone numbers, setting up the nucleus of resistance networks. The women held another demonstration two days later in Jabriyah where they were met with bullets.[21] Half a week later they went out again in a demonstration from the Klaib Mosque. On August 18 women marched from Mansuriyah to Qadisiyah. Raida al-Fodari, a recent graduate in philosophy from Kuwait University, was probably typical of other young middle-class women who took to the streets, forming part of a collectivity of women of all classes and ages. She recalled how Iraqi soldiers opened fire on the demonstrators.[22] Participants ran through houses and over rooftops. Sana 'Abd al-Rahman al-Nuri was shot and died the following day.[23] *Middle East Watch* reported: "Peaceful demonstrators were killed or wounded by gun fire, even though they presented no threat to soldiers."[24]

Raida al-Fodari said, "We had to let the world know that no one wanted Saddam Husain. We made videos of the demonstrations and sent them to the government in exile in Saudi Arabia and to the United Nations and other places. We made our point and then we had to stop to protect lives." Women also printed flyers about Iraqi defectors, which they dropped at places where Iraqi soldiers congregated. "We did this to demoralize them and to show that not all soldiers were pro-Saddam." The political threat the women's demonstrations posed to Iraq was evidenced not only by Iraq's brutal repression but also by other measures intended to counteract their effects. *Middle East Watch* announced that the Iraqi secret service forced people to make pro-Iraq demonstrations and to chant pro-Iraqi slogans that were broadcast on Iraqi television.[25]

The women's demonstrations signaled the appearance of a new public woman and a new private man. Women became more visible and men more invisible. Women became protectors and men the protected. During the resistance, gender roles and use of space were reversed. A new gender and national iconography were enacted. The same women who had publicly burned their abayas in the 1960s—coupling a refusal to shroud themselves with demands to participate more fully in society and to enjoy political rights—returned to their abayas.[26] Younger women who had never worn abayas now put them on.

The abaya was not a symbol of cultural defense, as its equivalent had been for Algerian women under French colonial rule. (During the liberation war in Algeria, however, some women removed their veils to look European and thus camouflage their clandestine activities.[27]) The abaya did not signal a retreat of women to the privacy of the home. On the contrary, the abaya facilitated women's public roles and movements under siege. The abaya rendered women anonymous, hid their sexual attractiveness, and facilitated the carrying of arms and information. The abaya had no religious or cultural significance, but became a weapon in the defense of women and the nation. Raida al-Fodari said: "People started wearing abayas during the occupation because we couldn't show [our] beauty to the soldiers. They might take us. There were many stories of rapes near our house. They catch women and kill them, they shoot them in the head. Also [with abayas] everyone looks alike and women can hide things under their abayas." Badriya Ghanem, one of the women of privileged background who had been educated at mid-century, and one of those who had rejected the abaya three decades earlier, told how she had taken it up again. "We didn't want the Iraqis to see us. We wanted to show them we were angry. So we dressed in black wearing abayas and sunglasses."[28]

At checkpoints where women had to present identity cards Iraqi soldiers remarked on the difference between the faces on the cards and the plain-looking women with abayas. "Ours face had nothing to do with the identity cards we carried. But, no one asked us to remove our abayas. They couldn't."[29] Kuwaiti women urged non-Kuwaitis also to wear abayas for protection.[30] The abaya conferred anonymity and also stamped all who wore it "Kuwaitis." Indeed, it became a metaphor for national cohesion. Class distinctions, together with differences in ancestral origins or differences between Sunnis and Shiis, all disappeared in the defense of female selves and endangered Kuwaiti identity.

Women went into the streets and mosques to do political work and moved around the city tending to the needs of the community and the nation. It was women who more overtly mobilized community resistance.[31] They routinely passed through the armed checkpoints that webbed the city. Badriya Ghanem said, "We were running from area to area." Privileges of class were retracted and normal male protectors were invisible or absent. "We didn't have drivers. We didn't have anybody. Every woman was running." Fatuma 'Issa, a founder of the Girls Club, said that Iraqis asked: "Aren't there any men in Kuwait?"[32] Raida al-Fodari recalled: "During the air war women [in the armed resistance] went from area to area. We did it to make it easier for the men." In a reversal of normal roles, women became protectors of men. Occupied Kuwait became "a city-state of women."

Men, as the "important" members of society in normal times, now were more vulnerable. They were wanted by the Iraqis for their political, economic, and technical positions and expertise. (Women known to be in critical or high positions were also wanted.) Men eluded the invaders by fleeing the country or taking shelter underground, often quite literally hiding out in the *sirdabs*, the basement storage areas common in affluent Kuwaiti houses. Men, especially those in the military and police, also became invisible when they joined the underground resistance.[33] To render themselves anonymous, Kuwaiti men discarded their distinctive national dress (the *dishdasha*) for the generic shirts and trousers worn by Mediterranean Arabs, Asians, and Westerners.[34] While women "desexualized" themselves and announced their national identity through taking up the abaya, men "denationalized" themselves by removing the dishdasha.

The day after the first woman's demonstration, Hidaya Sultan, a pioneer in journalism in the 1960s, gathered a group of women to her house to produce a resistance paper.[35] Three days later, on August 9, the first issue of *al-Kuwaitiya* (The Kuwaiti Woman) was ready. This single sheet, handwritten on both sides, had both political and practical purposes. It affirmed allegiance to the Kuwaiti government in exile, keeping alive the idea of the Kuwaiti nation, national identity, and national sovereignty. The paper dispensed useful advice and relayed messages from the armed resistance. The practical information addressed daily concerns: food, water, shelter, health, and medicine. There were instructions on how to deal with chemical warfare, including a formula for producing a homemade gas mask using charcoal. *Al-Kuwaitiya* also circulated news gleaned from foreign media. Other women, such as Fatma Husain, another pioneering journalist from the 1960s, also produced clandestine papers.[36] All the pre-invasion newspapers—six Arabic and two English dailies—had been closed down. Two days after the women began *al-Kuwaitiya* the Iraqis started issuing their own newspaper, *al-Nida*, on the presses seized from *al-Qabas* newspaper.[37]

Women took charge of circulating the underground paper. Twenty to thirty women went to Sultan's house to pick up copies of the paper and smuggled them under their abayas through checkpoints to different locations where they would make photocopies and distribute them to other women or leave them in mosques.[38] Around early September, with mounting danger signs, only about seven women still came to take copies of the paper. Anyone caught with a newsletter risked being shot on the spot.[39] By the end of September when the dangers became too great women had to stop carrying the papers. By October it was not longer safe for women to meet in the mosques because Iraqi soldiers had started to enter and shoot. Thus, women adopted other means to communicate, such as queues in cooperatives and supermarkets which were open in the morning.[40]

Non-cooperation with the Iraqis and maintaining self-sufficiency were cornerstones of the resistance.[41] Badriya Ghanem affirmed: "We refused to let anyone take anything from the Iraqis. They had nothing to give but we did not want to be under their wing. We wanted our people to be independent. No one would go to them. No one would accept them. They saw that nobody accepted them. No one collaborated with them. There was constant refusal in every direction." Women were central to the offensive of organizing community needs. These included food, housing, health, and medicine, and the care of the young and old, the disabled and orphans, and persons living on their own.

Food constituted a focus of contest and defiance. Women shared what was in their family stores and bought food supplies from cooperatives for redistribution, while Kuwaiti merchants also opened their warehouses. Women also baked bread at home for distribution to others. Some young Kuwaiti men learned to bake bread and worked in small bakeries, allowed to function for limited hours. Women used their networks to distribute food supplies to those in need, especially taking care that milk and food reached infants. The distribution was done in local neighborhoods but was not confined to them.[42] *Middle East Watch* reported in November: "Because Iraq apparently considered the independent food-distribution system that came into existence after the invasion an impediment to its efforts to establish control in Kuwait, it started a campaign to terrorize those working in it." Some involved in food distribution were detained or executed.[43]

Households were no longer sites of private family life but were run as shelters and asylums. Women took in orphans, the sick and disabled, and those who were stranded. A single woman, whose family was abroad, recounted how she had lived alone for some time. Her strategy for safety was to create the appearance of family life. She borrowed children's clothes and put them out on the line, illustrating how women appropriated the functions of everyday domestic life as defense mechanisms.[44] Women took in armed resistance fighters who had to keep on the move. They also harbored stranded foreigners.[45] With the everpresent danger of attacks and chemical warfare, and in the absence of public shelters, women prepared shelters in the basements of their houses and stocked them with food, water, and homemade gas masks. They kept track of people and tried to make sure everyone had a refuge. "We all did it. But it was dangerous," Badriya Ghanem recalled. *Middle East Watch* reported: "In addition to the house-bound elderly and infirm, foreigners, draft-age men, and Kuwaiti government employees and military personnel live in hiding for fear of being arrested."[46]

A fundamental resistance offensive was ministering to the health and medical needs of the community. Concerned about the wounded in the first few days of the invasion, Raida al-Fodari and her sister Maliha, a science major at Kuwait University at the time of the invasion, attended a first-aid course Kuwaiti doctors gave at the Mubarak Hospital. Raida al-Fodari said:

> Some of the youth in the armed resistance took the courses to know how to treat their friends. Every three days there was another group. I spent one week taking courses. Then we went to the clinics. We had to make sure the clinics were kept operating. They needed women to give injections to people with diabetes and to do other injections. But the Iraqis came and took much of the equipment from the clinics and closed some of them.

Women also assisted in the distribution of medicine. Awatif al-Majid, a member of the Red Crescent Society, used to enter Mubarak Hospital posing as a pregnant woman and leave with medicines concealed under her abaya. There were various underground medicine chains. Badriya Ghanem explained: "We were organized. We took medicine to houses. We did not know anything about medicine but for the first month we were doctors." By the beginning of October only 20 out of 320 doctors were still working at the Mubarak Hospital.[47] The Iraqi occupation had placed the health services in Kuwait under the authority of an Iraqi military doctor. Checkpoints set up at hospital entrances discouraged Kuwaitis from entering. Some hospitals were reserved exclusively for Iraqi troops. Wounded resistance fighters were often treated in makeshift clinics. *Middle East Watch* reported: "At least four doctors are known to have been executed for suspicion of treating wounded resistance fighters at their homes, hoarding drugs or hiding medical instruments."[48] Kuwaiti nurses tended to the needs of children, treated armed resistance fighters, and helped bury the dead.[49]

The Iraqis attempted to run the public schools, but Kuwaiti women refused to teach and kept their children away as well. One woman recounted: "My cousin was a teacher. At the checkpoint they would say, 'You're a teacher. Did you go to work?' She would say, 'Yes, I just came back.' It would be mid-morning and he knew it was a lie."[50] Two sisters, Munira and Fatama al-Ujairi, who had graduated from Kuwaiti University in 1983, opened a school in Shamiya in October. They were conservative Islamic middle-class women who had decided not to work outside after graduation but to stay at home and raise their children. During the occupation they took the initiative to start a school with all the problems and dangers that it posed. They were members of the women's committee of the Islamic benevolent organization Jam'iyyat al-Takkaful. The first day only six children showed up, but by graduation in January there were seventy-nine.[51]

During occupation, Kuwaitis, especially men, were routinely rounded up and sent to prisons in Iraq. Women made routine visits to their relatives and others incarcerated in Baghdad, Basra, and other towns; they took food, medicines, blankets, heaters, and money. Sarah Saiyir took the initiative to organize buses to take Kuwaiti women to prisons in Iraq. The women were allowed in by Iraqi authorities, because they helped underwrite the costs of maintaining the prisoners and they also gave provisions and money to Iraqis themselves. Badriya Ghanem said: "We fed five camps. We gave our prisoners of war everything—food, blankets, and other things."[52] A poor working-class mother, Fatma Salim, had lost two sons (one had been in the army and the other in the armed resistance), but insisted on going with her remaining nine-year-old son when he was taken off to Iraq. The two were rotated to several prisons in Iraq for three and a half months.[53]

Women formed part of the underground armed resistance as well. Mainly organized by men with military backgrounds, it consisted of cells that were small, discrete, task-based units. Coordinators assigned tasks and they alone had contact with other cells, a model resembling the structure of the Algerian National Liberation Front (FLN). Among the tasks women assumed was the highly dangerous task of ferrying weapons and ammunition through checkpoints. The al-Fodari sisters, who both joined the underground armed resistance, described how they wound ammunition strips around themselves underneath their abayas. They also sewed ammunition into rice sacks and stowed weapons under car seats. Women also trained in hand-to-hand combat and in handling and planting explosives. Raida al-Fodari told how women competed in taking up dangerous tasks. When the air war began the activities of the women stepped up. They tracked explosions and would go to see if people were hurt. They also tried to obtain information about ammunition stores, to report to their leaders who relayed it abroad during the buildup to the ground war. The al-Fodari sisters said that mothers did not ask daughters about their comings and goings at odd hours at a time when normal rules and conventions were suspended.[54]

Women in the armed resistance gave their lives in defense of their country. One of the many women martyrs is Asrar Qabandi, a university-educated computer specialist working in the Ministry of Foreign Affairs who had gone underground three days after the invasion. Putting on a sari to pose as an Indian, she retrieved computer disks from the government's central records office in Jabriya. She routinely passed messages to the Kuwaiti government in exile and the international media, and clandestinely crossed the desert to Saudi Arabia smuggling money and ammunition for the armed resistance. In early November she was arrested while carrying a large sum of money through a checkpoint. She was imprisoned at Meshatil, an agricultural experimental station which the Iraqis had turned into a "rape farm." She was later killed, and her mutilated body was thrown in front of her house.[55]

Fatma al-'Issa related how the night the air war started she and friends found some Republican Guards stationed near their houses, and told them that the BBC had reported that the Iraqis had fled Kuwait. One of the women said maternalistically: "Run away. Go home. Your mothers are waiting for you. Go home and give us our home."

The Rhetoric of Reconstruction and the Politics of Political Rights

In the immediate aftermath of liberation, women wished to hold onto the newfound gender solidarity they had achieved under occupation and resistance. They wished to direct this cohesiveness and their enhanced gender consciousness toward building a re-visioned postliberation Kuwait. Women brought the issue of female suffrage back to center stage.

Young resistance fighter Raida al-Fodari expressed women's new gender consciousness: "The attitude of women toward themselves changed. They think of themselves as different persons. They found many things inside themselves they had never seen before. They gave their lives for their country. They should be given their rights." Sensitive to the interconnection between gender and nation she continued: "The government will need the people. The war has just started. We have to build the new Kuwait we dreamed of before the invasion. We are in a war now to make it more beautiful, better, freer than it was before." Her sister Maliha al-Fodari insisted:

> The woman should obtain the right to vote in recognition of all her sacrifices. She believes this is the least she should be given. If she doesn't get it now it may be a long time before she does. I think there should be a movement if the government doesn't give women the vote to women. During the resistance women know how to cope in front of soldiers who were shooting bullets near them. They know [now] what they want. They know what they need. They will fight and go out on demonstrations for this. Women helped in everything during resistance. Women didn't need lessons in political awareness. They spontaneously participated in resistance, even simple women. They saw their sons dying and being executed and they still came out in demonstrations.

If these were the views expressed by the new generation, the pioneering generation of women activists also expressed the hope that the solidarity and equality experienced during resistance would carry over into reconstruction. In capturing their experience in resistance when they were at center stage, Kuwaiti women likened it to the old seafaring culture of the pre-oil era when women took charge during the long months when men were out on the ships. They projected this indigenous model of participation in the affairs of their society onto their vision for a reconstructed Kuwait.

After liberation Kuwaiti women resumed the campaign for their political rights, begun in the 1960s. This time they also demanded that second-class citizens and bidun be accorded full citizenship.[56] As before, they grounded their demands for women's suffrage in the Constitution, but now women's roles in resistance added greater urgency to their case. In a speech at the Diplomatic Club early in 1992, Rasha al-Sabah, a vice-rector of Kuwait University at the time of the invasion and founder of the Joint Women's Resistance Committee in Cairo, spoke for other women when she stressed that reconstruction and democratization could not be achieved "without placing women at the core of the process." She insisted: "The prevention of Kuwaiti women from political participation and representation must be considered a form of discrimination against them as humans and citizens."[57]

Women articulated their demands for political rights in newspapers and journals, in pubic speeches, and in seminars and meetings. Lawyer Badriya al-Awadhi said:

> The restoration of democracy in the country is the right of all Kuwaitis. Since independence Parliament was dissolved three times and the promise to restore the National As-

sembly was kept and it was an extremely positive move. Unfortunately democracy has not been completely restored and with fifty per cent of the Kuwaiti population kept out of the political process democracy in Kuwait is standing on one leg. . . . If there were any doubt that Kuwaiti women were intelligent and capable then her role during the invasion granted her a certificate of distinction.

Amal al-Rushud told *al-Watan* newspaper that women could shoulder responsibilities better than men. "Women showed bravery during the occupation and on many occasions have sacrificed their lives for the nation. Women must be rewarded for that by allowing them to participate in politics and giving them their legitimate rights as indicated in the Constitution."[58] Veteran feminist Fatma Husain, who produced a clandestine paper during the occupation and after liberation was appointed managing editor of *al-Watan*, answered those pointing to the risks for women in electoral politics: "Such risks won't be as dangerous as the risks of the Iraqi invasion. It was the Kuwaiti women who during the occupation took part in military and other forms of resistance."[59] At a first-year memorial ceremony for Asrar Qabandi in January 1992, long-time feminist activist Nuriya al-Sadani declared that the matter of political rights for women "has now been settled for the country and society. The martyrs have written its end with their blood. There is no longer any room for bargaining on this issue."[60] al-Sadani's narration of the struggle and sacrifice of women martyrs was a feminist and nationalist act. Evocation of sister martyrs became a central trope in postliberation suffrage discourse.

In Kuwait there has been a dual political culture. Along side the Parliament the informal institution of the *diwaniya*, a regular "open house" in private homes (or private gathering places) is a site of political debate. The Parliament and the diwaniya have been exclusively male institutions, the former made so by an electoral law and the latter zealously preserved by custom. In 1990, six months before the invasion Rasha al-Sabah, protected by her status as a member of Kuwait's ruling family and her position with Kuwait University, inaugurated the first woman-run diwaniya, which was opened to both sexes. University professors, writers, and journalists formed the core of the diwaniya while parliamentarians and other political figures appeared periodically. Although secular liberals predominated, Islamists also frequented this diwaniya where women's suffrage commanded central attention.[61]

The "women's diwaniya" was one of the first to resume after liberation and with it the cause of women's political rights, which was articulated with renewed vigor. At a postliberation gathering, Kuwaiti University professor of psychology Najma al-Kharafi insisted: "When women ask for their right to vote and to be elected they don't intend to compete with men but to participate in rebuilding the country. It is not fair to take our traditions as an excuse not to give women their rights. We are all citizens of this land and our rights are ensured by the Constitution."[62] Writer Laila al-Othman urged women to unite in a campaign for their political rights: "During the occupation Kuwaiti women organized demonstrations and now they have to remember that and make serious moves to obtain their rights."[63]

While women were rhetorically adept in exploiting their resistance experience to strengthen their call for political rights, they were unable to redirect the practical and organizational skills they had honed in resistance. It was not long before class, kin, ethnic, and sectarian divisions resurfaced, dissipating the cohesion they had achieved under occupation. What women could do for their nation under siege they could not do for their gender in normal times.[64]

Women faced two fundamental problems. First, the women's associations founded in the 1960s and the 1970s were anachronistic by the 1990s. They were inadequate to the postliberation task of mounting a campaign for women's rights.[65] These associations, which reflected the class and kin divisions of their foundation and pre-invasion history, were vehicles for reproducing these divisions postliberation. Younger women, many newly politicized in the crucible of resistance, were more able to ignore class and kin differences than their elders. But by now there was added a distinct generational divide. Young women attempted to consolidate with senior women but were disaffected by women who they felt did not hear their voices. At the same time, these young women also felt unable to organize on their own. This was understandable in the early aftermath of liberation, when the purely physical tasks of rebuilding home and workplace, and the psychological demands, were high. Additionally, unlike their elders who constituted the founding generation of women's societies, the new generation had to fit into a scene in which the early associations held sway. Also now increasing divisions between "secularists" and "Islamists" added to women's difficulties in forging a broad gender alliance.

The second problem women faced was the lack of serious support from men, both those in political groups and those at the helm of government. At the Kuwaiti popular conference in exile in Saudi Arabia (November 1991) during the occupation, the Amir applauded the roles of women in resistance and affirmed the need to grant women fuller political roles after Kuwait was liberated. He reiterated this message shortly after liberation, during his end of Ramadan speech (March 1992), and on many other occasions. The ruler had the ability to issue a decree granting women their political rights during the period when the National Assembly was not functioning, to be subject to the vote of the Parliament once it resumed, but he did not do so, nor was he pressed to do so.

In the renewed democratization campaign after liberation, the issue of women's political rights could not be ignored and at the level of rhetoric it was not. The progressives and liberals of the Democratic Forum placed women's political rights on their agenda and were vociferous in calling for these rights in front of the media, especially the international media. As elections, set for fall 1992, drew near these ardent supporters became less outspoken. Democratic Forum candidates welcomed women to their diwaniyas only after setting up segregated facilities for them. It was explained that, despite wishes to have a gender-mixed diwaniyas, social norms and conservative opinion would not allow for this. While social norms could be contravened for the good of the country during resistance they could not be overlooked, or restructured, for the good of the country with the return to "normalcy." It was more than a supreme irony that women could not be present with men to discuss the issue of their own political rights. The timid adherence to a gender-segregated informal political culture did not bode well for the realization of a gender-integrated parliamentary democracy. If women and men could not sit together in a diwaniya to debate national issues—such as the right of women to vote and to be elected to Parliament—how could they sit together in the legislature? In accepting this contradiction, justified by a static construction of social norms, the "progressive" male candidates undercut the female suffrage plank in their platform.

Most Islamists meanwhile supported women's right to vote, but stood firmly against women's right to be elected to Parliament. Less surprisingly, the Islamists, clearer and more consistent about their conservative approach to culture and society, did not admit women to their diwaniyas. In the male politics regarding political rights for women, the secular progressives appear reluctant to see a translation of their progressive rhetoric into reality because of the fear that Islamists might gain more power if women had the right to vote. A patriarchal element operating in their politics should also not be discounted. For men of various groups, and for the state, women's political rights are subordinate to their own masculinist political interests and perceived power needs. For women their ability to vote and be elected is an ideological statement about their citizenship and a matter of exercise of their legitimate rights.

When voter registration opened early in 1992, women tried to register but were turned back. A group of fifty women marched to the Elections Department insisting on their full political rights.[66] When elections were held in the autumn of 1992, women appeared at several polling stations, as they had done on earlier occasions, but they were sent away. After elections, when the National Assembly reconvened, women's rights to vote and run for office did not command serious attention. Four months after the elections—on the third anniversary of the national liberation—veteran feminist Najat Sultan remarked:

> Kuwaitis have proved that they have the right stuff to fight an invading enemy and help liberate the country, but two years after the liberation of Kuwait they unfortunately have not proved their right to democracy. Every Kuwaiti has the constitutional right to participate in the political process, but every elected Parliament since 1962 has violated this right by isolating women and second class citizens from the political process.

She continued in words that evoked the experience of Algerian women in their national liberation struggle, "We had some brilliant resistance fighters who were women, nobody told them that they did not have the right to participate in fighting for their country."[67]

The nationalist and gender symbolism of dress resistance and postliberation is telling. Kuwaiti women, who had previously removed the abaya or who had never worn it, took it up during resistance. The abaya was assumed primarily as an instrument of mechanism which "desexualized" women and rendered them anonymous. However, it signaled a national identity. Kuwaiti men exchanged their dishdashas for shirts and trousers under occupation to obscure their national identity for self-protection. After national liberation, women shed their abayas in favor of cosmopolitan dress while men resumed their dishdasha, once again asserting their nationality. For Kuwaiti women the national dress, the abaya, signaled "protection" of females and their distancing from public life. Women understood this when they burned their abayas when the first Kuwaiti Parliament was opened in 1963, rejecting the symbol of their distancing from public life. In the national patriarchal order the dishdasha is a symbol of power. The female and male national dress symbolize the system of national gender inequality.

Adding complexity is another symbolic order of dress: the *hijab* or "Islamic dress" as opposed to (secular) national dress. This Islamic dress is a modern invention: a loose all-enveloping garment that includes a headscarf, plus a face veil for the more zealous. While the abaya has been on the decline since the 1960s, this new Islamic dress which made its appearance in the 1980s has increased since liberation. The spread of this dress signals the spread of Islamism.[68] While women's assumption of the hijab signals social conservatism, it does not include women's rejection of the vote. (Islamist women, however, do not demand the right to be elected to Parliament.) The hijab is a mode of dress that was chosen by women (not imposed as the abaya had been) and most saw it as enabling their movements in public, while adhering to a more conservative interpretation of Islam, rather than signaling their separation from society. This is not to suggest, however, that a restraining influence is not at work upon women. Moreover, the hijab is a political statement, announcing an Islamist sympathy.

The fate of democracy in Kuwait—integral to which is the fate of women's enjoyment of full political rights—is captive to the re-emergence of conservative forces in postliberation Kuwait. The struggle between secularists and Islamist forces is one strand of competing interests played out on gender ground. Within a year after liberation explosives were set off at the Medical Faculty of Kuwait University and at the home of its dean, who upheld a university ruling that women must not wear *niqabs* (face veils) and gloves in the dissection halls. In 1996 the plan to gender-segregate Kuwait University (within three years) was pushed through. These, and the noticeable spread of the hijab since liberation, are just some of the signs of the spread of Islamism in Kuwait. Other forms of gender control emerged in postliberation, such as the creation of a society to promote polygamy. Meanwhile, the stringent citizenship laws governing non-Kuwaiti spouses of Kuwaitis were imposed in postliberation Kuwait, causing gender-specific harm; as already noted, Kuwaiti women's non-Kuwaiti spouses are not eligible for citizenship nor can these Kuwaiti women pass their citizenship to their children. However, men married to non-Kuwaitis possess all of these rights. But this discrimination did not go unchallenged. In 1991, Badriya al-Awadhi, former dean of the Law Faculty at Kuwait University, created the Association of Kuwaiti Women Married to Non-Kuwaitis.[69] While a general principle was being fought for, the majority of actual cases involved Kuwaiti women married to biduns, the discriminated stateless within.

If Kuwaiti women did not vote in the 1992 elections, they were just as far away from voting in the 1996 elections. The politics of women's political rights is preventing women from gaining access to their constitutional rights. There are different layers to these politics. There are class and kinship interests at work which imply that these interests are best served through the preservation of the presently gendered political culture. There are patriarchal concerns operating that temper masculinist enthusiasm for political rights for women, especially the right to be elected. There is the states' concern for its longevity, which it seems to believe is best secured by preserving the gendered status quo in Kuwaiti political culture.

A significant restraining force in stalling on political rights for women is regional politics, specifically Saudi Arabian pressures. Saudi Arabia, which has no constitution and therefore no pretense to a democratic system and which has a repressive gender culture that shows no signs of changing, is adamantly opposed to the enfranchisement of women in neighboring Kuwait. The role Saudi Arabia played in the liberation of Kuwait, and its ongoing role in the politics of the region, exerts its own pressure.

Related to this is the contest between secular and Islamist forces. The Islamic fear factor appears to be the trump card preventing women's political empowerment (and along with women the empowerment of the other large segment of the disenfranchised). It is frequently repeated that if women gain the vote they will use it to vote Islamists into power. It is true that virtually all Islamists favor the vote for women, contending that women's votes will strengthen their cause. Since women's Islamist identity is their primary identity, the assumption that they will back their male counterparts is probably a correct one for the time being, until (as in other older Islamist movements, such as in Iran or Egypt) a more independent female Islamist strand starts to emerge.

Secularists are also probably correct not to assume that "their" women will predictably follow their lead. Secularist women may well demonstrate an independence leading to a functioning of democracy that could dislodge entrenched masculinist class and kin interests. It is an "admission" by secularist men that secularist women's Kuwaiti nationalist and gender ("feminist") identity might assert itself. A newly enfranchised gender could well unravel the fragile "holding pattern" that is the present state and society in Kuwait. The victor may not necessarily be (male) Islamists but a refigured, more democratic society could result.

While Kuwaiti women were able to play central roles in liberating their country they so far are unable to liberate themselves, if that liberation is measured in attaining their full political rights. A strong patriarchal class and kin structure still prevents women from forging a large, effective gender solidarity. The state's attempts to balance competing forces to keep its own rule intact, and entrenched male political groups efforts to retain or extend their power, do not bode well for women's political rights. Complicating this grid of patriarchal politics is the contest between secularists and Islamists, which, it appears, will hold democracy and women hostage in Kuwait for some time to come.

Notes

1. Originally nomadic bedouin whose pastoral practices have taken them back and forth in territories that later became marked by modern nation-state frontiers; many of the bidun settled in Kuwait but cannot prove having settled there prior to 1920. On the bidun and the violation of their rights, see Human Rights Watch/Middle East, *The Bedoons of Kuwait: "Citizens without Citizenship"* (New York: Human Rights Watch, 1995).

2. This also happened in Egypt, where in 1923 the first postindependence constitution proclaimed equal rights for all citizens and a subsequent law then removed these rights from those of the female gender. The Kuwaiti constitution and electoral law of 1962, drafted by Egyptian jurists, were based largely on these early Egyptian models.

3. I recorded women's oral histories of resistance during a stay in Kuwait from March 16 to April 8, 1991. I also moved around considerably and kept a journal of what I saw and heard in this early postliberation period.

4. This section draws on the detailed and penetrating study of the Kuwaiti scholar, Haya al-Mugni, *Women in Kuwait: The Politics of Gender* (London: Saqi, 1993), especially chap. 3–5.

5. I returned to Kuwait from September 1991 to August 1992 and again from January to March 1993, when I observed the process of reconstruction, listened to women debating the issue of political rights for the disenfranchised, and took part in discussions.

6. See al-Mugni, *Women in Kuwait*, chap. 2.

7. See, for example, the paper presented at the United Nations Conference in Nairobi (1985) by Lulua al-Qitami, "The Kuwaiti Woman: The Present and the Expected."

8. Interviews with women in Kuwait immediately following liberation.

9. See Kamala Nath, "Education and Employment among Kuwaiti Women," in *Women in the Muslim World*, ed. Lois Beck an Nikki Keddie (Cambridge, Mass.: Harvard University Press, 1978); al-Mugni, *Women in Kuwait*, 41–62.

10. See Rasha al-Sabah, "Kuwaiti Women and Political Rights," public lecture, Smith College, September 1992, on women's march to Seif Palace in the early 1960s and burning their abayas while demanding their political rights. Among Nuriya al-Sadani's books on the suffrage campaign see, for example, *al-Masirah al-Tarikhiyah lil Huquq Siyasiyah lil Mar'ah al-Kuwatiyah fi Fatra Ma*

Bain 1971–1982 (Kuwait: Matba'at Dar al-Siyasah, 1983); *Kitab Watha'iq Tarikh al-Huquq al-Siyasiyah lil-Mar'ah al-Kuwaitiyah* (Kuwait: Mafudha Press, 1994).

11. See Margot Badran, *Feminists, Islam, and Nation: Gender and the Making of Modern Egypt* (Princeton, N.J.: Princeton University Press, 1994), pp. 207–08. On this history of Kuwaiti women's suffrage struggle, see al-Sadani, *al-Masira* and al-Sadani, *Kitab*.

12. See al-Mughni, *Women in Kuwait*, chap. 3, "The Early Women's Organizations and the Campaign for Women's Rights." On the following discussion of the various women's societies, see also al-Mughni, chap. 4, "Contemporary Women's Organizations: Activities and Membership," and chap. 5, "The Politics of Contemporary Women's Organizations."

13. In addition to al-Sadani's books specifically on the struggle for suffrage (cited in note 10), she has written the following books on the general women's movement in Kuwait and her own activist experience: *Tarikh al-Mar'ah al-Kuwaitiyah*, 2 vols. (Kuwait: Matba'at Dar al-Siyasah, 1972–1980); and *al-Harakah al-Nisa'iyahh al-'Arabiyah fi al Qarn al-Ishrun* (Kuwait: Matba'at Dar al-Siyasah, 1982). The author is grateful for the conversations she has had with al-Sadani on the women's movement in Kuwait.

14. On the formation and foundational agenda of the Arab Feminist Union, see Margot Badran, *Feminists, Islam, and Nation*, pp. 223–250.

15. al-Mughni tells how deputies fled to the back seats in the National Assembly when WCSS women went to hear a parliamentary debate after the bill had been voted down. See al-Mugni, *Women in Kuwait*, pp. 131–132.

16. In Egypt during the constitutional monarchy several fatwas had been issued taking a position against political rights for women; it was not until after the 1952 revolution (in 1956) that a fatwa was finally issued allowing for women's rights to vote and to be elected.

17. al-Mugni, *Women in Kuwait*.

18. Information conveyed on April 3, 1991, by a Kuwaiti air force officer recently back from detention in Iraq.

19. In October 1991, the Islamic Care Society mounted an exhibition of photographs and materials illustrating the work of the women's resistance committees abroad. This was noted in "Kuwaiti Women's Role Praised," *The Kuwait Times*, October 24, 1991.

20. "Women have staged numerous nonviolent demonstrations." Eyewitnesses reported that Iraqi troops opened fire on some of the women demonstrators, "The Conduct of Iraqi Troops in Kuwait Toward Kuwaitis and Non-Westerners," *News from Middle East Watch* (September 1990): 5.

21. See Jadranka Porter, *Under Siege in Kuwait: A Survivor's Story* (London: Victor Gollanz, 1991), p. 61; Porter says that women shielded a sniper who fired on Iraqis and, as a result, ten women were "mowed down."

22. Interview with Raida al-Fodari, March 27, 1991. All other quotations from al-Fodari are from this interview.

23. "The conduct of Iraqi Troops in Kuwait," p.5.

24. "Kuwait: Deteriorating Human Rights Conditions Since the Early Occupation," *News from Middle East Watch* (November 1990): 14. "The Conduct of the Iraqi Troops in Kuwait" p. 5, speaks of the women's demonstrations and of "reports of nonviolent demonstrators being killed or wounded by Iraqi gunfire."

25. "Kuwait: Deteriorating Human Rights Conditions," p. 14.

26. al-Mughni observes the ways Kuwaiti women from different classes discarded the abaya, *Women in Kuwait*, pp. 54–55.

27. On this comparison, see Margot Badran, "Feminist Challenges by Muslim Arab Women: Egypt, Algeria, and Kuwait in the Nineteenth and Twentieth Centuries," paper delivered during Women's History Month, March 1992, Princeton University. On Algeria, see Marnia Lazreg, *The Eloquence of Silence: Algerian Women in Question* (London: Routledge, 1994).

28. Interview with Badriya Ghanem, March 24, 1991. All other quotations from Ghanem are from this interview.

29. Interview with Ghanem, March 24, 1991.

30. Badriya Ghanem, pp. 29–31. Anh Nga Longva, "Kuwaiti Women at a Crossroads: Privileged Development and the Constraints of Ethnic Stratification," *International Journal of Middle Eastern Studies* 25 (1993): 443–456, argues that in normal times the abaya was/is a national marker. "The abaya was a discourse by the Kuwaiti women that was aimed principally at the non-Kuwaiti audience" (p. 448–449). The Kuwaiti abaya sent a national signal and also a class signal. Currently, the abaya is typically worn by lower or modest middle strata women; the bedouin abaya is different from the urban abaya. Longva argues that Kuwaiti women working in arenas with expatriate women tended to wear the abaya to set themselves apart from the foreigners (p. 451).

31. Young men provided assistance but they were in a vulnerable category and many had to make themselves invisible. In November *Middle East Watch* reported: "The rumor of impending conscription that lead many men between the ages of 17 and 45 to go in hiding has also deprived neighborhood committees of many of the volunteers who had serviced the house-bound." "Kuwait: Deteriorating Human Rights Conditions."

32. Interview with Fatuma 'Issa, March 29, 1991. All other quotations from 'Issa are from this interview.

33. See "The Conduct of Iraqi Troops in Kuwait," p. 2, and "Kuwait: Deteriorating Human Rights Conditions," pp. 16–17, on the dangers of leaving and returning.

34. See Longva, "Kuwaiti Women," p. 448, on the dishdasha as a national marker for men of all classes.

35. Interview with Hidiya Sultan, March 1992; she is currently editor-in-chief of *al-Majlis*. All other quotations from Sultan are from this interview.

36. Interview with Fatuma 'Issa and Rabi'a Issa, March 29, 1991. Fatma Husain is currently editor of *al-Watan*.

37. *Al-Qabas* resumed publication from London and *al-Anba'* resumed publication from Cairo.

38. Interview with Hidiya Sultan, March, 1991. Badriya Ghanem (interview on March 24, 1991) told how single copies were picked up at a mosque and passed from house to house.

39. A number of underground newsletters circulated in Kuwait after the invasion, but the harsh punishment inflicted on those distributing them made it all but impossible for them to survive. In their house-to-house searches for weapons and Westerners, Iraqi troops also looked for and seized typewriters and reproduction equipment." "Kuwait: Deteriorating Human Rights Conditions," p. 14. A man was "accused of distributing resistance literature and tortured"; "Mahmoud Khalifa al-Jassem was publicly executed after he printed a leaflet about food consumption which Iraqi troops seem to have thought was "hostile propaganda." "The Conduct of Iraqi Troops in Kuwait," pp. 6 and 7, respectively. An employee of the Ministry of the Interior was killed by an Iraqi patrol which found a "hostile leaflet" in his car. "Kuwait: Deteriorating Human Rights Conditions," p. 14.

40. Interview with Raida and Maliha al-Fodari, March 27, 1991. They said that in mid-December 1990 Iraqis started entering the mosques. "They [Iraqis] shot at one mosque because they thought some of the resistance were hiding in the mosque." Mary Ann Tetreault, "Civil Society in Kuwait: Protected Spaces and Women's Rights," *The Middle East Journal* 47 (2) (Spring 1993), 274–291 said, "Resistance efforts to sustain Kuwaitis physically, emotionally, and spiritually were centered around the mosque, the only public space that the occupiers showed any hesitance in breaching" (pp. 278–279).

41. During the Palestinian intifada women also played key roles in creating and maintaining community self-sufficiency. See, for example, Islah Abdul Jawwad, "The Evolution of the Political Role of the Palestinian Women's Movement in the Uprising," in Joost R. Hiltermann, ed. Behind

the Intifada: Labor and Women's Movements in the Occupied Territories (Princeton: Princeton University Press, 1991).

42. Interview with Ghanem, March 24, 1991.

43. "Kuwait: Deteriorating Human Rights Conditions," p. 11.

44. Conversation in March with anonymous woman.

45. See Porter, *Under Siege in Kuwait*. Porter was a journalist with the *Arab Times* who remained in Kuwait throughout the occupation and moved from place to place.

46. "Kuwait: Deteriorating Human Rights Conditions," p. 11.

47. See the section "Medical Situation" in "Kuwait: Deteriorating Human Rights Conditions," pp. 8–10. For an interview with a Kuwaiti doctor see "Dr. [Sulaiman Falah Al] Ali Recollects Iraqi Occupation," *Arab Times*, December 23, 1991, p. 3.

48. "Kuwait: Deteriorating Human Rights Conditions," p. 9.

49. See "Director Lauds Role of Nurses During Occupation," *Arab Times*, December 31, 1991.

50. From the author's Kuwait journal.

51. Interview with Munira and Fatma al-Ujairi, March 28, 1991.

52. From the author's Kuwait journal.

53. Interview with Fatma Saleh and her son Nasir, March 26, 1991.

54. On women's roles in armed resistance, see Lazreg, *The Eloquence of Silence*, and Mariam Helie Lucas, "Women, Nationalism and Religion in the Algerian Struggle," in *Opening the Gates: A Century of Arab Feminist Writing*, ed. Margot Badran and Miriam Cooke (Bloomington: Indiana University Press, 1990), pp. 104–114.

55. See Nuriya al-Sa'dani, *Asrar Qabandi* (Kuwait: n.p., 1991) and John Martin Levins, "The Secret War of Asrar Qabandi," *Arab Times*, January 13–24, 1993, an article published on the third anniversary of Qabandi's murder.

56. On discrimination against women, second-class citizens, and bidun relating to citizenship and political rights, see Human Rights Watch, *The Bedoons of Kuwait*.

57. Lima Khalafawi, "Dr. Rasha Laments Slow Implementation of Rights," *Arab Times*, April 11, 1992.

58. "'Women Capable of Entering Politics,'" *Arab Times*, January 4, 1992.

59. "'Women to Enroll for Elections,'" *Arab Times*, December 29, 1991.

60. "Call for Women Vote Right at Memorial," *Arab Times*, January 16–17, 1992.

61. The diwaniya of Rasha al-Sabah (cousin of the present Amir) recalls Nazli Fazil's precedent-breaking salon in Cairo in the 1880s. She was also protected by her status—as the daughter of Prince Mustafa Fazil and niece of the then deposed Khedive Isma'il—and received leading intellectuals and statesmen of the day. Women's rights were also a topic of debate at the salon, where Qasim Amin, author of *Tahrir al-Mar'a*, took part in discussions. However, unlike in Rasha al-Sabah's diwaniya, women did not attend Nazli Fazil's salon. See Badran, *Feminists, Islam, and Nation*.

62. "Women Off the Shelf," *Arab Times*, November 4, 1991. The debates in this diwaniya have received wider attention by being frequently reported in the press. See for example: Lima Khalafawi, "It's Time—Women Want the Vote," *Arab Times*, October 24, 1991; "Women Meet on Political Rights—'Open your Diwaniyas Men...Let's Talk,'" *Arab Times*, December 4, 1991. Rasha al-Sabah's diwaniya was held at an alternative location because her own diwaniya had been ravaged when her house had been taken over as an Iraqi military command site, arms depot, and interrogation center.

63. "'Women Be Given their Rights,'" *Arab Times*, December 30, 1991.

64. Taghreed al-Qudsi-Ghabra, "Women in Kuwait: Educated, Modern, and Middle Eastern," *The Washington Report on Middle East Affairs* (July 1991): p. 29. The author, at his early postliberation moment, cautioned against women being co-opted by other groups, stressing the need for women to form their own agenda.

65. See the results of a survey of women *al-Watan* conducted on women's societies: "Women Societies under Fire: Vital Issues Neglected," *Arab Times*, April 23–24, 1992.

66. "Political Rights Sought," *Arab Times*, March 10, 1992.

67. "On Rights: Women," *Arab Times*, February 25–26, 1993.

68. See Nesta Ramazani, "Islamic Fundamentalism and the Women of Kuwait," *Middle East Insight* (January–February 1988): 21–26.

69. Interview with Badriya al-Awadhi, April 1992. See al-Mughni, *Women in Kuwait*, p. 147, and Human Rights Watch, *The Bedoons of Kuwait*, p. 81

Philippine Muslim Women

Tradition and Change

Muslims constitute the largest minority group in the Philippines. Estimates in 1990 placed their number at between five and six million or about 8.6% of the country's total population of 63 million.[1] Muslims are concentrated in the southern parts of the islands of Palawan and Mindanao and are distinguished by varied ethnolinguistic characteristics[2] as well as different economic activities.[3] Despite these variations, their common bond is that they are Muslims, which is a key aspect of their identity in a predominantly Christian country.[4] Because of this religious distinction and because the Muslim areas are geographically isolated from the political and economic centers of the country, Muslims exhibit cultural norms and traditions that differ from the rest of the Philippines.

Philippine Muslim society was shaped by its customs and the Islamic traditions that came to the Philippines in the fourteenth century[5] by way of Malaysia. The culture and traditions of the Muslim societies in the Philippines, therefore, are more akin to their Malaysian and Indonesian neighbors than they are to the rest of the country. These cultural variations are manifested in social relations and practices which include the position and role of women.

Sixty percent of the estimated five to six million Muslims in the Philippines are women.[6] While obviously a numerical majority, in terms of their roles in the decision-making process—particularly in the public sphere—they constitute a minority within a minority.

This chapter traces the evolving roles of Philippine Muslim women and explains the factors that have helped bring these roles about, using discrete periods in Philippine history as the framework. These periods brought with them policies, institutions, and situations that either acted as agents of change for women or goaded women to action. Using the historical framework also offers a convenient scheme for presenting, in a chronological fashion, the influences and events that have affected Philippine Muslim women. The following sections present Muslim women in the context of other movements, particularly the Philippine women's movement[7] and the Moro National Liberation Front (MNLF). I then discuss Islamic resurgence, which has brought about visible signs of religious piety, and conclude with an assessment of the changes in Muslim women's roles.

Philippine Muslim Women in the Pre-American Period

Philippine Muslim society before the coming of the Americans was characterized by three functional categories: the aristocrats or royalties, the commoners, and the slaves.[8] The sultans,[9] *datus*,[10] and their families formed the aristocratic or royal class. The majority of the Muslims belonged to the commoner group. They were referred to as freemen, but they owed loyalty and tribute to the datu. If necessary, they were pressed into labor and service as fighting men. The slaves, as the property of their masters, could be bought and sold. Female slaves sometimes served as wives or concubines of their masters or were given as presents.[11] There was a very strong perception of rank and order, with the commoners and slaves always tending to follow the datus and their families.

During this period, the Muslim woman did not have the freedom to make choices for herself, especially in matters of education and marriage. Parents made the decisions and she was expected to follow them.[12] Among the Maranao and the Maguindanao, adolescent girls were isolated in a small room called a *lamin* or *bilik*.[13] This isolation of young ladies continued to be observed among many Muslim families even in the late 1940s.[14] Women were taught proper behavior and how to read the Quran in their homes by a *guru* (teacher).[15] They were also trained in the art of traditional singing and playing musical instruments, particularly the *kulintang*, (a set of eight gongs that vary in size and tone[16]) and the *gabang* (a native xylophone). Women appeared in public only to perform dances and play musical instruments on various occasions, such as weddings, a girl's coming of age (when her ears are pierced and her teeth filed and stained), or circumcision ceremonies. Sometimes they performed for the crews of foreign vessels[17] whenever the sultan invited the crews to his home for state dinners. Thomas Forrest, a British captain who was in Mindanao in 1774, noted that:

> men never mix with women in amusement of this kind [singing] or even touch them, bow to them, or take notice of them by look, or otherwise, as they pass; yet not seeming to avoid them. . . . In the streets, women seldom speak but to women; and the paths being narrow, they follow one another, as in a string. In their houses, they talk with freedom to anybody, as in Europe.[18]

Women's activities were centered in the home, and they were expected to take care of household and child-rearing activities. In addition, they engaged in income-generating activities in the confines of their home, such weaving, sewing, embroidery,[19] and small-scale-food production.[20] Men were not expected to do household activities unless the women were temporarily incapable of performing the tasks. Women's involvement in the decision-making process was largely confined to domestic affairs, usually involving money and family. Role differentiation between men and women was obviously connected to the distinction between public and private space.

While prevailing practices tended to limit women to private spaces, historical records indicate that there were exceptional women whose involvement in politics affected the course of events in Muslim Mindanao. One of them, Fatimah, daughter of Sultan Azim ud-Din (who was imprisoned by the Spaniards in Manila) went to Jolo to negotiate for the release of fifty Christians held captive by Sultan Bantilan.[21] Several women were political pawns to consolidate alliances among the ruling families. Sulu[22] princesses were usually the women given in such alliances, as, for example, when the Sultan of Sulu arranged the marriages of his children to those of the Rajah Muda of Maguindanao in 1608.[23] A daughter of Rajah Bongsu of Sulu married Sultan Qudarat of Maguindanao and another daughter married Baratamay, the ruler of Buayan in 1657.[24] Two hundred years later, the practice of "political alliances through marriage" still continued; Datu Uto of Buayan, who was reputed to be the most powerful datu along the Pulangi river in the late 1800s,[25] solidified his friendships with other datus either by marrying their daughters or arranging marriages between them and his daughters.[26] These were marriages brokered by fathers and male relatives, usually without the consent of the future bride.

Some women were reputed to be powers behind the sultans, like Myong, wife of Sultan Pahar ud Din of Maguindanao, who was "said to have governed the sultan."[27] Inchi Jamila lobbied, although unsuccessfully, to have her son, Amirul Kiram, assume the position of sultan after Jamal ul Kiram's death in 1881. When the new ruler, Sultan Badar-ud-Din II (the older half-brother of Amirul Kiram) made a pilgrimage to Mecca, Inchi Jamila was one of the two regents who served in the sultan's absence.[28] Her desire to have Amirul Kiram declared sultan continued after Badar-ud-Din's death, when she convoked the Ruma Bechara (council) twice to have them elect Amirul Kiram as sultan, to no avail. She later sent a message to the Spanish officials, expressing her willingness and that of her son (who refused to surrender) to accept Spanish sovereignty.[29] Her son eventually became sultan, but not through her efforts; it happened only after Sultan Harun ar-Rashid asked the Spanish government to relieve him of the position.[30] Amirul Kiram took the name Jamal ul Kiram II and was the sultan when the Americans came to Sulu.

Inchi Jamila was not an invisible power here; she was an active participant in Sulu politics of her time. Known as *"The* Sultana" because she was the wife of a sultan, she wielded real power behind the throne and "usually controlled the affairs of the state."[31] She was described as a "very bright woman, with a decided genius for organization and command. . . . "[32] Women's involvement in state affairs was definitely not confined to Sulu; her high level of activity at that time negates the preconceived notion that Philippine Muslim women were all secluded and had no say in public affairs.

Rajah Putri, the wife of Datu Uto of Buayan, was another influential woman. Together with her mother, Paya Sabi, she was held in high esteem not only by their people but also by the Spanish.[33] She signed a capitulation to the Spanish although the Datu rejected it. Later on, she, together with Datu Uto sent letters to the Spanish affirming their loyalty and submission.[34]

Site Cabil, also known as Ampy and Sultana Nur al Azam, governed as sultana for about four or five years.[35] Interestingly, her name is included in Dalrymple's list of sultans of Sulu but it is not included in Sulu genealogy. Such omission, according to Majul, might be due to her being female.[36] Aside from her family linkages, there is nothing else known about her or her rule. It is significant, however, to know that a woman actually ruled in Sulu.

Women's capability to rule was recognized by Charles Wilke, an American explorer who was in Sulu in the mid-1800s. He noted that the women enhanced their capability by associating with slaves from whom they learned about other religions and other countries,[37] thus providing them some knowledge of the world outside the sultanate.

There is some ambivalence, however, regarding the roles of women during this period. Forrest and Dampier wrote about isolation practices and how women were not expected to converse with men in public. Yet they also mentioned upper-class women who were "allowed the freedom to converse with her *pagally* (Platonic friend of the opposite sex) and may give or receive presents from them." Wives of the sultan who were "always coopt [*sic*] up will yet look out of their cages when a stranger passes by and demand of him if he wants a *pagally* and will invite them to their friendship. . . . "[38] Forrest noted that women here "have as much liberty of going abroad as in Europe."[39] This observation was shared by Dalrymple, who asserted that the Sulus do not, "like the Mahometans [*sic*] of Hindustan, confine their women. On the contrary, they mix in society as in Europe."[40] These writers, however, did not specify whether all the women they referred to were married or not, or whether the married ones tended to have more freedom to venture out of the house than the unmarried women. Their observations, however, indicate that while there were customs that required distance from and isolation of women, this was not uniformly observed among the Muslims in the Philippines.

Philippine Muslim Women during the American Period

The first American troops arrived in Jolo in May 1899 to establish American control over the sultanate. Having learned their lessons from Spain's experiences,[41] the immediate goal of the Americans was to pacify the areas and establish an infrastructure aimed at "civilizing" the Muslims. They concluded a treaty with the Sultan,[42] which reduced the latter's position to a spiritual leader. Despite the loss of political power of the Sultan, he and his family and the rest of the aristocracy maintained their social and political standing, because followers continued to consult them in their affairs. An American governor performed the political functions of the Sultan.

The Americans introduced public health and education programs to the Muslim areas. In introducing these programs, the Americans always had to convince the Muslims of the sincerity of their purposes and that they did not have any ulterior designs against the Muslims and their religion.

Public schools based on the American model were established in the Muslim areas. In its first year, there were about 200 students attending the school in Jolo, a few of whom were Muslims. The reluctance of Muslim parents to send their children to public schools was due to their fear that the American schools might convert their children to Christianity. Although the enrollment of Muslim children increased each year, they were outnumbered by Christians. The strong opposition to the education of females is demonstrated by a reaction of a datu who said: "You can put my boy in school if you like but not my daughter. Women are not supposed to know anything anyway."[43] It was only after a prominent datu came to observe the schools and concluded that the teaching was not confined to religion that Muslims slowly began to send their children to public schools.[44] Still, the numbers were considerably lower than those of Christian students. This helps to explain why the level of literacy in the Muslim areas is lower compared to the rest of the country.

The Americans, who were intent in their pacification campaign, tried not to touch on Islam for fear that it would bring about violent opposition to American rule. However, their Christian bias was obvious in statements made by Governor Pershing when the Cotabato Girls' School was opened in 1913. Pershing hoped that the girls would be influenced by teachers who practiced Christianity. He further asserted that without education, the girls could only "become wives or concubines of the datus who offer the greatest sums for their purchase."[45] The girls were taught personal cleanliness, housekeeping, cooking, embroidery, and English.[46] It is evident that the focus of the curriculum was on enhancing the domestic roles of women. For all the American opposition to the practice of arranged marriages of the area, Pershing indicated that the local officials should find similarly trained husbands for these girls to assure them of their honorable places as wives.[47]

Subsequent U.S. administrators recognized the abilities of women and the value of educating them. In a letter to the Secretary of Interior in 1919, Governor Frank Carpenter acknowledged that some women who belonged to the aristocracy had a strong influence not just on the sultan and datus, but also on the rulers' followers. Carpenter felt that this situation might be used to further the aims of the American government in administering the Muslim areas.[48] This must have been on Carpenter's mind when the American government established the girls' dormitory and school in Jolo in 1916. It was run by a Christian Filipina and financed by American women in New York. The aim of this school, according to Carpenter, was to prepare women for leadership in their own communities.[49] Because the royal families were always perceived as role models and leaders of the people, the American government in Sulu made special efforts to convince them to send their daughters to school. To induce them further, the government shouldered the expenses for the education of girls in this special school. One father's concern was manifested by Datu Tambuyong, father of Princess Indataas, when he required the American authorities to sign an agreement that his daughter "would not be allowed to talk or dance with men."[50] Arrangements also had to be made to ensure that the school would observe Islamic dietary laws.[51]

By 1920, there were fifty Muslim girls enrolled in the school, eight of whom held the rank of princess.[52] In addition to the goal of educating these women, it was also the school's intention (as indicated in Carpenter's letter) to amalgamate the Muslims into the Christian populations of the country. It was of special concern to them that the girls studying in the boarding school become "determined monogamists" and therefore, would help end polygamy "through the most effective of means—intolerance on the part of the women."[53] Carpenter was determined that the government would not undertake a religious objective, that is, engage in converting people to Christianity. However, he felt it to be politically and economically expedient that all peoples of the Philippines share the same beliefs, standards, and ideals. At that time, the Philippines had already become a predominantly Christian country, with the majority of the people professing Catholicism. Carpenter further emphasized that the government's objective was to make the Muslims be like the other Filipinos.[54] Women were to be intruments of this undertaking.

In recognition of women's roles in the U.S.'s civilizing mission, Governor Carpenter recommended that Princess Tarhata Kiram, a niece and adopted daughter of Sultan Jamal ul Kiram II, be sent to the United States to study. Carpenter described her as a nominal Muslim, but he gave instructions that no attempt should be made to convert Tarhata Kiram to Christianity; conversion would "destroy her status and value among her people."[55] Tarhata Kiram registered at the University of Illinois at Urbana-Champaign. Her course of studies and activities were closely monitored by the Bureau of Insular Affairs in Washington, D.C., the Department of Interior, and Governor Carpenter in the Philippines. She was to be prepared for leadership and was to direct graduates of the girls' school in Jolo in community work upon her return to the Philippines. Basically, the idea was that since Tarhata Kiram was well respected by her people, she would come to the United States, learn more about American ways, and influence Muslim women, who in turn would influence their husbands. Carpenter thought that it would be an effective way of reducing Muslim resistance to American rule. Tarhata's guardians at the University of Illinois also had to be sure that she took courses that would give her some of the accoutrements of a lady, such as courses in voice and piano. She was, after all, going to be a role model for Muslim women.

Tarhata Kiram returned to the Philippines in 1924, without finishing her degree. By then her sponsor, Frank Carpenter, was no longer governor and the new administrators had other priorities. The Bureau of Non-Christian Tribes assigned her to be a charity worker for Jolo.[56] As listed in official records, however, her position was "government agent" together with her aunt, Dayang Dayang Hadji Piandao. Whoever occupied such a position was to function as a link between the government and the Muslims.[57]

In an effort to bring about Muslim–Christian cooperation, Tarhata started a women's club in Jolo. This was part of a nationwide effort of women in different municipalities to organize themselves. They were engaged mainly in social and civic activities and charity work.

Tarhata Kiram later taught at one of the schools in Jolo until she became the fourth wife of Datu Tahil in 1926, to the disappointment of the U.S. administrators. Tarhata Kiram's independence of character was manifested in her decision to marry Datu Tahil despite two objections by Sultan Jamal ul Kiram II: that Tarhata Kiram was going to be the fourth wife, and because Datu Tahil did not deliver the promised dowry. The newspapers reported that she eventually divorced her husband but did not elaborate on the divorce procedure.[58]

Throughout the American period, Tarhata Kiram and Dayang Dayang Hadji Piandao exerted their influence in state affairs.[59] This may, however, have more to do with the type of personality of the sultan than anything else. When the sultan's mother, the Sultana Inchi Jamila, was alive, she was known to have been the power behind the throne (as previously discussed). These were exceptional women, members of the aristocracy, who were educated and had the personality to do as they did. Certainly, this was not the norm, but they set the pace and they were considered role models by Muslim women.

When Sultan Jamalul Kiram II died in 1936, the Ruma Bechara (council) petitioned the Philippine Commonwealth government to recognize Dayang Dayang Hadji Piandao as Sultana of Sulu since the sultan did not have a direct heir. The government rejected the petition because of a policy that there should be only one government—the duly constituted civil government—and that the sultanate had ended with the death of Sultan Jamal ul Kiram II.[60]

Aside from Inchi Jamila, Dayang Dayang Hadji Piandao, and Tarhata Kiram, there were other Muslim women who were recognized not only by fellow Muslims but also by U.S. administrators for their abilities. William Cameron Forbes, the Governor General of the Philippines from 1909 to 1913, noted the wife of Inok, a war leader of Datu Piang in the Cotabato valley, who became the leader of her people upon the death of her husband. When the municipal government was organized in Buluan, Cotabato, she was appointed municipal president, by virtue of an overwhelming demand of Muslim men in that region. She was an active force in the establishment of schools in the area and in the education of girls. It is interesting to note that, for all her accomplishments and her distinction of being perhaps the first Muslim woman municipal president, she was not named in Forbes' book.[61] Another woman, Panglima Fatima Tandubas of the islands of Tawi-Tawi, succeeded her husband who died in battle, led her forces to victory, and eventually became a local leader and dignitary.[62]

The American government in the Philippines was very concerned with slavery and polygamy which, according to them, violated the basic principles of the laws of the United States. Governor Carpenter recognized this, but did not make it an issue because it could result in active resistance of the Muslims against the U.S. government.[63] Domestic matters, like marriage, divorce, adoption, and inheritance, were therefore left under the jurisdiction of the spiritual leaders and the sultan for arbitration. The government only interfered if cases were brought to court.[64]

Although Islam allows a man up to four wives, if he could be fair and just to all of them (Quran, S. 4:3), having more than one wife was not the usual case among Philippine Muslims in the pre-American and American periods.[65] Divorce was not a frequent occurrence and infidelity was rare, but concubinage was fairly common among the sultans and members of royalty.[66] Also, the forces of custom and public opinion were so strong that there were few violations of moral code.[67] Sydney Cloman, an American administrator in Sulu, observed that when infidelity did occur, it was difficult to protect the guilty from death and destruction[68] at the hands of the men in the community.

While there were exceptions, the practice of arranged marriages continued even during this time. Usually, the bride accepted the arrangement out of a sense of duty to the family and because family honor was at stake.

Independence Period: Government Policies and Muslim Women

The United States granted political independence to the Philippines on July 4, 1946. The 1950s and 1960s saw an increase in the number of Muslim men involved in national politics. Members of the aristocracy vied for elective positions, and women were elected to local government positions. Santanina Rasul was elected board member of Sulu, Tarhata Alonto Lucman was governor of Lanao, and Titina Anni was mayor of Siasi. Santanina Rasul was a teacher and a journalist who was one of the founders of the newspaper *The Sulu Star*. She was also among the first Muslim women to pursue higher education in Manila. She attended the University of the Philippines, where she graduated *cum laude* with a B.A. in political science, thus making her the first Muslim to graduate from college with that distinction. She comes from a politically prominent family, as does her husband, Abraham Rasul, a former judge and former ambassador to Saudi Arabia. In 1987, Santanina Rasul became the first Muslim woman to be elected senator. She was reelected in 1992.

Titina Anni belongs to one of the four competing prominent families in Sulu.[69] Her brother and, later on, her husband, served as governors, and one of her sons is currently a congressman. Another son is serving as an assemblyman in the Autonomous Regions of Muslim Mindanao, while yet another son is the present mayor. Titina Anni's arranged marriage at the age of sixteen, plus her own political skills, consolidated the political bases of the Sangkula and Anni families, which later helped get her elected mayor for three terms.[70] Tarhata Alonto Lucman, on the other hand, is the sister of former Senator Domocao Alonto and the widow of former congressman and sultan, Rashid Lucman.

All three women come from prominent families whose positions, once determined by lineage, are now legitimized by elections. But, as this description indicates, the family's socioeconomic and political positions, more than anything else, are important factors for the success of these Muslim women.

In the 1950s, government policies toward the Muslims could be described in one word: integration. One of the ways by which this could be achieved was through education. In 1955, the Congress of the Philippines passed Republic Act 1382[71] establishing the Mindanao State University (MSU). It was envisioned to serve as an instrument for the economic and social growth of Mindanao and to cater to the needs of deserving but economically deprived students who could not pursue their education. More important, it was to serve as a venue for exposing Muslims and Christians to each other's cultures in the hope that Muslims would eventually be integrated into the national body politic. In the first ten years of the university, there were more Christian students (81%) than Muslims (19%) at the college level. Over time, more Muslims attended MSU as it established satellite campuses in other parts of Mindanao.

In 1957, Republic Act 1888 created the Commission on National Integration. The act declared it a policy of Congress to integrate the non-Christian Filipinos into the body politic.[72] The intent of the law was for overall moral, material, economic, political, and social advancement of the minorities; for some reason, however, the education programs became the main thrust of the Commission on National Integration. It offered scholarships to minorities who satisfied eligibility requirements, one of which was the indigent status of the participant. Muslims have been the major beneficiaries of the program. The Commission's scholarship program, plus Mindanao State University, opened the doors to higher education for many Muslims, including women who went into such professions as medicine, law, and education. Many Muslim women pursued graduate education in Manila. And, just as women from the aristocracy were among the first to take advantage of American education, they were also the first ones to pursue higher education.

At the elementary school level, the Muslims appeared to have started to overcome the initial rejection of public schools and even sent their children to Catholic schools like the Notre Dame schools in Cotabato and Jolo.[73]

With the increasing educational attainment of Muslim women came their increasing politicization and active involvement in the larger society. More than anything else, the public school system and MSU made education available to women of varying backgrounds and provided them an option of breaking away from their traditional roles.

Except for the passage of the Women's Suffrage Act in 1934, one cannot speak of a piece of legislation that was primarily directed at women (much less Muslim women) until the 1980s. The programs and policies implemented in Mindanao in the 1970s, which had to do mainly with political and economic development of the area, were responses to the agitation of Muslims, particularly the Moro National Liberation Front (MNLF). At that time, the MNLF was engaged actively in a war of secession from the Republic of the Philippines.[74]

During this period, President Ferdinand Marcos issued numerous decrees that were supportive of Islam. For example, Muslim holidays were declared official holidays and Islam was declared part of Philippine national heritage. Interestingly, the government recognized the sultans again (albeit without giving them political powers), in an attempt to win them over to the government's side in the conflict with the MNLF. There were other programs as well, such as the establishment of Maharlika Village to provide housing for Muslims. The government also created agencies that would implement develop-

ment programs in the Muslim areas, so that all Muslims, men and women, would benefit from it. Among them were the Southern Philippine Development Authority and
Amanah Bank. Many Muslim women who pursued college education found employment in these agencies.

The Muslims are bound by their *adat* (custom) and Islamic laws, in addition to the
fact that they are subject to the laws of the Philippines. Conflicts naturally came about as
to which law should be applied to particular cases. In response to this situation, President
Marcos commissioned a group of Muslim scholars to work on the codification of Muslim
Personal Laws in 1974. Three years later, in February 1977, Marcos signed Presidential
Decree No. 1083, promulgating the Code of Muslim Personal Laws as part of the laws of
the country. The Muslim Code has provisions for *shariah* courts to adjudicate cases. It
also provides that when a conflict exists between provisions of the Muslim Code and the
general laws of the Philippines, the code provisions would prevail. The Code is applicable
only to Muslim areas.

Among the subjects covered by the Code of Muslim Personal Law are marriage, divorce, inheritance, and guardianship of persons. The Code is faithful to the Quranic provisions in these aspects and followed the Shafii school of law. Theoretically, a woman may
acquire divorce through *khul*, *faskh*, and *tafwid* but this hinges on whether the petition for
divorce by the woman satisfies the conditions allowed. In addition to this, ideas of family
solidarity, honor, and shame come in when a woman wants to divorce a husband. In many
instances, the woman is prevailed upon by the elders to try to keep the marriage. The
greatest range of rights for divorce still remains with the husband.[75] It must be noted,
however, that the rate of divorce varies among different Muslim groups. It is considered
"detestable" among the Tausugs and is not as common as polygyny, but is more frequent
among the Maranaos.[76]

The code upholds a man's right to four wives, as specified by the Quran. Although it
is common among Tausug husbands to get the consent of the first wife before marrying
another, the code requires filing a written notification to contract a marriage with the
shariah clerk of court. Notice should then be given to the wife or wives. If the wife or wives
object, the matter is brought to an arbitration council that decides whether or not to uphold the objection of the wife or wives. This, however, has not always been followed, and
there are incidents where the first wife was not notified at all prior to a husband's subsequent marriage.

The code includes provisions on the rights and duties of the wife; it specifies that a
husband's consent is necessary before a wife can acquire any property by "gratuitous title
except from relatives within the prohibited degrees in marriage." If a woman wants to pursue a profession or engage in business, she also needs a husband's consent. If the husband
refuses, then the matter can be brought to an arbitration council.[77]

A great majority of Muslims are aware that the Code of Muslim Personal Laws now
exists. However, they are not familiar with the provisions of the code[78] and continue to rely
on the male elders, *imams* and *ustadz*, for the interpretation of these provisions.

Interestingly, there was no woman involved in the codification of Muslim laws despite
the fact that there already was at least one Muslim woman lawyer, as well as other educated
Muslim women at that time. It seems that a main concern of the Commission was to bring
Philippine Muslim laws in conformity with those observed in other Muslim countries.
There are no specific provisions that could possibly help women or guarantee justice and

fairness for her in cases of divorce or subsequent remarriage of the husband. These are left to be specified by the *qadis*, the arbitration council. The major accomplishment of the Muslim Code of Personal Laws was to formalize and systematize Islamic laws (some of which were already being observed), for implementation in the Muslim areas in the Philippines.

Two important pieces of legislation affect all women in the Philippines: The New Family Code,[79] which took effect in 1988 and the "Women in Development and Nation-Building Act" (Republic Act 7192) of February 1992. Some of the provisions of the Family Code run counter to those of the Code of Muslim Personal Laws. While the Muslim laws require a husband's consent in a woman's choice or exercise of profession, the Family Code gives the woman the right to exercise her career or profession as well as the right to accept gifts through donation without need of her husband's consent.[80] Perhaps the differences in these laws can be seen in terms of their varying intents and purposes. The Code of Muslim law seeks primarily to preserve the unity of the family while affirming the role of the man as its head, but the New Family Code and Women in Development Act seek to guarantee equal status for women and empower them as equal participants in the areas of family, politics, economy, and social life.

The Women in Development and Nation-Building Act seeks to "ensure the fundamental equality between man and woman."[81] Women of legal age, regardless of civil status, have equal capacity to enter into contracts as men. They can also obtain loans and have equal access to all government and private sector programs granting loans and agricultural credit. Married women are given rights equal to those of married men in applying for passports, visas, and other travel documents without need to seek consent of their spouses.[82]

Considering the fact that Muslim women in the Philippines are also Filipinos, and that the Family Code and Women in Development Act are of general application, is the Muslim woman then to choose which law would be applicable to her? Or, since she is a Muslim and the Code of Muslim Personal laws say that the Code is binding in the Muslim area, must the Muslim woman move to a non-Muslim area if she wants to secure the full benefits of the Women in Development Act and the New Family Code? According to the Code of Muslim Personal Laws, in case of a conflict between any of its provisions and laws of general application, the Muslim Personal Laws shall prevail. It would be interesting to see if a Muslim woman can have the option to choose the law to be applied that would be to her advantage. In the two particular provisions mentioned here, obviously, there is a conflict.

Muslim Women and the Philippine Women's Movement

Since the American period in the Philippines, the government has always encouraged, although informally, the formation of women's associations. The focus of these women's groups, however, was very different from those that later evolved in the 1980s. In the 1930s until the late 1960s, these organizations were the form of women's clubs that were initiated and supported by wives of government officials. They were primarily sociocultural groups whose involvement in women's welfare was mainly in the areas of maternal health and child care. Muslims were also involved in this to some extent, although the more active members were those who came from the aristocracy, some of whom were also wives of government officials. These were not political organizations, but their members were very active in politics, campaigning primarily for local and national candidates.[83]

Aside from women's clubs, Muslim women in Jolo and Cotabato were involved in the counterpart associations of the local Lions Club and the Jaycees. Together with Christian women, they initiated social and civic projects like cleanliness and beautification campaigns for their towns. Again, the women involved here were wives of politicians and business leaders, hence, they were upper-class and middle-class women. The majority of the members of these organizations were Christians.

A distinction must be made between these women's associations and women's movements. Women's associations can be any grouping of women — sociocultural groups, religious associations of women and others, which were formed on the basis of shared interests of the women. Women's movements, on the other hand, may involve women representing various interests and goals, but they are interested in effecting changes that would benefit women in different aspects of life. In most instances, they are premised on the idea that women have been deprived, discriminated against, or not allowed to realize their full potentials because of certain constraints that reflect a patriarchal society.

The contemporary women's movement in the Philippines is a nonmonolithic, sectoral movement representing women of varied interests.[84] Actually, we can speak of two parallel movements: one that is encouraged and supported by the government and another that developed out of national liberation movements that were very active during the time of President Marcos. The first group is primarily concerned with increasing political and economic opportunities for women. Government support and encouragement for these groups comes in the form of seminars, training programs, and help to set up nongovernmental organizations (NGOs). These NGOs are usually involved in literacy, nutrition, reproductive-health programs, and income-generating activities. Government agencies help them secure funding; this is facilitated by a provision in the Women in Development Act requiring a substantial portion of official development assistance funds from foreign governments and multilateral agencies and organizations to be allotted to support programs and activities for women.[85] The major sources of funds have been United Nations agencies and the Canadian and European governments. Aside from women-run NGOs, there are also other organizations that fall into this category. They are included in an umbrella organization, the National Council of Women of the Philippines (NCWP). The NCWP envisions the total and active participation of women in decision-making processes, in government, and in all stages of development — national, economic, political, social, and cultural.[86] The members of the board of the NCWP are professional women who are members of various organizations like Soroptimist Club, Zonta Club, and others. Aside from a representative of women agricultural workers, most of the members of the board are wives of politicians or government officials, and are educators and businesswomen.

The parallel movement is represented by GABRIELA[87] (General Assembly Binding Women for Reforms Integrity, Equality, Leadership, and Action), an umbrella organization for over 100 women's groups; in the late 1980s, this included about 28,000 women members.[88] Among these groups are Kilusan ng Manggagawang Kababaihan (Women Workers' Movement, KMK), KALAYAAN (Association of Women for Freedom), SAMAKANA (Organization of United Nationalist Women), PILIPINA, NOWRP (National Organization of Women Religious in the Philippines), EATWOT (Ecumenical Association of Third World Theologians), and SAMAKA (Organization of Students and Young Women). These organizations adhere to four major principles: restoration of democracy; attainment of a genuine and sovereign Philippines where women will be true and equal partners of men in developing and preserving national patrimony; enhancement of the development of women at the grassroots level and rejection of any move that dehumanizes women; and national liberation is incomplete without women's liberation.[89] The concerns of these organizations go beyond increasing women's political and economic participation. Rather, they are for raising women's consciousness and providing them with the skills necessary for sociocultural transformation. They offer a commitment to breaking the feudal and patriarchal structures that are responsible for the inferior status of women vis-à-vis men. Many of these organizations were involved with the leftist movement, especially during the period of martial law. Some of these groups do run NGOs, but their concern it is not just a matter of having more women in congress or more women enterpreneurs or more women-run NGOs. There are deeper issues that need to be addressed. There are issues of sovereignty and democracy, as well as the need to support the struggles of women workers, peasants, and urban poor.

Considering the differences in the historical experiences and cultural orientation of Philippine Muslim women, it is difficult to lump Muslim women's movements with the non-Muslim movements noted previously, nor can we consider them as forming a single, unified Muslim women's movement. There are Muslim women members of GABRIELA, but there are also women's movements that are exclusively Muslim.

There are several kinds of Muslim women's groups that are involved in the Muslim women's movement: (1) those that are encouraged by the government and are included in the National Council of Women of the Philippines; (2) those that are concerned with promoting Islamic views on women; (3) those that try to combine activities for women with promotion of Islam, and (4) those that are concerned with national liberation.

The first type is represented by the Philippine Muslim Women's Association (PHILMUSLIMA) and the Muslim Professional and Businesswomen's Association of the Philippines (MPBWAP). The PHILMUSLIMA was organized in the 1950s upon the encouragement of a Muslim senator, Domocao Alonto. Most of the members of this association were members of political families, and connected to the old aristocracy, like Tarhata Alonto Lucman, Maryam Abubakar Ututalum and Santanina Rasul, who are all wives of Muslim political leaders. In 1965, they were the ones who represented the Philippine Muslim women in the Afro-Asian Islamic Conference in Bandung, Indonesia.[90] The Philippine Muslim Women's Association was primarily a social and civic organization, and was not concerned with political issues.

In 1975, PHILMUSLIMA was reorganized, and Zorayda Abbas Tamano became its president. She is the daughter of the first Muslim judge of the Court of First Instance, and a wife of Mamintal Tamano, a former senator and former head of the Commission on National Integration. Under her leadership, the PHILMUSLIMA became involved with NCWP. Tamano was one of the commissioners in the National Commission on the Role of Filipino Women and she is also chair of the Alliance of Women of the Cultural Communities (AWOCC). Tamano sees PHILMUSLIMA as an integral part of the national women's movement. While intending to foster cooperation between Muslims and non-Muslims and to make its members aware of women's issues,

PHILMUSLIMA is also interested in educating Muslim women on their duties, obligations, rights, and privileges.[91]

In 1993, PHILMUSLIMA, together with AWOCC, organized a series of consultations with Muslim women in four cities in Mindanao (Basilan-Zamboanga, Cotabato, Marawi, and Davao) to discuss issues relevant to women in preparation for the Philippine participation in the United Nations Women's Conference in Beijing (1995). Among the issues discussed in Cotabato and Davao were marriage, divorce, and polygyny. It is interesting to note that the women expressed the need for a strict enforcement of the Shariah. They contended that women must address the problem of polygynous husbands whose actions are not punished by law. This seems rather inconsistent, because if they registered disapproval of polygynous practices of the men, how could they insist on strict implementation of the Shariah that allows it? The documents did not elaborate whether it was the question of "justice and fairness" to the four wives that they were concerned with or polygyny itself. This raises the question: Are the women knowledgeable of the provisions of the Quran and the Code of Muslim Personal Laws?

The other issues discussed in the consultations had to do mainly with lack of healthcare services, the need for more women in government offices and in the legislature, and Muslim women's representations in the Human Rights Committee. Interestingly, one of the problems discussed in Basilan was about the campaign of the *ulama* against women's participation in politics. This campaign could be indicative of a development that might be pushing back women's rights.

Although the issues discussed have so far remained just that—issues—PHILMUSLIMA and AWOCC have taken a significant step in identifying the problems that beset Muslim women.

The other organization that falls under this first category is the Muslim Professional and Businesswomen's Association of the Philippines (MPBWAP), organized in 1974, with Santanina Rasul as its first president. MPBWAP claims that it is "the first nongovernmental organization established by and for Filipino Muslim women which focused on direct participation in the development process."[92] The association was primarily involved in literacy programs, which Rasul started on her own by writing a reading primer in 1966. Rasul eventually established the "Mabassa Kita (Let's Read) Foundation." Aside from the literacy program, the foundation is now involved in maternity, child care, and livelihood skills programs.

The current president of MPBWAP is Amina Rasul-Bernardo, a daughter of Santanina Rasul. Together with Lourdes Mastura, the wife of Congressman Michael Mastura (who is also a descendant of the royal house in Maguindanao), they are the two Muslim Commissioners in the National Commission on the Role of Filipino Women. Rasul-Bernardo claims that the MPBWAP is also interested in the women's agenda and that it has active women leaders in the Muslim communities. She concedes, however, that the association has to work within the "realities of their environment." For the MPBWAP, women have to be educated first and be provided with skills that will help them increase their income before they can avail themselves of the provisions of recent legislations affecting women. The MPBWAP is careful about espousing causes that might threaten and alienate the men; Rasul-Bernardo expressed fear of losing men's support if that happens.[93] Rasul-Bernardo, who is a product of the University of the Philippines (like her mother), believes that the liberating influence which urban women enjoy does not exist in the rural areas. This is a position that GABRIELA and the MNLF women would not agree to. It is probably because MPBWAP has chosen to focus on literacy and livelihood skills programs.

Like PHILMUSLIMA, MPBWAP is a member of the National Council of Women of the Philippines (NCWP). Its decision to be involved with the NCWP was motivated by the desire for networking with women whose primary interests lie more in increasing the income and economic opportunities of women rather than advocating for women's rights.[94] Both PHILMUSLIMA and MPBWAP consider their organizations to be integral parts of the women's movement in the Philippines that is primarily centered in Manila. Their leaders are educated Muslim women who come from traditionally political families and are nationally visible. Not all Muslim women, however, see PHILMUSLIMA and MPBWAP as its leaders envisioned it. There are those who see these organizations as primarily political tools of their leaders, and therefore stay away from them. There is an MPBWAP chapter in Zamboanga that was organized by the sister of Rasul but it is not active at the moment. To some Muslims in Zamboanga, the association furthers the political ambitions of the family and gives the message that they are the only ones who can represent the Muslim women.

The second type of Muslim women's group, the ones concerned with promoting Islamic views on women, is exemplified by the Muslim Women Fellowship of the Philippines. It was organized in 1986 by fifteen women in Cotabato City. The Islamic emphasis of this association is indicated in its articles of incorporation filed with the Securities and Exchange Commission of the Philippines. Its first purpose is to instill in Muslim women their basic role in the community. At first glance, it seems like the organization is not much different from other women's organizations. However, a closer look at its statement reveals the missionary nature of the fellowship. It plans to hire missionaries and teachers who will teach "people from other faith about Islam." It also plans to build schools and solicit donations from members and the general public, as well as local and foreign governments, to finance their projects and to help the needy members.[95]

The Sarang Bangun Foundation is typical of the third type of Muslim women's organization. It combines women's activities with the promotion of Islam. Sarang Bangun was named after Desdemona Tan (who died in 1987), the first wife of the Chairman of the Moro National Liberation Front, Nur Misuari. Tan, who came from a very prominent family in Jolo, Sulu, was strongly involved in the peace negotiations between the MNLF and the Philippine government in 1986. Her revolutionary name was Sarang Bangun.

The Sarang Bangun foundation was initially organized to care for the widows and orphans of the war with the MNLF. But because these children have now grown, the foundation has expanded its programs to include a grade school where Islamic studies are offered, a cooperative for women, skills and livelihood training, and Quran and Arabic courses for adults. Their programs are not limited to Muslims, but are also open to those who profess other religions. As an officer of the Sarang Bangun emphasizes, everyone needs to understand Islam in order to eliminate the age-old prejudices that date back to Spanish rule in the country. They have also started to hold seminars on women's rights in the Quran and have invited the local imam to speak. No woman has spoken in the seminars because they have yet to find a woman who is knowledgeable about the Quran, particularly its provisions on women.[96] Funding for Sarang Bangun comes from a variety of sources, including Muslim countries, with the largest support coming from the Islamic

Development Bank, which is financing the construction of their orphan care center in Jolo. Sarang Bangun is a nongovernmental organization.

Women of the Moro National Liberation Front

The women of the MNLF represent the last category of Muslim women's groups. Its initial emphasis was on liberation of their BangsaMoro (Moro[97] nation) homeland and people, seeking to secede from the Republic of the Philippines to establish its own BangsaMoro Republik. The MNLF itself is a movement that has affected the lives of many Muslims, and it is the largest and most organized Muslim movement in the country.

The MNLF was organized in 1969, as a response to what its members believed were repressive and oppressive policies adopted by the Spanish, American, and Philippine governments toward the Muslims. The MNLF sees itself as a popular revolutionary movement[98] whose initial goal was to establish a sovereign nation that would chart its own destiny. It has been engaged in an armed conflict with the government of the Philippines,[99] which escalated into full warfare in the early 1970s. The war left destruction in several places in Mindanao but it also pushed the government to deliver infrastructure, development programs, and policies that would benefit the Muslims.

In 1976, the MNLF entered into the Tripoli Agreement with the government, which would have provided for autonomy in thirteen provinces in the Muslim areas of the country[100] within the context of Philippine sovereignty. The agreement was not implemented by the government and, at the moment, it is once more the subject of negotiations between representatives of the Philippine government and the MNLF.

While most of the members of the MNLF are men, they have a considerable number of women members who refer to themselves as BangsaMoro women. Several of them have been part of the movement since its early years. They were among the core group of individuals who started organizing the MNLF in the Muslim areas in 1970. While women were not formally considered members at that time (they were "sympathizers"), they were nevertheless active organizers who went to Muslim villages to explain the purposes of the MNLF to the Muslim masses.

In 1972, the women in this core group organized the Women's Committee. According to one of its first members, organizing in the rural areas where women were less educated was difficult because of traditional perceptions of male–female roles. For one thing, it was felt that the job of fighting a war belongs to the men and it was unthinkable for a Muslim woman to be a revolutionary. There were, however, families who did not register any objection to their daughters' joining the movement. This was largely because they already had other family members in the MNLF. These families were aware of the risks involved and they felt a strong sense of commitment to justice for the Muslims. A woman MNLF member noted that as the war wore on, there were families who literally "offered" their children—male and female— to the cause of the revolution.[101]

Women in the MNLF come from various backgrounds. There are women who descended from the old aristocracy, from political families, from middle-class families, and from the rural masses. They represent various ethnolinguistic groups, such as Maranaos, Tausugs, and Maguindanaons. There are women with college and graduate school education, as well as women who never went to school. There were those who were educated in the *madrasah*,[102] those who came from public schools as well as from Catholic schools.

Many came from the Notre Dame schools in Cotabato and Jolo. They learned of the MNLF through Muslim associations in the universities, through their relatives and family members who had already joined, and through the recruiting efforts of the MNLF on campus. Others joined when the MNLF recruiters organized meetings in their *barangay* (villages).

In an interview of twenty-five women of the MNLF,[103] 68% indicated that they joined the movement because of government and military oppression, and because they want justice for themselves and their family members.[104]

Women's involvement with the MNLF was not an open situation. There were those who joined the men in the hills, and others who remained "outside" but performed vital functions for the movement. The latter were students, employees, agricultural workers, and mothers who helped the movement in various capacities while continuing with their daily lives. Some who were suspected of cooperating with the MNLF were arrested and questioned, and some were placed under house arrest.

Women's involvement was crucial to the MNLF, especially during the period of martial law—which was also the height of the armed confrontations between government military forces and the MNLF. They served as communication links between the members in the hills and those in the cities. They delivered medicine, supplies, food, messages, and information to the forces. Using the multiple folds of their traditional skirts (*malong*), some of the women smuggled ammunitions and small arms to the men in the hills.

While women suspected of sympathizing or helping the MNLF were generally questioned and then allowed to return to their families or put under house arrest, they were not usually held in military stockades, as had happened with women involved in other liberation movements in the Philippines. Perhaps the military felt that the Muslim women were so occupied in their traditional ways that they would not be involved in the revolution actively. This was not the case. Women were as active as they possibly could be, and there were instances of women who fought with men in the front lines. There were exceptional cases, like Farouza, who was killed when government forces attacked Jolo in 1974, as well as the wife of a commander in Basilan who took over her husband's place and led 150 men when her husband was killed in battle.[105]

The MNLF gave these women military training primarily to protect themselves from abuses committed by the military. Whenever the military launched their offensives and they happened upon women, there were always instances of abuse and the MNLF leadership felt it was necessary to train women to use firearms. Plus, in case of emergency, it might be necessary to put women in the frontlines. Women were also trained to make bombs and bullets for use by the men in the field. The main task of the women in times of battle, however, was to provide moral support to the men and take care of wounded fighters.

Those who did not go to the hills prepared food for the men, sewed uniforms, made insignias, and engaged in income-producing activities to support the war efforts.[106] They collected regular contributions, which they referred to as *sadaqa*, from MNLF members and sympathizers who were not in the battlefields. They also took care of the moneylending[107] operations of the movement, the proceeds of which were used for maintenance of the forces and various other projects. A major task of the women continues to be recruitment and consciousness raising. As the MNLF negotiates with the government over the implementation of the Tripoli Agreement, women disseminate information on the progress of the negotiations to the people. It is interesting to note that many MNLF women are aware of the major provisions of the agreement.

Although the MNLF women perform numerous tasks, they have not been directly involved in the negotiations with the Philippine government. Sometime before the 1986 peace talks initiated by President Corazon Aquino, the Women's Committee passed a resolution requesting involvement in the peace process. So far, their involvement has been in the secretariat, and their main task is to provide research and clerical support to the men who negotiate with the government representatives.

In the early 1980s, the MNLF leadership felt that it was necessary to tap professional Muslim women who would further articulate the issues affecting the Muslims and help in providing financial support to the movement. In 1986, the BangsaMoro Women's Professional and Employees Association was organized. There are about 350 to 400 members of the association, most of whom come from the urban areas and are government employees. Like the MNLF Women's Committee, they continue to engage in consciousness-raising among the Muslims. They are concerned with empowerment of women and increasing women's roles in politics, society, and the economy. There are plans for the establishment of a women's center that will help the orphans and the widows of the war; the center will be independent of the Muslim politicians, who, they feel are not genuinely concerned with their welfare. They coordinate their activities with the Women's Committee of the MNLF, because there are many women who are involved in both groups.

Despite the increasing role of women in the MNLF, few are in actual positions of leadership. The MNLF operates on a committee system, with the Central Committee headed by the Chairman, Nur Misuari. There are various committees with their specific concerns (such as finance and economic affairs, education, transportation and communication, sanitation, intelligence, propaganda, foreign affairs, social welfare, and women), on the local, provincial, and national levels. The Chairpersons of these committees on the national level are members of the Central Committee. There is only one woman in the Central Committee—the Chairman of the Women's Committee. She is a voting member of the Central Committee, which means that women only have one vote in the Central Committee. So far, this limited participation in decision-making at the higher level has not affected the involvement and enthusiasm of the MNLF women. They continue to be involved, committed, and efficient in the tasks that they set out to do.

In 1994, when the MNLF women were interviewed, there was a ceasefire being observed by the MNLF and the government forces. Because it was generally a more peaceful time, the women claimed that they could engage in other undertakings. They have not abandoned their earlier roles but have expanded their activities and their goals. They have started to discuss women's rights in Islam in their meetings, and in September 1994 they participated in a seminar on the shariah where a local imam, Udstadz Abirin, gave a lecture on "Women's Rights in the Quran." The Chairman of the MNLF is now encouraging its women members to read the Quran and learn about the rights of women as provided for in Islam. This is an interesting development because the MNLF has been criticized as being too secular, and because many Muslim women are not aware of the Quranic provisions on women.

Women's involvement in the MNLF was motivated primarily by their desire for meaningful and positive changes for Muslims. They believe that armed struggle is justified, because the problems of land grabbing, military abuses, government oppression and neglect have persisted for years. They expect justice and equal treatment.

The war years brought about a change in the way the MNLF women and their families perceived the traditional roles, duties, and privileges of Muslim women. Those who joined the MNLF in the hills broke away from the traditional notion that a Muslim woman leaves the home only when she marries. They were separated from their families and joined with men—some of whom they never knew before—in a cause that they believed was worth fighting for. An MNLF woman who came from a politically and economically prominent family told how the women fighters learned to sleep anywhere and make do with whatever there was. Class and gender distinctions were set aside as women from the traditional elite nursed wounded fighters and prepared food in the camps. At an MNLF camp in North Cotabato, men and women conversed freely but, perhaps still in keeping with traditions, the men are protective of the women and the women seem to accept this.

The MNLF brought a new level of political consciousness and activism to its women members. While MNLF's only mode of political participation before was voting or helping campaign for candidates seeking public office, members are now engaged in national liberation, political activism, consciousness-raising, organizing seminars, mobilizing people, and agitating for the implementation of the Tripoli Agreements. The women involved exhibit a feeling that they can achieve their goals. When asked what they see in the future for themselves, if and when the government does implement the Tripoli Agreement, practically all the women interviewed said they believe that women will be actively involved, and those who are qualified will have positions in the autonomous government. Their answers demonstrate their confidence in the capability of women to share in the work of governing their nation.[108]

In June 1996, the MNLF, under pressure from the Organization of Islamic Conference and the Philippine government, agreed to the creation of the Southern Philippines Council for Peace and Development (SPCPD). The MNLF Chairman, Nur Misuari, has been designated to head this body, which will oversee development programs and implement the terms of the peace agreement, as well as pave the way for the creation of an autonomous region in Mindanao. In July 1996, Misuari filed his candidacy for the governorship of the Autonomous Region for Muslim Mindanao. These developments, in effect, replace the original MNLF goal of secession from the Philippines, but it is still too early to assess the implications of these events on the MNLF women, their goals, and their aspirations of participating in the building of their Moro nation.

There is no single unified Muslim women's movement in the Philippines; this is largely due to the nature of the leadership, their goals, and their agenda. PHILMUS-LIMA and MBPWAP focus more on opening up opportunities for women in politics and economics. Basically, what this means is more women in government positions—both elective and appointed—in the bureaucracy, and in business activities. These organizations are encouraged and supported by the government in many ways and, in turn, the groups are supportive of government policies and programs for women.

The MNLF Women's Committee had concentrated on issues of national liberation for the Muslims, and on their rights to self-determination and autonomy. Their activities in the MNLF expanded over time, from sympathizers, recruiters, and supporting roles at the height of the armed conflict, to some degree of participation in the decision-making process. They have become more visible participants in the movement. They are well aware of the problems and situations of Muslims in the Philippines, and, at the same time, they feel they can do something about it. MNLF women leaders recognize that the MNLF has brought out leadership abilities in them and helped them realize their potentials. The MNLF, in effect, has acted as an agent of change for these Muslim women. The BangsaMoro Women's Professional and Employees Association, which was established under the auspices of the MNLF (many of their members are also involved with the MNLF), is also engaged in consciousness-raising but is now talking about women's empowerment in society. In the absence of war, they claim they now have time for other things. While their primary concern before was national liberation, now they are talking about women's rights. They are still, however, in the process of defining their position in a postwar setting. In times of war, there was a breakdown of the gender barriers; after the war, it remains to be seen whether the men they worked with will continue to see them as equal partners in the struggle for justice.

Islamic Resurgence and Muslim Women

There are many indicators of Islamic resurgence in the Philippines. One of them is the increasing number of Islamic schools called madrasah (plural, *madaris*). The most rapid growth of these schools can be seen in the mid 1970s, when about 80% of these schools (now totalling more than 2,000) were established in Mindanao.[109] These schools have helped Muslims learn about Islam and have also provided women with new opportunities for employment as teachers in the schools. There are also Egyptian teachers, particularly in Marawi, as well as local Muslims who have returned from studies and training in the Middle East. Since they are now recognized by the government, the madaris serve as alternative schools for those who still refuse to send their children to public or Christian schools.[110] Students attending the madaris have the chance to obtain scholarships to Muslim countries if they qualify, and to further their learning about Islam. There are also Islamic schools that combine government-approved standard curricula for grade schools and high schools with courses in Arabic language, Islamic theology, philosophy, and science.[111]

This resurgence is also manifested in the growing number of women who are now studying the Quran and wearing the head cover, be it a scarf, a *kombong*, or a hijab. Traditionally, both men and women wear a head cover that is part of their ethnic attire. For the men, it is the *kopia*, while the women wear the kombong, a long piece of soft material that is twisted into a turban.[112] The Muslims, however, were not particular about wearing them before. In the 1960s, Muslims studying in the universities in the Manila area never wore them, nor did the Muslim women of Marawi in 1972. Those, however, who have gone to the *hajj* always wore them (white for women) as a sign that they have made the pilgrimage. Older women usually wear the kombong. Others have scarves loosely covering their heads. There are also women who wear the hijab and the Islamic dress. In the early 1970s, it was unusual to see a woman wearing a hijab, but they are now a common sight in Marawi, Jolo, Cotabato and other Muslim areas.

In the study conducted in Cotabato in 1994, eighteen of the twenty-five women interviewed all started wearing the head cover (this includes the hijab, kombong, and the scarf) in the late 1970s. Only two women wore the hijab. They wear their head covers because they believe it is a requirement of the religion and it identifies them as Muslims. One woman admitted that she did not wear it before because she was embarrassed to do so. It made her look different, and some people see it as a sign of backwardness. But now, more than anything else, it gives her a sense of identity and she is uncomfortable without it.

In September 1993, Muslim men and women demonstrated against the Notre Dame University in Cotabato City, which prohibited the use of hijab for medical and nursing students when working in the hospital. The demonstration was organized by the Islamic Resistance Against Hijab Prohibition (IRAHP). The university administration claimed that it was implementing Department of Health Memorandum No. 11-A s. 1961, which prescribed a standard uniform for all government health personnel under the control and supervision of the Department of Health. The First National Muslim Youth Consultative Assembly of 1993 passed a resolution appealing the department memorandum. On June 21, 1994, Secretary of Health Juan Flavier issued Memorandum Order 1 s. 1994 which amended the previous memorandum and allowed "female health personnel of Islamic faith to wear the head veil prescribed by their religion while on duty, provided that the sterility of vital areas is ensured."[113] This decision of the health department was welcomed by Muslims and serves as a reminder of Muslims' determination to struggle for their religion. A Muslim woman who was refering to the demonstration, said, "that was part of our *jihad.*"

The situation in a Catholic-run college in Zamboanga is different. Pilar College is open to girls of different religious and ethnic backgrounds. Around 1991, Muslim students of this all-girls' school started wearing the veil. The school authorities called a meeting and pointed out that since it was an all-girls' school, wearing the veil was not necessary. Shortly after, the students were told that they could not wear it. The nuns who run the school invited some Muslims to talk to the students about veiling and said that veiling was customary in Saudi Arabia before Islam and is not really required by the religion. There were some girls who insisted on wearing the hijab but, eventually, even these girls stopped.

Conclusion

Throughout the periods covered in this chapter, numerous factors have affected the lives of Philippine Muslim women. Among others, there were government programs, legislation, education, women's groups, a revolutionary movement, and Islamic resurgence, all of which acted as agents of change for them. Of all these factors, however, education comes out as the one that has had a tremendous impact on women, especially if we think in terms of the number of Muslim women it has affected. The scholarship programs of the Commission on National Integration and the opening up of universities in Mindanao made higher education accessible to women, many of whom are now in various professions like law, medicine, and education, as well as in other occupations.

Memberships in women's groups, as well as participation in the revolution, have politicized and raised the consciousness of women and have given them the opportunity to rediscover and believe in themselves.

The worldwide Islamic resurgence has also affected Philippine Muslim women. The coming of Muslims from other countries to teach in the Islamic schools, the Muslim women's increasing participation in the hajj, and the establishment of more schools that teach the Quran and Arabic have all heightened their Islamic consciousness. Government policies and programs that recognize Islam as part of the national heritage have helped them develop a sense of pride as Muslims in a country where they were once objects of curiosity because they are not Christians.

All these factors have worked to bring about a strong sense of identity and a new awareness of their roles and capabilities as Muslim women.

Although men are still regarded as the most qualified to interpret the Quran, there are educated Muslim women who are now reading it and interpreting the provisions for themselves, particularly the passages on marriage and divorce. In a recently concluded symposium at the Institute of Islamic Studies at the University of the Philippines, Muslim women argued that the message of the provision on marriage is essentially monogamy, considering the requirement of justice and fairness to the wives.

As noted earlier, there were various women who have influenced the political decision-making process in the Sulu and Maguindanao sultanate, and educated women who have held political positions—like senators, governors, mayors, and numerous barangay councilors. Most of these women belong to the aristocracy, the traditional elites or royalties who held power before the coming of the Spanish and whose descendants still continue to hold sway. For many of those who sought elective offices and succeeded, their hereditary positions of power and influence were legitimized by the election process after the sultanates declined. In a sense, we can say that involvement in public life has been so much a tradition among the aristocracy that their roles really did not change. Rather, the roles were expanded and legitimized by new structures.

Perhaps the middle and lower classes have experienced the most in terms of changed roles. Education accounted mainly for the changes as it enabled them to break through traditional class barriers. In many ways, education "democratized" the opportunities for them.

Many Muslim women, however, are still unaware of specific contents of the Code of Muslim Personal Laws, recent legislations (particularly the Women in Development Act and the New Family Code), and their implications on the rights and roles of Muslim women. Unless Muslim women's groups undertake an active dissemination campaign on the rights of women included in these legal instruments, the ordinary Muslim woman may never fully know her rights and what she is entitled to. But once she knows, she will need to determine a way to reconcile Islamic laws that affect her as a woman and the provisions of current legislations that give her equal footing with men both in family affairs and in nation-building.

Notes

1. Cesar Adib Majul, "Philippines," in *The Oxford Encyclopedia of the Modern Islamic World*, ed. John L. Esposito, (New York: Oxford University Press, 1995).

2. Philippine Muslims comprise numerous tribal groups, the major ones being the Maranao, Maguindanao, Tausug, Yakan, Samal, Sangil, Jama Mapun, Palawani, Molbog, Illanun, Kalagan, and Kalibugan. The Badjau are also generally included in this classification, although not all consider themselves Muslims.

3. Muslim communities are primarily agricultural and, depending on the natural resources in

their areas, engage in farming, fishing, cloth and mat weaving, woodcarving, and metalcraft. Tausugs and Samals also engage in barter trade with neighboring islands and with Malaysia.

4. About 85% of Filipinos are Christians. The Spanish, who colonized the Philippines for over 350 years, and tried to subjugate the Muslims, were met with resistance by the latter who refused to give up their lands and their religion.

5. For the coming of Islam to the Philippines, see Cesar Adib Majul, *Muslims in the Philippines* (Quezon City: University of the Philippines for the Asian Center, 1973), particularly chap. 2.

6. "Muslim Women Cry Bias," *Philippine Daily Inquirer*, October 23, 1994.

7. Materials on the Philippine women's movement and on Muslim women from Juan Manolo Alcasabas, Dr. Esperanza Angeles, Dr. Cesar A. Majul, Dr. Carol Sobritchea, and Daisy Soriano have been very useful for this study. Steven Breedlove, of Connelly Library's Inter-library Loan Section, La Salle University, helped borrow materials from libraries in the United States. Discussions with Raquel Zaraspe Ordonez, President of the Coalition, for the Advancement of Filipino Women, have been very helpful for the section on women's movement.

8. Peter Gowing, *Muslim Filipinos: Heritage and Horizon* (Quezon City: New Day, 1979), p. 47.

9. Sultans occupied the highest position in the state. They exercised political power and provided spiritual leadership to the people.

10. Datus exercised power over their followers, took care of them, utilized their services when necessary, and administered justice. It was a patron–client type of relationship.

11. Peter Gowing, *Muslim Filipinos*, pp. 53–54. In 1669, the Sultan of Sulu gave the Dutch Governor General of Batavia a gift of twelve pearls and a female slave. See Cesar A. Majul, *Muslims in the Philippines*, p. 176.

12. Luis Q. Lacar, "Philippine Muslim Women: Their Emerging Role in a Rapidly Changing Society," in *Mindanao: Land of Unfulfilled Promise*, ed. Mark Turner, R. J. May, and Lulu R. Turner (Quezon City: New Day, 1992), p. 109.

13. Labi Hadji Sarip, "A Profile of Economic Activities of Maranao Women in Molundo, Marantao, and the Islamic City of Marawi, Lanao del Sur," *Dansalan Quarterly* 7 (1–2) (1985–1986): 7–8. William Dampier, who was in Mindanao in 1686, included in his account a report that a fourteen-year-old princess was kept in a room and "never stirs out, and that she did not see any man but her father and Raja Laut, her uncle." See William Dampier, *A Voyage to the New World* (London: New Argonaut, 1927), p. 229.

14. Personal interview with Bai Malagan (a Barangay council member), Dinaig, Maguindanao, July 17, 1994.

15. Santanina Rasul, "The Muslim Woman: Her Role in Contemporary Philippine Society," in F. Landa Jocano, *Filipino Muslim: Their Social Institutions and Cultural Achievements* (Quezon City: Asian Center, 1983), p. 35.

16. Aminah Usodan-Sumagayan, "The Changing Role of Maranao Women in a Maranao Rural Society," *Dansalan Quarterly* 9 (4) (1988): 186.

17. Dampier, *A Voyage to the New World*, p. 233, 246.

18. Thomas Forrest, *A Voyage to New Guinea and the Moluccas 1774–1776* (Kuala Lumpur: Oxford University Press, 1969), p. 246.

19. *Ibid.*

20. Usodan-Sumagayan, "Changing Role," pp. 186–202.

21. Majul, *Muslims in the Philippines*, p. 242.

22. Sulu is a predominantly Muslim province in the southern tip of the Philippines.

23. See Anne Lindsey Reber, "The Sulu World in the Eighteenth and Early Nineteenth Centuries: A Historiographical Problem in British Writing on Malay Piracy" (master's thesis, Cornell University, 1966).

24. Majul, *Muslims in the Philippines*, p. 17.

25. Majul, *Muslims in the Philippines*, p. 310.

26. See Reynaldo C. Ileto, *Magindanao, 1860–1888: The Career of Datu Uto of Buayan*, Data Paper: Number 82, Southeast Asia Program (Ithaca, N.Y.: Cornell University, 1971), p. 34.

27. Forrest, *A Voyage to New Guinea*, pp. 205–206.

28. Majul, *Muslims in the Philippines*, 302.

29. The ensuing political struggles between claimants to the position of sultan eventually convinced the Spanish of the popularity of Amirul Kiram. The Spanish then proposed that Amirul Kiram go to Manila to take the oath of office. He refused to do so and the Spanish eventually installed Harun ar Rashid. Senate Document no. 136, 56th Congress, 1st sess., 14 (1903) and *Report of the War Department*, 1903, vol. 3, 390–392 cited by William Cameron Forbes, *The Philippine Islands*, vol. 2 (Boston: Houghton Mifflin, 1928) p. 39.

30. Majul, *Muslims in the Philippines.*, p. 306.

31. Charles Hagadorn, "Our Friend, The Sultan of Jolo," *The Century Illustrated Monthly Magazine* 60, n.s., 38 (May–October 1900): 27.

32. Dean C. Worcester, *The Philippines and Their People* (New York: Macmillan, 1898), pp. 173-174.

33. Ileto, *Magindanao*, p. 34.

34. Majul, *Muslims in the Philippines*, p. 311, 312.

35. Alexander Dalrymple, "Essay Towards an Account of Sulu," *Journal of the Eastern Archipelago and Eastern Asia* 3 (1849): 564–565.

36. Majul, *Muslims in the Philippines*, p. 19. Majul also noted that the Patikul *khutbah*, one of the sources he used, mentions her name only as Azam, with the name Nur left out. Majul further speculates that this is probably due to a later disbelief that a woman ruled.

37. See Charles Wilke, "Narrative of United States Exploratory Expeditions during 1838, 1839, 1840–41, 1842, Phildelphia, 1884" in *The Philippine Islands 1493–1803*, vol. 43, ed. Emma Blair and James A. Robertson (Cleveland, Ohio: Arthur H. Clark, 1903–1909), pp. 163–154.

38. Dampier, *A Voyage to the New World*, p. 224.

39. Forrest, *A Voyage to New Guinea*, p. 327. Wilke also noted that women did go abroad, perhaps to the different islands in the region. See Wilke, "Narrative," p. 163.

40. Dalrymple, "Essay," p. 555.

41. Spanish advances into the Muslim areas of Mindanao were met with Muslim resistance for much of the three centuries that Spain colonized the country. It was only toward the end of Spanish rule that they were able to bring Sulu within their territorial jurisdiction.

42. The Bates Treaty was concluded by General Bates and Sultan Jamal ul Kiram II on August 20, 1899. It was abrogated when the Moro Province was created in 1903.

43. Dorothy M. Rogers, "A History of the American Occupation and Administration of the Sulu Archipelago 1899–1920" (master's thesis, University of San Francisco, 1959), p. 98, cited by Peter Gowing, *Mandate in Moroland: The American Government of Muslim Filipinos, 1899–1920* (Quezon City: Philippine Center for Advanced Studies, University of the Philippines, 1977), p. 304.

44. *Ibid.*

45. *Reports of the Governor of the Moro Province* (1913) p. 32, cited by Gowing, *Mandate in Moroland*, p. 216.

46. Gowing, *Mandate in Moroland*, p. 216.

47. *Ibid.*

48. Frank Carpenter to Secretary of Interior, January 27, 1919, p. 2.

49. *Ibid.*

50. Gowing, *Mandate in Moroland*, p. 306.

51. Sixto Y. Orosa, *The Sulu Archipelago and Its People*, 2nd ed. N.p.: New Mercury, 1970), p. 118.

52. *Ibid.*

53. Carpenter to Secretary of Interior, January 27, 1919, p. 3.

54. *Ibid.*, p. 3.

55. *Ibid.*, p. 4.

56. "Princess Tarhata's Changing Period of Romance," *Sunday Tribune Magazine*, May 20, 1934, p. 3.

57. "Resignation of Dayang Dayang Piandao Accepted," *The Tribune*, October 16, 1940.

58. "Princess Tarhata's Changing Period of Romance," p.3.

59. "Sultan of Sulu Now Bereft of all Political Standing," *New York Times*, July 21, 1934, p. 5.

60. Gowing, *Muslim Filipinos*, p. 56.

61. Forbes, *The Philippine Islands*, Vol. 2, p. 40.

62. *Ibid.*, pp. 40–41.

63. Manuscript Report of the Philippine Commission (1915), pp. 3120–3133, cited by Gowing, *Mandate in Moroland*, p. 286.

64. Gowing, *Mandate in Moroland*, p. 286.

65. Forrest, *A Voyage to New Guinea*, p. 327.

66. Hagadorn, "Our Friend," p. 28.

67. See Lloyd Buchanan, "The Nature of Moros," *The World's Work* 12 (May 1906): 7567. Also Katherine Mayo, *Isles of Fear* (New York: Harcourt, Brace, 1925), p. 322.

68. Sydney Amos Cloman, *Myself and A Few Moros* (Garden City, N.Y.: Doubleday, 1923), p. 156.

69. The other families are the Abubakars, Kirams, and Rasuls. See Eric Gutierrez, "Frontier Town Politics," *The Philippine Star*, May 16, 1995, p. 1.

70. Personal interview with Assemblyman Wilson Anni, Norristown, Pennsylvania, July 28, 1995.

71. "The Charter of the Mindanao State University," Republic Act no. 1382. Full text in Antonio Isidro, *Muslim–Christian Integration at the Mindanao State University* (Marawi City, 1968), pp. 450–455.

72. Republic Act 1888 (as amended by Republic Act 3852). See full text in Romulo B. Lumauig, *Laws Affecting the National Cultural Minorities of the Philippines* (Manila: n.p., 1968) pp. 6–13.

73. See Lacar, "Philippine Muslim Women," pp. 114–115.

74. For a discussion of the MNLF, its activities and goals, see Cesar A. Majul, *The Contemporary Muslim Movement in the Philippines* (Berkeley, Calif.: Mizan Press, 1985).

75. Thomas M. Kiefer, *The Tausug: Violence and Law in a Philippine Moslem Society*. New York: Holt, Rinehart and Winston, 1972, p. 46.

76. Juanito A. Bruno, *The Social World of the Tausug: A Study in Culture and Education*. Manila: Centro Escolar University Research and Development Center, 1973, cited by Peter Gowing, *Mandate in Moroland*, p. 82

77. See *Code of Muslim Personal Laws of the Philippines*, Art. 35.

78. In a study done in 1989, Zenaida S. Reyes determined that the majority of Muslims living in Mindanao (64%) and in the Manila area (78%) were aware of the existence of the Code. Only 16% to 22% of them, however, had specific knowledge of the provisions of the Code. See Zenaida S. Reyes, *Survey Report on the "Recognition and Promotion of Legal Rights of Muslims as a Precondition to National Unity and Development.* (Quezon City: University of the Philippines, 1989).

79. *The Family Code of the Philippines* (Executive Order No. 209, as amended by Executive Order No. 227), August 4, 1988.

80. See *The Family Code*, Arts. 73 and 92.

81. Republic of the Philippines, *Republic Act 7192*, Sect. 2.

82. *Ibid.*, Sect. 5.

83. Toribio B. Castillo, "The Changing Social Status of the Filipino Women during the American Administration" (master's thesis, University of Southern California, 1942), p. 99.

84. This was a subject of discussion in the Women's Consultative Planning Forum in 1988. See Women's Resource Center, *Proceedings of the Women's Consultative Planning Forum, January 29–31, 1988* (Quezon City: Women's Resouce and Research Center, 1988).

85. Republic of the Philippines, *Republic Act 7192*, Sect. 2.

86. Pamphlet of the National Council of Women of the Philippines.

87. The organization was named after Gabriela Silang, a Filipina woman who fought against the Spanish in the 18th century.

88. Lois A. West, "Feminist Nationalist Social Movements: Beyond Universalism and Towards a Gendered Cultural Relativism," *Women's Studies Forum*, 15 (1992): 570.

89. Epifanio San Juan, *Crisis in the Philippines: The Making of a Revolution* (South Hadley: Massachusetts: Bergin and Garvey, Inc., 1986), pp. 170–171. See also Lois A. West, "Feminist Nationalist Social Movements," and Dorothy Friesen, "The Women's Movement in the Philippines," *NWSA Journal*, 1 (Summer 1989): 676–688.

90. Rasul, "Muslim Women," p. 37.

91. "Report on the AWOCC–PHILMUSLIMA Series of Area Consultations in Preparation for the 1994 Ministerial Conference in Jakarta and the 1995 UN 4th World Conference on Women," N.p., September 13–14, 1993.

92. Amina Rasul Bernardo, "Muslim Women and the Management of Change in their communities," typescript, p. 6.

93. *Ibid.*

94. *Ibid.*, p. 9.

95. "Articles of Incorporation of the Muslim Women Fellowship of the Philippines," pp. 1, 8.

96. Telephone interview with Zenaida Tan Lim (an officer of the Sarang Bangun Foundation), April 29, 1995.

97. Moro was the term used by the Spanish for Muslims. It was adopted by members of the MNLF to indicate their rejection of the idea that they are part of the Philippine nation.

98. Letter, from Nur Misuari, Chairman of the Moro National Liberation Front, to Vivienne SM. Angeles, October 15, 1983, p. 5.

99. See Majul, *The Contemporary Muslim Movement*,

100. The thirteen provinces are: Sulu, Tawi-Tawi, Basilan, Zamboanga del Norte, Zamboanga del Sur, Lanao del Norte, Lanao del Sur, North Cotabato, South Cotabato, Maguindanao, Sultan Kudarat, Davao del Sur, and Palawan.

101. Telephone interview with the former Chair of the MNLF Women's Committee, February 22, 1995.

102. Local schools where students are taught the Quran and Arabic.

103. The field interview was conducted by the author in July 1994 in Cotabato City, North Cotabato, and Maguindanao, Philippines. Questionnaires were sent and followed by telephone interviews to respondents in Zamboanga, Philippines, and Islamabad, Pakistan. See Vivienne SM. Angeles, "Women and Revolution: Philippine Muslim Women's Participation in the Moro National Liberation Front," *Muslim World* 86 (April 1996): 130–147.

104. A respondent said: "My relatives were victims of the soldiers. My grandparents were victims of the Ilagas [armed Christian groups]. They were decapitated and my relatives were raped." To another respondent, it was the sight of victims of a massacre that made her realize the extent of atrocities committed against the Muslims.

105. Personal interview with Kumander Aladin (a commander of the Moro National Liberation Front), North Cotabato, July 15, 1994.

106. "Role of the Women in the BangsaMoro Revolution," *Mahardika* 9 (1982): p. 1.

107. Members of the Finance Committee take care of this. They lend money at 10% interest and proceeds are used for supplies and other expenses of the movement.

108. Some samples of responses are: "If the provisionary government includes women, how much more the autonomous government?" "If there are no women, nothing will happen." "Women will be partners in building the BangsaMoro Republic." "Women can be in management positions . . . if women are involved, maybe corruption will be less."

109. Lacar, *Philippine Muslim Women*, p. 113.

110. Amina P. Usodan-Sumagayan, "The Changing Role of Maranao Women," pp. 208–209.

111. Peter Gowing, *Muslim Filipinos*, p. 71.

112. Hadja Maimona Aida L. Plawan, "Growing Up," in *The Maranao Woman*. (Marawi City: Mindanao State University, 1979), p. 9.

113. Republic of the Philippines, Department of Health, Memorandum order 1 s. 1994, June 21, 1994.

Select Bibliography

Aarts, Paul. "The New Oil Order: Built on Sand?" *Arab Studies Quarterly* 16 (2) (Spring 1994): 1–12.

Abaza, Mona. *The Changing Image of Women in Rural Egypt*. Cairo: The American University in Cairo, 1987.

Abdo, Nahla. "Nationalism and Feminism: Palestinian Women and the Intifada." In *Gender and National Identity*, ed. Valentine M. Moghadam. London: Zed, 1994: 149–152.

Abduh, Muhammad. *al-Islam wal-Mar'ah fi Ra'y al-Imam Muhammad Abduh*, ed. Muhammad 'Imara. Cairo: n.p., n.d.

Abu Yahya, Muhammad Hassan. *Ahamm Qadaya al-Mar'ah al-Muslimah*. Amman: Maktabat al-Risalah al-Hadithah, 1991.

Abu Zahrah, Muhammad. *Tanzim al-Usrah wa-Tanzim al-Nasl*. Cairo: Dar al-Fikr al-'Arabi, 1976.

Abu Zayd, Hikmat. "Imkanat al-Mar'a al-'Aribiyya fi al-'Amal al-Siyasi." In *al-Mar'a wa-Dawruha fi Harakatt al-Wahda al-'Arabiyah*, ed. Ali Shalaq et al. Beirut: Markaz Dirasat al-Wahdah al-'Arabiyah, 1982: 163–164.

Abu Zayd, Nasr Hamid. *Mafhum al-Nass: Dirasah fi 'Ulum al-Qur'an*. Beirut: al-Markaz al-Thaqafi al-'Arabi, 1990.

———. *Naqd al-Khitab al-Dini*. 2nd ed. Cairo: Sina lil-Nashr, 1994.

———. *al-Ittijah al-'Aqli fi al-Tafsir: Dirasah fi Qadiyat al-Majas fi al-Qur'an 'inda al-Mu'tazila*. Beirut: Dar al-Tanwir lil-Tiba'ah wa-al-Nashr, 1993.

Afkhami, Mahnaz. "Women in Post-Revolutionary Iran: A Feminist Perspective." In *In the Eye of the Storm: Women in Post-Revolutionary Iran*, ed. Mahnaz Afkhami and Erika Friedl. London: I. B. Tauris, 1994: 5–18.

Ahmad, Eqbal. "Islam and Politics." In *The Islamic Impact*, ed. Yvonne Y. Haddad, Byron Haines, and Ellison Findly. Syracuse, N.Y.: Syracuse University Press, 1984: 7–26.

Ahmed, Leila. "Early Feminist Movements in the Middle East: Turkey and Egypt." In *Muslim Women*, ed. Freda Hussain. New York: St. Martin's, 1992: 111–126.

———. *Women and Gender in Islam*. New Haven, Conn.: Yale University Press, 1992.

Amanat, Abbas. *Resurrection and Renewal: The Making of the Babi Movement in Iran 1844–1850*. Ithaca, N.Y.: Cornell University Press, 1989.

Anni, Wilson. Personal interview, July 27, 1995.

Arberry, A. J., trans. *The Koran Interpreted*. New York: Macmillan, 1955.

Arkoun, Mohammed. *Rethinking Islam: Common Questions, Uncommon Answers*, trans. and ed. Robert D. Lee. Boulder, Colo.: Westview, 1994.

As'ad, Yusuf Mikha'il. *al-Mar'ah wa-al-Hurriyah*. Cairo: Dar Nahdat Misr, 1977.

Asfour, Gabir. *Hawamisah 'Ala Daftar al-Tanwir*. Kuwait: Dar Su'ad al-Sabah, 1994.

al-Ashqar, Umar Sulayman and Ahmad al-Qattan. *Zahrat Nisa'iyah*. Kuwait: Maktabat Dar al-Bayan, 1989.

Al-'Asimi, Malika. *al-Mar'ah wa Ishkaliyat al-Dimuqratiya: Qira'a fi al-Waqi' wa al-Khitab*. Casablanca: Afriqya al-Sharq, 1991.

'Ata, 'Abd al-Qadir Ahmad. *al-Liqa; bayn al-Zawjayn fi Daw' al-Kitab wa-al-Sunna*. Cairo: Dar al-Turath al-'Arabi, 1980.

al-'Attar, 'Abd al-Nasir Tawfig. *Dirasah fi Qadiyat Ta'addud al-Zawjat*. Cairo: Dar al-Ittihad al-'Arabi. 1968.

———. *Ta'addud al-Zawjat*. Cairo: Silsilat al-Buhuth al-Islamiyah, 1972.

al-'Awwadi, Badriyyah. *al-Mar'ah wa-al-Qanun*. Kuwait: n.p., 1990.

Azadi, Mina Yadigar. "Davari-yi zan dar Ikhtilafat-i Khanivadigi [Part 1]." *Zanan*, 1 (6) (August 1992): 22–28.

———. "Ijtihad va Marja'iyat-i Zanan." *Zanan* 1 (8) (November–December 1992): 24–32.

———. "Qizavat-i Zan [Part 1]." *Zanan* 1 (1) (May 1992): 20–26.

———. "Qizavat-i Zan [Part 2]." *Zanan* 1 (5) (June–July 1992): 17–25.

'Azzam, Henry. "al-Mar'ah al-'Arabiyah wa al-'Amal: Musharakat al-Mar'ah al-'Arabiyah fi al-Quwa al-'Amila wa dawruha fi 'Amaliyyat al-Tanmiya." In *al-Mar'ah wa-Dawruha fi Harakat al-Wahdah al-'Arabiyah*, ed. Ali Shalaq et al. Beirut: Markaz Dirasat al-Wahdah al-'Arabiyah, 1982: 265–301.

Badamchian, Asadallah. "Bidun-i Sharh . . ." *Zanan* 3 (#19) (August–September 1994): 9–11.

Badran, Margot. *Feminists, Islam, and Nation: Gender and the Making of Modern Egypt*. Princeton, N.J.: Princeton University Press, 1994.

Baffoun, Alya. *Research in the Social Sciences on North African Women: Problems, Trends and Needs*. UNESCO SS-81/CONF. 804/4. Paris: UNESCO, 1981.

al-Bahi, Muhammad. *al-Islam wa-Ittijah al-Mar'ah al-Mu'asirah*. Cario: Dar al-I'tisam, 1981.

al-Banna, Hasan. *al-Mar'ah al-Muslimah*. Cairo: Dar al-Kutab al-Salafiyah, 1983.

al-Baydawi, Abd Allah ibn Umar. *Anwar al-Tanzil wa-Asrar al-Ta'wil*. Vol. 1 of *Reproductio Phototypica Editionis 1846–1848*. Osnabruck: Biblio, 1968.

———. *Reproductio Phototypica Editionis 1846–1848*, vol. 1.

Belarbi, Aicha. *Research in the Social Sciences on Women in Morocco*. UNESCO SS-81/CONF. 804/7. Paris: UNESCO, 1981.

Bihishti, Ahmad. *Zanan-i-Namdar dar Qur'an, Hadith va Tarikh*. Tehran: Sazman-i Tablighat-i Islami, 1989.

Brand, Laurie A. *Palestinians in the Arab World: Institution Building and the Search for State*. New York: Columbia University Press, 1988.

Bruno, Juanito A. *The Social Worker of the Tausug: A Study in Culture and Education*. Manila: Centro Escolar University Research and Development Center, 1973.

al-Buti, Muhammad Ramadan. *Ila Kull Fatat Tu'min bi Allah*. Tunis: Maktabat al-Jadid, 1988.

———. *Tahdid al-Nasl Wiqayatan wa-Ilaja*. Damascus: Maktabat al-Farabi, 1976.

Carroll, Lucy. "Nizam-i-Islam: Processes and Conflicts in Pakistan's Programme of Islamisation, with Special Reference to the Position of Women." *Journal of Commonwealth and Comparative Politics* 20 (1982): 57–95.

Castillo, Toribio B. "The Changing Social Status of the Filipino Women during the American Administration." M.A. thesis, University of Southern California, 1942.

"The Charter of the Mindinao State University Public Act #1382." In *Muslim-Christian Integration at the Mindanao State University*, ed. Antonio Isidro. Marawi City: n.p., 1968: 1–5.

Cheneviere, Alain. *L'Oman et les Emirats du Golfe*. Paris: Hachette, 1990.

Cloman, Sydney Amos. *Myself and a Few Moros*. Garden City, N.Y.: Doubleday, 1923.

"Combatting Sexual Harassment at Work." *Mahjubah: The Islamic Magazine for Women* 4 (April 1994): 6.

"The Conduct of Iraqi Troops in Kuwait Toward Kuwaitis and Non-Westerners." *News from Middle East Watch* (September 1990): 5.

Cooke, Miriam. *War's Other Voices: Women Writers on the Lebanese Civil War*. Cambridge, Mass.: Cambridge University Press, 1988.

———. "WO-man, Retelling the War Myth." In *Gendering War Talk*, eds. Miriam Cooke and Angela Woollacott. Princeton, N.J.: Princeton University Press, 1988: 177–204.

Cornell, Vincent J. "Qur'an." In *The Oxford Encyclopedia of the Modern Islamic World*, vol. 3, ed. John L. Esposito. New York: Oxford University Press, 1994: 387–394.

Cromer, Evelyn Baring. *Modern Egypt*, 2 vols. New York: Macmillan, 1908.

Dajan, Souad. "The Struggle of Palestinian Women in the Occupied Territories: Between National and Social Liberation." *Arab Studies Quarterly* 16 (2) (Spring 1994): 13–26.

Dalrymple, Alexander. "Essay Towards an Account of Sulu." *The Journal of Eastern Archipelago and Eastern Asia* 3 (1849): 564–565.

Dampier, WIlliam. *A Voyage to the New World*. London: New Argonaut, 1927.

al-Din, Muhammad 'Alam. *al-Tarbiya al-Jinsiyya bayn al-Waqi' wa 'Ilm al-Nafs wa-al-din*. Cairo: Al-Hay'a al-Misriyya al-'Ammah lil-Ta'lif wa al-Nashr, 1970.

"Discrimination Against Women Persists Despite Progress." *Mahjubah: The Islamic Magazine for Women* 6 (June 1994): 29.

Ebtekar, Massoumeh. "Va Sara Khandid." *Farzaneh* (1) (Fall 1993): 121–130.

———. "Woman and Family in Human Development." *Mahjubah: The Islamic Magazine for Women* 13 (12) (December 1994): 54.

———. "Women and Family in Human Development." *Mahjubah: The Islamic Magazine for Women* 14 (6) (June 1995): 7–8.

Elson, Diane. "From Survival Strategies to Transformation Strategies: Women's Needs and Structural Adjustment." In *Unequal Burden: Economic Crises, Persistent Poverty, and Women's Work*, ed. Lourdes Beneria and Shelley Feldman. Boulder, Colo.: Westview, 1992: 26–48.

England, Paula. "The Separate Self: Androcentric Bias in Neoclassical Assumptions." In *Beyond Economic Man: Feminist Theory and Economics*, ed. Marianne A. Feber and Julie A. Nelson. Chicago: University of Chicago Press, 1993: 27–53.

Enloe, Cynthia. *Does Khaki Become You?* Boston: South End, 1983.

Esposito, John L. "Population Ethics/Islamic Perspectives." *Encyclopedia of Bioethics*, ed. Warren T. Reich. New York: Macmillan, 1995: 1977–1981.

———. *Women in Muslim Family Law*. Syracuse, N.Y.: Syracuse University Press, 1982.

Ethelston, Sally. "Gender, Population, Environment." *Middle East Report* 24 (190) (September–October 1994): 2–5.

Fa'iz, Ahmad. *Dustur al-Usra fi Zilala al-Qur'an*. Beirut: Mu'assasat al-Risalah, 1980.

Fakhro, Munira A. "The Uprising in Bahrain: An Assessment." Paper presented at the Third International Conference—Gulf 2000. Bellagio, Italy, July 1995.

———. *Women at Work in the Gulf: A Case Study of Bahrain*. London: Kegan Paul International, 1990.

Faludi, Susan. *Backlash: The Undeclared War Against American Women*. New York: Crown, 1981.

The Family Code of the Philippines. August 4, 1988. Executive Order no. 209 as amended by Executive Order no. 227.

Faraj, al-Sayyid Ahmad. *al-Mu'amara 'ala al-Mar'ah al-Muslimah: Tarikh wa-Watha'iq*. Al-Mansura: al-Wafa' lil-Tiba'a wa-al-Nashr, 1985.

Fargues, Philippe. "From Demographic Explosion to Social Rupture." *Middle East Report* 24 (190) (September–October 1994): 6–10.

Farkhundah, Nahid. "Shi'r-i Furugh bah Almani Tarjumah Shud, Vali . . . " *Zanan* 3 (18) (June–July 1994): 22–23.

Farrag, Ahmad. "Introduction." In *Al-Qada' wa-al-Qadar*, ed. Muhammad Mutawalli al-Sha'rawi. Cairo: Dar al-Shuruq, 1974: 5–7.

Farrukhzad, Furugh. "Tavalludi Digar." In *Tavalludi Digar*. Tehran: Murvarid, 1963–1964: 164–169.

al-Faruqi, Ismail Ragi. "Towards a New Methodology for Qur'anic Exegesis." *Islamic Studies* (March 1962): 35–52.

Fawzi, Husayn. *al-Mar'ah wa-Ara' al-Falsifah*. Landan: al-Nishirun Darf al-Mahdudah, 1985.

al-Fiqi, Muhammad Kamil. *La Tazlimu al-Mar'ah*. Cairo: Maktabat Wahbah, 1985.

Fischer, Michael. *Iran: From Religious Dispute to Revolution*. Cambridge, Mass.: Harvard Univeristy Press, 1980.

———. "The Religious Establishment and the Expanding State." In *Iran: From Religious Dispute to Revolution*. Cambridge: Harvard University Press, 1980: 108–123.

al-Fodari, Maliha, and al-Fodari, Raida. Personal interview, March 27, 1991.

Forrest, Thomas. *A Voyage to New Guinea and the Moluccas 1774–1776*. New York: Oxofrd University Press, 1969.

Gause III, F. Gregory. *Oil Monarchies: Domestic and Security Challenges in the Arab Gulf States*. New York: Council on Foreign Relations, 1994.

Gerami, Shahin. "The Role, Place, and Power of Middle-Class Women in the Islamic Republic." In *Identity Politics and Women: Cultural Reassertions and Feminisms in International Perspective*, ed. Valentine M. Moghadam. Boulder, Colo.: Westview, 1994: 329–348.

Ghabra, Shafeeq. "Democratization in a Middle Eastern State—Kuwait, 1993." *Newsletter of the Society for Gulf Arab Studies* 4 (2) (November 1994): 4–12.

al-Ghadban, Munir Muhammad. *al-Akhawat al-Mu'minat*. Zerka, Jordan: Maktabat al-Manar, 1982.

al-Ghannushi, Rashid. *al-Mar'ah bayna al-Qur'an wa-Waqi' al-Muslimin*. Tunis: Matba'at Tunis Qurtaj al-Sharqiyah, n.d.

Ghassoub, Mai. "Feminism—or the Eternal Masculine—in the Arab World." *New Left Review*, no. 161 (1987): 11.

al-Ghazali, Muhammad. *Our Beginnings in Wisdom*, trans. Isma'il R. al-Faruqi. New York: Octagon, 1975.

al-Ghazali, Zeinab. "Al-Tariq 'ila al-Sa'ada." In *Al-Da'iya Zeinab al-Ghazali: Masirat Jihad wa-Hadith min al-Dhikrayat min Khilal Kitabatiha*, compiled by Ibn al-Hashimi. Cairo: Dar al-I'tisam, 1989: 75–76.

———. "Al-Um wa Bina' al-Insan al-Salih." In *Al-Da'iya Zeinab al-Ghazali: Masirat Jihad wa-Hadith min al-Dhikrayat min Khilal Kitabatiha*, Compiled by Ibn al-Hashimi. Cairo: Dar al-I'tisam, 1989: 77–78.

Giele, Janet Z. "Introduction: The Status of Women in Comparative Perspective." In *Women: Roles and Status in Eight Countries*, ed. Janet A. Giele and Audrey C. Smock. New York: Wiley, 1977: 3–31.

Gorgi, Moneer. "Zan Va Zimamdari." *Farzaneh* 1 (1) (Fall 1993): 9–34.

Government of Pakistan. "National Conservation Strategy Report." Islamabad: Government of Pakistan, 1992.

Gowing, Peter G. *Muslim Filipinos: Heritage and Horizon*. Quezon City: New Day, 1979.

Gutierrez, Eric. "Frontier Town Politics." *The Philippine Star* May 16, 1995: 1.

Haddad, Yvonne Yazbeck. "Islam, Women and Revolution in Twentieth-Century Arab Thought." In *Women, Religion, and Social Change*, ed. Yvonne Yazbeck Haddad and Ellison Banks Findly. Albany: SUNY Press, 1985: 275–306.

Haeri, Shahla. *Law of Desire: Temporary Marriage in Shi'i Iran*. Syracuse: Syracuse University Press, 1989.

Hagadorn, Charles. "Our Friend, The Sultan of Jolo." *The Century Illustrated Monthly Magazine*, 60, n.s., 38, (May–October 1900): 26–29.

Haidar, Khalil Ali. *al-Sahway al-Islamiyah wa-al-Mar'ah*. Kuwait: al-Tanwir, 1989.

Hamoudah, 'Adil. *Al-Hijra 'ila al-'Unf*. Cairo: Sina lil-Nashr, 1987.

Haqju, Nasir. "In Qafilah ta bah Hahr Lang Ast." *Kayhan-i Hava'i*, no. 1113 (December 28, 1994): 8.

Hatem, Mervat. "Egypt's Middle Class in Crisis: The Sexual Division of Labor." *The Middle East Journal* 42 (3) (Summer 1988): 407–422.

———. "Towards the Develoment of Post-Islamist and Post-Nationalist Feminist Discourses in the Middle East." In *Arab Women: Old Boundaries, New Frontiers*, ed. Judith E. Tucker. Bloomington: Indiana University Press, 1993: 29–58.

Hermansen, Marcia K. "Fatimeh as a Role Model in the Works of Ali Shari'ati." In *Women and Revolution in Iran*, ed. Guity Nashat. Boulder, Colo.: Westview, 1983: 87–96.

Higgens, Patricia F. and Pirouz Shoar-Ghaffari. "Women's Education in the Islamic Republic of Iran." In *In the Eye of the Storm: Women in Post-Revolutionary Iran*, ed. Mahnaz Afkhami and Erika Friedl. London: I. B. Tauris, 1994: 19–43.

Hijab, Nadia. *Womanpower: The Arab Debate on Women at Work*. Cambridge: Cambridge University Press, 1988.

Hijazi, Mustafa. *al-Takhalluf al-Ijtima'i: Madkhal ila-Sicholojiyat al-Insan al-Maqhur*. Beirut: Ma'had al-Inma' al-'Arabi, 1976.

Hillmann, Michael C. *A Lonely Woman: Forugh Farrokhzad and Her Poetry*. Washington, D.C.: Three Continents, 1987.

Hodgson, Marshall. *The Venture of Islam*, vol. 2. Chicago: University of Chicago Press, 1974.

Hoffman Ladd, Valerie J. "Women's Religious Observances." In *The Oxford Encyclopedia of the Modern Islamic World*, vol. 4., ed. John L. Esposito. New York: Oxford University Press, 1995: 327–331.

Hourani, Albert Habib. *Arabic Thought in the Liberal Age, 1798–1939*. Cambridge: Cambridge University Press, 1983.

Ibrahim, Muhammad Zaki. *Ma'alim al-Mujtama' al-Nisa'i fi-al-Islam*. Cairo: Dar al-'Ashira al-Muhammadiyya, n.d.

Ibrahim, Sa'd al-Din. *al-Nizam al-Ijtima'i al-'Arabi al-Jadid*. Beirut: Markaz Diarasat al-Wahdah al-'Arabiyah, 1982.

Ileto, Reynaldo C. *Magindanao, 1860–1888: The Career of Datu Uto of Buayan*. Data Paper: Number 82, Southeast Asia Program. Ithaca, N.Y.: Cornell University, 1971.

Isidro, Antonio. *Muslim–Christian Integration at the Mindanao State University*. Marawi City: n.p., 1968.

Isma'ili, Amir, and Abu al-Qasim Sidarat, eds. *Javdanah Furugh Farrukhzad*. Tehran: Marjan, 1968.

Jabr, Muhammad Salama. *Hal Hunna Naqisat 'Aql wa-Din?* Kuwait: Dar al-Istambuli lil Nashr wa-al-Tawzi', 1989.

Jacobson, Jodi L. "Women's Work: Why Development Isn't Always Good News for the Second Sex." In *Third World 94/95*, ed. Robert J. Griffiths. Guilford, Conn.: Dushkin, 1994: 231–236.

al-Jamal, Ibrahim Muhammad. *Fiqu al-Mar'ah al-Muslimah: 'Ibadat, Mu'amalat, Suluk Fatawa*. Cairo: Maktabat al-Qur'an, 1982.

———. *Kaba'ir al-Nisa' wa-Sagha'irihin wa-Hafawatihin*. Cairo: Dar al-Bashir, 1989.

"Jaygay-i Zan Dar Jumhuri-yi Islami-yi Iran." *Zan-i Ruz*, April 7, 1984: 3, 58.

Jehangir, Asma, and Hina Jilani. *The Hudood Ordinances: A Divine Sanction?* Lahore: Rhotas, 1990.

Jilani, Hina. "Law as an Instrument of Social Control." In *Locating the Self: Perspectives on Women and Multiple Identities*, ed. Nighat Said Khan, Rubina Saigol, and Afiya Zia. Lahore: ASR, 1994: 96–105.

Jomier, J. "Quelques Positions Actuelles de l'Exegese Coranique en Egypte: Revelées pare une Polemique Recente." *Melanges* 1 (1954): 39–72.

Kamal, Nadia Takriti, and Mary Qawar. "The Status and Role of Women in Development of Jordan." Manpower Division, Ministry of Planning, Hashemite Kingdom of Jordan, 1990. Unpublished paper presented at the ILO meeting on "Women in the Jordanian Labor Force," held at the Royal Scientific Society, December 1990.

Kar, Mihrangiz. *Firishtah-'i 'Adalat va Pardah'ha-yi Duzakh.* Tehran: Rawshangaran, 1991.

———. "Huquq-i Siasi-yi zan dar Iran az Bahman-i 57 ta Imruz." *Zanan* 3 (20) (October–November 1994): 18–25.

———. "Jaygah-i zan dar Qavanin-i Kayfari-yi Iran." *Zanan* 2 (11) (June–July 1993): 16–25.

Keddie, Nikki, and Lois Beck. Introduction to *Women in the Muslim World*, ed. Lois Beck and Nikki Keddie. Cambridge, Mass.: Harvard University Press, 1978: 1–34.

Kerr, Malcolm H. *Islamic Reform: The Political and Legal Theories of Muhammad Abduh and Rashid Rida.* Berkeley: University of California Press, 1966.

Khalafallah, Muhammad Ahmad. *Al-Fann al-Qasasi fi al-Qur'an al-Karim.* Cairo: Maktabat al-Nahdah al-Misriyya, 1958.

———. "Huquq al-Mar'ah wa Qanun al-Ahwal al Shakhsiya." *al-Yaqzah al-Arabiyah* 1 (4) (June 1985): 48–56.

al-Khatib, Umm Kulthum Yahya Mustafa. *Qadiyyat Tahdid al-Nasl fi al-Shari'a al-Islamiyah.* Jeddah: al-Dar al-Su'uhiyah lil-Nashr wa-al-Tawzi', 1982.

al-Khuli, al-Bahi. *al-Islam wa-al-Mar'ah al-Mu'asirah.* Kuwait: Dar al-Qalam, n.d.

Khuri, Fuad Ishaq. *Tribe and State in Bahrain: The Transformation of Social and Political Authority in the Arab State.* Chicago: University of Chicago Press, 1980.

Kiefer, Thomas M. *The Tausug: Violence and Law in a Philippine Moslem Society.* New York: Holt, Rinehart and Winston, 1972.

Kirmanshahi, Zaynab al-Sadat. "Jaygah zan dar Fiqh-i Kayfari-yi Islam [Part 1]." *Zanan* 2 (13) (September 1993): 56–60.

———. "Jaygah zan dar Fiqh-i Kayfari-yi Islam [Part 2]." *Zanan* 1 (15) (December 1993–January 1994): 52–55.

———. "Jaygah zan dar Fiqh-i Kayfari-yi Islam [Part 3]." *Zanan* 3 (16) (February–March 1994): 38–44.

Konikoff, Adolf. *Transjordan: An Economic Survey.* Jersualem: Economic Research Institute of the Jewish Agency for Palestine, 1946.

Kurian, George Thomas. *The New Book of World Rankings.* New York: Facts on File, 1991.

"Kuwait: Deteriorating Human Rights Conditions Since the Early Occupation." *News from Middle East Watch* (November 1990): 14.

Lacar, Luis Q. "Philippine Muslim Women: Their Emerging Role in a Rapidly Changing Society." In *Mindanao: Land of Unfulfilled Promise*, ed. Mark Turner, R. J. May, and Lulu R. Turner. Quezon City: New Day, 1992: 109–125.

Lazreg, Narnia. *The Eloquence of Silence: Algerian Women in Question.* London: Routledge, 1994.

Lim, Zenaida Tan. Telephone interview, April 29, 1995.

Longva, Anh Nga. "Kuwaiti Women at a Crossroads: Privileged Development and the Constraints of Ethnic Stratification." *International Journal of Middle Eastern Studies* 25 (1993): 443–456.

Lucas, Mariam Helie. "Women, Nationalism and Religion in the Algerian Struggle." In *Opening the Gates: A Century of Arab Feminist Writing*, ed. Margot Badran and Miriam Cooke. Bloomington: Indiana University Press, 1990: 104–114.

Lumauig, Romulo B. *Laws Affecting the National Cultural Minorities of the Philippines.* Manila: n.p., 1968.

Lufti, Sahyr. "Wad' al-Mar'ah fi al-Usrah al-'Arabiyah wa-'Alaqatuh bi-Azmat al-Hurriyah wa-al-Dimuqratiyah." In *al Mar'ah wa-Dawruha fi Harakat al-Wahdah al-'Arabiyah*, ed. Ali Shalaq et al. Beirut: Markaz Dirasat al-Wahdah al-'Arabiyah, 1982: 119–136.

Madkur, Sallam. *Nazrat al-Islam ila Tanzim al-Nasl*. Cairo: Dar al-Nahdah al-'Arabiyah, n.d.

Mahasanah, Nasrin. "Wad' al-Mar'ah al-Urduniyah fi Tashri'at al-Qanuniyah." Unpublished study sponsored by the General Secretariat, National Assembly, Hashemite Kingdom of Jordan, 1994.

Majul, Cesar Adib. *The Contemporary Muslim Movement in the Philippines*. Berkeley, Calif.: Mizan, 1985.

———. *Muslims in the Philippines*. Quezon City: University of the Philippines for the Asian Center, 1973.

———. "Philippines." In *The Oxford Encyclopedia of the Modern Islamic World*, vol. 3, ed. John L. Esposito. New York: Oxford University Press, 1995: 326–328.

Malagan, Bai. Personal interview, July 17, 1994.

Mallon, Florencia E. "The Promise and Dilemma of Subaltern Studies: Perspectives from Latin American History." *AHR Forum* (December 1994): 1510.

al-Mawdudi, Aby al-A'la. *Harakat Tahdid al-Nasl*. Cairo: Mu'assasat al-Risalah, 1975.

Mayo, Katherine. *Isles of Fear*. New York: Harcourt, Brace, 1925.

al-Mazini, Ahmad. *Qalu fi al-Mar'ah wa lam 'Aqul...al-Mar'ah al-Kuwaitiya, Ila Ayn?* Kuwait: Dar al-Salasil, 1988.

Mernissi, Fatima. *Beyond the Veil*. New York: Schenkman, 1975.

———. *Islam and Democracy: Fear of the Modern World*. London: Virago, 1993.

———. *The Veil and the Male Elite: A Feminist Interpretation of Women's Rights in Islam*, trans. Mary Jo Lakeland. Reading, Mass.: Addison-Wesley, 1992.

———. "Virginity and Patriarchy." *Women's Studies International Forum* 5 (2) (1982): 183–191.

Milani, Farzaneh, *Veils and Words: The Emerging Voices of Iranian Women Writers*. Syracuse; N.Y.: Syracuse University Press, 1992.

Ministry of Planning, Hashemite Kingdom of Jordan. *Five Year Plan for Economic and Social Development, 1986–1990*. Amman: National Press, n.d..

Mir, Mustansir. "Tafsir." In *The Oxford Encyclopedia of the Modern Islamic World*, vol. 4, ed. John L. Esposito. New York: Oxford University Press, 1995: 169–176.

Mirza, Sarfaraz Hussain. *Muslim Women's Role in the Pakistan Movement*. Lahore: Research Society of Pakistan, 1969.

Moghadam, Valentine M., ed. *Modernizing Women: Gender and Social Change in the Middle East*. Boulder, Colo.: L. Rienner, 1993.

Moghissi, Haideh. *Populism and Feminism in Iran: Women's Struggle in a Male-Dominated Revolutionary Movement*. London: Macmillan, 1994.

Mojab, Shahrzad. "The Islamic Government's Policy on Women's Access to Higher Education: 1979–85." Office of Women in International Development, Working Paper No. 156. Michigan State University, Lansing, December 1987.

———. "Kunturul-i Dawlat Va Muqavimat-i Zanan Dar 'Arsah-'i Danishgah'ha-yi Iran." *Nimeye Digar* 1 (14) (Spring 1991): 35–76.

Mu'adh, Da'd. "Tajribat al-Ittihad al-Nisa'i (1974–1981)." *Al-Urdunn al-Jadid* 7 (Spring 1986): 60.

al-Mughni, Haya. *Women in Kuwait: The Politics of Gender*. London: Saqi, 1993.

Mumtaz, Mumtaz, and Farida Shaheed. *Women of Pakistan: Two Steps Forward, One Step Back?* London: Zed; Karachi: Vanguard, 1987.

Musfir, Said bin. *Risalah min Fatat Ghayyurah ila al-Rijal*. Riyadh: Dar al-'Asima, 1412H.

Naficy, Hamid. "Veiled Vision/Powerful Presences: Women in Post-Revolutionary Iranian Cinema." In *In the Eye of the Storm: Women in Post-Revolutionary Iran*, ed. Mahnaz Afkhami and Erika Friedl. London: I. B. Tauris, 1994: 131–150.

———. "Zan Va'Mas'alah-'i zan' Dar Sinima-yi Iran Ba'd az Inqilab." *Nimeye Digar* 1 (14) (Spring 1991): 123–169.

Najafabadi, Dari. "The Veil and Women's Rights in Islam." *Ittila'at*, no. 17829 (March 3, 1986): 13.

al-Najjar, Baqir. "Ma'uqat al-Istikhdam al-Amthal lil-Qiwa al-'Amila al-Wataniyah fi al-Khalij al-'Arabi wa Imkaniyat al-Hal." In *Conference of Experts on Policies for Arab Labor Mobility and Utilization*. Kuwait: Economic and Social Commission for West Asia [ESCWA] and Kuwait Institute of Planning, 1995.

Najmabadi, Afsaneh. "Power, Morality, and the New Muslim Womanhoo." In *The Politics of Social Transformation in Afghanistan, Iran, and Pakistan*, ed. *Myron Weiner and Ali Banauzizi*. Syracuse, N.Y.: Syracuse University Press, 1994: 336–389.

Nath, Kamala. "Education and Employment among Kuwaiti Women." In *Women in the Muslim World*, ed. Lois Beck and Nikki Keddie. Cambridge, Mass.: Harvard University Press, 1978: 172–188.

National Planning Council, Hashemite Kingdom of Jordan. *Five Year Plan for Economic and Social Development, 1981–1985* (Amman: Royal Scientific Society Press, n.d.).

"The New Family Code." In *The Philippine Country Report on Women, 1986–1995*. N.p.: National Commission on the Role of Filipino Women, n.d.: 1–64.

Odeh, Hanna. *Economic Development of Jordan, 1954–1971*. Hashemite Kingdom of Jordan: Ministry of Culture and Information, 1972.

"Oman." *The Europa World Yearbook*. N.p.: Europa, 1993: 1164–1170.

Ommi, Mahboobe. "Chigunah Bayad Raft?" *Farzaneh* 1 (2–3) (Winter–Spring 1993): 159–162.

———. "Fiminizm az Aghaz Ta'kunun," Parts 1-5. *Zan-i Ruz*, nos. 1342–1347 (December 14, 1991–January 25, 1992): 10–13; 24–25; 28–29; 58.

———. "Women's Studies: The Indispensible Cultural Factor." *Farzaneh* 1 (1) (Fall 1993): 1–4.

Orosa, Sixto Y. *The Sulu Archipelago and Its People*, 2nd ed. N.p.: New Mercury, 1970.

Oussedik, Fatma. *The Conditions Required for Women Themselves to Conduct Research on Women in the Arab Region*. UNESCO SS-81/CONF. 804/6. Paris: UNESCO, 1981.

Pakistan Commission on the Status of Women. "Report of the Commission on the Status of Women in Pakistan." Islamabad: n.p., 1986.

Pakizegi, Behnaz. "Legal and Social Positions of Iranian Women." In *Women in the Muslim World*, ed. Lois Beck and Nikki Keddie. Cambridge, Mass.: Harvard University Press, 1978: 216–226.

Pateman, Carole. *The Sexual Contract*. Stanford, Calif.: Stanford University Press, 1988.

People's Government Fulfilling an Agenda for Change: Social Sector. N.p.: November Planning Commission, Government of Pakistan, 1988.

Peterson, V. Spike, and Anne Sisson Runyan. *Global Gender Issues*. Boulder, Colo.: Westview, 1993.

Planning Commission, Government of Pakistan. "Eighth Five-Year Plan (1993–1998) Approach Paper." Islamabad: n.p., 1992.

Plascov, Avi. *The Palestinian Refugees in Jordan, 1948–1957*. London: Frank Cass, 1981.

Plawan, Hadja Maimona Aida L. "Growing Up." In *The Maranao Woman*. Marawi City: Mindanao State University, 1979: 8–16.

Porter, Jadranka. *Under Siege in Kuwait: A Survivor's Story*. London: Victor Gollanz, 1991.

"Princess Tarhata's Changing Period of Romance." *Sunday Tribune Magazine*, May 20, 1934: 3.

Proceedings of the Women's Consultative Planning Forum, January 29–31, 1988. Quezon City: Women's Resource and Research Center, 1988.

Qa'ini, Muhsin. "Kutak Zadan-i Zan: Yiki az Athar-i Riasat-i Mard [Part 1]." *Zanan* 1 (3) (June–July 1994): 54–59.

———. "Kutak Zadan-i Zan: Yiki az Athar-i Riasat-i Mard [Part 2]." *Zanan*, Part 2, 3 (19) (August–September 1994): 68–72.

Qanbas, 'Abd al-Halim Muhammad. *Mu'dilat wa Mushkilat Tuwajih al-Mar'ah al-Muslimah al-Mu'asirah*. Damascus: Dar al-Albab, 1986.

al-Qudsi-Ghabra, Taghreed. "Women in Kuwait: Educated, Modern, and Middle Eastern." *The Washington Report on Middle East Affairs* (July 1991): 29.

Qutb, Sayyid. *Fi Zilal al-Qur'an*, vol. 2. Beirut: Dar al-Shuruq, 1982.

Rahman, Fazlur. *Islam and Modernity Transformation of an Intellectual Tradition*. Chicago: University of Chicago Press, 1982.

―――. *Major Themes of the Qur'an*. Minneapolis: Bibliotheca Islamica, 1980.

Ramazani, Nesta. "Islamic Fundamentalism and the Women of Kuwait." *Middle East Insight* (January–February 1988): 21–26.

Rasul, Santanina. "The Muslim Woman: Her Role in Contemporary Philippine Society." In *Filipino Muslims: Their Social Institutions and Cultural Achievements*, ed. F. Landa Jocano. Quezon City: Asian Center, 1983: 31–38.

Reber, Anne Lindsey. "The Sulu World in the Eighteenth and Early Nineteenth Centuries: A Historiographical Problem in British Writing on Malay Piracy." M.A. thesis, Cornell University, 1966.

"Report on the AWOCC–PHILMUSLIMA Series of Area Consultations in Preparation for the 1994 Ministerial Conference in Jakarta and the 1995 UN 4th World Conference on Women." N.p., 13–14 September 1993.

Republic of the Philippines, Department of Health. Memorandum order 1 s. 1994, June 21, 1994.

"Resignation of Dayang Dayang Piandao Accepted." *The Tribune*, October 16, 1940: 1.

Reyes, Zenaida. *Survey Report on the Recognition and Promotion of Legal Rights of Muslims as a Precondition to National Unity and Development*. Quezon City: University of the Philippines, 1989.

Rida, Muhammad Rashid. *Tafsir al-Qur'an al-Hakim al-Shahir bi-Tafsir al-Manar*, vol. 5, Beirut: Dar al-Ma'arif, 1973.

Rizvani, Huma, ed. *Laviyih Aqa Shaykh Fazlallah Nuri*. Tehran: Nashr-i Tarikh-i Iran, 1983.

Rogers, Dorothy M. "A History of the American Occupation and Administration of the Sulu Archipelago 1890–1920." M.A. thesis, University of San Francisco, 1959.

"Role of the Women in the BangsaMoro Revolution." *Mahardika* 9 (1982): 1.

al-Rumaihi, Muhammad. "Athar al-Naft 'ala Wad' al-Mar'ah al-'Arabiyah fi al-Khalij." In *al Mar'ah wa-Dawruha fi Harakat al-Wahdah al-'Arabiyah*. Beirut: Markaz Dirasat al-Wahdah al-'Arabiyah, 1982: 231–251.

el Saadawi, Nawal. "The Political Challenges Facing Arab Women at the End of the 20th Century." In *Women of the Arab World: The Coming Challenge*, ed. Nahid Toubia. London: Zed, 1988: 8–26.

Saba, Manijeh. "Tahlili Az Dibachah'ha-yi *Zani-i Ruz* dar Dawrah-'i Ba'd az Inqilab." *Nimeye Digar* 1 (14) (Spring 1991): 8–34.

Sabri, Mustafa. *Qawli fi al-Mar'ah wa-Muqaranatuhu bi-Aqwal Muqallidat al-Gharb*. Beirut: Dar al-Ra'id al-'Arabi, 1982.

al-Sadani, Nuriya. *Asrar Qabandi*. Kuwait: n.p., 1991.

―――. "The Early Women's Organizations and the Campaign for Women's Rights." In *Women in Kuwait: The Politics of Gender*, ed. Haya al-Mughni. London: Saqi, 1993: 63–88.

―――. *Kitab Watha'iq Tarikh al-Huquq al-Siyasiyah lil-Mar'ah al-Kuwaitiyah*. Kuwait: Mafudha Press, 1994.

―――. *Tarikh al-Mar'ah al-Kuwaitiyah*, 2 vols. Kuwait: Matba'at Dar al-Siyasah, 1972–1980.

Sa'idzadah, Sayyid Muhsin. " . . . Va Amma Pasukh-i Ma." *Zanan* 2 (14) (October–November 1993): 50–57.

―――. "Zan Bah Didah-'i 'Aql va Kamal." *Zanan* 2 (9) (January–February 1993): 29–34.

Salih, Muhammad Tariq Muhammad. *Ilayki Ayyatuha al-Ukht al-Muslimah*. Cairo: Dar al-Kutub al-Salafiyah, 1984.

San Juan, Epifanio. *Crisis in the Philippines: The Making of a Revolution*. South Hadley, Massachusetts: Bergin and Garvey, 1986.

Sarimi, Suhayla. "Va in Manam/Zani Tanha . . . " *Zanan* 3 (16) (February–March 1994): 18–21.

Sarip, Labi Hadji. "A Profile of Economic Activities of Maranao Women in Molundo, Marantao, and the Islamic City of Marawi, Lanao del Sur." *Dansalan Quarterly* 7 (1–2) (1985–1986): 7–8.

Seikaly, May. "Women and Social Change in Bahrain." *International Journal of Middle Eastern Studies* 26 (1994): 415–426.

"Sexual Harassment at the United Nations." *Mahjubah: The Islamic Magazine for Women* 4 (April 1994): 5.

Sha'ban, Mahmud 'Abd al-Sami. *Nizam al-Usra bayn al-Masihiyah wa al-Islam. Dirasah Muqarana*, vol. 1. Cairo: Dar al-'Ulum, 1983.

Shaheed, Farida, and Khawar Mumtaz. *Women's Economic Participation in Pakistan*. Islamabad: UNICEF Pakistan, 1992.

Shakhatirah, Husayn Ibrahim. *Al-Mar'ah al-Urduniyah: Haqa'iq wa-Arqam*. Amman: Nadi Sahibat al-'Amal wa-al-Mihan, 1992.

al-Sharabasi, Ahmad. *al-Din wa-Tanzim al-Usrah*. Cairo: Dar wa-Matabi al-Shab, 1965.

Sharabi, Hisham. *Neopatriarchy: A Theory of Distorted Change in Arab Society*. New York: Oxford University Press, 1988.

al-Sha'rawi, Shaykh Mohamed Metwali. "Makanat al-Mar'ah fi al-Islam." In *Al-Qada' wa-al-Qadar*, ed. Shaykh Mohamed Metwali. Cairo: Dar al-Shuruq, 1975: 151–191.

Shariati, Ali. *Fatima is Fatima*, trans. Laleh Bakhtiar. Tehran: Shariati Foundation, 1981.

al-Sharif, Mahmus bin. *al-Islam wa-al-Hayat al-Jinsiyyah*. Cairo: Maktabat al-Anglo al Misriyya, 1960.

Sherkat, Shahla. "Chasmah-'i Agahi Agar Bijushad . . . " *Zanan* 1 (1) (February 1992): 2–3.

———. "Sal-i Usrat, Sal-i Ruyish." *Zanan* 2 (10) (March–April 1993): 2–3.

Shikhatra, Husayn. *Al-Mar'ah al-Urduniyah: Haqa'iq wa-Arqam*. Amman: Nadi Sahibat al-A'mal wa al-Mihan, 1992.

Shukri, Shukufrah, and Sashirah Labriz. "Mard: Sharik Ya Ra'is?!" *Zanan* 1 (2) (March 1992): 26–32.

———. "Tamkin." *Zanan* 1 (1) (February 1992): 58–63.

Skeet, Ian. *Oman: Politics and Development*. New York: St. Martin's, 1992.

Soffan, Linda Usra. *The Women of the United Arab Emirates*. London: Croom Helm, 1980.

Spellberg, Denise A. *Politics, Gender, and the Islamic Past: The Legacy of 'A'isha Bint Abi Bakr*. New York: Columbia University Press, 1994.

Sprachman, Paul. *Plagued By the West*. Delmar, N.Y.: Coward, McCann, and Geoghegan, 1981.

State of Bahrain. *Statistical Abstracts, 1990*. Bahrain, n.p., 1991: 17–18, 29, 195, 288.

Stowasser, Barbara Freyer. "Religious Ideology, Women and the Family: The Islamic Paradigm." In *The Islamic Impulse*, ed. Barbara Freyer Stowasser. London: Croom Helm, 1987: 262–296.

———. "The Status of Women in Early Islam." In *Muslim Women*, ed. Freda Hussain. New York: St. Martin's, 1984: 11–43.

———. *Women in the Qur'an, Traditions, and Interpretation*. New York: Oxford University Press, 1994.

———. "Women's Issues in Modern Islamic Thought." In *Arab Women: Old Boundaries, New Frontiers*, ed. Judith E. Tucker. Bloomington: Indiana University Press, 1993: 3–28.

al-Tabari, Abu Ja'far Muhammad ibn Jarir. *Jami' al-Bayan fi Tafsir'ay al-Qur'an*, vol. 8. ed. Mahmud M. Shakir and Ahmad M. Shakir. Cairo: Dar al-Ma'arif, 1972: 290–317.

Taha, Mahmoud Mohamed. *The Second Message of Islam*, trans. Abdullahi Ahmed an-Naim. Syracuse, N.Y.: Syracuse University Press, 1987.

al-Talidi, 'Abd Allah. *al Mar'ah al-Mutabarrijah wa Atharuha al-Sayyi' fi al-Ummah*. Beirut: Dar ibn Hazm, 1990.

Al-Talidi, Malika. *al-Mar'ah wa Ishkaliyat al-Dimuqratiyah: Qira'a fi al-Waqi' was al-Khitab*. Casablanca: Afriqiyah al-Sharq, 1991.

Taliqani, A'zam 'Ala'i. *Masa'il-i-Zanan*. Tehran: Mu'assisah-i Islami-yi- Zanan-i Iran, 1991.

al-Tall, Suhayr Salti. *Muqaddima Hawla Qadiyat al-mar'ah wa-al-Harakah al-Nisa'iyah fi al-Urdun*. Beirut: Al-Mu'assah al-'Arabiyah lil-Dirasat wa-al-Nashr, 1985.

Tawfiq, 'Abd al-Nasi. *Al-'Attar, Ta'addud al-Zawjat*. Cairo: Silsilat al-Buhuth al-Islamiyah, 1972.

Tetreault, Mary Ann. "Civil Society in Kuwait: Protected Spaces and Women's Rights." *The Middle East Journal* 27 (2) (Spring 1993): 274–291.

Thabit, Muzhgan Kiani. "Naqd-i Sukhanrani-yi Khanum Mihrangiz Kar." *Zanan* 2 (14) (October–November 1993): 42–49.

al-Tilmisani, Omar. *Dhikrayat . . . La Mudhakkarat*. Cairo: Dar al-Tawzi' wa-al-Nashr al-Islamiya, 1985.

Tohidi, Nayereh. "Modernity, Islamization and Women in Iran." In *Gender and National Identity: Women and Politics in Muslim Societies*, ed. Valentine M. Moghadam. London: Zed, 1994: 110–147.

Trust for Voluntary Organizations. *First Annual Report, 1992*. Islamabad: n.p., 1992.

al-Tuhami, Mukhtar. *Thalath Ma'arik Fikriyya: Al Sihafah wa-al-Fikr wa-al-Thawrah*. Cairo: the author, 1976.

'Ubayd, Thurayya Ahmad. *al-Ta'qibat, in al-Mar'ah wa-Dawruha fi Harakat al-Wahdah al-'Arabiyah*. Beirut: Markaz Dirasat al-Wahdah al-'Arabiyah, 1982.

United Nations, *Report of the Secretary General: Recommendations of Regional Inter-Governmental Preparatory Meetings*. A/CONF. 116/9, February 5, 1985.

United Nations. *Status of the Convention on the Elimination of All Forms of Discrimination Against Women*. A/CONF. 116/BP1, June 4, 1985.

United Nations. *The World's Women: Trends and Statistics, 1970–1990*. New York: United Nations, 1991.

United Nations Development Programme, *Human Development Report 1991*. New York: Oxford University Press, 1991.

'Uryan, Sa'id. "Dar Sayah." *Farzaneh* 1 (2–3) (Winter–Spring 1994): 305–312.

Usodan-Sumagayan, Aminah. "The Changing Role of the Maranao Women in a Maranao Rural Society." *Dansalan Quarterly* 9 (4) (1988): 165–228.

Uthman, Uthman Muhammad. *Ikhtilat al-Jinsayn fi Madarisina*. Cairo: Dar al-I'tisam, 1984.

van Sommer, Annie, and Samuel M. Zwemer. *Our Moslem Sisters: A Cry of Need from Lands of Darkness Interpreted By Those Who Heard It*. New York: Fleming H. Revell, 1907.

Vatandoust, Gholam-Reza. "The Status of Iranian Women During the Pahlavi Regime." In *Women and the Family in Iran*, ed. Asghar Fathi. Leiden: E.J. Brill, 1985: 107–130.

Vatikiotis, Panayiotis J. *Politics and the Military in Jordan, A Study of the Arab Legion 1921–1957*. New York: Praeger, 1967.

"Violence Against Women." *Mahjubah: The Islamic Magazine for Women* 5 (May 1994): 23–24.

Voll, John O. Foreword to *Toward an Islamic Reformism: Civil Liberties, Human Rights, and International Law*, by Abd Allahi Ahmad An-Naim. Syracuse, N.Y.: Syracuse University Press, 1990.

Wadud-Muhsin, Amina. *Qur'an and Woman*. Kuala Lumpur: Penerbit Fajar Bakti Sdn., Bhd., 1992.

Weiss, Anita M. "The Consequences of State Policies for Women in Pakistan." In *The Politics of Social Transformation in Afghanistan, Iran, and Pakistan*, ed. Myron Weiner and Ali Banuazizi. Syracuse, N.Y.: Syracuse University Press, 1994: 412–444.

———. "Implications of the Islamization Program for Women." In *Islamic Reassertion in Pakistan: The Application of Islamic Laws in a Modern State*, ed. Anita M. Weiss. Syracuse, N.Y.: Syracuse University Press, 1986: 97–113.

———. *Walls within Walls: Life Histories of Working Women in the Old City of Lahore*. Boulder, Colo.: Westview, 1992.

Wilke, Charles. "Narrative of United States Exploratory Expeditions during 1838, 1839, 1840–41, 1842, Phildelphia, 1844." In *The Philippine Islands 1493–1803*, ed. Emma Helen Blair and James A. Robertson. Cleveland, Ohio: Arthur H. Clark, 1906: 128–192.

Wilson, Mary C. *King Abdullah, Britain and the Making of Jordan*. New York: Cambridge University Press, 1987.

"Women and Development in the EROPA Conference." *Mahjubah: The Islamic Magazine for Women* 7 (July 1994): 20.

Worcester, Dean C. *The Philippine Islands and Their People*. New York: Macmillan, 1898.

Yagan, Fathi. *al-Islam wa-al-Jins*. Alexandria: Mu'assasat al-Risalah, 1972.

Yahya, Muhammad Kamal. *al-Judhur al-Tarikhiyah li-Tahrir al-Mar'ah al-Misriyah fi al-'Asr al-Hadith*. Cairo: al-Hay'a al-Misriyah al-'Ammah li al-Kitab, 1983.

Yahya, Yahya Bashir Haj. *al-Mar'ah wa-Qadaya al-Hayat fi al-Qissah al-Islamiyah al-Mu'asirah*. Kuwait: Dar Hawwa', 1994.

Yaljin, Miqdad. *al-Bayt al-Islami*. Cairo: Kitab al-Hilal, 1972.

Yasin, Bu'Ali. "Matabbat fi Masirat al-Mar'ah al-'Arabiyya 'Ala Tariq al-Tahurrur wa-al-Musawat." *al-Wahda* 1 (9) (June 1985): 41–54.

Yeganeh, Nahid. "Women's Struggles in the Islamic Republic of Iran." In *In the Shadow of Islam: The Women's Movement in Iran*, ed. Azar Tabari and Nahid Yeganeh. London: Zed, 1982: 26–74.

Youssef, Nadia H. "The Status and Fertility Patterns of Muslim Women." In *Women in the Muslim World*, ed. Lois Beck and Nikki Keddie. Cambridge, Mass.: Harvard University Press, 1978: 69–99.

Yusuf, Husayn Muhammad. *Ahdaf al-Usrah fi al-Islam wa-al-Tayyarat al-Mudaddah*. Cairo: Dar al-I'tisam, 1975.

Zahidi, Shams al-Sadat. "Muqi'iyat-i Zanan dar Jimi'ah-'i Danishgahi." *Zanan* 3 (21) (December 1994–January 1995): 2–21.

Zahidi, Zuhrah. "I'adah-'i Haythiyat-i Havva." *Zanan* 3 (16) (February–March 1994): 2–6.

Zakaria, Fouad. "The Standpoint of Contemporary Muslim Fundamentalists." *Women of the Arab World: The Coming Challenge*, ed. Nahid Toubia. London: Zed, 1988: 27–35.

Zebiri, Kate. *Mahmud Shaltut and Islamic Modernism*. Oxford: Clarendon Press, 1993.

Zia, Afiya Shehrbano. *Sex Crime in the Islamic Context: Rape, Class and Gender in Pakistan*. Lahore: ASR, 1994.

"Zimbabwe Women in Uphill Fight for Equality." *Mahjubah: The Islamic Magazine for Women* 12 (December 1994): 25.

Zwemer, Samuel Marinus, and Amy E. Zwemer. *Moslem Women*. West Medford, Mass.: The Central Committee of the United Study of Foreign Missions, 1926.

Index